CASENOTE™ LEGAL BRIEFS

EVIDENCE

Adaptable to courses utilizing Strong, Broun and Mosteller's casebook on Evidence

NORMAN S. GOLDENBERG, SENIOR EDITOR

PETER TENEN, MANAGING EDITOR

STAFF WRITERS

RICH LOVICH
KEMP RICHARDSON
CHRIS MIAO
RICK BRODY
BILL CARERO
JEFF BERKE

ALSO AVAILABLE!
EVIDENCE
OUTLINE
This Casenote Legal Briefs volume is now cross-referenced to the new *Casenote Law Outline* on Evidence
by Prof. Kenneth Graham

PUBLISHED BY CASENOTES PUBLISHING CO., INC. 1640 5th ST., SUITE 208 SANTA MONICA, CA 90401

ISBN 0-87457-076-X

FORMAT OF THE CASENOTE LEGAL BRIEF

CASE CAPSULE: This bold-faced section (first three paragraphs) highlights the procedural nature of the case, a short summary of the facts, and the rule of law. This is an invaluable quick-review device designed to refresh the student's memory for classroom discussion and exam preparation.

NATURE OF CASE: This section identifies the form of action (e.g., breach of contract, negligence, battery), the type of proceeding (e.g., demurrer, appeal from trial court's jury instructions) and the relief sought (e.g., damages, injunction, criminal sanctions).

FACT SUMMARY: The fact summary is included to refresh the student's memory. It can be used as a quick reminder of the facts when the student is chosen by an instructor to brief a case.

CONCISE RULE OF LAW: This portion of the brief summarizes the general principle of law that the case illustrates. Like the fact summary, it is included to refresh the student's memory. It may be used for instant recall of the court's holding and for classroom discussion or home review.

FACTS: This section contains all relevant facts of the case, including the contentions of the parties and the lower court holdings. It is written in a logical order to give the student a clear understanding of the case. The plaintiff and defendant are identified by their proper names throughout and are always labeled with a (P) or (D).

ISSUE: The issue is a concise question that brings out the essence of the opinion as it relates to the section of the casebook in which the case appears. Both substantive and procedural issues are included if relevant to the decision.

HOLDING AND DECISION: This section offers a clear and in-depth discussion of the rule of the case and the court's rationale. It is written in easy-to-understand language. When relevant, it includes a thorough discussion of the exceptions listed by the court, the concurring and dissenting opinions, and the names of the judges.

CONCURRENCE / DISSENT: All concurrences and dissents are briefed whenever they are included by the casebook editor.

EDITOR'S ANALYSIS: This last paragraph gives the student a broad understanding of where the case "fits in" with other cases in the section of the book and with the entire course. It is a hornbook-style discussion indicating whether the case is a majority or minority opinion and comparing the principal case with other cases in the casebook. It may also provide analysis from restatements, uniform codes, and law review articles. The editor's analysis will prove to be invaluable to classroom discussion.

CROSS-REFERENCE TO OUTLINE: Wherever possible, following each case is a cross-reference linking the subject matter of the issue to the appropriate place in the *Casenote Law Outline*, which provides further information on the subject.

WINTER v. G.P. PUTNAM'S SONS
938 F.2d 1033 (1991).

NATURE OF CASE: Appeal from summary judgment in a products liability action.

FACT SUMMARY: Winter (P) relied on a book on mushrooms published by Putnam (D) and became critically ill after eating a poisonous mushroom.

CONCISE RULE OF LAW: Strict products liability is not applicable to the expressions contained within a book.

FACTS: Winter (P) purchased The Encyclopedia of Mushrooms, a book published by Putnam (D), to help in collecting and eating wild mushrooms. In 1988, Winter (P), relying on descriptions in the book, ate some wild mushrooms which turned out to be poisonous. Winter (P) became so ill he required a liver transplant. He brought a strict products liability action against Putnam (D), alleging that the book contained erroneous and misleading information that caused his injury. Putnam (D) responded that the information in the book was not a product for purposes of strict products liability, and the trial court granted its motion for summary judgment. The trial court also rejected Winter's (P) actions for negligence and misrepresentation. Winter (P) appealed.

ISSUE: Is strict products liability applicable to the expressions contained within a book?

HOLDING AND DECISION: (Sneed, J.) No. Strict products liability is not applicable to the expressions contained within a book. Products liability is geared toward tangible objects. The expression of ideas is governed by copyright, libel, and misrepresentation laws. The Restatement (Second) of Torts lists examples of the items that are covered by §402A strict liability. All are tangible items, such as tires or automobiles. There is no indication that the doctrine should be expanded beyond this area. Furthermore, there is a strong public interest in the unfettered exchange of ideas. The threat of liability without fault could seriously inhibit persons who wish to share thoughts and ideas with others. Although some courts have held that aeronautical charts are products for purposes of strict liability, these charts are highly technical tools which resemble compasses. The Encyclopedia of Mushrooms, published by Putnam (D), is a book of pure thought and expression and therefore does not constitute a product for purposes of strict liability. Additionally, publishers do not owe a duty to investigate the contents of books that they distribute. Therefore, a negligence action may not be maintained by Winter (P) against Putnam (D). Affirmed.

EDITOR'S ANALYSIS: This decision is in accord with the rulings in most jurisdictions. See Alm v. Nostrand Reinhold Co., Inc., 480 N.E. 2d 1263 (Ill. 1985). The court also stated that since the publisher is not a guarantor of the accuracy of an author's statements, an action for negligent misrepresentation could not be maintained. The elements of negligent misrepresentation are stated in § 311 of the Restatement (Second) of Torts.

[For more information on misrepresentation, see Casenote Law Outline on Torts, Chapter 12, § III, Negligent Misrepresentation.]

NOTE TO THE STUDENT

OUR GOAL. It is the goal of Casenotes Publishing Company, Inc. to create and distribute the finest, clearest and most accurate legal briefs available. To this end, we are constantly seeking new ideas, comments and constructive criticism. As a user of *Casenote Legal Briefs,* your suggestions will be highly valued. With all correspondence, please include your complete name, address, and telephone number, including area code and zip code.

THE TOTAL STUDY SYSTEM. Casenote Legal Briefs are just one part of the Casenotes TOTAL STUDY SYSTEM. Most briefs are (wherever possible) cross-referenced to the appropriate *Casenote Law Outline,* which will elaborate on the issue at hand. By purchasing a Law Outline together with your Legal Brief, you will have both parts of the Casenotes TOTAL STUDY SYSTEM. (See the advertising in the front of this book for a list of Law Outlines currently available.)

A NOTE ABOUT LANGUAGE. Please note that the language used in *Casenote Legal Briefs* in reference to minority groups and women reflects terminology used within the historical context of the time in which the respective courts wrote the opinions. We at Casenotes Publishing Co., Inc. are well aware of and very sensitive to the desires of all people to be treated with dignity and to be referred to as they prefer. Because such preferences change from time to time, and because the language of the courts reflects the time period in which opinions were written, our case briefs will not necessarily reflect contemporary references. We appreciate your understanding and invite your comments.

EDITOR'S NOTE. Casenote Legal Briefs are intended to supplement the student's casebook, not replace it. There is no substitute for the student's own mastery of this important learning and study technique. If used properly, *Casenote Legal Briefs* are an effective law study aid that will serve to reinforce the student's understanding of the cases.

REF. # 1064-95-995

SUPPLEMENT REQUEST FORM

At the time this book was printed, a brief was included for every major case in the casebook and for every existing supplement to the casebook. However, if a new supplement to the casebook (or a new edition of the casebook) has been published since this publication was printed and if that casebook supplement (or new edition of the casebook) was available for sale at the time you purchased this Casenote Legal Briefs book, we will be pleased to provide you the new cases contained therein AT NO CHARGE when you send us a stamped, self-addressed envelope.

TO OBTAIN YOUR FREE SUPPLEMENT MATERIAL, **YOU MUST FOLLOW THE INSTRUCTIONS BELOW PRECISELY** OR YOUR REQUEST WILL NOT BE ACKNOWLEDGED!

1.   Please check if there is in fact an existing supplement and, if so, that the cases are not already included in your Casenote Legal Briefs. Check the main table of cases as well as the supplement table of cases, if any.

2.   **REMOVE THIS ENTIRE PAGE FROM THE BOOK.** You MUST send this ORIGINAL page to receive your supplement. This page acts as your proof of purchase and contains the reference number necessary to fill your supplement request properly. No photocopy of this page or written request will be honored or answered. Any request from which the reference number has been removed, altered or obliterated will not be honored.

3.   Prepare a STAMPED self-addressed envelope for return mailing. Be sure to use a FULL SIZE (9 X 12) ENVELOPE (MANILA TYPE) so that the supplement will fit and AFFIX ENOUGH POSTAGE TO COVER 3 OZ. **ANY SUPPLEMENT REQUEST NOT ACCOMPANIED BY A STAMPED SELF-ADDRESSED ENVELOPE WILL ABSOLUTELY NOT BE FILLED OR ACKNOWLEDGED.**

4.   MULTIPLE SUPPLEMENT REQUESTS: If you are ordering more than one supplement, we suggest that you enclose a stamped, self-addressed envelope for each supplement requested. If you enclose only one envelope for a multiple request, your order may not be filled immediately should any supplement which you requested still be in production. In other words, your order will be held by us until it can be filled completely.

5.   Casenotes prints two kinds of supplements. A "New Edition" supplement is issued when a new edition of your casebook is published. A "New Edition" supplement gives you all major cases found in the new edition of the casebook which did not appear in the previous edition. A regular "supplement" is issued when a paperback supplement to your casebook is published. If the box at the lower right is stamped, then the "New Edition" supplement was provided to your bookstore and is *not* available from Casenotes; however, Casenotes will still send you any regular "supplements" which have been printed either before or after the new edition of your casebook appeared and which, according to the reference number at the top of this page, have not been included in this book. If the box is not stamped, Casenotes will send you any supplements, "New Edition" and/or regular, needed to completely update your Casenote Legal Briefs.

*NOTE:*REQUESTS FOR SUPPLEMENTS WILL NOT BE FILLED UNLESS THESE INSTRUCTIONS ARE COMPLIED WITH!

6.   Fill in the following information:

Full title of CASEBOOK _____ **EVIDENCE** _____

_____

CASEBOOK author's name ___ **Strong, Broun and Mosteller** ___

_____

Date of new supplement you are requesting _____

_____

Name and location of bookstore where this Casenote Legal Brief

was purchased _____

_____

Name and location of law school you attend _____

_____

Any comments regarding Casenote Legal Briefs _____

_____

NOTE: IF THIS BOX IS STAMPED, NO NEW EDITION SUPPLEMENT CAN BE OBTAINED BY MAIL.

PUBLISHED BY CASENOTES PUBLISHING CO., INC. 1640 5th ST, SUITE 208 SANTA MONICA, CA 90401

PLEASE PRINT

NAME _____   PHONE _____

ADDRESS/CITY/STATE/ZIP _____

Announcing the First *Totally Integrated* Law Study System

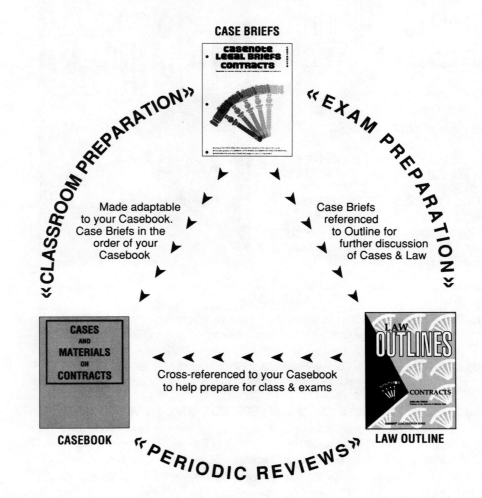

CASE BRIEFS

«CLASSROOM PREPARATION»

«EXAM PREPARATION»

Made adaptable to your Casebook. Case Briefs in the order of your Casebook

Case Briefs referenced to Outline for further discussion of Cases & Law

CASES AND MATERIALS ON CONTRACTS

Cross-referenced to your Casebook to help prepare for class & exams

CASEBOOK

LAW OUTLINE

«PERIODIC REVIEWS»

Casenotes Integrated Study System Makes Studying Easier and More Effective Than Ever!

Casenotes has just made studying easier and more effective than ever before, because we've done the work for you! Through our exclusive integrated study system, most briefs found in this volume of Casenote Legal Briefs are cross-referenced to the corresponding area of law in the Casenote Law Outline series. The cross-reference immediately follows the Editor's Analysis at the end of the brief, and it will direct you to the corresponding chapter and section number in the Casenote Law Outline for further information on the case or the area of law.

This cross-referencing feature will enable you to make the most effective use of your time. While each Casenote Law Outline focuses on a particular subject area of the law, each legal briefs volume is adapted to a specific casebook. Now, with cross-referencing of Casenote Legal Briefs to Casenote Law Outlines, you can have the best of both worlds – briefs for all major cases in your casebooks and easy-to-find, easy-to-read explanations of the law in our Law Outline series. Casenote Law Outlines are authored exclusively by law professors who are nationally recognized authorities in their field. So using Casenote Law Outlines is like studying with the top law professors.

Try Casenotes new totally integrated study system and see just how easy and effective studying can be.

Casenotes Integrated Study System Does The Work For You!

LAW OUTLINES from CASENOTE™

the Ultimate Outline

▶ **WRITTEN BY NATIONALLY RECOGNIZED AUTHORITIES IN THEIR FIELD.**

▶ **FEATURING A FLEXIBLE, SUBJECT-ORIENTED APPROACH.**

▶ **CONTAINS: TABLE OF CONTENTS; CAPSULE OUTLINE; FULL OUTLINE; EXAM PREPARATION; GLOSSARY; TABLE OF CASES; TABLE OF AUTHORITIES; CASEBOOK CROSS REFERENCE CHART; INDEX.**

▶ **THE TOTAL LAW SUMMARY UTILIZING THE MOST COMPREHENSIVE STUDY APPROACH IN THE MOST EFFECTIVE, EASY-TO-READ FORMAT.**

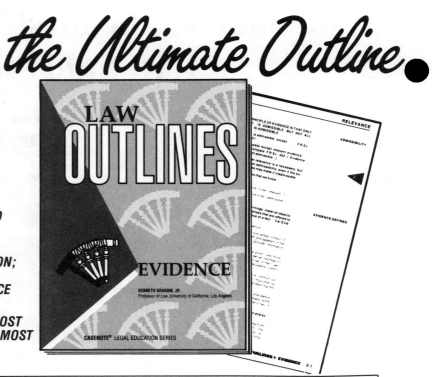

REF #	SUBJECT	AUTHORS	RETAIL PRICE
#5260 —	ADMINISTRATIVE LAW by **Charles H. Koch, Jr.,** Dudley W. Woodbridge Professor of Law, College of William and Mary. **Sidney A. Shapiro,** John M. Rounds Professor of Law, University of Kansas. (1994)		**(effective 7/1/95)** $17.95
#5040 —	CIVIL PROCEDURE by **John B. Oakley,** Professor of Law, University of California, Davis. **Rex R. Perschbacher,** Professor of Law & Associate Dean, Academic Affairs, University of California, Davis. (1993)		$18.95
	COMMERCIAL LAW (*see* 5700 SALES ● 5710 SECURED TRANS. ● 5720 NEG. INSTRUMENTS & PMT. SYST.)		
#5070 —	CONFLICT OF LAWS by **Luther L. McDougal, III,** W.R. Irby Professor of Law, Tulane University. **Robert L. Felix,** James P. Mozingo, III Prof. of Law, Univ. of S. Carolina. (1992)		$17.95
#5080 —	CONSTITUTIONAL LAW by **Gary Goodpaster,** Professor of Law, Univ. of California, Davis. (1994)		$20.95
#5010 —	CONTRACTS by **Daniel Wm. Fessler,** Professor of Law, University of California, Davis.		$17.95
#5050 —	CORPORATIONS by **Lewis D. Solomon,** Arthur Selwin Miller Research Prof. of Law, George Washington Univ. BUSINESS VEHICLES AND ALTERNATIVE **Daniel Wm. Fessler,** Prof. of Law, University of California, Davis **Arthur E. Wilmarth, Jr.,** Assoc. Prof. of Law, George Washington University (1994)		$19.95
#5020 —	CRIMINAL LAW by **Joshua Dressler,** Professor of Law, McGeorge School of Law. (1995).		$17.95
#5200 —	CRIMINAL PROCEDURE by **Joshua Dressler,** Professor of Law, McGeorge School of Law. (1993)		$16.95
#5800 —	ESTATE & GIFT TAX by **Joseph M. Dodge,** W.H. Francis Professor of Law, University of GENERATION-SKIPPING TAX INCLUDING THE FEDERAL Texas at Austin. (1993)		$17.95
#5060 —	EVIDENCE by **Kenneth Graham, Jr.,** Professor of Law, University of California, Los Angeles.		$18.95
#5300 —	FEDERAL COURTS by **Howard P. Fink,** Isadore and Ida Topper Prof. of Law, Ohio State University., et al.		TBA
#5210 —	FEDERAL INCOME TAXATION by **Joseph M. Dodge,** W.H. Francis Professor of Law, University of Texas at Austin.		$18.95
#5720 —	NEGOTIABLE INST. & PMT. SYST. by **Donald B. King,** Professor of Law, Saint Louis University **Peter Winship,** James Cleo Thompson, Sr. Trustee Prof., SMU (1995)		$17.95
#5030 —	PROPERTY by **Sheldon F. Kurtz,** Percy Bordwell Professor of Law, University of Iowa.		TBA
#5700 —	SALES by **Robert E. Scott,** Dean and Lewis F. Powell, Jr. Professor of Law, University of Virginia. **Donald B. King,** Professor of Law, Saint Louis University. (1992)		$17.95
#5710 —	SECURED TRANSACTIONS by **Donald B. King,** Professor of Law, Saint Louis University, et al.		TBA
#5000 —	TORTS by **George C. Christie,** James B. Duke Professor of Law, Duke University. **Jerry J. Phillips,** W.P. Toms Professor of Law & Chair, Committee on Admissions, University of Tennessee. (1990 w/ '92 supp.)		$18.95
#5220 —	WILLS, TRUSTS & ESTATES by **William M. McGovern,** Professor of Law, University of California, Los Angeles. (1990 w/ '92 supp.) (Calif. Supp. available)		$18.95

CASENOTE™ LEGAL BRIEFS

PRICE LIST — EFFECTIVE JULY 1, 1995 ● PRICES SUBJECT TO CHANGE WITHOUT NOTICE

Ref. No.	Course	Adaptable to Courses Utilizing	Retail Price
1265	ADMINISTRATIVE LAW	BONFIELD & ASIMOV	15.00
1263	ADMINISTRATIVE LAW	BREYER & STEWART	17.00
1280	ADMINISTRATIVE LAW	GELLHORN, B., S., R. & S.	15.00
1264	ADMINISTRATIVE LAW	MASHAW, MERRILL & SHANE	16.50
1282	ADMINISTRATIVE LAW	SCHWARTZ	16.00
1290	ADMIRALTY	HEALY & SHARPE	19.00
1291	ADMIRALTY	LUCAS	16.50
1351	AGENCY & PARTNERSHIP	HYNES	18.00
1350	AGENCY & PARTNERSHIP (ENT.ORG)	CONARD, KNAUSS & SIEGEL	19.00
1280	ANTITRUST	AREEDA & KAPLOW	16.50
1281	ANTITRUST (TRADE REGULATION)	HANDLER, B. P. & G.	15.50
1283	ANTITRUST	SULLIVAN & HOVENKAMP	16.00
1610	BANKING LAW	SYMONS & WHITE	13.00
1611	BANKING LAW	MACEY & MILLER	15.00
1303	BANKRUPTCY (DEBTOR-CREDITOR)	EISENBERG	17.00
1440	BUSINESS PLANNING	HERWITZ	11.50
1040	CIVIL PROCEDURE	COUND, F., M. & S	18.00
1043	CIVIL PROCEDURE	FIELD, KAPLAN & CLERMONT	18.00
1041	CIVIL PROCEDURE	HAZARD, TAIT & FLETCHER	17.00
1047	CIVIL PROCEDURE	MARCUS, REDISH & SHERMAN	17.00
1044	CIVIL PROCEDURE	ROSENBERG, S. & D.	17.00
1046	CIVIL PROCEDURE	YEAZELL, LANDERS, & MARTI6	15.00
1311	COMM'L LAW	FARNSWORTH, H., R., H. & 7.	17.00
1312	COMM'L LAW	JORDAN & WARREN	17.00
1310	COMM'L LAW (SALES/SEC.TR./PAY.LAW)	SPEIDEL, SUMMERS & WHITE	19.00
1313	COMM'L LAW	WHALEY	16.00
1320	COMMUNITY PROPERTY	BIRD	15.50
1630	COMPARATIVE LAW	SCHLESINGER, B., D., & H.	14.00
1048	COMPLEX LITIGATION	MARCUS & SHERMAN	15.00
1072	CONFLICTS	BRILMAYER	15.00
1071	CONFLICTS	CRAMTON, CURRIE & KAY	15.00
1070	CONFLICTS	REESE, ROSENBERG & HAY	18.00
1086	CONSTITUTIONAL LAW	BREST & LEVINSON	16.00
1082	CONSTITUTIONAL LAW	COHEN & VARAT	19.00
1080	CONSTITUTIONAL LAW	GUNTHER	17.00
1081	CONSTITUTIONAL LAW	LOCKHART, K., C. & S.	16.00
1085	CONSTITUTIONAL LAW	ROTUNDA	15.00
1087	CONSTITUTIONAL LAW	STONE, S., S. & T.	17.00
1017	CONTRACTS	CALAMARI, PERILLO & BENDER	21.00
1101	CONTRACTS	CRANDALL & WHALEY	18.00
1014	CONTRACTS	DAWSON, HARVEY & HENDRESON	17.00
1010	CONTRACTS	FARNSWORTH & YOUNG	16.00
1011	CONTRACTS	FULLER & EISENBERG	18.00
1100	CONTRACTS	HAMILTON, RAU & WEINTRAUB	17.00
1013	CONTRACTS	KESSLER, GILMORE & KRONMAN	21.00
1016	CONTRACTS	KNAPP & CRYSTAL	18.50
1012	CONTRACTS	MURPHY & SPEIDEL	20.00
1018	CONTRACTS	MURRAY	20.00
1015	CONTRACTS	ROSETT	19.00
1019	CONTRACTS	VERNON	18.00
1502	COPYRIGHT	GOLDSTEIN	16.00
1501	COPYRIGHT	NIMMER, M., M., & N.	17.50
1218	CORPORATE TAXATION	LIND, S. L. & R	12.00
1050	CORPORATIONS	CARY & EISENBERG (ABR. & UNA8R.)	17.00
1054	CORPORATIONS	CHOPER, MORRIS & COFFEE	19.50
1350	CORPORATIONS (ENTERPRISE ORG.)	CONARD, KNAUSS & SIEGEL	19.00
1053	CORPORATIONS	HAMILTON	19.00
1057	CORPORATIONS	O'KELLEY & THOMPSON	16.00
1056	CORPORATIONS	SOLOMON, S., B., & W.	17.00
1052	CORPORATIONS	VAGTS	15.00
1300	CREDITOR'S RIGHTS (DEBTOR-CREDITOR)	RIESENFELD	19.00
1550	CRIMINAL JUSTICE	WEINREB	16.00
1020	CRIMINAL LAW	BOYCE & PERKINS	20.00
1024	CRIMINAL LAW	DIX & SHARLOT	15.00
1028	CRIMINAL LAW	DRESSLER	19.00
1025	CRIMINAL LAW	FOOTE & LEVY	15.00
1027	CRIMINAL LAW	JOHNSON	15.00
1021	CRIMINAL LAW	KADISH & SCHULHOFER	17.00
1026	CRIMINAL LAW	KAPLAN & WEISBERG	16.00
1023	CRIMINAL LAW	LAFAVE	17.00
1022	CRIMINAL LAW	WEINREB	13.00
1205	CRIMINAL PROCEDURE	ALLEN, KUHNS & STUNTZ	15.00
1202	CRIMINAL PROCEDURE	HADDAD, Z., S. & B.	18.00
1200	CRIMINAL PROCEDURE	KAMISAR, LAFAVE & ISRAEL	17.00
1204	CRIMINAL PROCEDURE	SALTZBURG & CAPRA	15.00
1203	CRIMINAL PROCEDURE (PROCESS)	WEINREB	16.50
1303	DEBTOR-CREDITOR	EISENBERG	17.00
1302	DEBTOR-CREDITOR	EPSTEIN, LANDERS & NICKLES	16.00
1300	DEBTOR-CREDITOR (CRED. RTS.)	RIESENFELD	19.00
1304	DEBTOR-CREDITOR	WARREN & WESTBROOK	17.00
1223	DECEDENTS EST. (WILLS, TR. & EST.)	DUKEMINIER & JOHANSON	17.00
1224	DECEDENTS ESTATES	RITCHIE, ALFORD, EFFLAND & DORIS	19.00
1222	DECEDENTS ESTATES	SCOLES & HALBACH	19.50
1231	DECEDENTS ESTATES (TRUSTS)	WAGGONER, WELLMAN, A. & F.	18.00
	DOMESTIC RELATIONS (see FAMILY LAW)		
1670	EMPLOYMENT DISCRIMINATION	FRIEDMAN & STRICKLER	15.00
1671	EMPLOYMENT DISCRIMINATION	ZIMMER, SULLIVAN, R. & C.	15.00
1660	EMPLOYMENT LAW	ROTHSTEIN, KNAPP & LIEBMAN	17.50
1350	ENTERPRISE ORGANIZATION	CONARD, KNAUSS & SIEGEL	19.00
1342	ENVIRONMENTAL LAW	ANDERSON, MANDELKER & TARLOCK	14.00
1341	ENVIRONMENTAL LAW	FINDLEY & FARBER	16.00
1344	ENVIRONMENTAL LAW	PERCIVAL, MILLER, S. & L.	16.00
1343	ENVIRONMENTAL LAW	PLATER, ABRAMS & GOLDFARB	15.00
	EQUITY (see REMEDIES)		
1217	ESTATE & GIFT TAXATION	BITTKER & CLARK	13.00
1214	ESTATE & GIFT TAXATION	KAHN & WAGGONER	15.00
1213	ESTATE & GIFT TAX (FED. WEALTH TRANS.)	SURREY, MCDANIEL & GUTMAN	14.00
	ETHICS (see PROFESSIONAL RESPONSIBILITY)		
1064	EVIDENCE	STRONG, BROUN & MOUSTELLER	20.50
1065	EVIDENCE	GREEN & NESSON	18.00
1061	EVIDENCE	WALTZ & PARK	18.00
1063	EVIDENCE	LEMPERT & SALTZBURG	10.00
1062	EVIDENCE	MCCORMICK, SUTTON & WELLBORN	20.00
1066	EVIDENCE	MUELLER & KIRKPATRICK	15.00
1060	EVIDENCE	WEINSTEIN, M., A. & B.	20.50
1244	FAMILY LAW (DOMESTIC RELATION)	AREEN	20.00
1242	FAMILY LAW (DOMESTIC RELATION)	CLARK & GLOWINSKY	17.00
1245	FAMILY LAW (DOMESTIC RELATION)	ELLMAN, KURTZ & BARTLETT	18.00
1243	FAMILY LAW (DOMESTIC RELATION)	KRAUSE	22.00
1240	FAMILY LAW (DOMESTIC RELATION)	WADLINGTON	18.00
1231	FAMILY PROPERTY LAW (WILLS/TRUSTS)	WAGGONER, WELLMAN, A. & F.	18.00
1360	FEDERAL COURTS	BATOR ET AL. (HART & WECHSLER)	17.00
1362	FEDERAL COURTS	CURRIE	15.00
1363	FEDERAL COURTS	LOW & JEFFRIES	14.00
1361	FEDERAL COURTS	MCCORMICK, C. & W.	18.00
1510	GRATUITOUS TRANSFERS	CLARK, LUSKY & MURPHY	16.00
1650	HEALTH LAW	FURROW, J., J., & S.	15.50
1640	IMMIGRATION LAW	ALEINIKOFF & MARTIN	14.00
1371	INSURANCE LAW	KEETON	19.00
1372	INSURANCE LAW	YORK, WHELAN & MARTINEZ	17.00
1370	INSURANCE LAW	YOUNG & HOLMES	15.00
1394	INTERNATIONAL BUSINESS TRANSACTIONS	FOLSOM, GORDON & SPANOGLE	13.00
1393	INTERNATIONAL LAW	CARTER & TRIMBLE	14.00
1392	INTERNATIONAL LAW	HENKIN, P., S. & S.	15.00
1390	INTERNATIONAL LAW	OLIVER, F., B., S., & W.	20.00
1331	LABOR LAW	COX, BOK, GORMAN & FINKIN	17.00
1333	LABOR LAW	LESLIE	16.50
1332	LABOR LAW	MELTZER & HENDERSON	18.00
1330	LABOR LAW	MERRIFIELD, S. & C.	17.00
1471	LAND FINANCE (REAL ESTATE TRANS)	BERGER & JOHNSTONE	16.00
1620	LAND FINANCE (REAL ESTATE TRANS)	NELSON & WHITMAN	17.00
1470	LAND FINANCE	PENNEY, B. & C.	14.00
1450	LAND USE	WRIGHT & GITELMAN	21.00
1421	LEGISLATION	ESKRIDGE & FRICKEY	12.00
1590	LOCAL GOVERNMENT LAW	VALENTE & McCARTHY	20.00
1480	MASS MEDIA	FRANKLIN & ANDERSON	13.00
1312	NEGOTIABLE INSTRUMENTS (COMM. LAW)	JORDAN & WARREN	18.00
1313	NEGOTIABLE INSTRUMENTS (COMM. LAW)	WHALEY	16.00
1570	NEW YORK PRACTICE	PETERFREUND & McLAUGHLIN	23.00
1541	OIL & GAS	KUNTZ, L., A. & S.	16.00
1540	OIL & GAS	MAXWELL, WILLIAMS, M. & K.	16.00
1560	PATENT LAW	FRANCIS & COLLINS	21.00
1310	PAYMENT LAW (COMM LAW, SALES & SEC.TR.)	SPEIDEL, SUMMERS & WHITE	19.00
1313	PAYMENT LAW (COMM.LAW / NEG. INST.)	WHALEY	16.00
1431	PRODUCTS LIABILITY	KEETON, O., M., & G.	18.00
1430	PRODUCTS LIABILITY	NOEL & PHILLIPS	19.50
1091	PROF. RESPONSIBILITY (ETHICS)	GILLERS	11.00
1093	PROF. RESPONSIBILITY (ETHICS)	HAZARD, KONIAK, & CRAMTON	16.00
1092	PROF. RESPONSIBILITY (ETHICS)	MORGAN & ROTUNDA	12.00
1090	PROF. RESPONSIBILITY (ETHICS)	PIRSIG & KIRWIN	13.00
1033	PROPERTY	BROWDER, C., N., S.& W.	18.50
1030	PROPERTY	CASNER & LEACH	19.00
1031	PROPERTY	CRIBBET, JOHNSON, FINLEY & SMITH	19.50
1037	PROPERTY	DONAHUE, KAUPER & MARTIN	16.00
1035	PROPERTY	DUKEMINIER & KRIER	16.00
1034	PROPERTY	HAAR & LIEBMAN	18.50
1036	PROPERTY	KURTZ & HOVENKAMP	17.00
1032	PROPERTY	RABIN & KWALL	16.00
1621	REAL ESTATE TRANSACTIONS	GOLDSTEIN & KORNGOLD	16.00
1471	REAL ESTATE TRANS. & FIN. (LAND FINANCE)	BERGER & JOHNSTONE	15.00
1620	REAL ESTATE TRANSFER & FINANCE	NELSON & WHITMAN	17.00
1254	REMEDIES (EQUITY)	LAYCOCK	16.00
1253	REMEDIES (EQUITY)	LEAVELL, L., N. & K/F.	19.00
1252	REMEDIES (EQUITY)	RE & KRAUSS	21.00
1255	REMEDIES (EQUITY)	SHOBEN & TABB	20.50
1250	REMEDIES (EQUITY)	YORK, BAUMAN & RENDLEMAN	23.00
1312	SALES (COMM. LAW)	JORDAN & WARREN	17.00
1310	SALES (COMM. LAW)	SPEIDEL, SUMMERS & WHITE	19.00
1313	SALES (COMM. LAW)	WHALEY	16.00
1312	SECURED TRANS. (COMM. LAW)	JORDAN & WARREN	17.00
1310	SECURED TRANS.	SPEIDEL, SUMMERS & WHITE	19.00
1313	SECURED TRANS. (COMM. LAW)	WHALEY	16.00
1272	SECURITIES REGULATION	COX, HILLMAN, LANGEVOORT	16.00
1270	SECURITIES REGULATION	JENNINGS, MARSH & COFFEE	16.00
1271	SECURITIES REGULATION	RATNER	16.00
1215	TAXATION (BASIC FED. INC.)	ANDREWS	16.00
1217	TAXATION (ESTATE & GIFT)	BITTKER & CLARK	13.00
1212	TAXATION (FED. INC.)	FREELAND, LIND & STEPHENS	15.00
1211	TAXATION (FED. INC.)	GRAETZ & SCHENK	15.00
1214	TAXATION (ESTATE & GIFT)	KAHN & WAGGONER	15.00
1210	TAXATION (FED. INC.)	KLEIN & BANKMAN	16.00
1218	TAXATION (CORPORATE)	LIND, S., L. & R.	12.00
1213	TAXATION (FED. WEALTH TRANS.)	SURREY, MCDANIEL & GUTMAN.	14.00
1006	TORTS	DOBBS	17.00
1003	TORTS	EPSTEIN	18.50
1004	TORTS	FRANKLIN & RABIN	15.50
1001	TORTS	HENDERSON, P. & S.	18.50
1002	TORTS	KEETON, K., S.& S.	21.00
1000	TORTS	PROSSER, W., S., K., & P.	22.00
1005	TORTS	SHULMAN, JAMES & GRAY	20.00
1281	TRADE REGULATION (ANTITRUST)	HANDLER, B., P. & G.	15.50
1230	TRUSTS	BOGERT, O., H., & H.	18.00
1231	TRUSTS/WILLS (FAMILY PROPERTY LAW)	WAGGONER, WELLMAN A. & F.	18.00
1410	U.C.C.	EPSTEIN, MARTIN, H. & N.	13.00
1580	WATER LAW	TRELEASE & GOULD	17.00
1223	WILLS, TRUSTS & EST. (DEC. EST.)	DUKEMINIER & JOHANSON	17.00
1220	WILLS	MECHEM & ATKINSON	19.00
1231	WILLS/TRUSTS (FAMILY PROPERTY LAW)	WAGGONER, WELLMAN A. & F.	17.00

(SERIES XXXVII)

CASENOTES PUBLISHING CO. INC. ● 1640 FIFTH STREET, SUITE 208 ● SANTA MONICA, CA 90401 ● (310) 395-6500

PLEASE PURCHASE FROM YOUR LOCAL BOOKSTORE. IF UNAVAILABLE, YOU MAY ORDER DIRECT.*

4TH CLASS POSTAGE (ALLOW TWO WEEKS) $1.00 PER ORDER; 1ST CLASS POSTAGE $3.00 (ONE BOOK), $2.00 EACH (TWO OR MORE BOOKS)

*CALIF. RESIDENTS PLEASE ADD 8¼% SALES TAX

NOTES

A GLOSSARY OF COMMON LATIN WORDS AND PHRASES ENCOUNTERED IN THE LAW

A FORTIORI: Because one fact exists or has been proven, therefore a second fact that is related to the first fact must also exist.

A PRIORI: From the cause to the effect. A term of logic used to denote that when one generally accepted truth is shown to be a cause, another particular effect must necessarily follow.

AB INITIO: From the beginning; a condition which has existed throughout, as in a marriage which was void ab initio.

ACTUS REUS: The wrongful act; in criminal law, such action sufficient to trigger criminal liability.

AD VALOREM: According to value; an ad valorem tax is imposed upon an item located within the taxing jurisdiction calculated by the value of such item.

AMICUS CURIAE: Friend of the court. Its most common usage takes the form of an amicus curiae brief, filed by a person who is not a party to an action but is nonetheless allowed to offer an argument supporting his legal interests.

ARGUENDO: In arguing. A statement, possibly hypothetical, made for the purpose of argument, is one made arguendo.

BILL QUIA TIMET: A bill to quiet title (establish ownership) to real property.

BONA FIDE: True, honest, or genuine. May refer to a person's legal position based on good faith or lacking notice of fraud (such as a bona fide purchaser for value) or to the authenticity of a particular document (such as a bona fide last will and testament).

CAUSA MORTIS: With approaching death in mind. A gift causa mortis is a gift given by a party who feels certain that death is imminent.

CAVEAT EMPTOR: Let the buyer beware. This maxim is reflected in the rule of law that a buyer purchases at his own risk because it is his responsibility to examine, judge, test, and otherwise inspect what he is buying.

CERTIORARI: A writ of review. Petitions for review of a case by the United States Supreme Court are most often done by means of a writ of certiorari.

CONTRA: On the other hand. Opposite. Contrary to.

CORAM NOBIS: Before us; writs of error directed to the court that originally rendered the judgment.

CORAM VOBIS: Before you; writs of error directed by an appellate court to a lower court to correct a factual error.

CORPUS DELICTI: The body of the crime; the requisite elements of a crime amounting to objective proof that a crime has been committed.

CUM TESTAMENTO ANNEXO, ADMINISTRATOR (ADMINISTRATOR C.T.A.): With will annexed; an administrator c.t.a. settles an estate pursuant to a will in which he is not appointed.

DE BONIS NON, ADMINISTRATOR (ADMINISTRATOR D.B.N.): Of goods not administered; an administrator d.b.n. settles a partially settled estate.

DE FACTO: In fact; in reality; actually. Existing in fact but not officially approved or engendered.

DE JURE: By right; lawful. Describes a condition that is legitimate "as a matter of law," in contrast to the term "de facto," which connotes something existing in fact but not legally sanctioned or authorized. For example, de facto segregation refers to segregation brought about by housing patterns, etc., whereas de jure segregation refers to segregation created by law.

DE MINIMUS: Of minimal importance; insignificant; a trifle; not worth bothering about.

DE NOVO: Anew; a second time; afresh. A trial de novo is a new trial held at the appellate level as if the case originated there and the trial at a lower level had not taken place.

DICTA: Generally used as an abbreviated form of obiter dicta, a term describing those portions of a judicial opinion incidental or not necessary to resolution of the specific question before the court. Such nonessential statements and remarks are not considered to be binding precedent.

DUCES TECUM: Refers to a particular type of writ or subpoena requesting a party or organization to produce certain documents in their possession.

EN BANC: Full bench. Where a court sits with all justices present rather than the usual quorum.

EX PARTE: For one side or one party only. An ex parte proceeding is one undertaken for the benefit of only one party, without notice to, or an appearance by, an adverse party.

EX POST FACTO: After the fact. An ex post facto law is a law that retroactively changes the consequences of a prior act.

EX REL.: Abbreviated form of the term ex relatione, meaning, upon relation or information. When the state brings an action in which it has no interest against an individual at the instigation of one who has a private interest in the matter.

FORUM NON CONVENIENS: Inconvenient forum. Although a court may have jurisdiction over the case, the action should be tried in a more conveniently located court, one to which parties and witnesses may more easily travel, for example.

GUARDIAN AD LITEM: A guardian of an infant as to litigation, appointed to represent the infant and pursue his/her rights.

HABEAS CORPUS: You have the body. The modern writ of habeas corpus is a writ directing that a person (body) being detained (such as a prisoner) be brought before the court so that the legality of his detention can be judicially ascertained.

IN CAMERA: In private, in chambers. When a hearing is held before a judge in his chambers or when all spectators are excluded from the courtroom.

IN FORMA PAUPERIS: In the manner of a pauper. A party who proceeds in forma pauperis because of his poverty is one who is allowed to bring suit without liability for costs.

INFRA: Below, under. A word referring the reader to a later part of a book. (The opposite of supra.)

IN LOCO PARENTIS: In the place of a parent.

IN PARI DELICTO: Equally wrong; a court of equity will not grant requested relief to an applicant who is in pari delicto, or as much at fault in the transactions giving rise to the controversy as is the opponent of the applicant.

IN PARI MATERIA: On like subject matter or upon the same matter. Statutes relating to the same person or things are said to be in pari materia. It is a general rule of statutory construction that such statutes should be construed together, i.e., looked at as if they together constituted one law.

IN PERSONAM: Against the person. Jurisdiction over the person of an individual.

IN RE: In the matter of. Used to designate a proceeding involving an estate or other property.

IN REM: A term that signifies an action against the res, or thing. An action in rem is basically one that is taken directly against property, as distinguished from an action in personam, i.e., against the person.

INTER ALIA: Among other things. Used to show that the whole of a statement, pleading, list, statute, etc., has not been set forth in its entirety.

INTER PARTES: Between the parties. May refer to contracts, conveyances or other transactions having legal significance.

INTER VIVOS: Between the living. An inter vivos gift is a gift made by a living grantor, as distinguished from bequests contained in a will, which pass upon the death of the testator.

IPSO FACTO: By the mere fact itself.

JUS: Law or the entire body of law.

LEX LOCI: The law of the place; the notion that the rights of parties to a legal proceeding are governed by the law of the place where those rights arose.

MALUM IN SE: Evil or wrong in and of itself; inherently wrong. This term describes an act that is wrong by its very nature, as opposed to one which would not be wrong but for the fact that there is a specific legal prohibition against it (malum prohibitum).

MALUM PROHIBITUM: Wrong because prohibited, but not inherently evil. Used to describe something that is wrong because it is expressly forbidden by law but that is not in and of itself evil, e.g., speeding.

MANDAMUS: We command. A writ directing an official to take a certain action.

MENS REA: A guilty mind; a criminal intent. A term used to signify the mental state that accompanies a crime or other prohibited act. Some crimes require only a general mens rea (general intent to do the prohibited act), but others, like assault with intent to murder, require the existence of a specific mens rea.

MODUS OPERANDI: Method of operating; generally refers to the manner or style of a criminal in committing crimes, admissible in appropriate cases as evidence of the identity of a defendant.

NEXUS: A connection to.

NISI PRIUS: A court of first impression. A nisi prius court is one where issues of fact are tried before a judge or jury.

N.O.V. (NON OBSTANTE VEREDICTO): Notwithstanding the verdict. A judgment n.o.v. is a judgment given in favor of one party despite the fact that a verdict was returned in favor of the other party, the justification being that the verdict either had no reasonable support in fact or was contrary to law.

NUNC PRO TUNC: Now for then. This phrase refers to actions that may be taken and will then have full retroactive effect.

PENDENTE LITE: Pending the suit; pending litigation underway.

PER CAPITA: By head; beneficiaries of an estate, if they take in equal shares, take per capita.

PER CURIAM: By the court; signifies an opinion ostensibly written "by the whole court" and with no identified author.

PER SE: By itself, in itself; inherently.

PER STIRPES: By representation. Used primarily in the law of wills to describe the method of distribution where a person, generally because of death, is unable to take that which is left to him by the will of another, and therefore his heirs divide such property between them rather than take under the will individually.

PRIMA FACIE: On its face, at first sight. A prima facie case is one that is sufficient on its face, meaning that the evidence supporting it is adequate to establish the case until contradicted or overcome by other evidence.

PRO TANTO: For so much; as far as it goes. Often used in eminent domain cases when a property owner receives partial payment for his land without prejudice to his right to bring suit for the full amount he claims his land to be worth.

QUANTUM MERUIT: As much as he deserves. Refers to recovery based on the doctrine of unjust enrichment in those cases in which a party has rendered valuable services or furnished materials that were accepted and enjoyed by another under circumstances that would reasonably notify the recipient that the rendering party expected to be paid. In essence, the law implies a contract to pay the reasonable value of the services or materials furnished.

QUASI: Almost like; as if; nearly. This term is essentially used to signify that one subject or thing is almost analogous to another but that material differences between them do exist. For example, a quasi-criminal proceeding is one that is not strictly criminal but shares enough of the same characteristics to require some of the same safeguards (e.g., procedural due process must be followed in a parol hearing).

QUID PRO QUO: Something for something. In contract law, the consideration, something of value, passed between the parties to render the contract binding.

RES GESTAE: Things done; in evidence law, this principle justifies the admission of a statement that would otherwise be hearsay when it is made so closely to the event in question as to be said to be a part of it, or with such spontaneity as not to have the possibility of falsehood.

RES IPSA LOQUITUR: The thing speaks for itself. This doctrine gives rise to a rebuttable presumption of negligence when the instrumentality causing the injury was within the exclusive control of the defendant, and the injury was one that does not normally occur unless a person has been negligent.

RES JUDICATA: A matter adjudged. Doctrine which provides that once a court of competent jurisdiction has rendered a final judgment or decree on the merits, that judgment or decree is conclusive upon the parties to the case and prevents them from engaging in any other litigation on the points and issues determined therein.

RESPONDEAT SUPERIOR: Let the master reply. This doctrine holds the master liable for the wrongful acts of his servant (or the principal for his agent) in those cases in which the servant (or agent) was acting within the scope of his authority at the time of the injury.

STARE DECISIS: To stand by or adhere to that which has been decided. The common law doctrine of stare decisis attempts to give security and certainty to the law by following the policy that once a principle of law as applicable to a certain set of facts has been set forth in a decision, it forms a precedent which will subsequently be followed, even though a different decision might be made were it the first time the question had arisen. Of course, stare decisis is not an inviolable principle and is departed from in instances where there is good cause (e.g., considerations of public policy led the Supreme Court to disregard prior decisions sanctioning segregation).

SUPRA: Above. A word referring a reader to an earlier part of a book.

ULTRA VIRES: Beyond the power. This phrase is most commonly used to refer to actions taken by a corporation that are beyond the power or legal authority of the corporation.

ADDENDUM OF FRENCH DERIVATIVES

IN PAIS: Not pursuant to legal proceedings.

CHATTEL: Tangible personal property.

CY PRES: Doctrine permitting courts to apply trust funds to purposes not expressed in the trust but necessary to carry out the settlor's intent.

PER AUTRE VIE: For another's life; in property law, an estate may be granted that will terminate upon the death of someone other than the grantee.

PROFIT A PRENDRE: A license to remove minerals or other produce from land.

VOIR DIRE: Process of questioning jurors as to their predispositions about the case or parties to a proceeding in order to identify those jurors displaying bias or prejudice.

NOTES

TABLE OF CASES

Continued on next page

TABLE OF CASES (Continued)

Continued on next page

TABLE OF CASES (Continued)

CHAPTER 1
CHARACTERISTICS OF THE ADVERSARY SYSTEM

QUICK REFERENCE RULES OF LAW

1. **Examination of a Witness by the Trial Judge.** The trial judge may manage the trial and his actions create reversible error only where he has manifested to the jury a prejudice to one side. (United States v. Beaty)

   [For more information on examination of a witness by the trial judge, see Casenote Law Outline on Evidence, Chapter 11, § V, Order and Scope of Examination.]

2. **Judicial Discretion to Admit Testimony.** A trial judge has the discretion to admit testimony given by a witness at a previous trial if that witness is now unavailable. (State v. Maynard)

   [For more information on judicial discretion to admit testimony, see Casenote Law Outline on Evidence, Chapter 5, § II, Preliminary Questions of Fact.]

3. **The Admissibility of Confessions.** A statement may be adopted through the silence of a party. (State v. Walton)

   [For more information on the admissibility of confessions, see Casenote Law Outline on Evidence, Chapter 5, § II, Preliminary Questions of Fact.]

4. **Attorney-client Privilege.** A court may conduct an in camera review to determine whether privileged attorney-client communications fall within the crime-fraud exception. (United States v. Zolin)

   [For more information on attorney-client privilege, see Casenote Law Outline on Evidence, Chapter 8, § II, The Attorney-Client Privilege.]

5. **Errors in Ruling on Admissibility.** One who complains on appeal of exclusion of evidence must show affirmatively that he was injured thereby. (First Sec. Bank v. Burgi)

   [For more information on errors in ruling on admissibility, see Casenote Law Outline on Evidence, Chapter 5, § III, Evidentiary Errors.]

6. **Permissible Impeachment Evidence.** To raise and preserve for review the claim of improper impeachment with a prior conviction, a defendant must testify at trial. (Luce v. United States)

   [For more information on permissible impeachment evidence, see Casenote Law Outline on Evidence, Chapter 11, § VII, Impeachment of Witnesses.]

7. **Objections to Evidence.** When an objection is made to a question propounded to a witness, it should be sufficiently specific to inform the court and the opposing counsel of the real point of the objection. (Bragg v. Metropolitan St. Ry. Co.)

   [For more information on objections to evidence, see Casenote Law Outline on Evidence, Chapter 5, § I, Preserving Objections.]

8. **Preserving Objections.** The rules of evidence, procedure, and substantive law will be applied the same to all parties in a criminal trial, whether that party is represented by counsel or acting pro se. (Williams v. State)

   [For more information on preserving objections, see Casenote Law Outline on Evidence, Chapter 5, § I, Preserving Objections.]

9. **The Doctrine of Multiple Admissibility.** When an evidentiary fact is offered for one purpose, it is not admissible because it cannot be considered for other purposes. (Carbo v. United States)

    [For more information on the doctrine of multiple admissibility, see Casenote Law Outline on Evidence, Chapter 5, § IV, Limited Admissibility.]

10. **Preserving Objections.** The court has no duty to give a limiting instruction in the absence of a request. (Sherman v. Burke Contracting, Inc.)

    [For more information on preserving objections, see Casenote Law Outline on Evidence, Chapter 5, § I, Preserving Objections.]

11. **The Admission of Immaterial Evidence.** The admission of immaterial evidence does not necessarily require the reversal of a case where a court sits without a jury as the trier of fact. (Clark v. United States)

    [For more information on the admission of immaterial evidence, see Casenote Law Outline on Evidence, Chapter 5, § III, Evidentiary Errors.]

UNITED STATES v. BEATY
722 F.2d 1090 (3d Cir. 1983).

NOTES:

NATURE OF CASE: Appeals from convictions on drug related charges.

FACT SUMMARY: Beaty (D) and Ballouz (D) contended that the trial judge's actions prejudiced their defense and constituted reversible error.

CONCISE RULE OF LAW: The trial judge may manage the trial and his actions create reversible error only where he has manifested to the jury a prejudice to one side.

FACTS: Beaty (D) and Ballouz (D) were charged with attempting to import illegal drugs. At trial, Beaty (D) presented no evidence, yet his counsel vigorously cross-examined prosecution witnesses concerning the truth of their testimony. The trial judge cautioned him several times concerning the basis for such questioning. Ballouz (D) presented alibi evidence in the form of his testimony and the testimony of a witness, Mrs. Axelson. The court conducted examination of Mrs. Axelson in the presence of the jury which sought to examine her close relationship to Ballouz (D) and her credibility. Both defendants were convicted and appealed. Beaty (D) contended that the court's behavior chilled his counsel from adequately representing him. Ballouz (D) contended that the court showed partisanship toward the prosecution by cross-examining a key defense witness.

ISSUE: May the trial judge manage the trial but not manifest a prejudice to one side to the jury?

HOLDING AND DECISION: (Hunter, J.) Yes. A trial judge may manage the trial, and his actions are reversible error only where he manifests a prejudice to one side to the jury. In this case, the judge's comments to Beaty's (D) counsel were not such as would prejudice the fairness of the trial. Full cross-examination of witnesses was pursued showing no true chill was experienced. On the other hand, the cross-examination of a key defense witness was prejudicial error. It induced the jury into believing the judge questioned the veracity of the testimony and the credibility of the witness. This crossed the line from impartial manager to advocate. This prejudice deprived Ballouz (D) of a fair trial, and his conviction must be vacated.

EDITOR'S ANALYSIS: The judge is often viewed with great respect by jurors. Thus, any indication of favoritism by the judge may have a significant impact on the jury. Federal Rule of Evidence 614(b) codifies the judge's right to interrogate witnesses, yet it does not allow manifestations of partiality. Reversals based upon judicial partiality are rare.

[For more information on examination of a witness by the trial judge, see Casenote Law Outline on Evidence, Chapter 11, § V, Order and Scope of Examination.]

STATE v. MAYNARD

N.C. Sup. Ct., 184 N.C. 653, 113 S.E. 682 (1922).

NATURE OF CASE: Appeal from conviction for breaking and entering.

FACT SUMMARY: Maynard (D) contended that the trial judge erroneously admitted into evidence the testimony of an unavailable codefendant, which had been given at a preliminary hearing.

CONCISE RULE OF LAW: A trial judge has the discretion to admit testimony given by a witness at a previous trial if that witness is now unavailable.

FACTS: Maynard (D), Barnes, and two others were indicted for breaking into a storehouse. Barnes escaped from jail before trial after having given testimony at a preliminary inquiry. After evidence of Barnes' escape from custody was introduced at Maynard's (D) trial, the State (P) introduced a stenographer, who, after being duly sworn, testified that he had taken the stenographic notes of Barnes' evidence during the preliminary investigation. The stenographer further stated that his notes of the evidence had not been read to Barnes, nor signed by him at the close of his testimony, nor was a copy of the evidence filed with the court clerk. Although counsel for Maynard (D) objected, the court allowed the stenographer to state to the jury the evidence which Barnes had given in the preliminary investigation. The trial judge later denied a request by Maynard (D) that the judge instruct the jury that the stenographer's testimony was not admissible unless it appeared to the jury that Barnes was absent by the inducement or other act of Maynard (D). After being convicted, Maynard (D) appealed, arguing that the trial judge erred in allowing the stenographer to testify, and in refusing to give the requested instruction to the jury.

ISSUE: Does a trial judge have discretion to admit testimony given by a witness at a previous trial if that witness is now unavailable?

HOLDING AND DECISION: (Hoke, J.) Yes. Where, in a judicial proceeding before a court having power to compel the attendance of witnesses, administer oaths, and hear evidence pertinent to the inquiry, a witness has given evidence, and the defendants are present and have the right to cross-examine the witness, such testimony, when properly attested and verified, may be introduced and used during a second trial of the cause where the witness is unavailable. A witness is considered to be unavailable if he or she has died, has become hopelessly or permanently insane, is wrongfully absent from the trial by the acts and procurement of the defendants, or, when the witness has departed from the jurisdiction of the court and become a nonresident permanently. In these situations, the right and privilege of a defendant in a criminal case to confront his accuser and his witnesses, as mandated by the United States Constitution, is fully accorded by the opportunity given to cross-examine them at the former trial. The question of admitting the evidence and pertinent preliminary findings is for the court and not the jury. The trial judge's actions in admitting such testimony will not be disturbed on appeal absent a manifest abuse of discretion. Here, no reversible error appeared in the record. Affirmed.

EDITOR'S ANALYSIS: The Federal Rules provide that "Preliminary questions concerning the qualification of a person to be a witness, the existence of a privilege, or the admissibility of evidence shall be determined by the court. . . . In making its determination it is not bound by the rules of evidence except those with respect to privileges." See Federal Rule of Evidence 104(a).

[For more information on judicial discretion to admit testimony, see Casenote Law Outline on Evidence, Chapter 5, § II, Preliminary Questions of Fact.]

NOTES:

STATE v. WALTON
N.C. Sup. Ct., 172 N.C. 931, 90 S.E. 518 (1916).

NATURE OF CASE: Appeal from conviction for fornication and adultery.

FACT SUMMARY: Walton (D) objected to the introduction of a statement made by the female codefendant, to which he was silent when it was made, that he was the father of her child.

CONCISE RULE OF LAW: A statement may be adopted through the silence of a party.

FACTS: Walton (D) and a female codefendant were indicted for fornication and adultery. The woman, a Mrs. Harris, lived approximately one-and-a-half miles from the Amazon Mill, where Walton (D) was employed as the night watchman. Walton (D) visited Harris' home almost daily, during the day and at night, and was frequently seen performing chores there. On one occasion, a policeman went to her house to have her fill out a certificate of the birth of her child, and during this visit, Walton (D) stood some four or five feet away. When in answer to a question posed by the policeman as to the name of the father, Harris said that the child's father's name was John Walton (D). Walton (D) saying nothing, then exited the room. Walton's (D) motion to exclude the statement of paternity was denied, and he was subsequently convicted of the crimes charged. On appeal, Walton (D) argued that the declaration was improperly introduced into evidence at trial.

ISSUE: May a statement be adopted through the silence of a party?

HOLDING AND DECISION: (Allen, J.) Yes. If the declaration of Harris that Walton (D) was the father of her child was made in Walton's (D) presence and was heard by him, it was clearly competent. A declaration in the presence of a party to a cause becomes evidence, as showing that the party, on hearing such a statement, did not deny its truth; for if he is silent when he ought to have denied the statement, there is a presumption of his acquiescence. Where a statement is made, either to the person or within his hearing, that he was concerned in the commission of a crime, to which he makes no reply, the natural inference is that the imputation is well founded, or otherwise it would have been objected to. Here, Walton (D) was present when the declaration was made, and there is evidence that he heard it, as he was within four or five feet, and said nothing and left as soon as he was charged with being the father of the child. The evidence is ample to support the verdict. Affirmed.

EDITOR'S ANALYSIS: The Federal Rules state that "Hearings on the admissibility of confessions shall in all cases be conducted out of the hearing of the jury. Hearings on other preliminary matters shall be so conducted when the interests of justice require or, when an accused is a witness, if he so requests." Federal Rule of Evidence 104(c).

[For more information on the admissibility of confessions, see Casenote Law Outline on Evidence, Chapter 5, § II, Preliminary Questions of Fact.]

UNITED STATES v. ZOLIN
491 U.S. 554 (1989).

NATURE OF CASE: Appeal from decision in a tax return investigation action.

FACT SUMMARY: The Internal Revenue Service (P) contended that the crime-fraud exception to the attorney-client privilege should allow it to investigate documentary material relating to Church of Scientology (D) activities, but the trial court refused to inspect the allegedly privileged material absent independent evidence of crime or fraud.

CONCISE RULE OF LAW: A court may conduct an in camera review to determine whether privileged attorney-client communications fall within the crime-fraud exception.

FACTS: The Internal Revenue Service (P) sought to investigate the tax returns of L. Ron Hubbard, founder of the Church of Scientology (D). In the course of investigation, the IRS (P) sought access to documents that had been filed under seal in state court in connection with a suit by the Church (D) against one of its former members. The Church (D) objected to production of the documentary material on the grounds of the attorney-client privilege. The IRS (P) argued that the material fell within the crime-fraud exception to the privilege and urged the district court to listen to the tapes in making its privilege determination. Both the district court and the Ninth Circuit refused to apply the crime-fraud exception, finding no independent evidence to support it. The IRS (P) appealed, arguing that the crime-fraud exception did not have to be established by independent evidence (i.e., without reference to the content of the contested communications themselves) and that the applicability of the exception could be resolved by an in camera inspection of the allegedly privileged material.

ISSUE: May a court conduct an in camera review to determine whether privileged attorney-client communications fall within the crime-fraud exception?

HOLDING AND DECISION: (Blackmun, J.) Yes. A court may conduct an in camera review to determine whether privileged attorney-client communications fall within the crime-fraud exception. No express provision of the Federal Rules of Evidence (Fed. R. Evid.) bars the use of an in camera review of allegedly privileged communications to determine whether those communications fall within the crime-fraud exception. Although the Church (D) argues that Fed. R. Evid. Rule 104 (a) might be read with Rule 1101 (c) to establish that, in a summons-enforcement proceeding, attorney-client communications cannot be considered by the district court in making its crime-fraud ruling, there is no basis for holding that the documentary matter in this case must be deemed privileged under Rule 104 (a) while the question of crime or fraud remains open. Furthermore, disclosure of allegedly privileged materials to the district court for purposes of determining the merits of a claim of privilege does not have the legal effect of terminating the privilege. The question of the propriety of the review then becomes whether the policies underlying the privilege and its exceptions are better fostered by permitting such review or prohibiting it. The costs of imposing an absolute bar to consideration of communications in camera for the purpose of establishing the crime-fraud exception are too high. The standard that strikes the correct balance is that, before engaging in in camera review to determine the applicability of the crime-fraud exception, the judge should require a showing of a factual basis adequate to support a good-faith belief by a reasonable person that in camera review of materials may reveal evidence to establish the claim that the crime-fraud exception applies. Moreover, the party opposing the privilege, here the United States (P), may use any unprivileged evidence in support of its request for an in camera review, even if the evidence (here, transcripts of the tapes) is not independent of the contested communication. Reversed.

EDITOR'S ANALYSIS: As pointed out by Justice Blackmun in the Zolin case, the Supreme Court does not interpret Rule 104(a) in the same manner as it is interpreted under California law (Cal. Evid. Code Ann., 915 (a)). Under the Federal Rules of Evidence, Rule 104(a) provides that preliminary questions concerning the qualifications of a person to be a witness, the existence of a privilege, or the admissibility of evidence shall be determined by the court. In making its determination, it is not bound by the Rules of Evidence, except those with respect to privileges. However, Rule 104(a) does not by its terms, exclude from consideration all materials as of which a claim of privilege has been made. The comparable California evidence rule, § 915 (a), on the other hand, provides that a presiding officer may not require disclosure of any information "claimed to be privileged" under this division in order to rule on the claim of privilege. The Court in Zolin refused to read Rule 104(a) as if its text were identical to the California rule, thereby allowing a more flexible interpretation that lets the district court consider "non-independent" evidence in determining whether in camera review may take place.

[For more information on attorney-client privilege, see Casenote Law Outline on Evidence, Chapter 8, § II, The Attorney-Client Privilege.]

NOTES:

FIRST SEC. BANK v. BURGI
Utah Sup. Ct., 122 Utah 445, 251 P.2d 297 (1952).

NATURE OF CASE: Appeal from judgment of failure of deed and bill of sale.

FACT SUMMARY: Burgi (D) contended that the trial court erroneously excluded the testimony of his late father's attorney.

CONCISE RULE OF LAW: One who complains on appeal of exclusion of evidence must show affirmatively that he was injured thereby.

FACTS: Fred Burgi executed a warranty deed dated November 18, 1936, which purported to convey certain property to his son, Clyde (D). This conveyance was not recorded until February 7, 1950, five days after Fred's death. On January 29, 1937, Fred had executed a bill of sale which had assigned all of the stock of groceries, fixtures, and furnishings of the grocery business contained on the property later conveyed, to Clyde (D). The trial court found that there was no delivery of the deed or bill of sale, that they were executed for and with the intent that they would not be operative until after Fred's death, and concluded that the documents were testamentary in intent. Thus, the property and business were held to revert to the estate to be administered by the Bank (P). At trial, the judge, upholding an objection based upon privilege, refused to allow Clyde's (D) attorney to testify to the preparation of the deed in question. On appeal, Clyde (D) argued that he had been injured by the exclusion of the attorney's testimony, and that the judgment of the trial court should accordingly be reversed.

ISSUE: Must one who complains on appeal of exclusion of evidence show affirmatively that he was injured thereby?

HOLDING AND DECISION: (McDonough, J.) Yes. One who complains on appeal of exclusion of evidence must show affirmatively that he was injured thereby. Where an objection to evidence is sustained in an action at law, the general rule is that the record must disclose the substance of the proffered evidence before there can be a reversal because of its rejection. An offer of proof is the accepted method of bringing the substance of the evidence into the bill of exceptions. The reason for the rule is that judgments are not reversed unless error is made to appear, and without something in the record to disclose the substance of the rejected evidence, error does not appear. There is an exception when the question is in proper form, and clearly admits of an answer relevant to the issues and favorable to the party on whose side the witness is called. However, there is nothing in the record here to indicate that the attorney's evidence would be either competent, relevant, material or favorable to Clyde (D). Affirmed.

DISSENT: (Wade, J.) It seems clear that, had the objection not been sustained, the witness would have testified to facts relevant to the issue of delivery of the deed, which would have been favorable to Clyde (D), who called him. This evidence was not excluded on the ground that it would not be relevant, material or favorable to the party who called the witness, but on the ground that it was privileged.

EDITOR'S ANALYSIS: Where a party objects to the admission of certain evidence, Federal Rule of Criminal Procedure 51 requires that the offering party make known to the judge the specific grounds on which the claim of admissibility is made. The same result would be reached in a civil action, under Federal Rule of Civil Procedure 46, governing exceptions to orders of the court.

[For more information on errors in ruling on admissibility, see Casenote Law Outline on Evidence, Chapter 5, § III, Evidentiary Errors.]

NOTES:

LUCE v. UNITED STATES

469 U.S. 38 (1984).

NATURE OF CASE: Appeal from conviction for conspiracy and possession of cocaine with intent to distribute.

FACT SUMMARY: In the Government's (P) action against Luce (D) for conspiracy and possession of cocaine with intent to distribute, Luce (D) contended that the district court's ruling denying Luce's (D) motion to forbid the use of a prior conviction to impeach his credibility was an abuse of discretion.

CONCISE RULE OF LAW: To raise and preserve for review the claim of improper impeachment with a prior conviction, a defendant must testify at trial.

FACTS: Luce (D) was indicted on charges of conspiracy and possession of cocaine with intent to distribute, in violation of 21 U.S.C. §§ 846 and 841(a)(1). During his trial, Luce (D) moved for a ruling to preclude the Government (P) from using a 1974 state conviction to impeach him if he testified. Luce (D) made no commitment that he would testify if the motion was granted and did not make a proffer to the court as to what his testimony would be. In opposing the motion, the Government (P) represented that the conviction was for a serious crime — possession of a controlled substance. The district court ruled that the prior conviction fell within the category of permissible impeachment evidence under Federal Rule of Evidence 609(a). Luce (D) did not testify, and the jury returned a guilty verdict. The U.S. Court of Appeals for the Sixth Circuit affirmed the district court's decision. The court of appeals refused to consider Luce's (D) contention that the district court abused its discretion in denying Luce's (D) motion in limine without making a specific finding that the probative value of the prior conviction outweighed its prejudicial effect. The court of appeals held that when a defendant does not testify, the court will not review the district court's in limine ruling.

ISSUE: To raise and preserve for review the claim of improper impeachment with a prior conviction, must a defendant testify at trial?

HOLDING AND DECISION: (Burger, C.J.) Yes. To raise and preserve for review the claim of improper impeachment with a prior conviction, a defendant must testify at trial. Under Federal Rule of Evidence 609(a)(1), which directs the court to weigh the probative value of a prior conviction against the prejudicial effect to the defendant, to perform such balancing, a court must know the precise natures of the defendant's testimony, which is unknowable when, as here, a defendant does not testify. Were in limine rulings under Rule 609(a) reviewable on appeal, almost any error would result in the windfall of automatic reversal. Requiring Luce (D) to testify in order to preserve Rule 609(a) claims will enable the reviewing court to determine the impact any erroneous impeachment many have had in light of the record as a whole. Affirmed.

EDITOR'S ANALYSIS: As a method of impeachment, evidence of conviction of crime is significant only because it stands as proof of the commission of the underlying criminal act. There is little disagreement from the general proposition that at least some crimes are relevant to credibility. There is, however, much disagreement among cases and commentators about which crimes are usable for this purpose. Traditionally, use of felonies has been accepted and for crimes involving dishonesty or false statement without regard to the grade of the offense.

[For more information on permissible impeachment evidence, see Casenote Law Outline on Evidence, Chapter 11, § VII, Impeachment of Witnesses.]

NOTES:

BRAGG v. METROPOLITAN ST. RY. CO.
Mo. Sup. Ct., 192 Mo. 331, 91 S.W. 527 (1905).

NATURE OF CASE: Appeal from award of damages for negligence.

FACT SUMMARY: Metropolitan (D) contended that improper hypothetical questions had been asked at trial by counsel for Bragg (P).

CONCISE RULE OF LAW: When an objection is made to a question propounded to a witness, it should be sufficiently specific to inform the court and the opposing counsel of the real point of the objection.

FACTS: Bragg (P) sued Metropolitan (D) for injuries sustained when a car in which he was a passenger collided with a Missouri Pacific passenger train. At trial, Bragg (P) called a Dr. Snell, who had examined Bragg (P), to testify. Counsel for Bragg (P) recited the fact situation surrounding the injury, and then asked whether those facts were responsible for Bragg's (P) injuries. Counsel for Metropolitan (D) objected on the grounds that the question was incompetent and not a matter of expert knowledge, but the objection was overruled. Later, Metropolitan (D) called a Dr. Thompson as a witness, and a similar question was put to him by counsel for Bragg (P). Metropolitan (D) objected on the grounds that the question was not a proper hypothetical question, and was incompetent, irrelevant, and immaterial. This objection was also overruled. The jury returned a verdict for Bragg (P), and Metropolitan (D) appealed, arguing that the objections which were made at trial should have been sustained, and that the admission of the answer was error.

ISSUE: When an objection is made to a question propounded to a witness, should it be sufficiently specific to inform the court and the opposing counsel of the real point of the objection?

HOLDING AND DECISION: (Lamm, J.) Yes. When an objection is made to a question propounded to a witness, it should be sufficiently specific to inform the court and the opposing counsel of the real point in the objection. The question propounded to Dr. Snell was plainly directed to the ascertainment of a fact peculiarly within the realm of expert knowledge, i.e., whether the conditions found by Dr. Snell might result from the injuries and the accident outlined in the hypothetical question. It was not error, therefore, to permit Dr. Snell to answer the question asked, and it was also not error to permit Dr. Thompson to answer the hypothetical question which was asked of him. Metropolitan's (D) further ground of objection to the question asked of Dr. Thompson, that it was an improper hypothetical question, is vague and too nonspecific to afford a grounds for relief. The vice underlying any rule of practice tolerating the consideration, on appeal, of reasons and grounds not assigned in objections below is illustrated in the present case. On appeal, Metropolitan (D) has elaborated on the reasons for its objection to the question asked of Dr. Thompson, but these grounds are found nowhere in the record. Affirmed.

EDITOR'S ANALYSIS: If counsel is unable to understand the specific grounds of objection to a question he has propounded, he should ask that either the judge or opposing counsel state the ground. Wigmore states that "a specific objection sustained (like a general objection) is sufficient, though naming an untenable ground, if some other tenable one existed." 1 Wigmore, Evidence § 18 at 342 (3d ed. 1940).

[For more information on objections to evidence, see Casenote Law Outline on Evidence, Chapter 5, § I, Preserving Objections.]

NOTES:

WILLIAMS v. STATE
549 S.W.2d 183 (1977).

NATURE OF CASE: Appeal from conviction for robbery by firearm.

FACT SUMMARY: Williams (D) argued on appeal that the lower court's granting of his request to conduct his own defense at trial denied him a fair and impartial trial.

CONCISE RULE OF LAW: The rules of evidence, procedure, and substantive law will be applied the same to all parties in a criminal trial, whether that party is represented by counsel or acting pro se.

FACTS: Williams (D) was accused by the State (P) of committing robbery with a firearm. At trial, Williams (D) was partially represented by a court-appointed attorney, but Williams (D) also requested permission to pick his own jury and to cross-examine the complaining witness. The trial court granted both requests. During direct examination by the State (P), a witness alluded to a prior robbery by Williams (D), but Williams (D) did not raise an objection until after testimony concerning the robbery was brought out several times. His objection was sustained, and he did not request further relief. Williams (D) himself then proceeded to cross-examine the witness about the prior robbery. Williams (D) was convicted. On appeal, he contended that the trial court erred in admitting the prior offense evidence and also that he was denied a fair and impartial trial because the trial court granted him the right to conduct his own defense.

ISSUE: Will the rules of evidence, procedure, and substantive law be applied the same to all parties in a criminal trial, even those who are acting pro se?

HOLDING AND DECISION: (Dally, C.) Yes. The rules of evidence, procedure, and substantive law will be applied the same to all parties in a criminal trial, even those who are acting pro se. An accused has an absolute right under the U.S. Constitution to defend himself without benefit of counsel. Here, the court's charge instructed the jury not to consider testimony regarding other offenses Williams (D) might have committed unless it found beyond a reasonable doubt that Williams (D) committed the offenses and then only for the purpose of showing a common plan or systematic course of action or in determining the identity, intent, motive, or malice of Williams (D). Williams' (D) objection at trial to this testimony was a general objection which did not preserve error for review. Furthermore, the objection was untimely, and testimony regarding the first robbery was elicited by Williams (D) himself. Williams' (D) counsel now argues that the court should take into consideration Williams' (D) ignorance, as a layman, of the rules of evidence and procedure concerning preserving error and the rules excluding extraneous offenses. However, the right of self-representation is not a license to abuse the dignity of the courtroom. A defendant such as Williams (D) who elects to represent himself cannot thereafter complain that the quality of his own defense amounted to a denial of effective assistance of counsel. Affirmed.

EDITOR'S ANALYSIS: According to the concept of curative admissibility (a.k.a. "opening the door"), if a certain type of evidence is introduced by a party, he will most likely be precluded from objecting if the opposing party brings forth similar evidence. This is especially true in situations where the party, in a purposeful fashion, fails to object when the opposing party elicits inadmissible evidence. Cross-examination on an issue does not generally waive objection to it but may make the court's ruling on the initial objection harmless error.

[For more information on preserving objections, see Casenote Law Outline on Evidence, Chapter 5, § I, Preserving Objections.]

NOTES:

CARBO v. UNITED STATES
314 F.2d 718 (9th Cir. 1963).

NATURE OF CASE: Appeal from conviction for extortion and conspiracy.

FACT SUMMARY: Carbo (D), Sica, and others were convicted of extortion and conspiracy for their attempts to secure managerial control of a prize fighter.

CONCISE RULE OF LAW: When an evidentiary fact is offered for one purpose, it is not admissible because it cannot be considered for other purposes.

FACTS: Carbo (D), Sica, and others were convicted of extortion affecting commerce and of conspiracy arising out of their efforts to secure managerial control of Don Jordan, a welterweight fighter, by bringing pressure to bear upon his manager, Donald Nesseth, and a local promoter, Jackie Leonard. At trial, Sica moved to dismiss the indictment against him for the reason that he was unduly prejudiced by the charge that the conspiracy contemplated the use of "persons known to have underworld connections to execute the conspirators' demands by force and violence" and the enlistment of Sica for this purpose. Sica also objected to the introduction of testimony by Leonard and Nesseth to the effect that by reputation they knew of Sica as an underworld man and a strong-arm man. Both motions were overruled, and Sica appealed, arguing that he had been unfairly prejudiced by this testimony at trial.

ISSUE: Is an evidentiary fact inadmissible for all purposes if it is inadmissible for only one purpose?

HOLDING AND DECISION: (Merrill, J.) No. The common law rule disallows resort by the prosecution to any kind of evidence of a defendant's evil character to establish a probability of his guilt because of the danger of confusion of issues, unfair surprise, and undue prejudice. Here though, the prosecution relied on the reputation of Sica as a probative fact enabling the jury to infer that Sica had intervened with Leonard and Nesseth knowing that his presence would instill fear in them and intending to manipulate this fear for the benefit of Carbo (D); and further, to conclude that Carbo (D) had secured Sica's participation with full realization that his effectiveness was based upon the fear his reputation could inspire in the victims. In cases of extortion based upon fear of violence, the facts of fear, actual or anticipated, and its reasonableness are vital factors. The admission of this evidence was a proper case for application of the multiple admissibility doctrine, which states that when an evidentiary fact is offered for one purpose, it is not inadmissible because it does not satisfy the rules applicable to it in some other capacity, and because the jury might improperly consider it in the latter capacity. Here, the evidence was admitted to prove an element of the offense, and the trial judge took all steps to eliminate any prejudice flowing from the admission of the testimony. Affirmed.

EDITOR'S ANALYSIS: The Federal Rules provide that "when evidence which is admissible as to one party or for one purpose but not admissible as to another party or for another purpose is admitted, the court, upon request, shall restrict the evidence to its proper scope and instruct the jury accordingly." Federal Rule of Evidence 105.

[For more information on the doctrine of multiple admissibility, see Casenote Law Outline on Evidence, Chapter 5, § IV, Limited Admissibility.]

NOTES:

SHERMAN v. BURKE CONTRACTING, INC.
891 F.2d 1527 (11th Cir., 1990).

NATURE OF CASE: Appeal from award of damages in an action seeking recovery for racial discrimination.

FACT SUMMARY: Burke (D), defending against charges of racial discrimination, contended that the district court erred in admitting into evidence a telephone recording Sherman (P), a former employee, had made because the recording was inaudible and its contents were hearsay.

CONCISE RULE OF LAW: The court has no duty to give a limiting instruction in the absence of a request.

FACTS: Sherman (P) sued Burke (D), seeking recovery for two acts of racial discrimination. After leaving his job with Burke (D), a contractor, Sherman (P) found work with another contractor, Palmer. Sherman (P) alleged that Burke (D) persuaded Palmer to fire Sherman (P) because Sherman (P) had reported Burke (D) to the EEOC. At trial, Sherman (P) introduced into evidence a tape recording of a conversation which Sherman (P) had had with Palmer a few weeks after he left Palmer's employ. In that conversation, which Sherman (P) recorded without Palmer's knowledge, Palmer stated that Burke (D) had urged him to fire Sherman (P). The district court allowed the tape to be played before the jury, concluding that the recording was admissible to impeach Palmer, who had denied speaking with Burke (D). Burke (D) did not request a limiting instruction, and the court did not give one. Burke (D) was found guilty and, on appeal, contended that the district court had had a duty to instruct the jury, on its own initiative, that the tape could be considered only for impeachment purposes.

ISSUE: Does the court have a duty to give a limiting instruction in the absence of a request?

HOLDING AND DECISION: (Per curiam) No. The court has no duty to give a limiting instruction in the absence of a request. Under Fed. R. Evid. 105, when evidence which is admissible as to one party or for one purpose but not admissible as to another party or for another purpose is admitted, the court shall, upon request, restrict the evidence to its proper scope and instruct the jury accordingly. In this case, if Burke's (D) counsel had requested a limiting instruction, the court would have given one, having already recognized that the recording's sole value was as impeachment evidence. Under Fed. R. Evid. 105, the court had a duty to instruct only "upon request." Lawyers frequently choose for strategic reasons not to request limiting instructions. In order to find plain error in this context, therefore, a court must conclude that, as a matter of law, counsel's strategic choice resulted in a manifest miscarriage of justice. No such miscarriage occurred here. Affirmed in part, reversed in part, vacated in part.

EDITOR'S ANALYSIS: There is very little law that addresses the issue of plain error when a trial judge has failed to give limiting instructions with respect to evidence that is admissible for some purpose. Only one federal appellate court case has addressed this issue — Herndon v. Seven Bar Flying Serv., Inc., 716 F.2d 1322 (10th Cir. 1983). In Herndon, the appellant argued that plain error occurred when a trial judge failed sua sponte to instruct a jury that evidence of subsequent remedial measures was not admissible to prove negligence. The 10th Circuit recognized that such an instruction would have been appropriate if requested but held that, without such a request, reversal would be improper unless the trial court's failure to instruct constituted plain error. Like the Sherman court, it then concluded that the absence of an instruction in that case did not constitute plain error because it resulted in no manifest "miscarriage of justice."

[For more information on preserving objections, see Casenote Law Outline on Evidence, Chapter 5, § I, Preserving Objections.]

NOTES:

CLARK v. UNITED STATES
61 F.2d 695 (8th Cir. 1932).

NATURE OF CASE: Appeal from contempt citation.

FACT SUMMARY: Clark (D), a juror in a mail fraud case, was cited for contempt after withholding information regarding her previous association with the accused.

CONCISE RULE OF LAW: The admission of immaterial evidence does not necessarily require the reversal of a case where a court sits without a jury as the trier of fact.

FACTS: Clark (D) was accepted and acted as a juror in a celebrated mail fraud case. After a seven-week trial, the jury deliberated one week and was unable to reach a verdict. Throughout the deliberations the vote was eleven for conviction, and one for acquittal, the lone vote being Clark's (D). Clark (D) was then adjudged guilty of contempt for withholding, on voir dire examination, information as to her previous associations with the accused and other aspects of bias and prejudice. On appeal, one of the grounds of error asserted was the admission in evidence of the deliberations in the jury room.

ISSUE: Does the admission of immaterial evidence necessarily require the reversal of a case where a court sits without a jury as the trier of fact?

HOLDING AND DECISION: (Kenyon, J.) No. The testimony admitted of other jurors as to the statements and conduct of Clark (D) in the jury room were admissible as bearing on the question of the falsity of answers given by her on the voir dire examination. Assuming, however, that such testimony should have been excluded, there is sufficient evidence in the record to sustain the finding of the trial court as to the criminal contempt. The fact that immaterial evidence may have been admitted does not necessarily require the reversal of a case where a court sits without a jury as a trier of fact, as there is a presumption that it acts only upon the basis of proper evidence. If evidence appears to have been improperly admitted, the appellate court will reject it, and proceed to decide the case as if it was not in the record. The judgment of the court as to the contempt is affirmed, but the sentence is set aside and the case remanded to the trial court only for the purpose of resentencing.

DISSENT: (Gardner, J.) If the improper evidence is excluded, there is no substantial evidence to sustain the judgment of the trial court, and the evidence involved is not only immaterial but incompetent. While it is ordinarily presumed that the court sitting without a jury considers only the material and competent evidence, this is only a presumption, and it appears in this case that the court did consider and did rely upon this very evidence.

EDITOR'S ANALYSIS: Clarence Darrow, one of this country's most famous trial lawyers, once wrote: "Few judges are psychologists, or they would realize that nothing can be stricken out of a human consciousness after being once let in. Judges seem to be quite unaware that it is a hard task to put anything into the average mind, and, once in, an impossible one to take it out." Darrow, The Story of My Life 145 (Grosset's Universal ed.).

[For more information on the admission of immaterial evidence, see Casenote Law Outline on Evidence, Chapter 5, § III, Evidentiary Errors.]

NOTES:

NOTES

CHAPTER 2
LIMITATIONS OF THE ADVERSARY SYSTEM

QUICK REFERENCE RULES OF LAW

1. **Reversible Error.** A state may not knowingly use false evidence, including false testimony, to obtain a tainted conviction. (Napue v. Illinois)

   [For more information on reversible error, see Casenote Law Outline on Evidence, Chapter 5, § III, Evidentiary Errors.]

2. **Harmless Error.** A conviction is overturned based on noncompliance with pretrial discovery demands only where it is shown that the evidence not disclosed is material to the trial's outcome. (United States v. Bagley)

   [For more information on harmless error, see Casenote Law Outline on Evidence, Chapter 5, § III, Evidentiary Errors.]

3. **Prejudicial Error.** A defendant is entitled to have the question of his guilt determined on the evidence against him, not on whether a codefendant or government witness has been convicted on the same charge. (Leech v. People)

   [For more information on prejudicial error, see Casenote Law Outline on Evidence, Chapter 5, § III, Evidentiary Errors.]

4. **State Prisoners and Forfeiture.** State prisoners may not litigate, in a federal habeas proceeding, a constitutional claim that they forfeited before the state courts. (Engle v. Isaac)

5. **Admission of a Rape Victim's Character.** Rape shield laws protect the victim from revealing their sexual histories in both discovery and trial phases of the case. (State v. Miskell)

   [For more information on the admission of a rape victim's character, see Casenote Law Outline on Evidence, Chapter 6, § III, Character to Prove Conduct.]

NOTES

NAPUE v. ILLINOIS
360 U.S. 264 (1959).

NATURE OF CASE: Appeal from conviction for murder.

FACT SUMMARY: Napue (D) contended that the failure of the prosecutor to correct the testimony of a witness which he knew to be false deprived him of due process.

CONCISE RULE OF LAW: A state may not knowingly use false evidence, including false testimony, to obtain a tainted conviction.

FACTS: At the murder trial of Napue (D), Hamer, the principal state witness, then serving a 199-year sentence for the same murder, testified in response to a question by the assistant state's attorney that he had received no promise of consideration in return for his testimony. The assistant state's attorney had in fact promised him consideration, but did nothing to correct the witness' false testimony. The jury was apprised, however, that a public defender had promised "to do what he could" for Hamer. Napue (D) was found guilty of the murder charge, and was sentenced to 199 years in prison. On appeal, the Illinois Supreme Court affirmed the conviction, finding, contrary to the trial court, that the attorney had promised Hamer consideration if he would testify at Napue's (D) trial, and that the assistant state's attorney knew that Hamer had lied in denying that he had been promised consideration. It held, however, that Napue (D) was entitled to no relief since the jury had already been apprised that someone whom Hamer had tentatively identified as a public defender "was going to do what he could" in aid of Hamer. Napue (D) then brought this appeal, arguing that he had been denied due process of law.

ISSUE: May a state knowingly use false evidence, including false testimony, to obtain a tainted conviction?

HOLDING AND DECISION: (Warren, C.J.) No. A conviction obtained through use of false evidence, known to be such by representatives of a state, must fall under the Fourteenth Amendment. The same result obtains when a state, although not soliciting false evidence, allows it to go uncorrected when it appears. The principle that a state may not knowingly use false evidence including false testimony, to obtain a tainted conviction, implicit in any concept of ordered liberty, does not cease to apply merely because the false testimony goes only to the credibility of the witness. The jury's estimate of the truthfulness and reliability of a given witness may well be determinative of guilt or innocence, and it is upon such subtle factors as the possible interest of the witness in testifying falsely that a defendant's life or liberty may depend. Nor did the fact that the jury was apprised of other grounds for believing that Hamer may have had an interest in testifying against Napue (D) turn what was otherwise a tainted trial into a fair one. Had the jury been apprised of the true facts, it might well have concluded that Hamer had fabricated testimony in order to curry the favor of the very representative of the State (P) who was prosecuting the case in which Hamer was testifying, for Hamer might have believed that such a representative was in a position to implement any promise of consideration. Reversed.

EDITOR'S ANALYSIS: In a later case, the Court dealt with the conflict between possible coaching of witnesses and the Sixth Amendment right to counsel. In that case, the Court overturned an order that the defendant not consult with his attorney during an overnight recess, where the defendant had been on the stand and cross-examination was about to begin when the recess was called. See, Geders v. United States, 425 U.S. 80 (1976).

[For more information on reversible error, see Casenote Law Outline on Evidence, Chapter 5, § III, Evidentiary Errors.]

NOTES:

UNITED STATES v. BAGLEY
473 U.S. 667 (1985).

NATURE OF CASE: Appeal from narcotics and firearm violations.

FACT SUMMARY: The court of appeals reversed Bagley's (D) conviction due to the Government's (P) failure to adequately respond to Bagley's (D) pretrial discovery demand.

CONCISE RULE OF LAW: A conviction is overturned based on noncompliance with pretrial discovery demands only where it is shown that the evidence not disclosed is material to the trial's outcome.

FACTS: Bagley (D) was charged with federal narcotics and firearms violations. Prior to trial, he served the Government (P) with a discovery request asking for the names and criminal records of all prosecution witnesses but did not reveal agreements whereby the witnesses were compensated for information. The existence of such agreements was also requested by Bagley (D) before trial. Bagley (D) was convicted and subsequently learned of the agreements. He moved to vacate his sentence. The district court denied the motion, holding disclosure of the agreements would have had no impact on the outcome of the trial. The court of appeals reversed, holding the failure to disclose deprived Bagley (D) of his right to effective cross-examination. The Supreme Court granted a hearing.

ISSUE: Will a conviction be overturned due to a prosecution failure to adequately respond to a discovery request only where it is shown that the evidence was material to the trial's outcome?

HOLDING AND DECISION: (Blackmun, J.) Yes. A conviction will be overturned due to a prosecution failure to adequately respond to a discovery request only where it is shown that the evidence is material to the trial's outcome. The test of materiality is whether there is a reasonable probability that, had it been disclosed, the proceeding would have been different. The court of appeals did not consider materiality of the agreements in reversing the trial court. This was error. Reversed and remanded.

DISSENT IN PART: (White, J.) Materiality must be shown for reversal, thus the court of appeals should be reversed.

DISSENT: (Marshall, J.) A prosecution failure to fully disclose information on its only witness is reversible error regardless of materiality as defined by the majority.

DISSENT: (Stevens, J.) A prosecution silence to a specific discovery request is reversible error.

EDITOR'S ANALYSIS: The modern standard for defense discovery in criminal cases is Brady v. Maryland, 373 U.S. 83 (1963). Suppression of requested evidence was held to be a denial of due process. Since that case, the holding has been refined, as it was in this case, to require a level of materiality to be found before a conviction can be overturned.

[For more information on harmless error, see Casenote Law Outline on Evidence, Chapter 5, § III, Evidentiary Errors.]

LEECH v. PEOPLE
Colo. Sup. Ct., 112 Colo. 120, 146 P.2d 346 (1944).

NATURE OF CASE: Appeal from conviction for automobile theft.

FACT SUMMARY: Leech (D) contended that the introduction of evidence that a government witness had been convicted of the charge violated his right to a fair trial.

CONCISE RULE OF LAW: A defendant is entitled to have the question of his guilt determined on the evidence against him, not on whether a codefendant or government witness has been convicted on the same charge.

FACTS: On November 18, 1940, Leech (D) bought a new Pontiac automobile, for which he paid with his note for approximately $1,000, secured by a mortgage on the car. With installments on the note delinquent, Leech (D) and one Holman took the car to a place out of town where they concealed it from sight. The next morning Leech (D) reported the car stolen, and the insurance company later paid the claim on the basis of actual theft. Eventually an investigation of the incident led to charges of theft being filed against Leech (D) and Holman. When the case came to trial, Holman entered a plea of guilty, his sentence was postponed, and he testified against Leech (D). After being called as a witness by the district attorney, Holman was asked whether he had been charged with the same crime as Leech (D), whether he had entered a plea of guilty to the charge, and whether he now desired to testify concerning what he knew about the case. Holman answered in the affirmative to all questions, and Leech (D) was subsequently convicted of the charge. On appeal, Leech (D) contended that the posturing of these questions at trial deprived him of his constitutional right to a fair trial.

ISSUE: Is a defendant entitled to have the question of his guilt determined on the evidence against him, and not on whether a codefendant or government witness has been convicted on the same charge?

HOLDING AND DECISION: (Burke, J.) Yes. A defendant is entitled to have the question of his guilt determined upon the evidence against him, not on whether a codefendant or government witness has been convicted on the same charge. The questions asked at trial were neither incidental nor accidental, and were not the product of cross-examination. Because the questions were propounded by the People (P) on direct examination, there was prejudicial error at trial. Further, during trial, Leech's (D) attorney never made even a single objection to any testimony which was given, nor was a jury instruction tendered on behalf of Leech (D). Such actions, and particularly the failure to object to Holman's testimony, deprived Leech (D) of his right to a fair trial. Reversed and remanded.

EDITOR'S ANALYSIS: The Federal Rules of Criminal Procedure provide that: "Plain errors or defects affecting substantial rights may be noticed although they were not brought to the attention of the court." See, Federal Rule of Criminal Procedure 52(b).

[For more information on prejudicial error, see Casenote Law Outline on Evidence, Chapter 5, § III, Evidentiary Errors.]

ENGLE v. ISAAC
456 U.S. 107 (1982).

NATURE OF CASE: Appeal from judgment allowing litigation of a constitutional claim in a federal habeas corpus proceeding.

FACT SUMMARY: Isaac (D) and two other defendants (D) argued that federal due process rights had been violated because, at their respective homicide trials, the State (P) was not required to disprove their claim of self-defense, and, therefore, they were entitled to relief in a federal habeas corpus proceeding.

CONCISE RULE OF LAW: State prisoners may not litigate, in a federal habeas proceeding, a constitutional claim that they forfeited before the state courts.

FACTS: Isaac (D) and other defendants (D) requested a federal writ of habeas corpus after they were found guilty of homicide by a State of Ohio (P) court. On appeal, Isaac (D) and the other defendants contended that their federal due process rights were violated and a colorable constitutional claim was raised because, at their respective homicide trials, the State (P) was required to disprove their claim of self-defense. They further contended that they should be able to litigate, in a federal habeas proceeding, their constitutional claim even though neither Isaac (D) nor the other defendants (D) had challenged the constitutionality of the self-defense instruction at trial.

ISSUE: May state prisoners litigate, in a federal habeas proceeding, a constitutional claim that they forfeited before the state courts?

HOLDING AND DECISION: (O'Connor, J.) No. State prisoners may not litigate, in a federal habeas proceeding, a constitutional claim that they forfeited before the state courts. In this case, failure to comply with Ohio Rule of Criminal Procedure 30, which requires contemporaneous objections to jury instructions, bars appellate consideration of an objection and bars the challenge of the constitutionality of those instructions in a federal habeas proceeding. The writ of habeas corpus holds an honored position in our jurisprudence but entails great costs by extending the ordeal of the trial for both society and the accused. Rather than enhancing legal safeguards already available to the accused, ready availability of habeas corpus may diminish their sanctity by suggesting to the trial participants that there may be no need to adhere to these safeguards during the trial itself. The states possess primary authority for defining and enforcing the criminal law. In criminal trials, they also hold the initial responsibility for vindicating constitutional rights. Federal intrusions into state criminal trials frustrate both the states' sovereign power to punish offenders and their good-faith attempts to honor constitutional rights. Issuance of a habeas writ also undercuts the states' ability to enforce their procedural rules. Here, Isaac (D) and the other defendants (D) seek cause for their defaults because they claim that they could not have known, at the time of their trials, that the State's (P) self-defense instructions raised constitutional questions. However, the Constitution guarantees criminal defendants only a fair trial and a competent attorney. It does not insure that defense counsel will recognize and raise every conceivable constitutional claim. Where the basis of a constitutional claim is available, and other defense counsel have perceived and litigated that claim, the demands of comity and finality counsel against labeling alleged unawareness of the objection as cause for procedural default. Because Isaac (D) and the other defendants failed to comply with the State's (P) procedures for raising their constitutional claims, and because they have not demonstrated cause for the default, they are barred from asserting a federal habeas corpus claim. Reversed and remanded.

EDITOR'S ANALYSIS: The federal habeas corpus writ has its roots in English common law and was made a part of the U.S. Constitution in Article I. Lately, however, changes in the federal habeas corpus law have tremendously reduced its applicability and range from the popularity it held prior to the late 1970s. As can be seen in Isaac, the U.S. Supreme Court is loath to enforce a writ of habeas corpus unless the fundamental unfairness of the state court decision overshadows the costs, both in time and effort, to the state and federal judicial systems. A procedural error, such as occurred in Isaac, absent a showing of cause and actual prejudice, will not warrant the issue of a writ of habeas corpus.

NOTES:

STATE v. MISKELL
N.H. Sup. Ct., 122 N.H. 842, 451 A.2d 383 (1982).

NATURE OF CASE: Appeal from order compelling answers to deposition questions.

FACT SUMMARY: Miskell (D) contended that the rape-shield law did not preclude the discovery of the victim's sexual past in discovery phases of trial.

CONCISE RULE OF LAW: Rape shield laws protect the victim from revealing their sexual histories in both discovery and trial phases of the case.

FACTS: Miskell (D) was charged with rape. At a pretrial deposition, the prosecutrix refused to answer defense counsel's questions concerning her sexual history. Defense counsel successfully moved to compel responses, contending that while the rape-shield statute prevented the introduction of such evidence at trial, it was discoverable. The prosecutrix, through private counsel, brought an interlocutory appeal from the order to compel.

ISSUE: Is a prosecutrix's sexual history discoverable under the rape-shield law?

HOLDING AND DECISION: (Batchelder, J.) No. A prosecutrix's sexual history is not discoverable under the rape-shield law. In enacting the rape-shield law, the legislature intended to protect the rape victim from embarrassment, prejudice, and other indignities. It thus intended to create a testimonial privilege which is fully applicable to pretrial discovery proceedings. The indignity is visited by having to answer the question at all, not just at trial. Reversed and remanded.

EDITOR'S ANALYSIS: Rape-shield laws were enacted to encourage the rape victim to prosecute the rapist. Many victims were afraid of having defense counsel manipulate the trial to one of judging the victim's purity. The rape-shield law intends to do this. By creating an evidentiary privilege, the law has chosen to exclude otherwise material evidence in order to protect the victim.

_____

[For more information on the admission of a rape victim's character, see Casenote Law Outline on Evidence, Chapter 6, § III, Character to Prove Conduct.]

NOTES:

20

CHAPTER 4*
BURDEN OF PROOF

QUICK REFERENCE RULES OF LAW

1. **Direct Evidence.** A jury will not he permitted to believe testimony that is contradicted by physical facts. (Scott v. Hansen)

   [For more information on direct evidence, see Casenote Law Outline on Evidence, Chapter 2, § III, Is the "Evidence" Relevant?]

2. **Inference.** It is proper to infer a fact at issue from other facts which have been established by circumstantial evidence. (United States v. Nelson)

   [For more information on inference, see Casenote Law Outline on Evidence, Chapter 2, § III, Is the "Evidence" Relevant?]

3. **Circumstantial Evidence.** A jury may not be permitted to reach its verdict merely on the basis of speculation or conjecture, but there must be evidence upon which logically its conclusion may be based. (Smith v. Bell Tel. Co. of Pennsylvania)

   [For more information on circumstantial evidence, see Casenote Law Outline on Evidence, Chapter 2, § III, Is the "Evidence" Relevant?]

4. **Proposed Inference.** The credibility of an uncontradicted and unimpeached witness does not in all cases present a jury question. (Colthurst v. Lake View State Bank of Chicago)

   [For more information on proposed inference, see Casenote Law Outline on Evidence, Chapter 2, § III, Is the "Evidence" Relevant?]

5. **Allocation of the Burden of Proof.** The burden of proof rests upon the party asserting the affirmative of an issue. (Delaware Coach Co. v. Savage)

   [For more information on allocation of the burden of proof, see Casenote Law Outline on Evidence, Chapter 4, § I, Burdens of Proof.]

6. **Burden of Proof.** The standard of proof in a civil action for common law deceit or fraud must be "clear and convincing," but general or punitive damages arising out of that deceit or fraud need be proved only by a preponderance of the evidence. (Riley Hill General Contractor, Inc. v. Tandy Corp.)

   [For more information on burden of proof, see Casenote Law Outline on Evidence, Chapter 4, § I, Burdens of Proof.]

7. **Proof Beyond a Reasonable Doubt.** Juveniles are constitutionally entitled to proof beyond a reasonable doubt when they are charged with violation of a criminal law. (In re Winship)

   [For more information on proof beyond a reasonable doubt, see Casenote Law Outline on Evidence, Chapter 4, § III, Presumptions in Criminal Cases.]

*There are no cases in Chapter 3.

NOTES

SCOTT v. HANSEN
Iowa Sup. Ct., 228 Iowa 37, 289 N.W. 710 (1940).

NATURE OF CASE: Appeal award of damages for personal injuries.

FACT SUMMARY: Scott (D) contended that there was no competent evidence demonstrating that he had been guilty of negligent or reckless conduct, and that the evidence against him could not have physically occurred.

CONCISE RULE OF LAW: A jury will not be permitted to believe testimony that is contradicted by physical facts.

FACTS: Hansen (P) brought suit to recover for personal injuries sustained when Scott's (D) automobile, in which Hansen (P) was riding as a guest, collided with a cow that was crossing the highway. Hansen (P) alleged that Scott's (D) operation of the car at the time of the collision was reckless, and that such reckless operation was the proximate cause of Hansen's (P) injuries. At the conclusion of the evidence, Scott (D) moved for a directed verdict, on the ground that there was no competent evidence to show that he had been guilty of recklessness in the operation of the car. Hansen (P) had, at trial, introduced evidence of black tire marks having the appearance of brake marks or skid marks that extended east from the point of collision. Hansen (P) also called a witness who testified that he saw the car hit the cow, that the car was traveling approximately 75 miles per hour, and, that when it was hit, the cow flew nearly 30 feet in the air without touching the pavement at all, which was a physical impossibility. The jury returned a verdict for Hansen (P), and Scott (D) appealed.

ISSUE: Will a jury be permitted to believe testimony that is contradicted by physical facts?

HOLDING AND DECISION: (Richards, J.) No. Hansen's (P) witness testified that the cow flew 30 feet through the air, and that the cow probably weighed 1,200 pounds. Hansen's (P) own testimony was that he was almost sure that Scott (D) at no time applied the brakes, and that in his opinion the speed was about 75 miles per hour when the car struck the cow. The rate of speed as estimated by Hansen (P) and his witness, together with the manner in which, allegedly, the cow was catapulted, was sufficient and effective, in Hansen's (P) opinion, to generate jury questions respecting the specifications that Scott (D) failed to reduce his speed and drove into the cow at about 75 miles per hour. However, this testimony by Hansen (P) and his witness is wholly inconsistent with the undisputed and established physical facts, leading to the inevitable conclusion that Hansen (P) and his witness were mistaken. The estimate of the rate of speed at the time of the collision as stated by Hansen (P) and his witness, together with the testimony concerning the exhibition of levitation credited to the cow by the witness, were in such conflict with incontestable facts that such testimony was so lacking in probative force or effect that a jury finding that the car's speed as it approached the cattle was not reduced, would be unwarranted. Reversed.

EDITOR'S ANALYSIS: Under the California Evidence Code, "direct evidence means evidence that directly proves a fact without an inference or presumption, and which in itself, if true, conclusively establishes the fact . . . the direct evidence of one witness who is entitled to full credit is sufficient for proof of any fact." See, Cal. Evid. Code §§ 410, 411 (West 1966).

[For more information on direct evidence, see Casenote Law Outline on Evidence, Chapter 2, § III, Is the "Evidence" Relevant?]

NOTES:

UNITED STATES v. NELSON
419 F.2d 1237 (9th Cir. 1969).

NATURE OF CASE: Appeal from conviction for robbery.

FACT SUMMARY: Nelson (D) contended that circumstantial evidence was improperly used to convict him because the fact that he participated in the robbery in question could only be inferred from circumstantial evidence.

CONCISE RULE OF LAW: It is proper to infer a fact at issue from other facts which have been established by circumstantial evidence.

FACTS: Nelson (D) and Frank Brewton were indicted for robbery of a federally insured institution. Brewton was found incompetent to stand trial. At trial, the Government (P) introduced evidence that Brewton had entered and robbed the bank, while an unidentified person sat in a car in an adjacent parking lot, racing the engine. After the robbery, Brewton and the other person fled at a high speed in the car, while they were pursued by a police officer. After a chase the car slowed down, Nelson (D) exited from the driver's side and ran, and was later captured with $125 in his possession. Nelson (D) asserted that since he was charged as a principal in the bank robbery, the Government (P) was required to prove that he had actual knowledge that Brewton intended to rob the bank. Nelson (D) also contended that such knowledge could only be a result of an inference which stemmed from an earlier inference that he was the man in the car, and such an inference based upon an inference was precluded by law. Nelson (D) also contended that circumstantial evidence which does not exclude every hypothesis but that of guilt is insufficient as a matter of law. The trial court denied Nelson's (D) motion for acquittal and convicted him of all charges. Nelson (D) appealed.

ISSUE: Is it proper to infer a fact at issue from other facts which have been established by circumstantial evidence?

HOLDING AND DECISION: (Browning, J.) Yes. It is proper to infer a fact at issue from other facts which have been established by circumstantial evidence. Circumstantial evidence is not inherently less probative than direct evidence. Here, the intermediate fact at issue was whether Nelson (D) was the driver of the car waiting in the parking lot. That fact was established to a moral certainty by circumstances proven by uncontradicted and unquestioned testimony. The trial court therefore properly refused to instruct the jury that one inference may not be based upon another inference to support a conclusion of fact. A verdict in a criminal case is sustained only when there is relevant evidence from which the jury could properly find or infer, beyond a reasonable doubt, that the accused is guilty. The denial of the motion for acquittal in this case is affirmed because the jurors reasonably could decide that they would not hesitate to act in their own serious affairs upon factual assumptions as probable as the conclusion that Nelson (D) planned and executed the robbery of the bank as a joint venture with Brewton in which each carried out a prearranged role. Affirmed.

EDITOR'S ANALYSIS: The court in this case concurs with the view of Professor Wigmore that there is no rule prohibiting the predication of an inference upon a previous inference. Issues similar to those raised in this case arise by the attempted predication of a presumption on a presumption, or a presumption upon an inference.

[For more information on inference, see Casenote Law Outline on Evidence, Chapter 2, § III, Is the "Evidence" Relevant?]

NOTES:

SMITH v. BELL TEL CO. OF PENNSYLVANIA
Pa. Sup. Ct., 397 Pa. 134, 153 A.2d 477 (1959).

NATURE OF CASE: Appeal from judgment of nonsuit.

FACT SUMMARY: Smith (P) contended that the trial court applied an incorrect standard for weighing his case, which was largely based upon circumstantial evidence, that Bell's contractor caused Smith's (P) sewer line to be crushed by construction of a telephone conduit.

CONCISE RULE OF LAW: A jury may not be permitted to reach its verdict merely on the basis of speculation or conjecture, but there must be evidence upon which logically its conclusion may be based.

FACTS: In 1948, Counties Contracting and Construction Company, under contract to Bell (D), constructed an underground conduit to carry telephone lines along Baltimore Avenue in Lansdowne, Pennsylvania. In 1950, after an inspection which revealed no structural or other defects, Smith (P) purchased a house on Baltimore Avenue. Sometime prior to March 25, 1951, Smith (P) discovered seepage in his basement, which proved to be sewage backed up from the sewer lateral running from his home to the street. In September 1956, as the seepage continued, Smith (P) and a friend tunnelled under the sidewalk, and found that the telephone conduit had crushed the sewer lateral and was blocking it. Smith (P) brought suit on September 19, 1957, and after presenting evidence, was given a nonsuit in the case. In support of the judgment of nonsuit, the trial court applied the standard that where a plaintiff's case is based on circumstantial evidence, and inferences to be drawn therefrom, such evidence must be so conclusive as to exclude any other reasonable inference inconsistent therewith, and that Smith (P) had not produced such evidence. Smith (P) appealed.

ISSUE: May a jury be permitted to reach its verdict merely on the basis of speculation or conjecture?

HOLDING AND DECISION: (McBride, J.) No. A jury may not be permitted to reach its verdict merely on the basis of speculation or conjecture, but there must be evidence upon which logically its conclusion may be based. The evidence must be such that by reasoning from it, without resort to prejudice or guess, a jury can reach the conclusion sought by the plaintiff, and not that that conclusion must be the only one which logically can be reached. The right of a litigant to have the jury pass upon the facts is not to be foreclosed just because the judge believes that a reasonable man might properly find either way. When a party who has the burden of proof relies upon circumstantial evidence and inferences reasonably deducible therefrom, such evidence, in order to prevail, must be adequate to establish the conclusion sought and must so preponderate in favor of that conclusion as to outweigh in the mind of the fact finder any other evidence and reasonable inferences therefrom which are inconsistent. Here, a likely inference under the conditions described is that the soil was normal and the crushing of the pipe was due to Bell's (D) negligence in not supporting a conduit which passed over Smith's (P) lateral with less than six inches

clearance. It is entirely reasonable for the jury to find that the accident resulted from the negligence of Bell (D). Reversed and remanded.

CONCURRENCE: (Bell, J.) The new rule dealing with verdicts based upon circumstantial evidence should read as follows: When a party who has the burden of proof relies, not upon direct evidence, but upon circumstantial evidence, such evidence, together with all inferences reasonably deducible therefrom, must, in order to prevail, be adequate to establish the conclusion sought and must so preponderate in favor of that conclusion as to outweigh any other reasonable or possible inference or deduction inconsistent therewith.

EDITOR'S ANALYSIS: It is essential to the preservation of the jury's role in the fact-finding process that the judiciary recognize that evidence might reasonably convince a jury even though it does not convince the court. The rule enunciated in this case has been applied in a far less liberal fashion than its language might indicate.

[For more information on circumstantial evidence, see Casenote Law Outline on Evidence, Chapter 2, § III, Is the "Evidence" Relevant?]

NOTES:

COLTHURST v. LAKE VIEW STATE BANK OF CHICAGO

18 F.2d 875 (8th Cir. 1927).

NATURE OF CASE: Appeal from judgment finding holder in due course status.

FACT SUMMARY: Colthurst (D) contended that the trial court erred in refusing to allow the jury to consider the credibility of opposition witnesses.

CONCISE RULE OF LAW: The credibility of an uncontradicted and unimpeached witness does not in all cases present a jury question.

FACTS: On April 19, 1924, the Bank (P) filed a petition alleging that it was the holder in due course, for value, and without notice of any defense, of a note in the amount of $3,200, with interest at six per cent, dated December 16, 1918, due in one year, and signed by Colthurst (D). Colthurst (D), in his answer, charged procurement of the note by fraud and denied that the Bank (P) held it in due course. At trial, the Bank (P) offered testimony that it had purchased the note on February 20, 1919, for $3,234.67 from the then holder, one W. F. Van Buskirk, to whom the note had been endorsed by a prior endorsee, and that it had no knowledge of any defenses existing in favor of the maker of the note. After the district court directed a verdict for the Bank (P), Colthurst (D) brought this appeal, alleging that the district court erred, first, because the Van Buskirk letters showed that the Bank (P) did not receive the note before maturity and therefore was not a holder in due course; second, because, even if the Van Buskirk letters properly were excluded, facts and circumstances in evidence tended to show that the Bank (P) was not a holder in due course; and third, that it was for the jury to pass upon the credibility of witnesses for the Bank (P).

ISSUE: Does the credibility of an uncontradicted and unimpeached witness in all cases present a jury question?

HOLDING AND DECISION: (Otis, J.) No. First, the Van Buskirk letters were properly excluded by the district court. Second, even if there were no direct testimony tending to show that the Bank (P) had knowledge of defenses existing against the note when it obtained possession of it, if in the evidence there were facts and circumstances from which such a conclusion reasonably could be inferred then a verdict should not have been directed. Here though, there were not in evidence any facts or circumstances which, whether considered separately or together, would have furnished any basis for such an inference. Third, the credibility of an uncontradicted and unimpeached witness is not in all cases a jury question. Were such not the case, a party could claim that it had an inherent right to have a jury pass upon his claim. Affirmed.

EDITOR'S ANALYSIS: A distinction must be drawn between the burden of persuasion and the burden of producing evidence. Although the burden of persuasion remains on the same party throughout the trial, the burden of producing evidence may and often does shift back and forth between the parties.

[For more information on proposed inference, see Casenote Law Outline on Evidence, Chapter 2, § III, Is the "Evidence" Relevant?]

NOTES:

DELAWARE COACH CO. v. SAVAGE
81 F. Supp. 293 (D. Del. 1948).

NATURE OF CASE: Appeal from denial of damages for negligence.

FACT SUMMARY: Delaware Coach (P) contended that it had sustained its burden of proof of negligence at trial seeking damages resulting from a trolley coach-truck collision.

CONCISE RULE OF LAW: The burden of proof rests upon the party asserting the affirmative of an issue.

FACTS: Delaware Coach (P) brought an action as a result of a collision in the City of Wilmington, Delaware, between one of its trolley coaches and a truck and trailer owned by Savage (D). As a result of the collision the driver of the trolley coach was killed, and his widow received from Delaware Coach (P) compensation for his death. This subrogation action was brought subsequently. At trial, a number of eyewitnesses to the collision testified, with Savage (D) producing a greater number of disinterested witnesses supporting his view. The trial court found that the accident was not an unavoidable accident, but was caused by the negligence of at least one of the drivers of the motor vehicles involved. The court found that there was no preponderance of the evidence on behalf of Delaware Coach (P) of negligence of Savage (D), and as a legal consequence Delaware Coach (P) had not sustained its burden of persuasion. After judgment was entered for Savage (D), this appeal was brought by Delaware Coach (P).

ISSUE: Does the burden of proof rest upon the party asserting the affirmative of an issue?

HOLDING AND DECISION: (Rodney, J.) Yes. The burden of proof rests upon the party asserting the affirmative of an issue, such as, in this case, the negligence of Savage (D). If an allegation, such as negligence, is alleged, the party asserting such fact must prove it by a preponderance of the evidence. The burden of proof of such fact continues through the case, and this burden of proof never shifts. The burden of going forward with the evidence may shift from time to time during a trial after the establishment of a prima facie case or due to some other development in the case, but the burden of proof of the main fact remains with the party who alleged such main fact. Upon the establishment of a prima facie case, the burden of evidence or the burden of going forward with the evidence shifts to the defensive party. It then becomes incumbent upon such defensive party to meet the prima facie case which has been established. For this purpose the defensive party need not produce evidence which preponderates or outweighs or surpasses the evidence of his adversary, but it is sufficient if such evidence is coequal, leaving the proof in equilibrium. If the defensive party, either by a preponderance of evidence or evidence sufficient to establish equilibrium, has met and answered the prima facie case, then the burden of going forward with the evidence returns to the original proponent charged with the burden of proof who must in turn, by a preponderance or greater weight of evidence, overcome the equilibrium thus established, or otherwise support his burden of proof by a preponderance of the evidence. In this case, Delaware

Coach (P) did not sustain its burden toward the fact-finding tribunal and show the negligence of Savage (D) by a preponderance of the evidence. Affirmed.

EDITOR'S ANALYSIS: The United States Supreme Court stated that an inference or presumption "does no more then require the [defensive party], if he would avoid the inference, to go forward with evidence sufficient to persuade that the nonexistence of the fact, which would otherwise be inferred, is as probable as its existence." See, Commercial Molasses Corporation v. New York Tank Barge Corporation, 314 U.S. 104.

[For more information on allocation of the burden of proof, see Casenote Law Outline on Evidence, Chapter 4, § I, Burdens of Proof.]

NOTES:

RILEY HILL GENERAL CONTRACTOR, INC. v. TANDY CORP.
Or. Sup. Ct., 303 Or. 390, 737 P.2d 595 (1987).

NATURE OF CASE: Appeal from remand for a new trial in an action for compensatory and punitive damages on claims for fraud, breach of warranty, and negligence.

FACT SUMMARY: Tandy Corp. (D) contended that the trial court gave inconsistent instructions on the burden of proof, citing both the "clear and convincing" and "preponderance of evidence" burdens as the standards for decision.

CONCISE RULE OF LAW: The standard of proof in a civil action for common law deceit or fraud must be "clear and convincing," but general or punitive damages arising out of that deceit or fraud need be proved only by a preponderance of the evidence.

FACTS: Riley Hill General Contractor, Inc. (P) brought an action for fraud, breach of warranty, and negligence against Tandy Corp. (D) arising out of Riley's (P) purchase of a computer that was manufactured and sold by Tandy (D). At trial, the court instructed the jury that the presumption against fraud must be overcome by clear and convincing evidence, "even though the burden of proof remains...as in all civil cases, proof by a preponderance of the evidence." The jury returned a verdict for Riley (P), and Tandy (D) appealed, contending that the instructions were inconsistent. The court of appeals reversed and remanded for a new trial on this basis. Riley (P) appealed.

ISSUE: Must the standard of proof in a civil action for common law deceit or fraud be "clear and convincing," while general or punitive damages arising out of that deceit or fraud need be proved only by a preponderance of the evidence?

HOLDING AND DECISION: (Jones, J.) Yes. The standard of proof for common law deceit or fraud must be "clear and convincing," but general or punitive damages arising out of that deceit or fraud need be proved only by a preponderance of the evidence. To be "clear and convincing," the evidence must be free from confusion, fully intelligible, distinct, and established to the jury that the defendant intended to deceive the plaintiff and did so with a reckless disregard for the truth. To be "clear and convincing" the truth of the facts asserted must be highly probable. However, the extent of damages need only be proved by a preponderance of the evidence, which means that, when weighed with that opposed to it, it has more convincing force and is more probably true and accurate. In this case, the trial court gave inconsistent jury instructions on the burden of proof. Furthermore, the court should not have made any reference to a "presumption" — that term should not be heard by a jury. The court of appeals is affirmed.

EDITOR'S ANALYSIS: In the Riley decision, Judge Jones discussed the origins of the word "preponderance," its Latin antecedent "praeponderare," and its meaning — "to outweigh, be of greater weight." Regarding the burden of proof or persuasion in civil actions, it is generally accepted that preponderance means the greater weight of evidence. At one time in the history of English law, the translation received a literal interpretation, with heads of witnesses being counted on each side and each item of testimony receiving a quantitative value or weight.

[For more information on burden of proof, see Casenote Law Outline on Evidence, Chapter 4, § I, Burdens of Proof.]

NOTES:

IN RE WINSHIP
397 U.S. 358 (1970).

NATURE OF CASE: Appeal from declaration of juvenile delinquency.

FACT SUMMARY: Winship (D) was declared a juvenile delinquent for stealing money from a woman's pocketbook.

CONCISE RULE OF LAW: Juveniles are constitutionally entitled to proof beyond a reasonable doubt when they are charged with violation of a criminal law.

FACTS: Section 712 of the New York Family Court Act defines a juvenile delinquent as "a person . . . less than sixteen years of age who does any act which, if done by an adult, would constitute a crime." During a 1967 adjudicatory hearing, a judge in the New York Family Court found that Winship (D) had entered a locker and stolen $112 from a woman's pocketbook, an act which if done by an adult, would constitute the crime of larceny. The judge acknowledged that the proof might not establish guilt beyond a reasonable doubt, but relied on a state statute which provided that in juvenile adjudicatory hearings, the standard of proof was a preponderance of the evidence, a lesser standard. On appeal, Winship (D) argued that a standard of proof beyond a reasonable doubt was required by the Fourteenth Amendment. The New York Court of Appeals upheld the constitutionality of the state juvenile standard of proof statute.

ISSUE: Are juveniles constitutionally entitled to proof beyond a reasonable doubt when they are charged with violation of a criminal law?

HOLDING AND DECISION: (Brennan, J.) Yes. The Due Process Clause protects the accused against conviction except upon proof beyond a reasonable doubt of every fact necessary to constitute the crime with which he is charged. The reasonable doubt standard is a prime instrument for reducing the risk of convictions resting on factual error. The accused during a criminal prosecution has at stake interest of immense importance, both because of the possibility that he may lose his liberty upon conviction and because of the certainty that he would be stigmatized by the conviction. Accordingly, a society that values the good name and freedom of every individual should not condemn a man for commission of a crime when there is a reasonable doubt about his guilt. The same considerations that demand extreme caution in fact-finding to protect the innocent adult apply as well to the innocent child. Therefore, juveniles, like adults, are constitutionally entitled to proof beyond a reasonable doubt when they are charged with violation of a criminal law. Reversed.

CONCURRENCE: (Harlan, J.) The requirement of proof beyond a reasonable doubt in a criminal case is bottomed on a fundamental value determination of our society that it is far worse to convict an innocent man than to let a guilty man go free. When one assesses the consequences of an erroneous factual determination in a juvenile delinquency proceeding in which a youth is accused of a crime, it must be concluded that, while the consequences are not identical to those in a criminal case, the differences will not support a distinction in the standard of proof.

EDITOR'S ANALYSIS: One older definition of "reasonable doubt" has been used extensively in charging juries: "It is that state of the case, which, after the entire comparison and consideration of all the evidence, leaves the minds of the jurors in that condition that they cannot say they feel an abiding conviction, to a moral certainty, of the truth of the charge." Commonwealth v. Webster, 59 Mass. (5 Cush.) 295, Am. Dec. 711 (1850).

[For more information on proof beyond a reasonable doubt, see Casenote Law Outline on Evidence, Chapter 4, § III, Presumptions in Criminal Cases.]

NOTES:

NOTES

CHAPTER 5
PRESUMPTIONS

QUICK REFERENCE RULES OF LAW

1. **Presumptions Affecting Burden of Proof.** An unexplained rear-end collision gives rise to a presumption of negligence. (McNulty v. Cusack)

   [For more information on presumptions affecting burden of proof, see Casenote Law Outline on Evidence, Chapter 4, § II, Presumptions in Civil Cases.]

2. **Thayer-Wigmore Presumptions.** An unexplained death by violence is presumed to be an accidental death. (O'Brien v. Equitable Life Assur. Society)

   [For more information on Thayer-Wigmore presumptions, see Casenote Law Outline on Evidence, Chapter 4, § II, Presumptions in Civil Cases.]

3. **The Effect of Presumptions.** A presumption survives even after conflicting evidence has been offered only where an injured person is unavailable because of injuries or death. (State of Maryland v. Baltimore Transit Co.)

   [For more information on the effect of presumptions, see Casenote Law Outline on Evidence, Chapter 4, § II, Presumptions in Civil Cases.]

4. **Authorized Inferences.** For a permissible presumption to be constitutional, there must be a rational connection between the basic facts that the prosecution proved and the ultimate fact presumed, and the ultimate fact presumed must be more likely than not to flow from the facts proved. (County Court of Ulster County v. Allen)

   [For more information on authorized inferences, see Casenote Law Outline on Evidence, Chapter 4, § III, Presumptions in Criminal Cases.]

NOTES

McNULTY v. CUSACK
Fla. Ct. App., 104 So. 2d 785 (1958).

NATURE OF CASE: Appeal from directed verdict awarding damages in negligence action.

FACT SUMMARY: McNulty (D) contended that the showing of a rear-end collision of two automobiles gave rise to an inference, rather than a presumption, of negligence.

CONCISE RULE OF LAW: An unexplained rear-end collision gives rise to a presumption of negligence.

FACTS: Annie B. Cusack (P) sued F. Jerome McNulty (D) as the result of a rear-end collision between their two cars, in which McNulty's (D) car ran into the rear of Cusack's (P) car at an intersection. The sole testimony as to negligence in the case was that of Cusack (P). After she rested her case, McNulty (D) also rested, offering no explanation of his actions of crashing his car into the rear-end of Cusack's (P) car. After a directed verdict was entered for Cusack (P), McNulty (D) brought this appeal. The sole issue on appeal was whether the showing of a rear-end collision and the circumstances under which it occurred, in the absence of explanation, gives rise to a presumption of negligence so as to authorize a directed verdict, or whether it only gives rise to an inference of negligence sufficient for presentation to the jury.

ISSUE: Does an unexplained rear-end collision give rise to a presumption of negligence?

HOLDING AND DECISION: (Allen, J.) Yes. There is a split of authority on whether or not a rear-end collision, coupled with circumstances under which it occurs, gives rise to an inference or a presumption of negligence. In those jurisdictions in which a presumption arises, when a prima facie case is made out by proving that the plaintiff was damaged in a rear-end collision, the duty of going forward with evidence of due care falls upon the defendant. If the testimony then shows a conflict of evidence from which different conclusions may reasonably be drawn by ordinary prudent persons, then the question becomes one of fact for the jury to determine under proper instructions from the court. In those jurisdictions where only an inference arises, there is no inference of negligence which arises from the mere fact that a collision occurred. In those jurisdictions, in the absence of explanation on the part of the defendant, or other evidence, the issue is presented to the jury. The facts in this case created a presumption of negligence and not an inference of negligence, and therefore, in the absence of an explanation from McNulty (D), a verdict should have been directed by the lower court in favor of Cusack (P). If McNulty (D) had a justifiable reason for not observing traffic rules, then it was his duty to go forward with the evidence to show that he was not negligent and thus, permit the case to go to a jury for the jury's determination on conflicting theories or facts. Affirmed.

EDITOR'S ANALYSIS: Professor Wigmore notes that: "It must be kept in mind that the peculiar effect of a presumption 'of law' (that is, the real presumption) is merely to invoke a rule of law compelling the jury to reach the conclusion in the absence of evidence to the contrary from the opponent." 9 Wigmore, Evidence § 2491 (3d ed. 1940).

[For more information on presumptions affecting burden of proof, see Casenote Law Outline on Evidence, Chapter 4, § II, Presumptions in Civil Cases.]

NOTES:

O'BRIEN v. EQUITABLE LIFE ASSUR. SOC'Y
212 F.2d 383 (8th Cir. 1954);
cert. denied, 348 U.S. 835.

NATURE OF CASE: Appeal from directed verdict denying award of insurance proceeds.

FACT SUMMARY: O'Brien (P) contended that she had made out a prima facie case for recovery of double indemnity insurance for the death of her husband, and therefore, the case should have been submitted to a jury.

CONCISE RULE OF LAW: An unexplained death by violence is presumed to be an accidental death.

FACTS: O'Brien (P) brought an action to recover double indemnity insurance for the alleged accidental death of her husband. The husband's insurance policy provided for the payment of an additional amount in the event of accidental death, so long as the death was not the result of committing or attempting to commit an assault or felony. O'Brien's (P) husband was killed by Robert Jackson on the evening of October 27, 1951, at the home of Jackson's estranged wife, Virginia. The Jacksons, who were the only witnesses to the shooting, testified that the insured was at the time of his death in the act of committing an assault or a felony or both. O'Brien (P) offered in evidence the policy, made proof of death by gunshot wounds inflicted by another, and rested. Equitable (D) then offered the testimony of the Jacksons, and at the close of the evidence, the trial court sustained Equitable's (D) motion for a directed verdict. On appeal, O'Brien (P) argued that she had presented evidence of an unexplained death by violence, which created a presumption of accidental death, and therefore, the issue should have been submitted to the jury.

ISSUE: Is an unexplained death by violence presumed to be an accidental death?

HOLDING AND DECISION: (Collet, J.) Yes. An unexplained death by violence is alone sufficient to make out a prima facie case of accidental death, whether the presumption utilized is one in favor of death by accident or against death by suicide. The presumption of accidental death, while accomplishing the function of evidence is so far as the plaintiff's initial burden of going forward is concerned, nevertheless is not evidence of the fact presumed and is merely a rule of procedure or rebuttable legal presumption. It casts upon the defendant the burden of going forward with substantial evidence to the contrary which, if adduced, destroys the procedural presumption on which the plaintiff has relied as an evidentiary substitute. Where a plaintiff's prima facie case vitally depends upon a rebuttable presumption which is destroyed, the prima facie case collapses with the presumption thereby placing upon the plaintiff the burden of going forward with evidence sufficient to avoid a directed verdict. Where, as here, a rebuttable procedural presumption has been utilized, at most the plaintiff makes out but a rebuttable prima facie case which is procedurally but not substantively significant. The testimony of the Jacksons amply destroyed any presumption of accidental death arguing from O'Brien's (P) bare showing of death by violence. The inferences to be drawn from all the evidence are as consistent with Equitable's (D) theory of death as they are with O'Brien's (P). Affirmed.

EDITOR'S ANALYSIS: One of the most troublesome issues in the area of presumptions concerns the continuing effect to be given a presumption once evidence contrary to the presumption has been introduced. The view taken by the court in this case, that once a presumption is countered it disappears, is commonly called the Thayer or Thayer-Wigmore doctrine of presumptions. This view has been adopted in many American jurisdictions.

[For more information on Thayer-Wigmore presumptions, see Casenote Law Outline on Evidence, Chapter 4, § II, Presumptions in Civil Cases.]

NOTES:

STATE OF MARYLAND v. BALTIMORE TRANSIT CO.

329 F.2d 738 (4th Cir.);
cert. denied, 379 U.S. 842;
reh. denied, 379 U.S. 917 (1964).

NATURE OF CASE: Appeal from denial of damages in wrongful death action.

FACT SUMMARY: The State of Maryland (P) argued that the trial judge erred in charging the jury not to consider the presumption of due care exercised by the decedent.

CONCISE RULE OF LAW: A presumption survives even after conflicting evidence has been offered only where an injured person is unavailable because of injuries or death.

FACTS: The State's (P) intestate was killed at a street corner in the City of Baltimore when struck by a bus owned by the Transit Company (D). At trial, witnesses for the State (P) testified that the decedent was crossing a street in downtown Baltimore and in a marked pedestrian crosswalk, with the "walk" signal showing, when he was struck by the bus. Witnesses for the Transit Company (D), however, testified that the decedent undertook to cross the street some distance from the intersection and the pedestrian crosswalk, and without the protection of the electric signal. The trial judge instructed the jury that "a decedent is presumed to have exercised ordinary care for his own safety . . . but where as here, evidence has been offered to show that the decedent failed to exercise ordinary care in a number of respects, . . . you are not to rely upon the presumption." After a general verdict was entered for the Transit Company (D), the State (P) appealed, arguing that the jury should have been instructed to consider the presumption of due care.

ISSUE: Does a presumption survive even after conflicting evidence has been offered, in cases where an injured person is unavailable because of injuries or death?

HOLDING AND DECISION: (Bell, J.) Yes. A presumption survives even after conflicting evidence has been offered. The trial court refused to instruct the jury to consider the presumption of due care because the Transit Company (D) had offered evidence which conflicted with the presumption. However, the presumption prevails and the jury should have been so instructed despite the fact that countervailing evidence was adduced upon the disputed presumption. The presumption involved in this case may be invoked only where the injured person is unavailable because of the injuries suffered or because of death. Such incapacity is the just reason for the existence of this presumption, and thus the presumption cannot also be applied in favor of the Transit Company (D). Reversed and remanded.

DISSENT: (Haynsworth, J.) Resolution by the jury of the factual question on the contributory negligence issue depended simply upon whether the jurors believed one set of witnesses or the other. No presumption artificially endowed with evidentiary weight was needful or useful to them in resolving the simple issue of credibility which was presented to them. In Maryland, the presumption that the decedent acted with due care for his own self-protection is no stronger and stands on no higher basis than the presumption that the driver of the bus that killed him acted with due care for the safety of pedestrians and others using the streets.

EDITOR'S ANALYSIS: The Federal Rules provide that: "In all civil actions . . . a presumption imposes; on the party against whom it is directed the burden of going forward with evidence to rebut or meet the presumption, but does not shift to such party the burden of proof in the sense of the risk of nonpersuasion, which remains throughout the trial upon the party on whom it was originally cast." See, Federal Rule of Evidence 301.

[For more information on the effect of presumptions, see Casenote Law Outline on Evidence, Chapter 4, § II, Presumptions in Civil Cases.]

NOTES:

COUNTY COURT OF ULSTER COUNTY v. ALLEN
442 U.S. 140 (1979).

NATURE OF CASE: Appeal from affirmance of issuance of habeas corpus.

FACT SUMMARY: Allen (D) claimed his criminal conviction was obtained by use of an unconstitutional statutory presumption making the presence of a firearm in an automobile presumptive evidence of its illegal possession by all persons then occupying the vehicle.

CONCISE RULE OF LAW: For a permissible presumption to be constitutional, there must be a rational connection between the basic facts that the prosecution proved and the ultimate fact presumed, and the ultimate fact presumed must be more likely than not to flow from the facts proved.

FACTS: New York law made the presence of a firearm in an automobile presumptive evidence of its illegal possession by all persons then occupying the vehicle. Allen (D) and others suffered a criminal conviction in a trial in which this statutory presumption was applied under instructions which were vague but which arguably suggested it was permissible rather than mandatory. After a writ of habeas corpus was granted on the ground that the statute was unconstitutional and an appellate affirmance of that decision, the United States Supreme Court addressed the question.

ISSUE: Does the constitutionality of a permissible presumption depend on there being a rational connection between the basic facts which the prosecution proved and the ultimate fact presumed and on the latter being more likely than not to flow from the former?

HOLDING AND DECISION: (Stevens, J.) Yes. For a permissible presumption to be constitutional, there must be a rational connection between the basic facts which the prosecution proved and the ultimate fact presumed and that the latter is more likely than not to flow from the former. The circumstances of this case indicate the presumption at issue was treated as being permissive, so the argument that a reasonable doubt standard should be used to assess its constitutional validity simply will not stand. Under the appropriate standard for permissive presumptions, the presumption here was constitutional. Reversed.

DISSENT: (Powell, J.) This presumption violates due process because it does not fairly reflect what common sense and experience tell us about passengers in automobiles and the possession of handguns.

EDITOR'S ANALYSIS: The Supreme Court has held that the existence of other evidence in the record sufficient to support a conviction is relevant in analyzing a purely permissive presumption but not in analyzing a mandatory presumption. *Turner v. United States*, 396 U.S. 398; *Leary v. United States*, 395 U.S. 6; *United States v. Romano*, 382 U.S. 136.

[For more information on authorized inferences, see Casenote Law Outline on Evidence, Chapter 4, § III, Presumptions in Criminal Cases.]

NOTES:

CHAPTER 6
THE ORDER OF PROOF

QUICK REFERENCE RULES OF LAW

1. **The Order of Proof.** The party who asserts the affirmative of an issue is entitled to begin and reply. (Liptak v. Security Benefit Association)

   [For more information on the order of proof, see Casenote Law Outline on Evidence, Chapter 4, § I, Burdens of Proof.]

2. **The Order of Proof.** A party must put in all his evidence before he rests. (Seguin v. Berg)

3. **The Order of Proof.** A trial judge must be given broad latitude in the control of causes before him, particularly jury cases. (Duran v. Neff)

   [For more information on order of proof, see Casenote Law Outline on Evidence, Chapter 4, § I, Burdens of Proof.]

4. **Cross-examination.** Cross-examination is limited to the scope of the direct examination. (Atkinson v. Smith)

   [For more information on cross-examination, see Casenote Law Outline on Evidence, Chapter 11, § V, Order and Scope of Examination.]

5. **Cross-examination.** Where the testimony of a witness on direct examination makes a prima facie case, or creates a presumption or inference as to the existence of a fact not directly testified to, the witness may be cross-examined to rebut such prima facie proof, presumption, or inference. (Eno v. Adair County Mut. Ins. Ass'n)

   [For more information on cross-examination, see Casenote Law Outline on Evidence, Chapter 11, § V, Order and Scope of Examination.]

6. **The Scope of Cross-examination.** An opposing party may cross-examine a witness on any matter in issue. (Boller v. Cofrances)

   [For more information on the scope of cross-examination, see Casenote Law Outline on Evidence, Chapter 11, § V, Order and Scope of Examination.]

7. **Judicial Discretion.** The trial court may, in its discretion, permit reopening of the evidence after both parties have rested. (Bommer v. Stedelin)

   [For more information on judicial discretion, see Casenote Law Outline on Evidence, Chapter 11, § V, Order and Scope of Examination.]

LIPTAK v. SECURITY BENEFIT ASS'N
Ill. Sup. Ct., 350 Ill. 614, 183 N.E. 564 (1932).

NATURE OF CASE: Appeal from award of damages for breach of contract.

FACT SUMMARY: Security Benefit (D) argued that, because it had the burden of proof at trial, that it should have been permitted to take the lead in presenting its case.

CONCISE RULE OF LAW: The party who asserts the affirmative of an issue is entitled to begin and reply.

FACTS: Liptak (P), as widow of Julius Liptak, brought suit against Security Benefit (D), a fraternal benefit society, to obtain the proceeds on a benefit certificate issued to the decedent on November 26, 1921, in the amount of $1,000. Security Benefit (D) entered a special plea setting out certain sections of its bylaws and alleging that before his death, the decedent was suspended for failure to pay premium assessments in accordance with the provisions of those bylaws. Liptak (P) countered by stating that one John R. De Bow, an officer of Security Benefit (D), had come to the home of the decedent and had received the payment for the month in question. When the case was called for trial, Security Benefit (D) admitted the issuance of the certificate, the relationship of the parties, the correctness of the bylaws, admitted the death of the insured and receipt of proof of death, and moved the court that it be permitted to take the lead in the examination of the jury on account of the fact that under the pleadings the burden of proof was upon Security Benefit (D). This motion was denied, and when similar motions were made later in the proceedings, those too were denied. The jury returned a verdict for Liptak (P) in the sum of $1,000, and Security Benefit (D) appealed, arguing that the trial court should have properly allowed it to take the lead in the interrogation of the jury, and in presenting its case.

ISSUE: Is the party who asserts the affirmative of an issue entitled to begin and reply?

HOLDING AND DECISION: (Stone, J.) Yes. The party who asserts the affirmative of an issue is entitled to begin and reply. The right to open and close is a substantial right coexistent with the burden of proof. Whenever the plaintiff has anything to prove in order to secure a verdict, the right to open and close belongs to him. The right to open and close is not a matter resting merely in the discretion of the trial, but is a substantial right in the person who must introduce proof to prevent judgment against him. If Liptak (P) was, under the pleadings and admissions of Security Benefit (D), entitled to judgment in the absence of proof supporting the special plea, then Security Benefit (D) carried the burden to go forward in the offer of proof and was entitled to open and close the evidence and arguments. The only controversy in the case was that raised on the affirmative special plea. Because the right of Security Benefit (D) to open and close was a substantial right, the case is reversed and remanded for further proceedings.

EDITOR'S ANALYSIS: This case represents the majority view concerning the order of proof in civil actions. As noted in this case, the defendant in a civil action will acquire the right to open and close only where the plaintiff has nothing to prove in order to secure a judgment.

———————————————

[For more information on the order of proof, see Casenote Law Outline on Evidence, Chapter 4, § I, Burdens of Proof.]

NOTES:

SEGUIN v. BERG

N.Y. Sup. Ct., 260 App. Div. 284, 21 N.Y.S.2d 191 (1940).

NATURE OF CASE: Appeal from damages award for negligence.

FACT SUMMARY: Seguin (P) contended that the trial court improperly refused to allow him to present rebuttal evidence at the conclusion of Berg's (D) proof.

CONCISE RULE OF LAW: A party must put in all his evidence before he rests.

FACTS: On January 2, 1938, the automobiles of Seguin (P) and Berg (D) collided on the state highway connecting Lake Placid and Saranac Lake as a result of which both cars were damaged. Each of the owners of the respective vehicles charged the other with negligence in causing the collision. In support of his action to recover damages, Seguin (P) offered his own testimony and that of the mechanic who repaired his car and then rested. At the conclusion of Berg's (D) proof, Seguin (P) called as witnesses three persons, who had been passengers in his car, who saw the collision and sought to explain their version of how it occurred. Upon objection by Berg (D), the evidence was excluded on the ground that it was not proper rebuttal. After the jury rendered a verdict in favor of Berg (D) on his counterclaim for damages, Seguin (P) brought this appeal, contending that the trial court erred in refusing to allow him to present the testimony of the three witnesses who were called after Berg (D) had rested.

ISSUE: Must a party put in all his evidence before he rests?

HOLDING AND DECISION: (Heffernan, J.) Yes. A party must put in all his evidence before he rests. He must exhaust all of his testimony in support of the issue on his side before the proof of his adversary is heard. The defendant should then produce evidence, and finally the evidence in rebuttal is received. The plaintiff cannot put in merely enough evidence to make out a prima facie case and reserve the rest to meet the emergency of later needs. He has no right to reopen his case after the defendant has closed although he may introduce proof in rebuttal. He may not however under the guise of rebuttal put in evidence tending to support the allegations of his pleading. Here though, Seguin (P) had the right to offer such testimony as he desired in support of his cause of action. It is true that the evidence which he sought to introduce in rebuttal, and which was excluded, would have been competent as part of his affirmative case. The evidence was clearly admissible in rebuttal for the purpose of contradicting the evidence on the part of Berg (D) to the effect that the collision was due solely to Seguin's (P) negligence. Evidence which would have been proper as part of a plaintiff's affirmative case, and which he has no right to introduce as affirmative evidence after the defendant has rested, may still be offered by the plaintiff if it tends to impeach or discredit the testimony of any of the defendants. Reversed and remanded.

EDITOR'S ANALYSIS: In this case, Berg (D) has asserted a counterclaim against Seguin (P) for the damages to his own car. Under N.Y. Civ. Practice Act § 424, where a defendant interposes a counterclaim and demands an affirmative judgment against the plaintiff, the mode of trial of an issue of fact arising thereupon is the same as if it arose in an action brought by the defendant against the plaintiff for the cause of action stated in the counterclaim and demanding the same judgment.

NOTES:

ATKINSON v. SMITH
New Brunswick Sup. Ct., 9 N.B. 309 (1859).

NATURE OF CASE: Appeal from award of damages for injury to property.

FACT SUMMARY: Smith (D) contended that the trial judge unreasonably restricted the questioning of counsel on cross-examination of Atkinson's (P) witnesses.

CONCISE RULE OF LAW: Cross-examination is limited to the scope of the direct examination.

FACTS: Atkinson (P) brought suit against Smith (D) for breaking and entering his close and cutting down a mill-dam. Smith (D) countered that the location in question was a branch of the Buctouche River, which was a public navigable river for driving logs and lumber. Smith (D) further argued that the public river had been obstructed by the mill-dam built across it, and that as he moved his lumber down the river, he was obliged to remove a part of the dam in order to allow the logs to pass. At trial, Smith's (D) counsel proposed on the cross-examination of one of Atkinson's (P) witnesses to ask certain questions concerning Smith's (D) justification for removing the dam, an area which had not been inquired into during the direct examination by counsel for Atkinson (P). After objection had been made, the trial judge ruled that that particular evidence could not be gone into until Smith (D) opened his case. The jury found that Smith's (D) justification had been proved, but gave a verdict for Atkinson (P) for an amount representing the excessive damage in cutting the dam. On appeal, Smith (D) argued that the trial judge unreasonably and improperly restricted the cross-examination by his counsel.

ISSUE: Is cross-examination limited to the scope of the direct examination?

HOLDING AND DECISION: (Parker, J.) Yes. Cross-examination is limited to the scope of the direct examination. The defendant has no right at trial to inquire into areas constituting a justification for his actions, if they have not been inquired into during the direct examination by opposing counsel. If a contrary rule existed, it would be impossible for the judges to decide on the relevancy of many questions put by the defendant's counsel, and it would be in the power of an ingenious counsel to multiply discussion to almost any extent. It would be inconvenient, and often unjust, to interrupt the course of the examination of the plaintiff's witnesses while constantly recurring arguments were gone into on the admissibility of proof of facts which constituted a portion of the argument of the defense. Affirmed.

EDITOR'S ANALYSIS: The rule which restricts cross-examination to the scope of the direct examination does not apply to a cross-examination for the purpose of impeachment. However, a cross-examination for impeachment purposes often presents the potential for injecting confusion into the issues or distracting attention from the central issues in the case.

[For more information on cross-examination, see Casenote Law Outline on Evidence, Chapter 11, § V, Order and Scope of Examination.]

DURAN v. NEFF
Fla. Dist. Ct. App., 366 So.2d 169 (1979).

NATURE OF CASE: Appeal from directed verdict against plaintiff in a medical malpractice case.

FACT SUMMARY: The trial judge refused to allow Duran (P) to put on her expert witness at 5:10 in the afternoon after Duran (P) requested a recess.

CONCISE RULE OF LAW: A trial judge must be given broad latitude in the control of causes before him, particularly jury cases.

FACTS: In a medical malpractice action filed by Duran (P) against Neff (D), Duran (P) sought and received the right to have her case presented first on a Monday morning. On Monday afternoon, at 5:10 p.m., Duran's (P) counsel suggested that the court take a short recess before permitting him to put on an expert witness, whose examination would be lengthy. The court declined and instead recessed until the next day. Duran (P) was unable to produce the expert witness on the following day, and directed verdict was rendered against her. Duran (P) appealed.

ISSUE: Must a trial judge be given broad latitude in the control of causes before him, particularly jury cases?

HOLDING AND DECISION: Yes. A trial judge must be given broad latitude in the control of causes before him, particularly jury cases. In this case, the trial judge did not abuse his discretion by refusing to take Duran's (P) expert's testimony late on the first day. Affirmed.

EDITOR'S ANALYSIS: It is generally true that a trial judge's discretion is very broad in controlling such things as order of proof and timing. However, there are circumstances in which the judge's broad discretion has strictures placed upon it. In Loinaz v. EG & G, Inc., 910 F.2d 1 (1st Cir. 1990), the appellate court held that reversible error had occurred when the trial judge refused the defendant's request to present the main witness during plaintiff's case, forcing the defense to rely on a deposition in lieu of in-court testimony.

[For more information on order of proof, see Casenote Law Outline on Evidence, Chapter 4, § I, Burdens of Proof.]

ENO v. ADAIR COUNTY MUT. INS. ASS'N.
Iowa Sup. Ct., 229 Iowa 249, 294 N.W. 323 (1940).

NATURE OF CASE: Appeal from award of proceeds under insurance policy.

FACT SUMMARY: Adair (D) contended that the trial court had improperly limited its cross-examination of a witness for Eno (P).

CONCISE RULE OF LAW: Where the testimony of a witness on direct examination makes a prima facie case, or creates a presumption or inference as to the existence of a fact not directly testified to, the witness may be cross-examined to rebut such prima facie proof, presumption, or inference.

FACTS: Eno (P), the owner of a barn which had been destroyed by fire, brought suit to recover on an insurance policy issued by Adair (D) insuring the property against loss by fire and lightning. Adair (D) admitted execution of the policy, and the occurrence of the fire, but alleged that Eno (P) had violated certain policy provisions by installing a gasoline engine in the barn without notice to or consent from Adair (D). The only witness on behalf of Eno (P) was her husband, who identified the policy and testified that the barn had been destroyed by fire. On cross-examination, the trial court sustained an objection to the question of what caused the fire. After a trial without a jury, judgment was rendered for Eno (P), and Adair (D) then appealed, arguing that the trial court erred in refusing to permit it to cross-examine the husband of Eno (P) as to the cause of the fire and the attendant circumstances.

ISSUE: Where the testimony of a witness on direct examination makes a prima facie case, or creates a presumption or inference as to the existence of a fact not directly testified to, may the witness be cross-examined to rebut such prima facie proof, presumption, or inference?

HOLDING AND DECISION: (Bliss, J.) Yes. Where the testimony of a witness on direct examination makes a prima facie case, or creates a presumption or inference as to the existence of a fact not directly testified to, the witness may be cross-examined to rebut such prima facie proof, presumption, or inference. Cross-examination affords one of the most effective means of detecting falsehood and discovering the truth, and the rules governing it should be applied in a broad and liberal spirit, with a view to effectuating substantial justice. Although the extent of cross-examination is left largely to the sound legal discretion of the trial court, who may broaden it where the witness is hostile to the cross-examiner, or restrict it where the witness appears too friendly and eager to agree with the cross-examiner, cross-examination is a right to be jealously guarded. Here, Adair (D) had a right to cross-examine the witness on the policy, because it determined in part whether Eno (P) was entitled to recover its proceeds. Similarly, the witness had testified that Eno (P) had suffered a total loss because of the fire, yet he knew of circumstances and conditions attending the starting of the fire which made it a debatable question whether Eno (P) was entitled to recover. These circumstances and conditions were connected with the matter raised during direct examination, and Adair (D) was entitled to cross-examine the witness as to the cause of the fire. Reversed and remanded.

EDITOR'S ANALYSIS: In England, it has been the rule that a witness called for any purpose may be cross-examined by the opposing party on the whole case, or any phase of it. By contrast, the American rule holds that a party has no right to cross-examine any witness except as to facts and circumstances connected with the matter stated in the direct examination.

[For more information on cross-examination, see Casenote Law Outline on Evidence, Chapter 11, § V, Order and Scope of Examination.]

NOTES:

BOLLER v. COFRANCES
Wis. Sup. Ct., 42 Wis. 2d 170, 166 N.W.2d 129 (1969).

NATURE OF CASE: Appeal from dismissal of negligence action.

FACT SUMMARY: Cofrances (D) contended that the trial judge erred in excluding a question regarding the deceased's alleged extramarital relationship.

CONCISE RULE OF LAW: An opposing party may cross-examine a witness on any matter in issue.

FACTS: Virginia M. Boller (P), the administratrix of Henry W. Boller, brought an action for negligence, arising out of an automobile accident that occurred in the city of LaCrosse on May 23, 1965. Henry W. Boller and his passenger, Catherine Case, were both killed in the accident. At trial, during the cross-examination of Virginia Boller, counsel for Cofrances (D) asked whether she was aware that her husband was having an affair with Mrs. Case. The court sustained Boller's (P) objection to the question, on the grounds that it was beyond the scope of direct examination. After Boller's (P) complaint was dismissed, Boller (P) appealed. Cofrances (D) also argued that the question was proper, and Boller's (P) answer should have been admitted into evidence.

ISSUE: May an opposing party cross-examine a witness on any matter in issue?

HOLDING AND DECISION: (Heffernan, J.) Yes. One of the major issues to be resolved by the jury was the evaluation, to the extent possible, at the loss Virginia Boller (P) sustained by losing the companionship of Henry Boller. Certainly, the existence of an affair with another woman and Virginia Boller's (P) knowledge of it were probative of the value to be placed upon Virginia Boller's (P) loss. Because the question was directly related to, and in impeachment of, her testimony on direct examination, the question was within the scope of direct examination. The rule against questioning any witness beyond the scope of direct examination has no intrinsic merit and does not demonstrably assist in the search for the truth. If a question is relevant and is otherwise admissible and the information solicited is within the knowledge of the witness, it should be within the sound discretion of the trial judge to determine whether or not questions on cross-examination prevent an orderly and cogent presentation of the evidence. Cross-examination is the greatest device for getting at the truth, and the scope-of-direct rule, which needlessly hampers its exercise, is not sound. The disputed question properly should have been allowed as eliciting evidence relevant to the issue or an impeachment. Affirmed.

EDITOR'S ANALYSIS: Wigmore notes that the rule adopted in this case allows "the opposite party . . . not only [to] cross-examine [the witness] in relation to the point which he was called to prove, but he may examine him as to any matter embraced in the issue. He may establish his defense by him without calling any other witnesses. If he is a competent witness to the jury for any purpose, he is so for all purposes." 6 Wigmore, Evidence (3d ed.) § 1885, p. 532.

[For more information on the scope of cross-examination, see Casenote Law Outline on Evidence, Chapter 11, § V, Order and Scope of Examination.]

NOTES:

BOMMER v. STEDELIN
Mo. Ct. App., 237 S.W.2d 225 (1951).

NATURE OF CASE: Appeal from denial of damages for negligence.

FACT SUMMARY: Bommer (P) argued that the trial court erred in refusing his request to reopen the case to present additional evidence.

CONCISE RULE OF LAW: The trial court may, in its discretion, permit reopening of the evidence after both parties have rested.

FACTS: Bommer (P) brought suit to recover damages for an automobile bailed to a public parking lot for storage and parking. The testimony showed that Bommer's (P) wife had delivered their car to a parking lot at the corner of 8th and Delmar, where she turned the car over to an attendant, who gave her a claim stub in return. When Bommer's (P) wife returned to pick up the car, the attendant crashed the car into a parked car, causing damage to the front end of the automobile. Bommer's (P) wife testified that a man who identified himself as Mr. Stedelin (D) came to the parking lot after the occurrence, that he identified himself as a vice-president of Glueck Realty Company, which owned the parking lot. After Bommer (P) had presented his case, Stedelin's (D) counsel requested a directed verdict, and the trial judge indicated he would direct a verdict, whereupon Bommer's (P) counsel requested leave to reopen the case in order to produce witnesses to testify to the ownership and operation of the parking lot by Glueck Realty Company, who would have been available within an hour. Leave to reopen the case was denied, and a verdict was directed for Stedelin (D) on the grounds that Bommer (P) failed to identify the ownership and management of the parking lot with Stedelin (D). Bommer (P) then brought this appeal, arguing that the trial judge abused his discretion in ordering a directed verdict.

ISSUE: May the trial court, in its sound discretion, permit reopening of the evidence after both parties have rested?

HOLDING AND DECISION: (Houser, Comm'r) Yes. The trial court may, in its sound discretion, permit reopening of the evidence after both parties have formally rested. Although a trial judge is vested with a wide latitude and broad discretion in the allowance or denial of leave to reopen a case for additional testimony, that discretion must be a sound judicial discretion, which cannot be exercised in an arbitrary manner. Here, the record shows that the request was made at 6 minutes before 1:00 p.m., that the jury was recessed until 2:00 p.m., and that counsel had assured the court that he could produce the required evidence within an hour. There was no showing of surprise to Stedelin (D) or of inconvenience to the court, parties, counsel, or jury, or that the adverse party would have been deceived or prejudiced in any manner by granting the leave. The court denied Bommer (P) the opportunity to offer evidence to prove that Stedelin (D) owned and operated the parking facility, while at the same time directing a verdict against Bommer (P) for failure to prove such fact. Reversed and remanded.

EDITOR'S ANALYSIS: The Federal Rules provide that "the court shall exercise reasonable control over the mode and order of interrogating witnesses and presenting evidence so as to (1) make the interrogation and presentation effective for the ascertainment of the truth, (2) avoid needless consumption of time, and (3) protect witnesses from harassment or undue embarrassment." Federal Rule of Evidence 611(a).

[For more information on judicial discretion, see Casenote Law Outline on Evidence, Chapter 11, § V, Order and Scope of Examination.]

NOTES:

CHAPTER 7
THE CONCEPT OF RELEVANCY

QUICK REFERENCE RULES OF LAW

1. **The Danger of Undue Prejudice.** Evidence of the poverty or wealth of a party to an action is inadmissible in a negligence action. (City of Cleveland v. Peter Kiewit Sons' Co.)

   [For more information on the danger of undue prejudice, see Casenote Law Outline on Evidence, Chapter 2, § V, Discretionary Exclusion of Relevant Evidence.]

2. **Relevant Evidence.** Unless excluded by some rule of law, any fact may be proved which logically tends to aid the trier of fact in the determination of the issue. (Plumb v. Curtis)

   [For more information on relevant evidence, see Casenote Law Outline on Evidence, Chapter 2, § III, Is the "Evidence" Relevant?]

3. **Issues of Relevance.** A defendant's lack of money may not be introduced to prove the probability that the defendant committed crime in order to obtain money. (State v. Mathis)

   [For more information on issues of relevance, see Casenote Law Outline on Evidence, Chapter 2, § III, Is the "Evidence" Relevant?]

4. **Precedential Relevance.** Evidence of a defendant's pecuniary condition is admissible where a plaintiff seeks exemplary damages. (Hall v. Montgomery Ward & Co.)

   [For more information on precedential relevance, see Casenote Law Outline on Evidence, Chapter 2, § VI, Precedential Relevance.]

5. **Evidence of Liability Insurance.** The inability to pay doctrine renders the existence, not the amount, of insurance coverage of the defendant relevant. (Reed v. General Motors Corp.)

   [For more information on evidence of liability insurance, see Casenote Law Outline on Evidence, Chapter 7, § VI, Liability Insurance.]

NOTES

CITY OF CLEVELAND v. PETER KIEWIT SONS' CO.
624 F.2d 749 (6th Cir. 1980).

NATURE OF CASE: Appeal from award of damages.

FACT SUMMARY: Kiewit (D) contended that the City (P) had repeatedly made prejudicial comments and introduced prejudicial testimony at trial by referring to Kiewit's (D) wealth and insurance.

CONCISE RULE OF LAW: Evidence of the poverty or wealth of a party to an action is inadmissible in a negligence action.

FACTS: In 1973, Kiewit (D), a contracting firm headquartered in Omaha, Nebraska, entered into a permit agreement with the City (P) whereby Kiewit (D) was permitted to use a portion of the City's (P) dock to load blast furnace slag on barges to be transported to another construction project. On October 24, 1973, approximately three weeks after Kiewit (D) had surrendered possession to the City (P), portions of the dock collapsed. The portion that collapsed included only a small section of the area which had been leased to Kiewit (D). The City (P) then filed suit against Kiewit (D), seeking recovery of $350,000 in compensatory damages plus interest. At trial, counsel for the City (P) repeatedly made comments, over objection, referring to Kiewit (D) as one of the largest construction corporations. Counsel for the City (P) also, over objection, referred several times to a general public liability insurance policy carried by Kiewit (D). The jury returned a verdict in favor of the City (P) for $350,000, and Kiewit (D) appealed, arguing that the remarks, argument, and questioning of witnesses by the City's (P) counsel regarding liability insurance and Kiewit's (D) financial resources, considered in total, were prejudicial.

ISSUE: Is evidence of the poverty or wealth of a party to an action inadmissible in a negligence action?

HOLDING AND DECISION: (Weick, J.) Yes. Evidence as to the poverty or wealth of a party to an action is inadmissible in a negligence action. Appealing to the sympathy of jurors through references to financial disparity is improper. In damage actions in which compensatory damages only are recoverable, evidence is not admissible to show the wealth or financial standing of either the plaintiff or the defendant, except in such cases as actions for defamation or injury to reputation, where the position or wealth of the parties is necessarily involved in determining the damages sustained. Furthermore, in a case such as this, when the existence of insurance protection in favor of a party is shown to the jury, a mistrial should be declared because of the prejudice inhering to that party. In light of the extensive comments made by counsel for the City (P) at trial, any curative instructions which the trial court eventually chose to give were plainly not sufficient to remove the probability of prejudice. The excessive size of the verdict demonstrates the prejudicial effect of the comments by counsel for the City (P). Reversed and remanded.

EDITOR'S ANALYSIS: Federal Rule of Evidence 403 provides that: "Although relevant, evidence may be excluded if its probative value is substantially outweighed by the danger of unfair prejudice, confusion of the issues, or misleading the jury, or by considerations of undue delay, waste of time, or needless presentation of cumulative evidence."

[For more information on the danger of undue prejudice, see Casenote Law Outline on Evidence, Chapter 2, § V, Discretionary Exclusion of Relevant Evidence.]

NOTES:

PLUMB v. CURTIS
Conn. Sup. Ct., 66 Conn. 154, 33 A. 998 (1895).

NATURE OF CASE: Appeal from judgment granting damages.

FACT SUMMARY: Curtis (D) contended that the trial court allowed in allegedly irrelevant evidence of an agent's financial condition.

CONCISE RULE OF LAW: Unless excluded by some rule of law, any fact may be proved which logically tends to aid the trier of fact in the determination of the issue.

FACTS: Hanford Plumb (P) sued Lewis Curtis (D) for building materials allegedly purchased by Curtis (D) through his agent Simeon Plumb. Plumb (P) had furnished materials for three houses, on Simeon Plumb's order, and Curtis (D) admitted responsibility for those materials. Thereafter, Plumb (P) furnished materials for an additional five houses, also on Simeon Plumb's order, but Curtis (D) denied liability, claiming that the materials had been sold to Simeon Plumb individually. Plumb (P) was allowed, over Curtis' (D) objection, to testify that Simeon Plumb was a man of no property, so far as he knew. Plumb (P) claimed that he had extended credit to Curtis (D), and was justified, on the basis of their previous relationship, in doing so. Curtis (D) denied that Simeon Plumb had any authority to buy on his credit the goods charged for the additional houses. The jury returned a verdict for Plumb (P), and Curtis (D) appealed, arguing that the evidence as to Simeon Plumb's financial condition was irrelevant to the controversy.

ISSUE: Unless excluded by some rule of law, may any fact be proved which logically tends to aid the trier of fact in the determination of the issues?

HOLDING AND DECISION: (Baldwin, J.) Yes. Unless excluded by some rule or principle of law, any fact may be proved which logically tends to aid the trier of fact in the determination of an issue. If the evidence offered conduces in any reasonable degree to establish the probability or improbability of the fact in controversy, it should go to the jury. The word relevant means that any two facts to which it is applied are so related to each other, that according to the common course of events, one either taken by itself or in connection with other facts proves or renders probable the past, present, or future existence or nonexistence of the other. The jury, in the present case, was to determine whether it was probable that Plumb (P), after charging all the materials furnished on the order of Simeon Plumb, for the construction of three houses in Bridgeport, to Curtis (D) as the principal for whom Plumb acted, or to Plumb individually. According to the common course of human conduct, a merchant is not likely to continue for several months to make almost daily sales on credit, of goods worth in the hundreds of dollars, to a man who, so far as he knows, is destitute of any means to pay for them. Thus, Plumb's (P) testimony, taken in connection with the other evidence already introduced in the case, fairly tended to throw light on the matter in controversy, and was properly received. Affirmed.

EDITOR'S ANALYSIS: Federal Rule of Evidence 401 provides that: "Relevant evidence means evidence having any tendency to make the existence of any fact that is of consequence to the determination of the action more probable or less probable than it would be without the evidence."

[For more information on relevant evidence, see Casenote Law Outline on Evidence, Chapter 2, § III, Is the "Evidence" Relevant?]

NOTES:

STATE v. MATHIS
N.J. Sup. Ct., 47 N.J. 455, 221 A.2d 529 (1966).

NATURE OF CASE: Appeal from conviction for murder.

FACT SUMMARY: Mathis (D) contended that the trial court erred in allowing the prosecutor to inquire into his employment status at the time of the crime.

CONCISE RULE OF LAW: A defendant's lack of money may not be introduced to prove the probability that the defendant committed crime in order to obtain money.

FACTS: Mathis (D) was charged with the murder of Stanley Caswell, an insurance debit collector. At trial, evidence was introduced showing that Mathis (D) was visiting with his father on the day of the crime, that Caswell was also there to see the father on a business matter, that Mathis (D) had been seen pushing Caswell into Caswell's car, and that Caswell's forehead was bloody at that time. The prosecutor cross-examined Mathis (D) as to how much money he had and when he last worked. The examination strongly suggested that the State (P) might be urging that Mathis (D) was in financial need, and therefore was likely to commit a robbery. Evidence had previously been introduced that money was missing from Caswell's body. Over objection, the trial court permitted the prosecutor to ask about Mathis' (D) employment status at the time of the crime, but only for credibility purposes, rather than to show proof of financial need. The State (P) then proceeded to call two neighbors of the father to testify that they never saw Mathis (D) working at his father's house, where he claimed that he worked repairing automobiles. After being convicted of murder in the first degree and sentenced to die, Mathis (D) brought this appeal, alleging that the trial court erred in allowing evidence of his then employment status to be introduced at trial.

ISSUE: May a defendant's lack of money be introduced to prove the probability that the defendant committed a crime in order to obtain money?

HOLDING AND DECISION: (Weintraub, J.) A defendant's lack of money may not be introduced to show the probability that the defendant committed a crime in order to obtain money. Whether Mathis (D) did or did not work with his father was not an issue in the case. Nor would it directly bear upon credibility, for there is nothing about working with one's father or not working with one's father which suggests a man cannot be a trustworthy witness. Thus, the evidence was not germane to the case, either with respect to the triable issues or as to Mathis' (D) reliability as a witness. The point that the State (P) made was that Mathis (D) lied when he said he worked for his father, and hence he did not earn money that way, and being otherwise essentially unemployed, he must have been destitute and therefore more likely to commit a robbery. Reversed and remanded.

EDITOR'S ANALYSIS: In commenting on the issue presented by this case, Professor Wigmore states that: "The lack of money by A might be relevant enough to show the probability of A's desiring to commit a crime in order to obtain money. But the practical result of such a doctrine would be to put a poor person under so much unfair suspicion and at such a relative disadvantage that for reasons of fairness this argument has seldom been countenanced as evidence of the graver crimes, particularly of violence." 2 Wigmore, Evidence, § 392, p. 341 (3d ed. 1940).

_____

[For more information on issues of relevance, see Casenote Law Outline on Evidence, Chapter 2, § III, Is the "Evidence" Relevant?]

NOTES:

HALL v. MONTGOMERY WARD & CO.
Iowa Sup. Ct., 252 N.W.2d 421 (1977).

NATURE OF CASE: Appeal from award of damages for mental anguish.

FACT SUMMARY: After Montgomery Ward (D) interrogated Hall (P) about his unauthorized use of Montgomery Ward's (D) floor cleaning equipment and forced him to sign documents he could not comprehend, Hall (P) brought this action for mental anguish and received a large exemplary damage award upon presenting Montgomery Ward's (D) balance sheet as evidence over objection.

CONCISE RULE OF LAW: Evidence of a defendant's pecuniary condition is admissible where a plaintiff seeks exemplary damages.

FACTS: Hall (P) was an employee of Montgomery Ward (D) who performed janitorial and maintenance services. At times, Hall (P) "borrowed" Montgomery Ward's (D) floor cleaning equipment to do moonlight floor cleaning jobs. Montgomery Ward's (D) agents interrogated Hall (P) regarding the equipment use and the use of materials for cleaning. Hall (P) was a mental incompetent, but during the course of the interrogation, he was forced to sign four documents including a form granting consent to be detained and interrogated, a confession of theft, and a promissory note in the amount of $5,000. Hall (P) did not, and expert testimony tended to show that he could not, understand the forms. Hall (P) alleged mental anguish in this suit for damages, and alleged recurring dreams along with strained family relations, but did not allege any physical injury. Hall (P) then introduced, over Montgomery Ward's (D) objection, the balance sheet for Montgomery Ward's (D) business. The jury awarded exemplary damages of $50,000, in addition to $12,500 in general damages. Montgomery Ward's (D) motion for a new trial was granted on the ground of error in overruling Montgomery Ward's (D) objection to the introduction of the balance sheet. Hall (P) appealed, and Montgomery Ward (D) cross-appealed.

ISSUE: Is evidence of a defendant's pecuniary condition admissible where a plaintiff seeks exemplary damages?

HOLDING AND DECISION: (Uhlenhopp, J.) Yes. The rule in this jurisdiction has been to deny admission to evidence of a defendant's pecuniary condition even though the plaintiff seeks smart money. The rationale is to prevent the fact finder from improperly considering the relative poverty or affluence of the parties rather than the issues of the case. The great weight of authority is to the contrary under modern law, based on the notion that the jury needs to know the extent of the defendant's holdings in order to determine how large of an exemplary damage award will make him smart. Thus, the prior decisions precluding such evidence are overruled. Evidence of a defendant's pecuniary condition is admissible where a plaintiff seeks exemplary damages. The balance sheet exhibit was thus properly received in evidence and the new trial award was error. Reversed and remanded.

EDITOR'S ANALYSIS: As the court notes, most jurisdictions today hold that the defendant's ability to pay is relevant and admissible when punitive or exemplary damages (sometimes called "smart money") are awarded. The evidence which would establish the financial condition of the defendant is discoverable prior to trial where a claim is made out justifying punitive damages.

[For more information on precedential relevance, see Casenote Law Outline on Evidence, Chapter 2, § VI, Precedential Relevance.]

NOTES:

REED v. GENERAL MOTORS CORP.
773 F.2d 660 (5th Cir. 1985).

NATURE OF CASE: Appeal from award of damages for personal injuries.

FACT SUMMARY: Reed (P) contended that proof of the amount of Boudreaux's (D) and Meche's (D) insurance coverage was relevant, and its admission into evidence was not error.

CONCISE RULE OF LAW: The inability to pay doctrine renders the existence, not the amount, of insurance coverage of the defendant relevant.

FACTS: Reed (P) and his passengers were seriously injured when their vehicle was struck by Boudreaux's (D) vehicle. At the time of the collision, Boudreaux (D) was engaged in an illegal race with Meche (D). Reed (P) sued Boudreaux (D), and their insurers, to mitigate his damages of $450,000, ascribing 70% liability to Boudreaux (D) and 30% to Meche (D). Both Meche (D) and Boudreaux (D) were jointly and severally liable under state law. Meche (D) appealed, as did his insurer, on the basis that evidence of the amount of his coverage was erroneously admitted. He argued that the jury was induced to find both defendants liable so that Reed (P) would not be limited in their recovery to Boudreaux's (D) $10,000 in coverage.

ISSUE: Is the amount of a defendant's insurance coverage relevant?

HOLDING AND DECISION: (Rubin, J.) No. The inability to pay doctrine renders the existence, not the amount, of insurance coverage of the defendant relevant. The existence of insurance coverage was relevant due to the state direct action statute allowing for the joinder of insurance companies. However, the amount of coverage was irrelevant. It went no distance toward proving the liability or lack thereof of any party in the suit. It clearly induced the jury to find both parties negligent so that the severe injuries would not be limited to the $10,000 in coverage. As a result, the trial court's denial of Meche's (D) motion for a directed verdict was proper, and the case is remanded for a new trial.

EDITOR'S ANALYSIS: Most jurisdictions do not allow direct suits against the defendant's insurance company. Likewise, even the existence of insurance coverage is usually inadmissible. Interestingly, while it is usually agreed that insurance coverage is not relevant to the resolution of a personal injury action, the existence and limits of insurance coverage are usually discoverable.

[For more information on evidence of liability insurance, see Casenote Law Outline on Evidence, Chapter 7, § VI, Liability Insurance.]

NOTES

CHAPTER 8
FORMALIZED APPLICATIONS OF THE RELEVANCY CONCEPT

QUICK REFERENCE RULES OF LAW

1. **Other Happenings.** In a negligence action wherein a dangerous condition is alleged, evidence showing injuries to persons other than the plaintiff because of the condition is not admissible to show dangerousness of the condition. (Diamond Rubber Co. v. Harryman)

2. **Limited Admissibility.** Evidence of occurrences similar to the one sued upon in a negligence action may be admitted to show dangerousness of a condition if the agency or instrumentality is demonstrated to be in substantially the same condition. (City of Bloomington v. Legg)

   [For more information on limited admissibility, see Casenote Law Outline on Evidence, Chapter 5, § IV, Limited Admissibility.]

3. **Discretionary Exclusion of Relevant Evidence.** In products liability cases involving a claim of defective design, the trial court has discretion under Fed. R. Evid. 403 to admit evidence of safety history concerning both the existence and nonexistence of prior accidents, provided that the proponent establishes the necessary predicate for the evidence. (Jones v. Pak-Mor Manufacturing Co.)

   [For more information on discretionary exclusion of relevant evidence, see Casenote Law Outline on Evidence, Chapter 2, § V, Discretionary Exclusion of Relevant Evidence.]

4. **Relevant Evidence.** Evidence of the price at a recent sale of property is relevant to prove the value of similar property in the same location. (Redfield v. Iowa State Highway Comm'n)

   [For more information on relevant evidence, see Casenote Law Outline on Evidence, Chapter 2, § III, Is the "Evidence" Relevant?]

5. **Circumstantial Evidence.** Evidence of tests and experiments conducted under circumstances approximately similar to the incident sued upon is admissible. (Carpenter v. Kuhn)

   [For more information on circumstantial evidence, see Casenote Law Outline on Evidence, Chapter 2, § III, Is the "Evidence" Relevant?]

6. **Judicial Discretion in Admissibility of Relevant Evidence.** Evidence of an experiment conducted under circumstances substantially similar to those existing at the time of the incident under the court's consideration may be admitted within the judge's discretion. (Foster v. Agri-chem, Inc.)

   [For more information on judicial discretion in admissibility of relevant evidence, see Casenote Law Outline on Evidence, Chapter 2, § V, Discretionary Exclusion of Relevant Evidence.]

7. **Personality Traits and Behavior Patterns — Civil Cases.** Evidence of habitual conduct of an animal is admissible to establish an observer's ability to identify that animal or to prove conduct conforming to the habit. (Rumbaugh v. McCormick)

8. **Character Evidence.** In a civil action where a party's character is not at issue and the credibility of a party as witness is not impeached, evidence of that party's character or reputation must be excluded by the trial judge. (Beach v. Richtmyer)

   [For more information on character evidence, see Casenote Law Outline on Evidence, Chapter 6, § III, Character to Prove Conduct.]

9. **Habit or Routine Practice.** The incompetence of a driver is to be shown by specific acts rather than opinions or conclusions of witnesses in cases where the owner of an automobile is alleged to have negligently entrusted the car to such driver. (Guedon v. Rooney)

   [For more information on habit or routine practice, see Casenote Law Outline on Evidence, Chapter 6, § VI, Evidence of Habit or Routine Practice.]

10. **Evidence of Habit.** Evidence of a habit of a person is admissible as tending to prove that his behavior on a specified occasion conformed to that habit even where there is an eyewitness to the event in question on such specified occasion. (Missouri-Kansas-Texas R.R. v. McFerrin)

    [For more information on evidence of habit, see Casenote Law Outline on Evidence, Chapter 6, § VI, Evidence of Habit or Routine Practice.]

11. **The Use of Character Evidence.** Evidence of character is inadmissible to prove the person acted consistently therewith on a particular occasion. (Reyes v. Missouri Pacific Railroad Company)

    [For more information on the use of character evidence, see Casenote Law Outline on Evidence, Chapter 6, § III, Character to Prove Conduct.]

12. **Evidence of a Business Custom.** Evidence of a business custom of equipment inspection is admissible as probative of the kind of inspection that was received by a particular piece of equipment subject to the business custom. (Eaton v. Bass)

    [For more information on evidence of a business custom, see Casenote Law Outline on Evidence, Chapter 6, § VI, Evidence of Habit or Routine Practice.]

13. **Discretionary Exclusion of Relevant Evidence.** If a defendant puts her prior conduct into issue by testifying as to her own past good behavior, she may be cross-examined as to specific acts of misconduct unrelated to the crime charged. (Washington v. Virginia Sue Renneberg and Milton Victor La Vanway)

    [For more information on discretionary exclusion of relevant evidence, see Casenote Law Outline on Evidence, Chapter 2, § V, Discretionary Exclusion of Relevant Evidence.]

14. **Introduction of Evidence of Own Good Character.** Evidence of the good character of a criminal defendant which tends to show that it is unlikely that such defendant committed the crime charged is admissible. (Edgington v. United States)

    [For more information on the introduction of evidence of own good character, see Casenote Law Outline on Evidence, Chapter 6, § III, Character to Prove Conduct.]

15. **Character Evidence.** Character evidence is relevant where the person's state of mind is an element of the crime charged. (United States v. Staggs)

    [For more information on character evidence, see Casenote Law Outline on Evidence, Chapter 6, § III, Character to Prove Conduct.]

16. **Personality Traits and Behavior Patterns — Criminal Cases.** A witness testifying to the good character of a criminal defendant may, on cross-examination, be questioned about specific instances of misconduct having some relationship to the good character trait in question for the limited purpose of testing the accuracy of the reputation testimony and not as substantive evidence. (Broyles v. Commonwealth)

17. **Admission of Character Evidence.** Evidence of a victim's character is admissible to corroborate the defendant's contention, pursuant to his plea of self-defense, that the victim was the aggressor. (Evans v. United States)

[For more information on the admission of character evidence, see Casenote Law Outline on Evidence, Chapter 6, § III, Character to Prove Conduct.]

18. **Evidence of Other Crimes.** Evidence of other offenses may be offered in a criminal trial if relevant for any purpose other than to show a propensity or disposition to commit the crime, subject to the power of the trial judge to exclude the evidence if it will create undue prejudice. (United States v. Woods)

   [For more information on evidence of other crimes, see Casenote Law Outline on Evidence, Chapter 6, § IV, The "Other Crimes" Loophole.]

19. **Personality Traits and Behavior Patterns — Criminal Cases.** A court need not make, prior to admitting post acts introduced to show motive or knowledge, a preliminary finding that the acts occurred. (Huddleston v. United States)

20. **Relevance of Precedential Evidence.** Under Fed. R. Evid. 404 (b), evidence of prior bad acts is admissible if: (1) sufficient proof exists for the jury to find that the defendant committed the prior act; (2) the prior act was not too remote in time; and (3) the prior act is introduced to prove a material issue in this case. (United States v. Hadley)

   [For more information on relevance of precedential evidence, see Casenote Law Outline on Evidence, Chapter 2, § VI, Precedential Relevance.]

21. **Scientific and Other Specialized Information.** Proof of negligence requires a finding established by a fair preponderance of the evidence which is the plaintiff's burden to produce. (Toy v. MacKintosh)

22. **Qualifications of an Expert Witness.** The foundation for admission of results of scientific tests or techniques cannot be sufficiently laid by only the testimony of an expert witness that such tests or techniques are generally accepted by the relevant scientific community absent a showing of academic qualifications enabling him to express such an opinion. (People v. Kelly)

   [For more information on the qualifications of an expert witness, see Casenote Law Outline on Evidence, Chapter 12, § III, Expert Opinions.]

23. **Expert Witnesses.** An expert opinion does not need to be generally accepted in the scientific community to be admissible. (William Daubert v. Merrell Dow Pharmaceuticals, Inc.)

   [For more information on expert witnesses, see Casenote Law Outline on Evidence, Chapter 12, § III, Expert Opinions.]

24. **Relevance and Expert Opinions.** Before admitting novel scientific evidence, the court must conclude that the proposed testimony constitutes (1) scientific knowledge that (2) will assist the trier of fact to understand or determine a fact in issue. (United States v. Martinez)

   [For more information on relevance and expert opinions, see Casenote Law Outline on Evidence, Chapter 2, § III, Is the "Evidence" Relevant?]

25. **Mathematical Odds.** Mathematical odds are not admissible as evidence to identify a defendant in a criminal proceeding so long as the odds are based on estimates, the validity of which has not been demonstrated. (State v. Sneed)

26. **Subsequent Remedial Measures.** Rule 407 of the Fed. R. Evid. is fully applicable in strict liability actions to exclude evidence of post-accident design changes. (Grenada Steel Industries, Inc. v. Alabama Oxygen Company, Inc.)

[For more information on subsequent remedial measures, see Casenote Law Outline on Evidence, Chapter 7, § II, Subsequent Remedial Measures.]

27. **Admissibility of Settlement Agreements.** Rule 408 of the Federal Rules of Evidence bars the admission of evidence of settlements between plaintiffs and third-party joint tortfeasors and former codefendants. (McInnis v. A.M.F., Inc.)

   [For more information on the admissibility of settlement agreements, see Casenote Law Outline on Evidence, Chapter 7, § III, Compromise and Settlement Negotiations.]

DIAMOND RUBBER CO. v. HARRYMAN
Colo. Sup. Ct., 41 Colo. 415, 92 P. 922 (1907).

NATURE OF CASE: Appeal from award of damages for negligence.

FACT SUMMARY: Diamond (D) maintained an iron pipe near a public sidewalk for bicycle tire inflation, over which Harryman (P) tripped and fell, and, at trial, Harryman (P) was permitted to show others had similarly tripped and fallen.

CONCISE RULE OF LAW: In a negligence action wherein a dangerous condition is alleged, evidence showing injuries to persons other than the plaintiff because of the condition is not admissible to show dangerousness of the condition.

FACTS: Outside of its place of business near the sidewalk, Diamond (D) maintained a "gooseneck," an iron pipe from which bicyclists could inflate their tires. Harryman (P) tripped and fell over the pipe and brought this negligence action to recover for injuries. Diamond (D) objected to Harryman's (P) introduction of evidence that others had tripped over the gooseneck pipe before his accident, but the trial court admitted testimony to that effect. Diamond (D) appealed.

ISSUE: In a negligence action wherein a dangerous condition is alleged, is evidence showing injuries to persons other than the plaintiff because of the condition admissible to show dangerousness of the condition?

HOLDING AND DECISION: (Gabbert, J.) No. The character of the obstruction was susceptible of proof. Proof in the form of testimony that others had tripped upon the obstruction would be subject to inquiry as to the care exercised by the others and conditions under which they tripped. In a negligence action wherein a dangerous condition is alleged, evidence showing injuries to persons other than the plaintiff because of the condition is not admissible to show dangerousness of the condition. Dangerousness should have been determined to have existed or not existed from the jury's consideration of evidence of the construction of the pipe. Reversed and remanded.

EDITOR'S ANALYSIS: A court is loathe to engage in "a trial within a trial." Proof of negligence causing an accident at one time cannot be probative of such an accident at another time. In some jurisdictions, however, such proof is admissible if a substantial identity of material circumstances is shown as between the two events.

NOTES:

CITY OF BLOOMINGTON v. LEGG
Ill. Sup. Ct., 151 Ill. 9, 37 N.E. 696 (1894).

NATURE OF CASE: Appeal from affirmation of award of damages for negligence.

FACT SUMMARY: Legg's (P) decedent, who watered his team of horses in the City's (D) public fountain erected for such purpose, was killed when one of the horses' bridles caught on a spout causing him to bolt and throwing the decedent to the ground and Legg (P) introduced evidence at trial that other similar accidents had occurred.

CONCISE RULE OF LAW: Evidence of occurrences similar to the one sued upon in a negligence action may be admitted to show dangerousness of a condition if the agency or instrumentality is demonstrated to be in substantially the same condition.

FACTS: When Legg's (P) decedent was watering his horses in a fountain erected for that purpose by the City (D), the bridle of one of the horses caught on the spout in the fountain and the horse bolted. The decedent was thrown to the ground and killed. Legg (P) brought this action in negligence seeking damages for the death on the ground that the spout was negligently placed in a spot where bridles would catch on it. Legg (P) sought to introduce evidence that the spouts had caused similar accidents previous to the one in which the decedent was killed. The trial court permitted the introduction of the evidence, and the City (D) appealed the judgment rendered for $1,000 damages upon the jury's verdict for Legg (P).

ISSUE: May evidence of occurrences similar to the one sued upon in a negligence action be admitted to show dangerousness of a condition if the agency or instrumentality is demonstrated to be in substantially the same condition?

HOLDING AND DECISION: (Phillips, J.) Yes. Evidence of other accidents occurring from the same cause has been held competent in this court to show that the cause of those accidents was the same unsafe or dangerous thing that caused the accident alleged. It is not competent, however, to show independent acts of negligence in each of the prior cases. Furthermore, if the unsafe condition or thing is not in substantially the same condition at the time of the accident sued upon as in each of the prior accidents, the evidence is inadmissible. Evidence of occurrences similar to the one sued upon in a negligence action may be admitted to show dangerousness of a condition if the agency or instrumentality is demonstrated to be in substantially the same condition. The trial court properly warned and instructed the jury as to the limitations of their proper consideration of the evidence offered, and the jury properly determined that the condition was dangerous. Affirmed.

EDITOR'S ANALYSIS: The purpose of the evidence in this case was to show that the condition which caused a number of accidents was an unsafe or dangerous one. The forbidden purpose for which the jury might have improperly used the evidence is to show that the defendant was negligent in maintaining the condition in the past, and that therefore the same must be true as to the incident under their consideration.

[For more information on limited admissibility, see Casenote Law Outline on Evidence, Chapter 5, § IV, Limited Admissibility.]

NOTES:

JONES v. PAK-MOR MANUFACTURING CO.
Ariz. Sup. Ct., 145 Ariz. 121, 700 P.2d 819 (1985).

NATURE OF CASE: Appeal from verdict in favor of plaintiff in a products liability action.

FACT SUMMARY: In a products liability suit against Pak-Mor Manufacturing Company (D), Pak-Mor (D) argued that it should be permitted to present evidence that no accidents had ever occurred that were similar to the accident suffered by Jones (P) while he was working on a Pak-Mor (D) machine.

CONCISE RULE OF LAW: In products liability cases involving a claim of defective design, the trial court has discretion under Fed. R. Evid. 403 to admit evidence of safety history concerning both the existence and nonexistence of prior accidents, provided that the proponent establishes the necessary predicate for the evidence.

FACTS: Jones (P) was injured while working on a garbage compactor manufactured by Pak-Mor (D). In the products liability action that followed, Jones (P) alleged improper design and sought recovery on theories of negligence and strict liability. Before trial, Jones (P) moved to exclude all evidence of the absence of prior, similar accidents. In response, Pak-Mor (D) offered to prove that the compactor had been in use since 1947, that thousands had been sold, and that there had never been any report of a claim based on any injury similar to the one alleged by Jones (P). Pak-Mor (D) argued that this evidence was relevant to show that its product was neither defective nor unreasonably dangerous. The trial court, however, granted Jones' (P) motion, ruling that such evidence was inadmissible under Arizona law. After verdict and judgment for Jones (P), Pak-Mor (D) appealed, claiming that the exclusion rule was in error. The court of appeals affirmed, and Pak-Mor (D) again appealed. The Arizona Supreme Court accepted review.

ISSUE: In products liability cases involving a claim of defective design, does the trial court have discretion under Fed. R. Evid. Rule 403 to admit evidence of safety history concerning both the existence and nonexistence of prior accidents?

HOLDING AND DECISION: (Feldman, J.) Yes. In products liability cases involving a claim of defective design, whether based on negligence, strict liability, or both, the trial court has discretion under Fed. R. Evid. 403 to admit evidence of safety history concerning both the existence and nonexistence of prior accidents, provided that the proponent establishes the necessary predicate for the evidence. Here, both the trial judge and the court of appeals correctly noted the existence of Arizona decisions admitting evidence of prior accidents but excluding evidence of the absence of prior accidents. Although the trial court had discretion to admit evidence of prior accidents, the rule relating to inadmissibility of evidence of the absence of prior accidents is a per se rule. However, recent cases indicate that this rule of per se inadmissibility is manifestly incompatible with modern principles of evidence. This court believes that a blanket rule of inadmissibility is essentially a rule of relevancy. Safety history, including the presence or absence of prior accidents under similar use, is evidence which may make ultimate facts more probable or less probable than they would be without the evidence, and, thus, evidence of safety-history is relevant. Once evidence is shown to be relevant, Rule 402 provides that it is admissible unless "otherwise provided" by constitutional provision, statute, or rule. Several rules of evidence provide for per se inadmissibility, subject to enumerated exceptions, but no specific rule mandates rejection of evidence of safety history. The rule that applies to safety history evidence is Rule 403, which requires the court to weigh the benefit to be gained by admission against the harm that may result from admission. Pak-Mor (D) claims that this rule should apply to evidence of the absence of prior accidents in cases such as the one at bar. On the other hand, Jones (P) argues that the policy of product liability law should be to foster the manufacture and distribution of safe products and to discourage the distribution of unsafe products by a per se exclusion of relevant evidence of lack of prior accidents. But safety is not promoted by giving manufacturers, sellers, and distributors an incentive to refrain from learning about their products. The present rule, providing discretionary admission of prior accidents and automatic exclusion of evidence of lack of prior accidents, does just that. The law is better served by a rule that gives manufacturers and distributors the utmost incentive to acquire, record, and maintain information regarding the performance of their products. Thus, evidence of safety history is admissible on issues pertaining to whether the design caused the product to be defective, whether the defect was unreasonably dangerous, and whether it was the cause of the accident. With that said, however, the appellate court's ruling in this case does not constitute reversible error. Here, although Pak-Mor (D) stated that over the past twenty-six years it had no reports of injuries like those to Jones (P), this absence of reports is not a relevant fact absent a showing that if there had been accidents, Pak-Mor (D) would have known of them. There may, in fact, be no lawsuits filed against Pak-Mor (D), but there is no way of knowing what workers' compensation claims have been filed or what injuries have been sustained but not reported. Affirmed.

EDITOR'S ANALYSIS: The Arizona Supreme Court emphasized, in the Jones decision, that its rejection of the per se inadmissibility rule was applicable to defective design cases and not to those involving manufacturing flaws. Cases involving manufacturing flaws do not implicate the inherent design or quality of the entire line of products in question but only of a particular unit or number of units of that product. In such cases, the fact that the product as a whole has a demonstrated safety history is irrelevant.

[For more information on discretionary exclusion of relevant evidence, see Casenote Law Outline on Evidence, Chapter 2, § V, Discretionary Exclusion of Relevant Evidence.]

CARPENTER v. KURN
Mo. Sup. Ct., 348 Mo. 1132, 157 S.W.2d 213 (1941).

NATURE OF CASE: Appeal from award of damages for wrongful death.

FACT SUMMARY: After her husband was allegedly struck by a train, Carpenter (P) brought this wrongful death action in which testimony was admitted as to an experiment that was not exactly duplicative of the accident sued upon.

CONCISE RULE OF LAW: Evidence of tests and experiments conducted under circumstances approximately similar to the incident sued upon is admissible.

FACTS: Carpenter (P) sought damages for the wrongful death of her husband who was struck by a train and killed. At trial, the judge admitted testimony regarding an experiment carried out to determine the circumstances of the accident. In the experiment, a person stood on the train tracks and observed the view of another person standing thereon at different distances. The engineer's view from a locomotive cab was alleged to be materially different from the experimenters' view from standing on the tracks. Carpenter (P) won a judgment of $20,000 from which she appealed as being inadequate.

ISSUE: Is evidence of tests and experiments conducted under circumstances approximately similar to the incident sued upon admissible?

HOLDING AND DECISION: (Tipton, J.) Yes. Any dissimilarity between the event sued upon and the experiment goes to the weight that the fact finder will ascribe to the test, rather than to the admissibility of it. In order for such experimental evidence to be admitted, however, the circumstances under which the experiment was conducted must be substantially the same as those at the time of the occurrence under the court's consideration. Thus, evidence of tests and experiments conducted under circumstances approximately similar to the incident sued upon is admissible. In this case, the viewpoints in the experiment and those in the actual accident were essentially the same, and the evidence was properly admitted. Affirmed.

EDITOR'S ANALYSIS: As the court notes, some similarity must be demonstrated between the circumstances of the experiment and those of the incident in question before the evidence is admissible at all; but if the prima facie similarity is shown, the jury may still consider any other dissimilarity in weighing the evidence. There is no clear line between the showing for admissibility and that required to convince the jury.

[For more information on circumstantial evidence, see Casenote Law Outline on Evidence, Chapter 2, § III, Is the "Evidence" Relevant?]

REDFIELD v. IOWA STATE HIGHWAY COMM'N
Iowa Sup. Ct., 251 Iowa 332, 99 N.W.2d 413, 85 A.L.R.2d 96 (1959).

NATURE OF CASE: Appeal from award of damages for condemnation compensation.

FACT SUMMARY: Redfield (P) appealed an unsatisfactory damages award for the condemnation of his real property and alleged error in striking expert testimony as to the sale price of similar property in the same location.

CONCISE RULE OF LAW: Evidence of the price at a recent sale of property is relevant to prove the value of similar property in the same location.

FACTS: Redfield (P) was the owner of some 97 acres of land, which he purchased for the purpose of developing into a residential subdivision. The Commission (D) condemned 77.2 acres of this land for the construction of a highway. The condemnation commission fixed damages at $70,000, and the Commission (D) took possession of the land. Redfield (P) filed this action and was awarded $60,000 to compensate for the inadequacy of the compensation by the Commission (D). Redfield (P) produced a witness to testify as to the value of the property and the witness testified as to the price paid for a comparable piece of land in the same location. The evidence of that sale price was stricken, and the jury awarded damages based on one of the other widely varying estimates made by other experts. Redfield (P) appealed the unsatisfactory award on the ground of error in striking the evidence of the sale price.

ISSUE: Is evidence of the price at a recent sale of property relevant to prove the value of similar property in the same location?

HOLDING AND DECISION: (Garret, J.) Yes. The extreme differences among the values placed on the subject property by the various experts points up the fact that the actual records of sales of comparable properties from which the witnesses gained their knowledge are more reliable evidence than the mere opinions of experts. Such information offered here was stricken from the evidence, and the rule heretofore prevailing in Iowa is that such evidence is not admissible. Redfield (P) urged that this court change the rule, and it is advisable to do so. As a California case noted, the first thing that a buyer seeks to find out in purchasing property, or a seller in selling, is what price similar property in the same place has recently commanded. This is the information used by experts in formulating their opinions as to value. The majority rule, recognizing this, is that evidence of the price at a recent sale of property is relevant to prove the value of similar property in the same location. Iowa will join those jurisdictions. Reversed and remanded.

EDITOR'S ANALYSIS: The rationale for disallowing evidence of the sale price of similar properties in the same location is the avoidance of collateral issues. This purpose is not substantially furthered or the facts of the sale will seldom be in question, and the jury will determine the degree of similarity between the two compared parcels as regards value.

FOSTER v. AGRI-CHEM, INC.
Or. Sup. Ct., 235 Or. 570, 385 P.2d 184 (1963).

NATURE OF CASE: Appeal from denial of damages for negligence.

FACT SUMMARY: In a suit alleging that Agri-Chem (D) improperly spread too much fertilizer on Foster's (P) land so as to cause a lower crop yield, Agri-Chem (D) countered with evidence of experiments showing that higher concentrations of fertilizer did not produce lower crop yields.

CONCISE RULE OF LAW: Evidence of an experiment conducted under circumstances substantially similar to those existing at the time of the incident under the court's consideration may be admitted within the judge's discretion.

FACTS: Foster (P) contracted with Agri-Chem (D) for the spreading of fertilizer on Foster's (P) farmland. At harvest, Foster (P) alleged that his fertilized land produced 10,550 bushels fewer per acre of wheat. In addition to evidence of harvests from the land in previous years, Foster (P) introduced evidence of wheat yields of neighboring farmers. Agri-Chem (D) countered with evidence of an experiment which showed that the same and higher concentrations as that added by it to Foster's (D) failed to decrease crop yield from properly tended land. The trial court admitted this evidence and the verdict was rendered for Agri-Chem (D). Foster (P) appealed, alleging that the experiment was not conducted under circumstances substantially similar to those of his fields.

ISSUE: May evidence of an experiment conducted under circumstances substantially similar to those existing at the time of the incident under the court's consideration be admitted within the judge's discretion?

HOLDING AND DECISION: (Denecke, J.) Yes. An experiment is only admissible if performed under conditions substantially similar to those existing in the case being tried. Furthermore, the judge has wide discretion as to the admission of such evidence. The tests and experiments proffered by Agri-Chem (D) were not conducted pursuant to this litigation. No decisions have come forth from Oregon courts that point up this distinction, however, since the experiment in this case and others carried out purely for the gathering of scientific knowledge are free from any taint of interest or bias with respect to the case at hand, great latitude should be shown by the judge, who can admit such evidence within his discretion. Evidence of an experiment conducted under circumstances substantially similar to those existing at the time of the incident under the court's consideration may be admitted within the judge's discretion. Thus, the trial court's admission of the experiment evidence in this case was proper. Reversed [on other grounds.]

EDITOR'S ANALYSIS: The relaxation of the rule requiring substantial similarity between the experiment conditions and the principal event conditions turns on whether the experiment was conducted for purposes of the litigation or not. The judge's wide discretion in determining admissibility also gives him the opportunity to exclude such evidence on grounds of logical irrelevancy.

[For more information on judicial discretion in admissibility of relevant evidence, see Casenote Law Outline on Evidence, Chapter 2, § V, Discretionary Exclusion of Relevant Evidence.]

NOTES:

RUMBAUGH v. McCORMICK
Ohio Sup. Ct., 80 Ohio St. 211, 88 N.E. 410 (1909).

NATURE OF CASE: Appeal from admission of evidence of habit.

FACT SUMMARY: McCormick (P) brought this action alleging that Rumbaugh's (D) dog killed one of his sheep and introduced evidence of the dog's habit of coming to McCormick's (P) property and attacking sheep.

CONCISE RULE OF LAW: Evidence of habitual conduct of an animal is admissible to establish an observer's ability to identify that animal or to prove conduct conforming to the habit.

FACTS: McCormick (P) alleged that Rumbaugh's (D) dog killed his sheep in this action for damages. McCormick (P) introduced evidence that the dog had been driven away from his property and sheep on several prior occasions. Rumbaugh (D) contended that McCormick (P) owned a dog strongly resembling Rumbaugh's (D), and that McCormick (P) was mistaken as to the identity of the dog that killed his sheep. In a consolidated action, Blair also alleged the killing of sheep by the dog, and evidence of the habit of the dog to kill sheep was admitted. Rumbaugh (D) appealed.

ISSUE: Is evidence of habitual conduct of an animal admissible to establish an observer's ability to identify that animal or to prove conduct conforming to the habit?

HOLDING AND DECISION: (Price, J.) Yes. No better means of qualification as to the identity of the guilty animal can be suggested than frequently seeing him upon the sheep of the two plaintiffs. Where there is a conflict as to identity of an animal, observation of him on prior occasions acting in the same manner as the animal causing the injury tends to show such identity. Furthermore, the reason for precluding evidence of character in cases of conduct consistent therewith on a particular occasion with respect to persons is not present with animals governed by instinct rather than by reason. Such evidence offered to show conduct of an animal, as opposed to a person, is admissible. Thus, evidence of habitual conduct of an animal is admissible to establish an observer's ability to identify that animal or to prove conduct forming to the habit. There was, therefore, no error in admitting such evidence in this case. Affirmed.

EDITOR'S ANALYSIS: The admissibility of evidence of a dog's habit does not always have the intended effect, inasmuch as the admissibility does not control the weight of the evidence. It is up to the jury to decide that the animal in fact had the habit testified to, and whether the dog acted in conformity with such a habit if shown. It is commonly known that animals do not always do what they have been observed to have done in the past.

BEACH v. RICHTMYER
N.Y. Sup. Ct., 275 App. Div. 466, 90 N.Y.S.2d 232 (1949).

NATURE OF CASE: Appeal from denial of motion to vacate judgment and verdict for negligence.

FACT SUMMARY: Beach (P) was a passenger in a car owned by Carpenter and driven by her chauffeur, Harris, who was killed when the car crashed into a truck operated by Richtmyer (D), and Beach (P) introduced evidence of Harris' good moral character.

CONCISE RULE OF LAW: In a civil action where a party's character is not at issue and the credibility of a party as witness is not impeached, evidence of that party's character or reputation must be excluded by the trial judge.

FACTS: Beach (P) was a passenger in a car owned by Carpenter and driven by Harris, Carpenter's chauffeur. The car collided with a truck driven by Richtmyer (D). Richtmyer (D) was exonerated in an action by Beach (P) against him and Carpenter and Harris, who was killed in the accident. The jury found a verdict in the sum of $20,000 for Beach (P) and $8,000 for her husband from Harris' administrator and Carpenter, both of whom appealed the denial of their motions to vacate for alleged error in the admission of testimony of Harris' good moral character in response to Carpenter's uncorroborated testimony that she did not give Harris consent to drive the car on the night of the accident.

ISSUE: In a civil action where a party's character is not at issue and the credibility of a party as witness is not impeached, must evidence of that party's character or reputation be excluded by the trial judge?

HOLDING AND DECISION: (Heffernan, J.) Yes. There is a statutory presumption that the owner of an automobile consents to the use to which the driver of the car puts it. The trier of fact found below that Carpenter consented to Harris' use of the car over Carpenter's uncorroborated testimony that she did not. That testimony was insufficient in law, by itself, to destroy the presumption, and the finding must be upheld. The evidence of Harris' good moral character, however, was improperly admitted. The character or reputation of a party is not a proper subject of inquiry in a civil action unless such character is at issue. Nothing in this case put Harris' character at issue. Furthermore, since Harris was dead and gave no evidence on the accident, his credibility could not have been impeached. In a civil action where a party's character is not at issue and the credibility of the party as witness is not impeached, evidence of that party's character or reputation must be excluded by the trial judge. Judgments affirmed as to Richtmyer (D), and reversed as to the other defendants, with new trials granted.

EDITOR'S ANALYSIS: The probative value of character evidence in showing conduct consistent with a party's character is outweighed by the possible prejudicial effect of such evidence when improperly considered by the finder of fact and by the likelihood of such improper consideration.

GUEDON v. ROONEY
Or. Sup. Ct., 160 Or. 621, 87 P.2d 209, 120 A.L.R. 1298 (1939).

NATURE OF CASE: Appeal from denial of motion to strike testimony.

FACT SUMMARY: In attempting to establish Rooney's (D) negligence for hiring a driver who caused the accident resulting in Guedon's (P) injuries, Guedon (P) elicited testimony that the driver drove recklessly in general.

CONCISE RULE OF LAW: The incompetence of a driver is to be shown by specific acts rather than opinions or conclusions of witnesses in cases where the owner of an automobile is alleged to have negligently entrusted the car to such driver.

FACTS: Guedon (P) elicited testimony from a police officer that Wilson, an employee of Rooney (D), generally drove in a reckless manner. The officer was not permitted to state the times and places when and where he observed Wilson driving recklessly. Rooney (D) moved to strike all of the testimony in this action for personal injuries from an automobile accident, but the motion was denied. Rooney (D) appealed.

ISSUE: Is the incompetence of a driver to be shown by specific acts rather than opinions or conclusions of witnesses in cases where the owner of an automobile is alleged to have negligently entrusted the car to such driver?

HOLDING AND DECISION: (Bailey, J.) Yes. Under the view held by the overwhelming weight of authority, it is the duty of the jury, and not the witness, to draw inferences and reach conclusions from the facts presented. It was therefore error for the trial court to permit the police officer to state his conclusions as to the manner of Wilson's operation of an automobile at times other than the moment of the collision. The incompetence of a driver is to be shown by specific acts rather than by opinions or conclusions of witnesses in cases where the owner of an automobile is alleged to have negligently entrusted the car to such driver. The trial court's exclusion of evidence of Wilson's past driving conduct was based on the character nature of the evidence, but upon remand the court will proceed in a manner not inconsistent with this opinion. Reversed and remanded.

EDITOR'S ANALYSIS: As a matter of practicality, the evidence of the past conduct of a driver permits the jury to determine more fairly the driver's road performance better than the opinion of an observer. In negligent entrustment cases, reputation evidence is also relevant, however, to demonstrate the probability that the alleged entrustor was aware of the driver's incompetence.

[For more information on habit or routine practice, see Casenote Law Outline on Evidence, Chapter 6, § VI, Evidence of Habit or Routine Practice.]

MISSOURI-KANSAS-TEXAS R.R. v. McFERRIN
Tex. Sup. Ct., 156 Tex. 69, 291 S.W.2d 931 (1956).

NATURE OF CASE: Appeal from award of damages for negligence evidence.

FACT SUMMARY: After McFerrin's (P) decedent was killed in a railroad crossing accident, the Railroad's (D) fireman testified that the decedent had failed to stop his automobile at the crossing, but McFerrin (P) testified that the decedent habitually stopped at railroad crossings whenever she was with him.

CONCISE RULE OF LAW: Evidence of a habit of a person is admissible as tending to prove that his behavior on a specified occasion conformed to that habit even where there is an eyewitness to the event in question on such specified occasion.

FACTS: McFerrin's (P) decedent was killed when one of the Railroad's (D) trains struck his automobile at a crossing. The Railroad's (D) fireman testified that the decedent failed to stop his automobile at the crossing, but rather merely slowed down. McFerrin (P) testified over objection that the decedent had always stopped at railroad crossings when she was in the car with him. This evidence of habit was intended to show that the decedent had stopped on the occasion in question.

ISSUE: Is evidence of a habit of a person admissible as tending to prove that his behavior on a specified occasion conformed to that habit even where there is an eyewitness to the event in question on such specified occasion?

HOLDING AND DECISION: (Calvert, J.) Yes. In some jurisdictions no habit evidence can prove conduct on a particular occasion if there is an eyewitness to the conduct in question. However, if there is no such eyewitness the evidence is admissible. In a few jurisdictions, it is admissible in all cases, whether or not there is an eyewitness. Here, the only eyewitness is an employee of the party defendant. Furthermore, the habit evidence was here introduced via one witness and did not constitute a waste of time, which is the reason behind the exclusion of such evidence. Thus, evidence of a habit of a person is admissible as tending to prove that his behavior on a specified occasion conformed to that habit even though there is an eyewitness to the event in question on such specified occasion. If more witnesses are necessary, the court must balance the inconvenience of examining them against the probative value of the evidence sought to be derived therefrom. Reversed on other grounds.

EDITOR'S ANALYSIS: Analysis of the admissibility of habit evidence in general is tricky at best. The problem centers around the difficulty of distinguishing between character evidence, generally inadmissible to show conduct in conformity therewith, and habit evidence, which is sometimes admissible. The habit must constitute regular, patterned routine conduct, as opposed to something "usually" done.

[For more information on evidence of habit, see Casenote Law Outline on Evidence, Chapter 6, § VI, Evidence of Habit or Routine Practice.]

REYES v. MISSOURI PACIFIC R.R. CO.
589 F.2d 791 (5th Cir. 1979).

NATURE OF CASE: Appeal from denial of damages for personal injuries.

FACT SUMMARY: The Railroad (D) contended that evidence of Reyes' (P) past intoxication convictions was relevant to prove he was intoxicated and thus comparatively negligent at the time of the accident.

CONCISE RULE OF LAW: Evidence of character is inadmissible to prove the person acted consistently therewith on a particular occasion.

FACTS: Reyes (P) sued the Railroad (D) when he was run over by a train. The Railroad (D) introduced into evidence Reyes' (P) four prior misdemeanor convictions for public drunkenness to prove he was drunk at the time of the accident. The trial court denied recovery, and Reyes (P) appealed, contending evidence of his convictions was offered as proof of his character and behavior in compliance therewith at the time of the accident.

ISSUE: Is character evidence admissible to prove consistent behavior on a specified occasion?

HOLDING AND DECISION: (Hill, J.) No. Evidence of character is inadmissible to prove the person acted consistently therewith on a particular occasion. Character denotes disposition and is too unreliable to allow an inference of compatible behavior. Its marginal relevancy is outweighed by the significant prejudice which it caused. As a result the admission of such evidence was error. Reversed and remanded.

EDITOR'S ANALYSIS: The court distinguished inadmissible character evidence from evidence of habit. The latter type is more reliable as it indicates a constant pattern of behavior rather than a mere disposition. Evidence of habit is admissible to show consistent behavior.

[For more information on the use of character evidence, see Casenote Law Outline on Evidence, Chapter 6, § III, Character to Prove Conduct.]

NOTES:

EATON v. BASS
214 F.2d 896 (6th Cir. 1954).

NATURE OF CASE: Appeal from denial of damages for wrongful death.

FACT SUMMARY: At trial of Eaton's (P) negligence claim based on an alleged failure to inspect the trucks, Bass (D) offered its mechanic's testimony that Bass' (D) trucks were customarily inspected.

CONCISE RULE OF LAW: Evidence of a business custom of equipment inspection is admissible as probative of the kind of inspection that was received by a particular piece of equipment subject to the business custom.

FACTS: Eaton (P) brought this action against Bass (D) for wrongful death alleging that Bass (D) allowed its truck to be operated with defective brakes causing a fatal accident. Bass (D) offered evidence in the form of testimony by a shop foreman charged with inspection and repair duties that the truck in question was subject to a routine business custom of inspection of brakes and all other safety equipment, and that no trucks left his shop for the road without such inspection. He did not recall the inspection of the particular truck in question. The jury rendered a verdict for Bass (D), and Eaton (P) appealed.

ISSUE: Is evidence of a business custom of equipment inspection admissible as probative of the kind of inspection that was received by a particular piece of equipment subject to the business custom?

HOLDING AND DECISION: (Miller, J.) Yes. While the evidence of the customary inspection procedures would not be admissible to show that Bass (D) was not negligent because they used a generally accepted inspection custom, the evidence can be admitted for a more limited purpose. That purpose is to show that the particular truck in question received the same inspection and repair as the others subject to the custom. Evidence of a business custom of equipment inspection is admissible as probative of the kind of inspection that was received by a particular piece of equipment subject to the business custom. This leaves for the jury to decide whether such inspection was sufficient to render Bass (D) nonnegligent in permitting operation of the truck involved in the accident. Affirmed.

EDITOR'S ANALYSIS: The evidence of habit, or routine practice, is probative of conduct in conformity therewith on a particular occasion, but it does not establish such conduct nor give rise to a legal presumption that such conduct occurred. Nonetheless, habit evidence, particularly routine business practices, can produce a strong inference in favor of the proponent.

[For more information on evidence of a business custom, see Casenote Law Outline on Evidence, Chapter 6, § VI, Evidence of Habit or Routine Practice.]

WASHINGTON v. VIRGINIA SUE RENNEBERG AND MILTON VICTOR LA VANWAY
Wash. Sup. Ct., 83 Wash.2d 735, 522 P.2d 835 (1974).

NATURE OF CASE: Appeal from convictions of grand larceny and aiding and abetting grand larceny.

FACT SUMMARY: Virginia and Milton LaVanway (D) appealed from their convictions of grand larceny and aiding and abetting grand larceny, respectively, contending that the lower court erred when it permitted the State (P) to question them about their drug addiction.

CONCISE RULE OF LAW: If a defendant puts her prior conduct into issue by testifying as to her own past good behavior, she may be cross-examined as to specific acts of misconduct unrelated to the crime charged.

FACTS: Virginia (D) and Milton (D) LaVanway were charged by the State (P) with grand larceny and aiding and abetting grand larceny, respectively. Virginia (D) was charged with stealing approximately $250 from the cash register of a restaurant from which she had been discharged from employment. Milton (D) was charged with helping Virginia (D) steal the money. The court indicated in a pretrial ruling that any testimony as to drug addiction would be inadmissible in the State's (P) case. However, after Virginia (D) took the stand at trial and testified to her work experience, college attendance, glee club membership, and so on, the court allowed the State to (P) question her regarding her drug addiction.

ISSUE: If a defendant puts her prior conduct into issue by testifying as to her own past good behavior, may she be cross-examined as to specific acts of misconduct unrelated to the crime charged?

HOLDING AND DECISION: (Brachtenberg, J.) Yes. If a defendant puts her prior conduct into issue by testifying as to her own past good behavior, she may be cross-examined as to specific acts of misconduct unrelated to the crime charged. Admissibility of evidence of prior drug addiction can be considered on two different grounds: first, that it relates to the witness' credibility, and second, that it is an unrelated act of misconduct, admissible to contradict character evidence. The more restrictive ground of character impeachment dictates admissibility here. Virginia (D) voluntarily put her character before the jury. Implicit in her testimony is the painting of a picture of a person most unlikely to commit grand larceny. While Milton's (D) character was not so clearly put in evidence, it was introduced sufficiently to subject Milton (D) to the same questions asked of his wife. The State (P) was entitled to complete the tapestry with his admitted drug addiction. At the LaVanways' (D) request, the lower court instructed the jury that evidence of prior misconduct was to be considered only as bearing on credibility and on the weight to be given the witness' testimony. As that instruction was the LaVanways' (D) choice, they cannot now claim error. Affirmed.

EDITOR'S ANALYSIS: Although the LaVanways' (D) attorney elicited favorable testimony about their lives in order to show that the LaVanways (D) were not the type of people who would be involved in grand larceny, this tactic seemed to backfire in that the LaVanways (D) put their characters "in issue" with such door-opening testimony. The prosecutor then was permitted to rebut such testimony by bringing into evidence the LaVanways' (D) use and addiction to drugs. Note the similarity to the concept of curative admissibility, in which a party is prevented from objecting to introduction of inadmissible evidence by an opposing party once she has introduced like evidence.

[For more information on discretionary exclusion of relevant evidence, see Casenote Law Outline on Evidence, Chapter 2, § V, Discretionary Exclusion of Relevant Evidence.]

NOTES:

EDGINGTON v. UNITED STATES
164 U.S. 361 (1896).

NATURE OF CASE: Appeal from conviction for making a false deposition.

FACT SUMMARY: In Edgington's (D) trial for making a false deposition to aid in fraudulently obtaining a pension claim for his mother, Edgington (D) offered evidence that his character was such that it was unlikely that he would commit the crime, which was excluded.

CONCISE RULE OF LAW: Evidence of the good character of a criminal defendant which tends to show that it is unlikely that such defendant committed the crime charged is admissible.

FACTS: Edgington (D) was convicted of making a false deposition in order to fraudulently obtain a pension for his mother. During the trial, Edgington (D) offered evidence of his good character in order to show that it was not likely that he committed the crime, but the evidence was excluded by the trial judge. Edgington (D) appealed his conviction on the ground that the exclusion was improper and constituted reversible, prejudicial error.

ISSUE: Is evidence of the good character of a criminal defendant which tends to show that it is unlikely that such defendant committed the crime charged admissible?

HOLDING AND DECISION: (Shiras, J.) Yes. It is the accepted rule that evidence of good character of a criminal defendant which tends to show that it is unlikely that such defendant committed the crime charged is admissible. Here, Edgington (D) was charged with a species of crimen falsi, and thus evidence of his honesty was material and relevant. The error of the trial judge in refusing to admit the evidence was sufficient to require reversal. Reversed and remanded.

EDITOR'S ANALYSIS: The right of a defendant in a criminal proceeding to give evidence of his good character is accepted by the majority of jurisdictions and by the Federal Rules of Evidence and Rule 404(a)(1). The risk is run by such criminal defendant, however, that the prosecution will offer character evidence in rebuttal which does more harm to the defendant than the good character evidence accomplished. The prosecutor may only offer bad character evidence after the good character evidence has been admitted.

[For more information on the introduction of evidence of own good character, see Casenote Law Outline on Evidence, Chapter 6, § III, Character to Prove Conduct.]

UNITED STATES v. STAGGS
553 F.2d 1073 (7th Cir. 1977).

NATURE OF CASE: Appeal from conviction for assault.

FACT SUMMARY: The trial court barred as evidence of Staggs' (D) character, that he was more likely to hurt himself than another, as irrelevant character evidence.

CONCISE RULE OF LAW: Character evidence is relevant where the person's state of mind is an element of the crime charged.

FACTS: Staggs (D) was arrested after pointing a gun at federal agents sent to apprehend him for desertion from the Marines. He was charged with assault. The agent testified that Staggs (D) pointed the gun and spoke to him indicating he would shoot. Staggs (D) contended he was not intending to shoot the agent and was seeking to injure himself so he could not be returned to the Marines. The court refused to allow Staggs (D) to present evidence through a psychologist that he had character traits making it more likely he would attempt to injure himself than the agent. The court held that the evidence was inadmissible character evidence. Staggs (D) appealed his conviction on the basis that this failure to allow the testimony was error.

ISSUE: Is character evidence relevant and admissible if the person's state of mind is an element of the crime charged?

HOLDING AND DECISION: (Swygert, J.) Yes. Character evidence is relevant and admissible where the person's state of mind is an element of the crime charged. In this case, the crime of assault requires a specific intent to commit. As a result, Staggs' (D) state of mind was an element of the cause of action and evidence of his character was relevant and admissible. Reversed and remanded.

EDITOR'S ANALYSIS: Proving intent extrinsically is one of the most difficult chores in litigation. This case illustrates where the outward indications of intent are ambiguous, the character of the person is admissible to show his state of mind. If this case had involved a general intent crime, the state of mind would be irrelevant.

[For more information on character evidence, see Casenote Law Outline on Evidence, Chapter 6, § III, Character to Prove Conduct.]

NOTES:

BROYLES v. COMMONWEALTH
Ky. Ct. App., 267 S.W.2d 73, 47 A.L.R.2d 1252 (1954).

NATURE OF CASE: Appeal from conviction for murder.

FACT SUMMARY: Broyles (D) was convicted of murder in a trial wherein the prosecutor inquired of Broyles' (D) character witnesses if they had knowledge of or had heard of Broyles' (D) prior conviction for drunk driving, reckless driving, and disorderly conduct on cross-examination after the witnesses had testified of Broyles' (D) reputation for peace and quietude.

CONCISE RULE OF LAW: A witness testifying to the good character of a criminal defendant may, on cross-examination, be questioned about specific instances of misconduct having some relationship to the good character trait in question for the limited purpose of testing the accuracy of the reputation testimony and not as substantive evidence.

FACTS: Broyles (D) introduced the testimony of witnesses of his reputation for peace and quietude in his trial for murder. On cross-examination, the trial court permitted the prosecutor to inquire of the witnesses whether they knew of or had heard of Broyles' (D) prior convictions for drunken driving, reckless driving, and disorderly conduct. One witness answered in the affirmative. Broyles (D) appealed the ensuing conviction on the ground that the convictions were irrelevant to the good character trait in question.

ISSUE: May a witness testifying to the good character of a criminal defendant be questioned on cross-examination about specific instances of misconduct having some relationship to the good character trait in question for the limited purpose of testing the accuracy of the reputation testimony, though not as substantive evidence?

HOLDING AND DECISION: (Combs, J.) Yes. When a criminal defendant offers evidence in the form of reputation testimony of a good character trait, the witness may be cross-examined as to specific instances of misconduct on the part of the defendant. However, the instances elicited must bear some relationship to the particular trait in question. Broyles' (D) disorderly conduct and other convictions contradict the trait for peace and quietude testified to and might be inferred to show an attitude of disrespect for the law. A witness testifying to the good character of a criminal defendant may, on cross-examination, be questioned as to specific instances of misconduct having some relationship to the good character trait in question and for the limited purpose of testing the accuracy of the reputation testimony, but not as substantive evidence. The court properly permitted the inquiry into the convictions. Reversed on other grounds.

EDITOR'S ANALYSIS: At the time this case was decided, reputation evidence was the only permissible method of proving a good character trait of a criminal defendant. In jurisdictions where personal opinion testimony is admitted, those witnesses may also be asked about specific instances of misconduct relevant to the good character trait asserted.

[For more information on the use of character evidence to impeach, see Casenote Law Outline on Evidence, Chapter 6, § V, Character to Impeach.]

NOTES:

EVANS v. UNITED STATES
277 F.2d 354 (D.C. Cir. 1960).

NATURE OF CASE: Appeal from conviction for second-degree murder.

FACT SUMMARY: Evans (D) contended evidence of the victim's character toward aggression was relevant when the defense of self-defense was raised.

CONCISE RULE OF LAW: Evidence of a victim's character is admissible to corroborate the defendant's contention, pursuant to his plea of self-defense, that the victim was the aggressor.

FACTS: Evans (D) was charged with second-degree murder. She pled self-defense and offered testimony that the victim was drunk at the time of the incident, and that he had a character trait of aggression when drunk. She contended this proved the victim was the aggressor and corroborated her self-defense plea. The court refused to allow the character evidence as improper. Evans (D) was convicted and appealed.

ISSUE: Is evidence of a victim's character admissible to corroborate the defendant's contention that the victim was the aggressor?

HOLDING AND DECISION: (Bazelon, J.) Yes. Evidence of a victim's character is admissible to corroborate the defendant's contention pursuant to his plea of self-defense, that the victim was the aggressor. Instigation is a prime element of self-defense, and thus any character trait toward or against aggression on the part of the victim is relevant to show whether self-defense is applicable. Therefore, the failure to allow such evidence was reversible error. Reversed and remanded.

DISSENT: (Fahy, J.) The relationship between the evidence and the fact to be proved was too tenuous to be admissible.

EDITOR'S ANALYSIS: In this case, aggression was relevant to the victim's state of mind. Aggression is a character trait, thus evidence of aggression goes some distance in proving an element of the defense. In this case, therefore, character evidence was deemed admissible. General evidence of character to prove behavior consistent with such character is generally irrelevant.

[For more information on the admission of character evidence, see Casenote Law Outline on Evidence, Chapter 6, § III, Character to Prove Conduct.]

HUDDLESTON v. UNITED STATES
485 U.S. 681 (1988).

NATURE OF CASE: Review of conviction based on buying and selling stolen goods.

FACT SUMMARY: In a prosecution based on dealing in stolen goods, the trial court did not make a preliminary finding as to the accuracy of evidence of similar acts introduced to show motive and knowledge, prior to admission of the evidence.

CONCISE RULE OF LAW: A court need not make, prior to admitting post acts introduced to show motive or knowledge, a preliminary finding that the acts occurred.

FACTS: Huddleston (D) was indicted on charges of buying and selling stolen goods. At trial, the prosecution sought to introduce evidence of prior similar transactions by Huddleston (D). The court, without making any preliminary findings that the alleged prior acts had occurred, admitted the evidence based on Fed. R. Evid. 404(b), which permits the introduction of evidence of prior acts to show motive or knowledge. Huddleston (D) was convicted, and the court of appeals affirmed. The Supreme Court accepted review.

ISSUE: Must a court make, prior to admitting past acts introduced to show motive or knowledge, a preliminary finding that the acts occurred?

HOLDING AND DECISION: (Rehnquist, C.J.) No. A court need not make, prior to admitting past acts introduced to show motive or knowledge, a preliminary finding that the acts occurred. Fed. R. Evid. 404(b) prohibits the use of evidence of prior acts to prove conduct in conformity therewith, but permits the introduction of such evidence to prove knowledge, motive, opportunity or the like. Huddleston (D) argues that the court must preliminarily find that the prior acts did in fact occur. However, this runs contrary to the structure of the Rules of Evidence. Relevant evidence is to be admitted. Evidence of prior conduct, if relevant to show a legitimate item such as motive or knowledge, is equally admissible. It is for the jury to decide whether the prior act occurred. The only determination the court need make is that the evidence is relevant, which is to say, that a jury could find that the prior acts do in fact show motive or knowledge. Here, the court appears to have done just that. Affirmed.

EDITOR'S ANALYSIS: Fed. R. Evid. 404(b) is essentially an exclusionary section. It prohibits otherwise relevant evidence of prior acts to be introduced to prove conduct in conformity therewith. The rationale behind this is that the possibility of prejudice inherently outweighs whatever probative value exists. However, prior acts introduced to prove other than acts in conformity therewith are admissible.

UNITED STATES v. WOODS
484 F.2d 127 (4th Cir.);
cert. denied, 415 U.S. 979 (1973).

NATURE OF CASE: Appeal from conviction for murder.

FACT SUMMARY: After the death of Woods' (D) eight-month-old adoptive son from apparent cyanosis and respiratory difficulty, Woods (D) was put on trial for murder, during which trial the prosecution offered medical testimony that the child died by smothering and that, of the nine children in Woods' (D) care since 1945, seven had died similarly.

CONCISE RULE OF LAW: Evidence of other offenses may be offered in a criminal trial if relevant for any purpose other than to show a propensity or disposition to commit the crime, subject to the power of the trial judge to exclude the evidence if it will create undue prejudice.

FACTS: Woods (D) had custody of and sole access to her eight-month-old adoptive son Paul when five instances of breathing difficulties and cyanosis afflicted him. The final episode resulted in a coma and the ultimate death of Paul. In Woods' (D) trial for the murder of the boy, medical evidence was received to the effect that to a 75% certainty, the boy died as a result of a homicide by smothering. The prosecution then offered evidence that since 1945, Woods (D) had custody of nine children, who together had suffered over 20 cases of cyanosis resulting in the deaths of seven of them. Woods (D) was convicted and appealed.

ISSUE: May evidence of other offenses be offered in a criminal trial if relevant for any purpose other than to show a propensity or disposition to commit the crime, subject to the power of the trial judge to exclude the evidence if it will create undue prejudice?

HOLDING AND DECISION: (Winter, J.) Yes. While evidence of past criminal acts is generally inadmissible to show that the defendant in question committed the crime of which he is accused, if the past acts are such that it appears that the defendant engaged in a common plan or scheme including the crime in question, or if the past acts show that the defendant has placed his signature on his handiwork by committing the acts in the same way, the evidence is admissible. Furthermore, a developing approach to this problem is to balance the actual need of the evidence in order to prove the crime against the degree to which the jury will probably be roused by the evidence to overmastering hostility. Under this approach, this case presents an occasion to admit the evidence of the other deaths, even to prove the corpus delicti of the crime. Evidence of other offenses may be offered in a criminal trial if relevant for any purpose other than to show a propensity or disposition to commit the crime, subject to the power of the trial judge to exclude the evidence if it will create undue prejudice. The evidence should have been admitted here. Affirmed.

DISSENT: (Widener, J.) The evidence of the past occurrences offered in this case does not fit into any recognized exception to the rule excluding evidence of past acts to prove a crime in question in a criminal proceeding. The majority gives no reason for its ruling, though it purports not to rely upon the inapplicable signature or lack of accident exceptions.

EDITOR'S ANALYSIS: The danger of admitting past acts in proving a crime is that the jury will try the defendant on the basis of the past acts rather than the prosecutor's proof of the crime in question. Technically, the relevancy of prior conduct is always in question when it is being used to show that a defendant also engaged in certain unrelated conduct. However, where relevant, nonprejudicial and necessary to the prosecutor's case, the evidence is sometimes admitted, though the judge has discretion to exclude it.

[For more information on evidence of other crimes, see Casenote Law Outline on Evidence, Chapter 6, § IV, The "Other Crimes" Loophole.]

NOTES:

UNITED STATES v. HADLEY

918 F.2d 848 (9th Cir., 1990), cert. dismissed, __U.S.__, 113 S. Ct. 486 (1992).

NATURE OF CASE: Appeal from conviction for aggravated sexual abuse and abusive sexual conduct.

FACT SUMMARY: Hadley (D), a former elementary school teacher, appealed his conviction for aggravated sexual abuse, contending that the district court abused its discretion by improperly admitting evidence of prior acts of sexual abuse.

CONCISE RULE OF LAW: Under Fed. R. Evid. 404 (b), evidence of prior bad acts is admissible if: (1) sufficient proof exists for the jury to find that the defendant committed the prior act; (2) the prior act was not too remote in time; and (3) the prior act is introduced to prove a material issue in this case.

FACTS: Hadley (D), a former elementary school teacher at the Bureau of Indian Affairs School on the Navajo Reservation, was prosecuted by the United States (P) for aggravated sexual abuse and abusive sexual conduct. These charges arose from allegations that Hadley (D) had committed forcible anal intercourse and other acts of sexual abuse against a male student at the school. The student testified to three separate incidents of sexual molestation by Hadley (D). In addition, over Hadley's (D) objection, the district court allowed other government witnesses to testify that Hadley (D) had forcibly sodomized them as minors. The jury found Hadley (D) guilty of the three crimes perpetrated against the male student. Hadley (D) appealed, arguing that the district court abused its discretion by improperly admitting evidence of prior acts of sexual abuse and explanatory expert witness testimony.

ISSUE: Under Fed. R. Evid. 404(b), is evidence admissible if: (1) sufficient proof exists for the jury to find that the defendant committed the prior act; (2) the prior act was not too remote in time; and (3) the prior act is introduced to prove a material issue in this case?

HOLDING AND DECISION: (Wallace, J.) Yes. Under Fed. R. Evid. 404(b), evidence is admissible if: (1) sufficient proof exists for the jury to find that the defendant committed the prior act; (2) the prior act was not too remote in time; and (3) the prior act is introduced to prove a material issue in this case. In addition, if used to prove intent, the prior act must be similar to the offense charged. Here, sufficient evidence of the prior acts existed for a jury to reasonably conclude that the acts occurred and that Hadley (D) was the actor. The witnesses testified in detail about the sexual abuse inflicted upon them by Hadley (D). This testimony clearly amounted to more than unsubstantiated innuendo. Thus, the jury reasonably could have concluded that Hadley (D) previously sodomized and abused these witnesses. One witness testified to a regular pattern of sodomy and sexual molestation that began when he was ten years old and lasted five years. Hadley (D) argued that this act was too remote in time to justify admissibility because he had stopped abusing the witness ten years previous to the abuse for which he was convicted here. We have previously refused to adopt an inflexible rule regarding remoteness in the context of Rule 404(b). The similarity of the prior act to the offense charged here outweighs concerns regarding its remoteness. The district judge did not abuse his discretion in admitting this testimony. Furthermore,

Hadley (D) contended that the prior act evidence was not introduced to prove a material element in the case. The district judge found that the prior acts had to do with the alleged activities of Hadley (D) of a sexually gratifying nature. Also, the evidence helped to demonstrate specific intent and was similar to the offense charged; on that basis, it was properly admitted. Because the evidence was highly probative on the question of intent, although highly prejudicial, the prejudicial effect was limited by the instructions given by the court. Affirmed.

EDITOR'S ANALYSIS: Although, in the past, admissibility of other offenses in cases such as Hadley was often limited in prosecutions for sex crimes, these limitations are disappearing. This process began when proof of other offenses was limited to offenses involving the same parties. Admissibility was permitted to show familiarity between the parties. Currently, some courts are allowing admission of other sex offenses to show a propensity for the type of behavior at issue.

[For more information on relevance of precedential evidence, see Casenote Law Outline on Evidence, Chapter 2, § VI, Precedential Relevance.]

NOTES:

TOY v. MACKINTOSH
Mass. Sup. Ct., 222 Mass. 430, 110 N.E. 1034 (1916).

NATURE OF CASE: Appeal from award of damages for negligence.

FACT SUMMARY: Toy (P) underwent an operation by Mackintosh (D) requiring the extraction of teeth, one of which allegedly fell into Toy's (P) throat during the operation and caused injury, and the jury found for Toy (P) upon a jury instruction not setting forth the evidentiary standard or the burden of proof required, despite the absence of any proof of the claim.

CONCISE RULE OF LAW: Proof of negligence requires a finding established by a fair preponderance of the evidence which is the plaintiff's burden to produce.

FACTS: Mackintosh (D) performed an operation on Toy (P) which required the extraction of several teeth. Toy (D) alleged that during the operation, Mackintosh (D) negligently let a tooth fall in Toy's (P) throat and later lodge in his lung. Toy (P) testified that he later coughed up the tooth and thereafter the dizziness, partial loss of speech, pains, and numbness that had plagued him since the operation ceased. Toy (P) offered no evidence other than his own testimony, and Mackintosh (D) introduced the testimony of several experts to the effect that his conduct was nonnegligent, and that the tooth, lodged as alleged, could not have caused the injuries claimed. The jury was not instructed as to the plaintiff's burden of proving negligence by a fair preponderance of the evidence. The verdict was for Toy (P) and Mackintosh (D) appealed.

ISSUE: Does proof of negligence require a finding established by a fair preponderance of evidence the burden of which is upon the plaintiff?

HOLDING AND DECISION: (Crosby, J.) Yes. Toy (P) offered no expert medical or dental evidence of his claim. He was under an obligation as a plaintiff to produce a fair preponderance of evidence of negligence to make out such a case. Mackintosh (D) produced witnesses who gave evidence that the alleged acts of Mackintosh (D) were not negligence and that the injuries alleged could not have occurred from the cause alleged. The preponderance of the evidence therefore did not serve to establish the finding of negligence made by the jury in reaching its verdict. The trial judge did not instruct the jury of the plaintiff's burden to prove by a fair preponderance of the evidence that negligence occurred and that it was the cause of the injury alleged. Proof of negligence requires a finding established by a fair preponderance of evidence which is the plaintiff's burden to produce. The lack of instruction was erroneous. Exceptions sustained.

EDITOR'S ANALYSIS: Expert medical testimony that the injuries alleged were caused by the lodging of the tooth would have supplied evidence of causation in this case. First, however, it must have been shown that Mackintosh (D) dropped the tooth and that his conduct in doing so fell below the standard of care to which he was bound in performing the operation.

[For more information on the weight of burdens of proof, see Casenote Law Outline on Evidence, Chapter 4, § I, Burdens of Proof.]

NOTES:

PEOPLE v. KELLY
Cal. Sup. Ct., 17 Cal. 3d 24, 549 P.2d 1240 (1976).

NATURE OF CASE: Appeal from conviction for extortion.

FACT SUMMARY: Kelly (D) was convicted of extortion after tapes were made of the extorting voice on the victim's telephone and of Kelly's (D) voice, and the tapes were compared by a police expert who identified Kelly's (D) voice by the comparison and who presented the sole evidence that the voiceprint analysis method of comparison was accepted by the scientific community.

CONCISE RULE OF LAW: The foundation for admission of results of scientific tests or techniques cannot be sufficiently laid by only the testimony of an expert witness that such tests or techniques are generally accepted by the relevant scientific community absent a showing of academic qualifications enabling him to express such an opinion.

FACTS: The police taped telephone calls made to one Waskins threatening him. The tapes were compared by a police expert, Nash, to tapes obtained of Kelly's (D) voice over the telephone. Using a method known as voiceprint analysis, Nash gave the opinion that the voice on the extortion tape was Kelly's (D). Nash testified at Kelly's (D) trial and gave the only evidence on the voiceprint analysis method and the results of his test. Though having no formal degree in the field, Nash stated that the method was generally accepted by the scientific community. Kelly (D) appealed his conviction for extortion on the ground that the prosecution had not established the reliability of the voiceprint analysis.

ISSUE: Can the foundation for admission of results of scientific tests or techniques be sufficiently laid by only the testimony of an expert witness that such tests or techniques are generally accepted by the relevant scientific community absent a showing of academic qualifications enabling him to express such an opinion?

HOLDING AND DECISION: (Richardson, J.) No. It is questionable whether a sole witness is ever qualified to testify to the views of an entire scientific community. When, as here, the witness is a leading proponent of such a scientific technique, more caution is appropriate. Furthermore, in this case, Nash was without a formal degree in the area of voiceprint analysis, despite his extensive work and hours of classroom training. Under these circumstances, the prosecution failed to establish the reliability of the test employed. The foundation for admission of results of scientific tests or techniques cannot be sufficiently established by only the testimony of an expert witness that such tests or techniques are generally accepted by the relevant scientific community absent a showing of academic qualifications enabling him to express such an opinion. Reversed.

EDITOR'S ANALYSIS: In modern practice in progressive juris-dictions, no specific training or education is required of an expert in a given field, rather the court may determine from the qualifications alleged whether the witness is an expert in the field. Formal degrees and licenses are particularly relevant, of course. Fields that are not technically "scientific" are not excluded, but the foundation for evidence must satisfy the judge that some specialized knowledge is possessed by the expert and that the field can produce reliable results.

[For more information on the qualifications of an expert witness, see Casenote Law Outline on Evidence, Chapter 12, § III, Expert Opinions.]

NOTES:

DAUBERT v. MERRELL DOW PHARMACEUTICALS, INC.
___U.S.___, 113 S. Ct. 2786 (1993).

NATURE OF CASE: Review of summary judgment dismissing product liability action.

FACT SUMMARY: Daubert's (P) proffered expert witnesses were excluded because the opinions they intended to introduce were not based on methods generally accepted in the scientific community.

CONCISE RULE OF LAW: An expert opinion does not need to be generally accepted in the scientific community to be admissible.

FACTS: Daubert (P) and Schuller (D) filed a lawsuit against Merrell Dow Pharmaceuticals, Inc. (D), alleging that they suffered in utero injuries due to maternal ingestion of the drug Bendectin. Merrell (D) moved for summary judgment, introducing expert opinions to the effect that there was no causal link between Bendectin and birth defects. Daubert (P) and Schuller (P) countered with a series of declarations from eight medical experts, contending that such a link existed. The district court held that the plaintiff's experts had used methodologies not generally accepted in the scientific community. Specifically, they had based their opinions on in vitro and animal studies, as well as chemical structure analysis. Merrell's (D) motion for summary judgment was granted, dismissing the action. The Ninth Circuit affirmed, and the Supreme Court granted review.

ISSUE: Does an expert opinion need to be generally accepted in the scientific community to be admissible?

HOLDING AND DECISION: (Blackmun, J.) No. An expert opinion does not need to be generally accepted in the scientific community to be admissible. The admissibility of expert opinions is governed by Fed.R.Evid. 702. The Rule provides that "If scientific . . . or other specialized knowledge will assist the trier of fact to understand the evidence or to determine a fact in issue," an expert may testify thereto. Nothing in this Rule provides that general scientific acceptance is a condition to admissibility. This being so, the broad relevance requirement of Fed.R.Evid. 401 takes over, which also provides no such requirement. Consequently, no such requirement should be inferred. However, this does not mean that there are no limits on admissibility of expert testimony. The Rule requires "knowledge," so guesses or speculation are inadmissible. A necessary corollary to this is that the expert must base his opinion on sound principles and valid deductions. In this analysis, such factors as peer review, publication, and even general acceptance may be relevant. No one issue will be determinative, however. Here, the courts below held general acceptance to be determinative, and this was erroneous. Reversed.

CONCURRENCE AND DISSENT: (Rehnquist, C.J.) Everything in the present opinion going beyond the main holding that general acceptance is not required is dicta and should not have been included.

EDITOR'S ANALYSIS: The "general acceptance" rule was first enunciated in Frye v. U.S., 293 F. 1013 (1923). For seventy years after Frye, the general acceptance requirement was adopted by most courts, although the rule was a matter of great controversy. The present opinion appears to have settled this issue.

[For more information on expert witnesses, see Casenote Law Outline on Evidence, Chapter 12, § III, Expert Opinions.]

NOTES:

UNITED STATES v. MARTINEZ
3 F.3d 1191 (8th Cir., 1993).

NATURE OF CASE: Appeal from conviction of aggravated sexual abuse and sexual abuse of a minor.

FACT SUMMARY: Martinez (D) appealed his conviction for aggravated sexual abuse and sexual abuse of a minor, contending that the DNA evidence used to convict him should have been ruled inadmissible.

CONCISE RULE OF LAW: Before admitting novel scientific evidence, the court must conclude that the proposed testimony constitutes (1) scientific knowledge that (2) will assist the trier of fact to understand or determine a fact in issue.

FACTS: Martinez (D), an American Indian security guard, allegedly lured a girl away from a pow wow she was attending and raped her. Evidence gathered at the hospital shortly after the occurrence included semen stains. Using DNA profiling to isolate and analyze the semen, the FBI concluded that only one in 2,600 American Indians would be expected to produce the identical genetic characteristics as Martinez (D). At trial, the court admitted the DNA test results and the profiling analysis evidence but not the statistical probability evidence. Upon conviction, Martinez (D) appealed, arguing that none of the DNA evidence was admissible.

ISSUE: Before admitting novel scientific evidence, must the court conclude that the proposed testimony constitutes (1) scientific knowledge that (2) will assist the trier of fact to understand or determine a fact issue?

HOLDING AND DECISION: (Larson, J.) Yes. Before admitting novel scientific evidence under Fed. R. Evid. 702, the district court must conclude, pursuant to Fed. R. Evid. 104(a), that the proposed testimony constitutes (1) scientific knowledge that (2) will assist the trier of fact to understand or determine a fact issue. Under Fed. R. Evid. 702, in assessing the reliability of novel scientific evidence, courts should consider: (1) whether the scientific technique can be (and has been) tested; (2) whether the technique or theory has been subjected to peer review and publication; (3) the known rate of error of the technique and the existence and maintenance of standards controlling the technique's operation; and (4) whether the technique is generally accepted. DNA profiling is still relatively new as a forensic tool and has been the subject of heated controversy in both the legal and scientific communities. However, it is generally conceded that the principles of DNA profiling are recognized as reliable and that the procedures associated with it are not so new or novel as to warrant disagreement. In this case, the district court did not err in admitting the profiling evidence. The district court held a preliminary hearing, including the submission of evidence and expert testimony on the subject of DNA profiling. The court thus undertook a broad inquiry, determining that the underlying principle was generally well accepted by the scientific community, the testing protocol and procedures were generally accepted as reliable, and the FBI properly followed the protocol, accurately performing the prescribed procedures. The court further balanced the probative value against the prejudicial effect of the evidence and concluded that the evidence of a DNA match was properly admitted. Affirmed.

EDITOR'S ANALYSIS: The court of appeals also barred Martinez (D) from raising an argument that the exclusion of evidence showing that, as a matter of probability, one in 2,600 Native Americans could have provided DNA matching the samples found on the victim here prejudiced him because the jury would conclude that he was the only possible source of the DNA found on the victim. Martinez (D) was barred from raising this argument by the doctrine of invited error. After the district court decided to admit the DNA match evidence, the court invited counsel to comment on the propriety of admitting statistical evidence of the likelihood of a match. Martinez' (D) counsel suggested that the court exclude the probability evidence. Thus, having specifically requested that the district court exclude the statistical evidence, Martinez (D) could not subsequently complain about its exclusions.

[For more information on relevance and expert opinions, see Casenote Law Outline on Evidence, Chapter 2, § III, Is the "Evidence" Relevant?]

NOTES:

STATE v. SNEED
N.M. Sup. Ct., 76 N.M. 349, 414 P.2d 858 (1966).

NATURE OF CASE: Appeal from conviction of first-degree murder.

FACT SUMMARY: Sneed (D) appealed from his conviction for first-degree murder, contending that the testimony of Dr. Thorp, whereby the mathematical probability that Sneed (D) was the individual who purchased the gun presumably used in the crime as opposed to someone else was estimated, was erroneously admitted since the validity of the estimates upon which the testimony was based had not been demonstrated.

CONCISE RULE OF LAW: Mathematical odds are not admissible as evidence to identify a defendant in a criminal proceeding so long as the odds are based on estimates, the validity of which has not been demonstrated.

FACTS: Sneed (D) was tried for first-degree murder. The State (P) sought to introduce the evidence of Dr. Thorp, a mathematician, as evidence that Sneed (D) had been properly identified as the individual who purchased the gun which was presumably used in the murder. Evidence was introduced that Sneed (D) had used the name Crosset within a week of the murder, and that someone named Crosset had purchased the gun presumably used in the crime on the morning of the murder. Dr. Thorp made certain estimates based upon the number of times the person named Crosset appeared in telephone books, and estimates made based upon the description of the individual who purchased the gun contained in the gun shop's register. Dr. Thorp testified that the laws of probability indicated that the chances of someone accidently implicating Sneed (D) as the individual who purchased the gun, as opposed to Sneed (D) making the purchase himself, were 240 billion to one. The testimony was admitted, and Sneed (D) was convicted. From this decision, Sneed (D) appealed, contending that Dr. Thorp's testimony was erroneously admitted because the validity of his estimates had not been demonstrated.

ISSUE: Are mathematical odds admissible as evidence to identify a defendant in a criminal proceeding, if the validity of the estimates upon which the odds are based has not been demonstrated?

HOLDING AND DECISION: (Wood, J.) No. Mathematical odds are not admissible as evidence to identify a defendant in a criminal proceeding so long as the odds are based upon estimates, the validity of which has not been demonstrated. No testimony was received from Dr. Thorp as to why these particular items were chosen to base his estimates. The basis for using the phone books and the register descriptions may be common knowledge to mathematicians, but this basis is not set forth in the record and is not of such common knowledge that judicial notice may be taken of such basis. Scientific principles are admissible when their validity is demonstrated and becomes accepted. Since the estimates upon which Dr. Thorp based his odds are as of yet unproven, his testimony was erroneously admitted. Reversed with directions to award new trial.

EDITOR'S ANALYSIS: The court's decision in the present case leaves the door open for the admission of such testimony, if the validity of the estimates utilized has been demonstrated and is not in question. The decision in the instant case raises certain implications regarding the use of life expectancy and annuity tables in evaluating damages in wrongful death cases. See Mapes Casino, Inc. v. Maryland Casualty Co., 290 F. Supp. 186 (D. Nev. 1968).

[For more information on the admission of scientific evidence, see Casenote Law Outline on Evidence, Chapter 12, § III, Expert Opinions.]

NOTES:

**GRENADA STEEL INDUSTRIES v.
ALABAMA OXYGEN CO., INC.**
695 F.2d 883 (5th Cir. 1983).

NATURE OF CASE: Appeal from denial of recovery in a products liability action.

FACT SUMMARY: Grenada (P) contended the district court erred in excluding evidence of post-accident design changes by Sherwood-Selpac Corp. (SSC) (D) in a suit for strict products liability.

CONCISE RULE OF LAW: Rule 407 of the Fed. R. Evid. is fully applicable in strict liability actions to exclude evidence of post-accident design changes.

FACTS: Grenada (P) sued SSC (D) for damages arising from a fire allegedly caused by a defective valve on an acetylene tank. Grenada (P) was precluded from introducing evidence of SSC's (D) post-accident design changes. It was denied recovery and appealed, contending the exclusion of such evidence or culpable conduct were sought to be proved. Therefore, it argued, since strict liability does not depend upon finding of negligence or fault, the exclusion did not apply in strict liability cases.

ISSUE: Is Rule 407 fully applicable in strict liability actions to exclude evidence of post-accident design changes?

HOLDING AND DECISION: (Rubin, J.) Yes. Fed. R. Evid. 407 is fully applicable in strict liability cases to exclude evidence of post-accident design changes. The policy behind Rule 407, which is equally applicable in strict liability cases, is to encourage manufacturers to make necessary repairs to protect the public. Further, manufacturers may decide to change designs for many reasons other than the fact the original design rendered the product unreasonably dangerous. Admitting such evidence could improperly suggest the change was made solely in recognition of a design detect. As a result the evidence was properly excluded in this case. Affirmed.

EDITOR'S ANALYSIS: The rule illustrated in this case is followed in the First, Second, Third, Fourth, and Sixth Circuits, as well as the Fifth after this case. The Eighth Circuit, however, has consistently held that Rule 407 is inapplicable in strict liability cases because negligence is not the issue. The issue involved, in its basic form, is one of legal relevancy. It is believed that evidence of subsequent remedial measures is substantially more prejudicial than probative when offered to prove negligence or culpable conduct.

[For more information on subsequent remedial measures, see Casenote Law Outline on Evidence, Chapter 7, § II, Subsequent Remedial Measures.]

NOTES:

McINNIS v. A.M.F., INC.
765 F.2d 240 (1st Cir. 1984).

NATURE OF CASE: Appeal from denial of damages defense verdict in personal injury action.

FACT SUMMARY: McInnis (P) appealed from a defense verdict in favor of A.M.F., Inc. (AMF) (D) in her personal injury action, contending that the trial judge erred in admitting evidence that she had released codefendant Poirier from liability prior to instituting suit against AMF (D).

CONCISE RULE OF LAW: Rule 408 of the Federal Rules of Evidence bars the admission of evidence of settlements between plaintiffs and third-party joint tortfeasors and former codefendants.

FACTS: McInnis' (P) leg was severed when her motorcycle was involved in an accident with an automobile driven by Poirier. She settled with Poirier for $60,000 prior to instituting suit against AMF (D). She contended in part that her injuries were due to the fact that the clutch housing on the motorcycle shattered. At trial, AMF (D), over the objections of McInnis (P), was allowed to introduce evidence of the $60,000 settlement. From a decision in favor of AMF (D), McInnis (P) appealed, contending that evidence of the settlement was admitted in violation of Federal Rule of Evidence 408.

ISSUE: Does Rule 408 of the Federal Rules of Evidence bar the admission of evidence of settlements between plaintiffs and third-party joint tortfeasors or former codefendants?

HOLDING AND DECISION: (Pettine, J.) Yes. Rule 408 of the Federal Rules of Evidence bars the admission of evidence of settlements between plaintiffs and third-party joint tortfeasors and former codefendants. Rule 408 excludes evidence of settlements and settlement negotiations in order to promote the voluntary compromise and settlement of disputes among parties to litigation. It is also a recognition that such evidence is of questionable relevance on the issues of liability or of the value of claims, as there are other motivations for the compromise of claims. [The court first made clear that the rule applied to all settlements, whether offered against a settling defendant or a settling plaintiff.] The trial record is clear that the evidence of the settlement was admitted for the purpose as being relevant to the issue of causation. It is clear to see that evidence of causation or noncausation is fully subsumed under Rule 408's prohibition against the introduction of settlements on the issue of the validity or nonvalidity of a claim. Regardless of the manner in which the purpose for admitting evidence of the settlement is couched, it is clear that AMF (D) could not be held liable for the injuries sustained in the accident. The fact of settlement cannot be reasonably found to be indicative of the cause of McInnis' (P) injuries, and the admission of this evidence was prejudicial error. Reversed and remanded for new trial.

EDITOR'S ANALYSIS: Rule 408 differs from the rule applicable in most common law jurisdictions in that it also precludes the admission of admissions of fact in settlement negotiations. Also implicit in the court's decision in the present case is a recognition that for Rule 408 to have full effectiveness, a dispute must be considered to exist prior to the filing of a formal complaint. For a further discussion, see McCormick § 274, at 811-12.

[For more information on the admissibility of settlement agreements, see Casenote Law Outline on Evidence, Chapter 7, § III, Compromise and Settlement Negotiations.]

NOTES:

NOTES

CHAPTER 9
JUDICIAL NOTICE

QUICK REFERENCE RULES

1. **Jury Notice.** Jurors may take judicial notice of the commonly accepted meaning of all English words and may thus use a standard English dictionary in recalling such meaning where no special or legal significance of its use is involved. (Palestroni v. Jacobs)

   [For more information on jury notice, see Casenote Law Outline on Evidence, Chapter 3, § I, Definitions and Distinctions.]

2. **Judicial Notice.** A trial court may in its discretion take judicial notice of facts of a verifiable certainty outside the general common knowledge if the judge or the party requesting judicial notice notifies the opponent so as to permit him to adduce contradictory sources. (Fringer v. Venema)

   [For more information on judicial notice, see Casenote Law Outline on Evidence, Chapter 3, § I, Definitions and Distinctions.]

3. **Judicial Notice of Adjudicative Facts.** A judicially noticed fact must be one not subject to reasonable dispute in that it is either: (1) generally known within the territorial jurisdiction of the trial court or (2) capable of accurate and ready determination by resort to sources whose accuracy cannot reasonably be questioned. (State v. Vejvoda)

   [For more information on judicial notice of adjudicative facts, see Casenote Law Outline on Evidence, Chapter 3, § II, Judicial Notice of Adjudicative Facts.]

4. **Proffered Evidence.** A motion for nonsuit should be granted where the evidence proffered does not support the inference suggested of the defendant's liability. (Clayton v. Rimmer)

   [For more information on proffered evidence, see Casenote Law Outline on Evidence, Chapter 5, § II, Preliminary Questions of Fact.]

5. **Authentication of a Writing.** An unauthenticated written source reciting overages of results from various experiments is inadmissible as either expert opinion or as evidence of an experiment when used to establish the circumstances of a particular event or fact in issue. (Hughes v. Vestal)

   [For more information on authentication of a writing, see Casenote Law Outline on Evidence, Chapter 13, § II, Authentication of Documents.]

6. **Judicial Notice.** A court may take judicial notice of information illustrating the character of a process or event giving rise to a claim. (Potts v. Coe)

   [For more information on judicial notice, see Casenote Law Outline on Evidence, Chapter 3, § II, Judicial Notice of Adjudicative Facts.]

NOTES

PALESTRONI v. JACOBS
N.J. Super. Ct., 8 N.J. Super. 438, 73 A.2d 89;
reversed, 10 N.J. Super. 266, 77 A.2d 183 (1950).

NATURE OF CASE: Motion to set aside verdict for jury misconduct.

FACT SUMMARY: The attending court officer delivered to the jury upon request a dictionary of the English language which it consulted during its deliberations in this breach of contract action.

CONCISE RULE OF LAW: Jurors may take judicial notice of the commonly accepted meaning of all English words and may thus use a standard English dictionary in recalling such meaning where no special or legal significance of its use is involved.

FACTS: Palestroni (P) brought this breach of contract action against Jacobs (D) for failure to pay and Jacobs (D) counterclaimed for failure to complete performance. After the trial, the jury began deliberations but interrupted them to consult an English language dictionary provided upon request for the attending court officer. The verdict was rendered for Palestroni (P) and Jacobs (D) moved to set aside the verdict for the jury's misconduct in referring to the dictionary which was not offered and received as evidence.

ISSUE: May jurors take judicial notice of the commonly accepted meaning of all English words and thus use a standard English dictionary in recalling such meaning where no special or legal significance of its use is involved?

HOLDING AND DECISION: (Waesche, J.) Yes. In considering and weighing the evidence, jurors are expected to rely upon their own common sense and general knowledge. The ordinary and generally accepted meaning of English words is a matter of common knowledge, which jurors are expected to know. Jurors may take judicial notice of the commonly accepted meanings of all English words and thus use a standard English dictionary in recalling such meaning where no special or legal significance of its use is involved. Motion to set aside verdict and judgment denied.

EDITOR'S ANALYSIS: Certain facts fall within a category subject to "jury notice." This consists of a multitude of nonevidentiary background information which will facilitate comprehension of the evidence presented. Included in this background information is the general nature of things and the commonly accepted meanings of ordinary words.

[For more information on jury notice, see Casenote Law Outline on Evidence, Chapter 3, § I, Definitions and Distinctions.]

FRINGER v. VENEMA

Wis. Sup. Ct., 26 Wis. 2d 366, 132 N.W.2d 565;
reh'g denied, 26 Wis. 2d 376a, 133 N.W.2d 809 (1965).

NATURE OF CASE: Appeal from award of damages for permitting an animal to escape.

FACT SUMMARY: At trial of Fringer's (P) suit to recover damages when Venema's (D) bull escaped onto Fringer's (P) land under a statute imposing strict liability for such escape by animals over the age of six months, the trial judge took judicial notice of the bull's being over six months old due to the fact that it had fertilized 15 heifers.

CONCISE RULE OF LAW: A trial court may in its discretion take judicial notice of facts of a verifiable certainty outside the general common knowledge if the judge or the party requesting judicial notice notifies the opponent so as to permit him to adduce contradictory sources.

FACTS: Fringer (P) brought suit to recover damages incurred when Venema's (D) bull escaped onto his land. The suit was based on a statute imposing strict liability for such escape by an animal over the age of six months. The bull had managed to fertilize 15 heifers during its escape, and from this fact, the trial judge took judicial notice that the bull was over the age of six months. The court was not requested to take such judicial notice and did not advise the parties that it intended to do so. Venema (D) appealed and introduced affidavits of farmers and a veterinary obstetrician that it is possible for a bull of less than six months old to sire heifers.

ISSUE: May a trial court in its discretion take judicial notice of facts of a verifiable certainty outside the general common knowledge if the judge or the party requesting judicial notice notifies the opponent so as to permit him to adduce contradictory sources?

HOLDING AND DECISION: (Beilfuss, J.) Yes. Venema (D) urged that the trial judge erred in taking judicial notice of the bull's age being more than six months because the age at which bulls can fertilize is not a matter of common knowledge, and it is not impossible for a bull of less than six months to fertilize a heifer. A trial judge need not confine the matters of which he can take judicial notice to those of common knowledge. A trial court may in its discretion take judicial notice of facts of verifiable certainty outside the general common knowledge if the judge or the party requesting judicial notice notifies the opponent so as to permit him to adduce contradictory sources. It is error to take judicial notice, however, of facts that are disputable or to take judicial notice without notifying the parties who may wish to contradict the noticed fact. Reversed and remanded.

EDITOR'S ANALYSIS: Judicial notice is usually restricted to facts about which the judge cannot be wrong. Under the Federal Rules of Evidence (Rule 201(b)), facts outside the general knowledge, may be noticed if they are capable of accurate and ready determination by resort to sources whose accuracy cannot be reasonably questioned.

[For more information on judicial notice, see Casenote Law Outline on Evidence, Chapter 3, § I, Definitions and Distinctions.]

NOTES:

STATE v. VEJVODA
Neb. Sup. Ct., 231 Neb. 668, 431 N.W.2d 461 (1989).

NATURE OF CASE: Appeal from conviction of drunk driving.

FACT SUMMARY: Vejvoda (D) contended that the State (P) failed to prove that Hall County was the venue for his trial because the court improperly took judicial notice that locations mentioned in Vejvoda's (D) trial were within Hall County.

CONCISE RULE OF LAW: A judicially noticed fact must be one not subject to reasonable dispute in that it is either: (1) generally known within the territorial jurisdiction of the trial court or (2) capable of accurate and ready determination by resort to sources whose accuracy cannot reasonably be questioned.

FACTS: Vejvoda (D) was prosecuted by the State (P) for drunk driving after Vejvoda's (D) car was observed by a police officer at "7th and Vine Streets," and later Vejvoda (D) was apprehended on a street called "Oak." The police officer never identified the city or the county where he observed and apprehended Vejvoda (D). The court, however, took judicial notice that the driving occurred in Hall County. Vejvoda (D) was convicted. On appeal, the district court affirmed Vejvoda's (D) conviction and sentence. Vejvoda (D) appealed again, contending that the State (P) failed to prove that Hall County was the venue for his trial because the court improperly took judicial notice that the locations mentioned in Vejvoda's (D) trial were within Hall County.

ISSUE: Must a judicially noticed fact be one that is not subject to reasonable dispute in that it is either: (1) generally known within the territorial jurisdiction of the trial court or (2) capable of accurate and ready determination by resort to sources whose accuracy cannot reasonably be questioned?

HOLDING AND DECISION: (Shanahan, J.) Yes. Under Nebraska Evidence Rule 201(2), which pertains to judicial notice of adjudicative facts, a judicially noticed fact must be one not subject to reasonable dispute in that it is either: (1) generally known within the territorial jurisdiction of the trial court; or (2) capable of accurate and ready determination by resort to sources whose accuracy cannot reasonably be questioned. Judicial notice of an adjudicative fact is a species of evidence which is received without adherence to the Nebraska Evidence Rules and is established as fact without formal evidentiary proof. However, when a fact is not generally known within the territorial jurisdiction of the trial court, judicial notice may be taken only if an adjudicative fact can be verified by sources whose accuracy cannot reasonably be questioned. Judicial notice should be used sparingly in a criminal case, lest prejudicial error result from denial of a defendant's constitutional or statutory rights. Here, the trial court's sua sponte judicial notice was permissible at the point in Vejvoda's (D) trial where adduction of evidence had been concluded and the case was ready for submission to the fact-finding process. However, on this record, one cannot conclude that the location of the municipal microcosm known as Vine Street or 8th and Oak Streets was known throughout the length and breadth of Hall County and, therefore, a fact known within the territorial jurisdiction of the trial court. Although the location of streets within Grand Island, Nebraska is readily verifiable by reference to a city map, the trial court took an impermissible step by judicially noticing the inference that because Vejvoda (D) was driving on Vine, 8th, and Oak Streets, he was driving in Grand Island, Hall County, Nebraska. The court's locational inference necessary for venue was not an adjudicative fact capable of accurate and ready determination by resort to sources whose accuracy cannot reasonably be questioned. The trial court erred in taking judicial notice of the inference that Vejvoda (D) was driving in Grand Island and therefore that Vejvoda's (D) drunk driving occurred in Grand Island. However, the police officer's testimony supplied a sufficient evidentiary basis for a fact-finder's determination that Vejvoda's (D) drunk driving occurred in Grand Island, Hall County, Nebraska. Therefore, the trial court's error is harmless because such an error could not materially influence a jury in a verdict adverse to a substantial right of Vejvoda (D). Affirmed.

EDITOR'S ANALYSIS: Under Nebraska Evidence Rule 201(7), judicial notice in a civil action is fundamentally different from judicial notice in a criminal case. In a civil action, the judge must instruct the jury to accept as conclusive any fact judicially noticed. In a criminal case, the judge must instruct the jury that it may, but is not required to, accept as conclusive any fact judicially noticed. In a civil action, the judicially noticed fact is conclusively established and binds the jury, whereas in a criminal case, a jury ultimately has the freedom to find that an adjudicative fact has not been established notwithstanding judicial notice by the trial court.

[For more information on judicial notice of adjudicative facts, see Casenote Law Outline on Evidence, Chapter 3, § II, Judicial Notice of Adjudicative Facts.]

NOTES:

CLAYTON v. RIMMER
N.C. Sup. Ct., 262 N.C. 302, 136 S.E.2d 562 (1964).

NATURE OF CASE: Appeal from denial of nonsuit in personal injury action.

FACT SUMMARY: Clayton (P), whose automobile collided with Rimmer's (D), relied solely on evidence of Rimmer's (D) 126-foot skid marks leading to the point of impact and marks past that point as probative of Rimmer's (D) excessive speed.

CONCISE RULE OF LAW: A motion for nonsuit should be granted where the evidence proffered does not support the inference suggested of the defendant's liability.

FACTS: Clayton (P) was negotiating a left turn onto a road upon which Rimmer (D) was traveling north. Skid marks 126 feet in length were present leading to the point of impact, and scuff marks appeared past the point where the debris from the accident was scattered. From this evidence, Clayton (P) sought to establish that Rimmer (D) was traveling in excess of the 55-mile-per-hour speed limit. Rimmer (D) moved for nonsuit, but the trial court denied the motion, finding that 211 feet of stopping time is required of a car traveling at 50 miles per hour according to a text on driving. The figure of 211 feet included 55 feet of reaction time and 156 feet of braking time. Rimmer (D) appealed.

ISSUE: Should a motion for nonsuit be granted where the evidence proffered does not support the inference suggested of the defendant's liability?

HOLDING AND DECISION: (Per curiam) Yes. Neither Clayton (P) nor his wife saw the Rimmer (D) vehicle as it approached them; the only evidence of Rimmer's (D) speeding is the testimony regarding the skid marks. The evidence does not support an inference that Rimmer (D) was speeding in light of the ordinary stopping time of 211 feet for a car traveling at 50 miles per hour. A motion for nonsuit should be granted where the evidence proffered does not support the inference suggested of the defendant's liability. Reversed.

EDITOR'S ANALYSIS: The court took judicial notice of the "ordinary" stopping time from a text which was supported as accurate by foundational evidence, but which was published by the state motor vehicle department. While the court may not have properly assessed the meaning of stopping time set forth in relation to the skid marks actually present, judicial notice may be taken of works not offered in evidence and not supported by foundational evidence of its accuracy if considered reliable.

[For more information on proffered evidence, see Casenote Law Outline on Evidence, Chapter 5, § II, Preliminary Questions of Fact.]

NOTES:

HUGHES v. VESTAL
N.C. Sup. Ct. 264 N.C. 500, 142 S.E.2d 361 (1965).

NATURE OF CASE: Appeal from denial of damages for negligence.

FACT SUMMARY: Vestal (D) introduced a chart depicting average stopping distances at various speeds taken from the state motor vehicle department handbook as evidence that Hughes (P) was contributorily negligent in causing an automobile accident between the parties by speeding.

CONCISE RULE OF LAW: An unauthenticated written source reciting overages of results from various experiments is inadmissible as either expert opinion or as evidence of an experiment when used to establish the circumstances of a particular event or fact in issue.

FACTS: Hughes (P) brought an action for personal injuries resulting from an automobile accident between himself and Vestal (D), alleging Vestal's (D) negligence in improperly parking his vehicle on a thoroughfare. Vestal (D) countered with an allegation of contributory negligence on Hughes' (P) part by speeding. To show the speed of the Hughes (P) vehicle, Vestal (D) introduced a chart appearing in the back of the state motor vehicle department handbook reporting average stopping distances at various speeds determined by various experiments and tests. Hughes' (P) objections to this evidence as unauthenticated and inadmissible were overruled and the jury found Hughes (P) contributorily negligent, precluding recovery. Hughes (P) appealed.

ISSUE: Is an unauthenticated written source reciting averages of results from various experiments admissible either as expert opinion or as evidence of an experiment when used to establish the circumstances of a particular fact or event in issue?

HOLDING AND DECISION: (Moore, J.) No. No foundation was laid for the chart introduced as it was not identified, authenticated, or verified by any recognized method. An "experiment" for purposes of the law of evidence involves the reenactment of the occurrence under substantially similar circumstances and is introduced with testimony of the experimenter. Expert opinion as to a matter may be introduced in the form of the expert's testimony with respect to the specific matter under scrutiny. An unauthenticated written source reciting the averages of results from various experiments is inadmissible, however, either as an expert opinion or as evidence of an experiment when used to establish the circumstances of a particular fact or event in issue. In effect the trial judge took judicial notice of the manual from which the chart came. This was improper. While the work would so qualify for notice as to probable stopping distances within certain limits, it cannot establish precise stopping distances in particular cases. Such a work can be referred to or judicially noticed for illustrative purposes, but it cannot be used as controlling or even as a significant collateral basis for a determination. New trial ordered.

EDITOR'S ANALYSIS: The chart was here offered in evidence, but the court accepted it for purposes most akin to judicial notice. The extent of the use of the information in determining the fact in issue is important to the propriety of judicial notice of it. Clayton v. Rimmer seems to be distinguished because the same chart was only used to "illustrate" that Clayton had failed to adequately demonstrate that Rimmer was speeding by the sole evidence of skid marks. The distinction may often be elusive.

[For more information on authentication of a writing, see Casenote Law Outline on Evidence, Chapter 13, § II, Authentication of Documents.]

NOTES:

POTTS v. COE
145 F.2d 27 (D.C. 1944).

NATURE OF CASE: Motion to vacate dismissal of suit to compel patent registration.

FACT SUMMARY: The court of appeals affirmed a district court dismissal of a suit to compel registration of a patent, which had been assigned to Teletype Corporation, based on judicial notice of the type of enterprise engaged in by Teletype as being a gradual step-by-step development (as opposed to innovation) not entitled to patent protection.

CONCISE RULE OF LAW: A court may take judicial notice of information illustrating the character of a process or event giving rise to a claim.

FACTS: Coe (D), Commissioner of Patents, denied registration of a patent for an automatic stock quotation board. Potts (P), a nominal plaintiff, allegedly invented the board and assigned his right to patent it to Teletype Corporation, which claimed the patent. The district court dismissed a suit to compel registration, and the court of appeals affirmed on the ground that Teletype's method of research and development was a step-by-step process rather than an invention or innovation and was therefore ineligible for patent protection. The court took judicial notice of congressional hearings on the relationship of corporate research in general to the law of patents. Potts (P) and Teletype moved to vacate the affirming opinion on the ground that such judicial notice constituted raising and deciding an issue not presented by the record.

ISSUE: May a court take judicial notice of information illustrating the character of a process or event giving rise to a claim?

HOLDING AND DECISION: (Arnold, J.) Yes. Patent protection is not afforded to a device developed through the step-by-step progress of scientific or technical knowledge. Corporations often take assignments of patent rights from individuals in their employ to satisfy the requirement that there be an individual inventor of a device in question. Thus, what may seem to be a startling innovation may actually be the result of a gradual advance in technology. The process used by corporations such as Teletype of developing devices over long periods and then crediting their "invention" to an employee who assigns his patent claim by contract was the subject of congressional hearings. The court used the hearings to illustrate what was obvious in their absence regarding corporate research and patent law. A court may take judicial notice of information illustrating the character of a process or event giving rise to a claim. It appears that the reason for this motion is not really the use of judicial notice but the application of the law in a manner unacceptable to Teletype. However expensive step-by-step scientific development may be, the results of it are not protected by patent law. Motion denied.

EDITOR'S ANALYSIS: For judicial notice purposes, "legislative facts" include information helpful in determining what is the law and/or the rationale behind it. Legislative facts need not be indisputable to be noticed. "Adjudicative facts" are those relating to the dispute between the parties at bar and typically will not be noticed if there is any real chance that the court could be wrong in assuming them true.

[For more information on judicial notice, see Casenote Law Outline on Evidence, Chapter 3, § II, Judicial Notice of Adjudicative Facts.]

NOTES:

CHAPTER 10
REAL AND DEMONSTRATIVE EVIDENCE

QUICK REFERENCE RULES OF LAW

1. **Demonstrative Evidence.** Court permission to use demonstrative evidence constitutes reversible error only where such evidence is used for dramatic effect or emotional appeal rather than to aid the reasoning of the jury. (Smith v. Ohio Oil Co.)

   [For more information on demonstrative evidence, see Casenote Law Outline on Evidence, Chapter 2, § VI, Precedential Relevance.]

2. **Preliminary Facts.** The admission as evidence of an instrumentality alleged to have caused an injury must be predicated upon a foundational showing that the object is what it purports to be and that it is in a condition reasonably the same as when it allegedly caused the injury. (Gallagher v. Pequot Spring Water Co.)

   [For more information on preliminary facts, see Casenote Law Outline on Evidence, Chapter 5, § II, Preliminary Questions of Fact.]

3. **Precedential Evidence.** The admission of evidence regarding an instrumentality allegedly involved in an injury must be predicated upon a foundational showing that the evidence relates to the actual object in question in substantially the same condition as when the alleged injury occurred. (Semet v. Andorra Nurseries, Inc.)

   [For more information on precedential evidence, see Casenote Law Outline on Evidence, Chapter 2, § VI, Precedential Relevance.]

4. **Demonstrative Evidence.** Videotaped reenactments are admissible if they portray facts shown by sworn testimony. (Clark v. St. Thomas Hospital)

   [For more information on demonstrative evidence, see Casenote Law Outline on Evidence, Chapter 2, § VI, Precedential Relevance.]

5. **Authentication by Chain of Custody.** Photographic evidence is admissible so long as the trial court, in its discretion, finds sufficient foundational evidence to indicate the evidence is what its proponent says it is. (Fisher v. State)

   [For more information on authentication by chain of custody, see Casenote Law Outline on Evidence, Chapter 13, § III, Authentication of Objects.]

6. **Discretionary Exclusion of Evidence.** In order for a photograph to be admitted into evidence, it must be material and relevant. (Evansville School Corp. v. Price)

   [For more information on discretionary exclusion of evidence, see Casenote Law Outline on Evidence, Chapter 2, § V, Discretionary Exclusion of Relevant Evidence.]

7. **In-court Demonstration of Injured Plaintiff.** An in-court demonstration of an injured plaintiff conducted by a testifying witness or by counsel is permissible in the measurable discretion of the trial court. (Ensor v. Wilson)

8. **Jury Viewing.** A jury viewing is not evidence; it is a vehicle to allow the digestion of competent evidence. (McDowell v. Schuette)

9. **Jury Misconduct.** Jury misconduct which results in prejudice to a litigant and impairs his right to a fair and impartial trial requires a new trial. (George C. Christopher & Son, Inc. v. Kansas Paint & Color Co., Inc.)

NOTES

SMITH v. OHIO OIL CO.
Ill. App. Ct., 10 Ill. App. 2d 67, 134 N.E.2d 526 (1956).

NATURE OF CASE: Appeal from award of damages for personal injuries.

FACT SUMMARY: Smith (P) brought an action for personal injuries sustained in an automobile accident against Ohio (D) and during presentation of medical evidence, used a skeleton as demonstrative of the witness' explanations.

CONCISE RULE OF LAW: Court permission to use demonstrative evidence constitutes reversible error only where such evidence is used for dramatic effect or emotional appeal rather than to aid the reasoning of the jury.

FACTS: Smith (P) brought an action for personal injuries against Ohio (D) after an automobile accident in which one of Ohio's (D) trucks struck the Smith (P) vehicle. During presentation of medical evidence as to Smith's (P) injuries, the medical witness used a human skeleton to aid in his explanations. The jury awarded a verdict of $50,000, and Ohio (D) appealed, alleging that the gruesome nature of the skeleton rendered its use as demonstrative evidence improper.

ISSUE: Does court permission to use demonstrative evidence constitute reversible error only where such evidence is used for dramatic effect or emotional appeal rather than to aid the reasoning of the jury?

HOLDING AND DECISION: (Scheineman, J.) Yes. Demonstrative evidence, such as models, maps, photographs and X rays, has no probative value in and of itself. It merely serves as a visual aid to the jury in comprehending the testimony of a witness. It must be relevant and actually explanatory. The use of such demonstrative evidence may be permitted within the discretion of the court. However, court permission to use demonstrative evidence constitutes reversible error where such evidence is used for dramatic effect or emotional appeal rather than to aid the reasoning of the jury. Here, the medical witness made only limited use of the skeleton where useful in explaining pelvic injuries and other esoteric physiological matters. The mere allegation of the skeleton's being "gruesome" is not sufficient to establish that dramatic effect or emotional appeal was the reason for the use of the evidence. Affirmed.

EDITOR'S ANALYSIS: As scientific advances cause proofs at trial to become increasingly more technical, the importance of demonstrative evidence is augmented. Whether classified as "demonstrative" or "real," evidence that would result in prejudice, confusion, or a waste of time can be excluded though relevant. See Federal Rules of Evidence, Rule 403.

[For more information on demonstrative evidence, see Casenote Law Outline on Evidence, Chapter 2, § VI, Precedential Relevance.]

NOTES:

GALLAGHER v. PEQUOT SPRING WATER CO.
Conn. Cir. Ct., 2 Conn. Cir. 354, 199 A.2d 172 (1963).

NATURE OF CASE: Appeal of award of damages for personal injuries.

FACT SUMMARY: At trial, 18 months after Gallagher's (P) father poured some of Pequot's (D) grape soda into a glass allegedly discovering a foreign substance therein, Gallagher (P) produced the bottle containing an unidentified substance which was admitted into evidence.

CONCISE RULE OF LAW: The admission as evidence of an instrumentality alleged to have caused an injury must be predicated upon a foundational showing that the object is what it purports to be and that it is in a condition reasonably the same as when it allegedly caused the injury.

FACTS: During Gallagher's (P) wedding reception, her father poured some of Pequot's (D) grape soda into her glass. A foreign substance was allegedly thereupon discovered, described variously as a bloodsucker or a cockroach. Gallagher (P) brought an action for personal injuries due to sickness caused by the incident. At trial, 18 months later, Gallagher (P) produced what her witness claimed was the bottle in question, filled with a substance which neither the witness nor other evidence identified. Over objection, the bottle was admitted, and the jury awarded $2,500 in damages, which the court remitted to $1,000. Pequot (D) appealed, assigning error to the admission of the bottle without a proper foundation.

ISSUE: Must the admission as evidence of an instrumentality alleged to have caused an injury be predicated upon a foundational showing that the object is what it purports to be and that it is in a condition reasonably the same as when it allegedly caused the injury?

HOLDING AND DECISION: (Kosicki, J.) Yes. Ordinarily, the admission of an object as evidence requires only a foundation based upon the identification of it by a witness with sufficient knowledge of what it is. However, in this case the evidence was not offered to identify the bottle from which the objectionable material came, but as real evidence of what substance was in the bottle. The substance and not the bottle allegedly caused the injury. The substance was not identified by any evidence or testimony, but the bottle and the substance were admitted over objection. The trial was long after the incident, and no assertion was made that the substance had not changed since then. The admission as evidence of an instrumentality alleged to have caused an injury must be predicated upon a foundational showing that the object is what it purports to be and that it is in a condition reasonably the same as when it allegedly caused the injury. Sufficient foundation was not here laid. Judgment set aside; new trial ordered.

EDITOR'S ANALYSIS: Where there is a logical possibility that a tangible object offered as "real" evidence (i.e., something that was itself involved in the transaction or occurrence under scrutiny) has changed or is not the actual object it is alleged to be, a foundation must be laid establishing identity and substantial similarity of condition. "Demonstrative" evidence need only be asserted by a testifying witness to fairly represent a matter within his personal knowledge about which he is testifying.

[For more information on preliminary facts, see Casenote Law Outline on Evidence, Chapter 5, § II, Preliminary Questions of Fact.]

NOTES:

SEMET v. ANDORRA NURSERIES, INC.
Pa. Sup. Ct., 421 Pa. 484, 219 A.2d 357 (1966).

NATURE OF CASE: Appeal from nonsuit in personal injury action.

FACT SUMMARY: Semet (P) sought to introduce testimony and photographs regarding a ladder from which he fell though neither his witness nor other evidence could establish that the ladder examined and photographed was the same one as was involved in the accident.

CONCISE RULE OF LAW: The admission of evidence regarding an instrumentality allegedly involved in an injury must be predicated upon a foundational showing that the evidence relates to the actual object in question in substantially the same condition as when the alleged injury occurred.

FACTS: Semet (P) was stringing electrical wiring and ordered an Andorra (D) employee to secure a ladder against the side of the house for Semet (P) to climb. The employee did so and himself climbed and descended the ladder without incident, whereupon Semet (P) climbed the ladder and fell, sustaining injuries. At trial for the personal injuries, Semet (P) offered the testimony of an expert witness who had discovered a ladder through inquiring of unnamed Andorra (D) employees and then tested and photographed the ladder to which he was directed. The testimony and the photographs were not admitted on the ground that there had been no showing that the ladder examined and photographed was the one from which Semet (P) had fallen. A judgment of nonsuit was entered, and Semet (P) appealed the affirmation of the judgment.

ISSUE: Must the admission of evidence regarding an instrumentality allegedly involved in an injury be predicated upon a foundational showing that the evidence relates to the actual object in question in substantially the same condition as when the alleged injury occurred?

HOLDING AND DECISION: (Bell, J.) Yes. Semet (P) sought to introduce expert testimony for the purpose of explaining the mechanical function of the ladder and the reasons for its collapse. His expert, however, was directed to a ladder by persons unknown, who, though they were Andorra (D) employees, were not shown to have personal knowledge as to whether the ladder shown to the expert was the one from which Semet (P) had fallen. The testimony and photographs were therefore properly excluded. The admission of evidence regarding an instrumentality allegedly involved in an injury must be predicated upon a foundational showing that the evidence relates to the actual object in question in substantially the same condition as when the alleged injury occurred. Affirmed.

EDITOR'S ANALYSIS: Tests and experiments may be conducted and their results admitted into evidence even where the actual objects involved in the incident in question are not used. However, in those cases, the expert witness will be testifying that his experiments or tests were performed under substantially similar circumstances in all material respects. Pursuant to such testimony, objects introduced into evidence will be merely "demonstrative," and must only be alleged to fairly represent what the experimenter knows. If tests of what is alleged to be the actual object involved are offered, the foundation of identity and substantial similarity of condition of the object is required, as this is "real" evidence of what happened.

_____

[For more information on precedential evidence, see Casenote Law Outline on Evidence, Chapter 2, § VI, Precedential Relevance.]

NOTES:

CLARK v. ST. THOMAS HOSPITAL
Tenn. Ct. App., 676 S.W.2d 347 (1984).

NATURE OF CASE: Appeal from denial of damages for personal injuries.

FACT SUMMARY: Clark (P) contended that a videotaped reenactment of his accident portraying the Hospital's (D) version was inadmissible.

CONCISE RULE OF LAW: Videotaped reenactments are admissible if they portray facts shown by sworn testimony.

FACTS: Clark (P) slipped and fell while a patient at St. Thomas (Hospital) (D). The Hospital (D) contended that he was laid down on the ground after his knees buckled. They produced a videotaped reenactment of this version based upon the testimony of a Hospital (D) employee who witnessed the accident. Clark (P) appealed the adverse jury verdict on the basis that the tape was inadmissible.

ISSUE: Are videotaped reenactments admissible if based on sworn testimony?

HOLDING AND DECISION: (Todd, J.) Yes. Videotaped reenactments are admissible if based upon sworn testimony. Demonstrative evidence including reenactments are common. So long as the tape reasonably reflects the testimony, it is admissible. Improper portions, those not based on the testimony, are inadmissible. Thus, the verdict was correct. Affirmed.

EDITOR'S ANALYSIS: Videotape is merely a technological change in the presentation of evidence. The core evidence is the testimony. The tape is no different in kind from a model or other exhibit. The trial court does, as with all demonstrative evidence, have discretion to disallow it.

[For more information on demonstrative evidence, see Casenote Law Outline on Evidence, Chapter 2, § VI, Precedential Relevance.]

NOTES:

FISHER v. STATE
Ark. Ct. App., 7 Ark. App. 1, 643 S.W.2d 571 (1982).

NATURE OF CASE: Appeal from conviction for theft.

FACT SUMMARY: Fisher (D) contended videotape of her theft was inadmissible because the State (P) failed to authenticate it sufficiently to satisfy the foundational requirements.

CONCISE RULE OF LAW: Photographic evidence is admissible so long as the trial court, in its discretion, finds sufficient foundational evidence to indicate the evidence is what its proponent says it is.

FACTS: Fisher (D) was charged with theft and at trial a videotape of her actions was offered. The operator of the machine could not testify as to the foundation for the substance of the acts depicted, however, he testified as to the proper functioning of the camera and equipment and of the chain of possession of the evidence. Fisher (D) was convicted and appealed contending no proper foundation for the tape was offered, rendering it inadmissible.

ISSUE: Is photographic evidence admissible upon a foundational showing of adequate authentication?

HOLDING AND DECISION: (Cooper, J.) Yes. Photographic evidence is admissible so long as the trial court, in its discretion, finds sufficient foundational evidence to authenticate it. In this case, the trial court found that testimony concerning the proper functioning of the equipment and the chain of possession established the foundational requirement of authentication. It cannot be said that this finding was an abuse of discretion. The tape can be used as substantive evidence of guilt. Affirmed.

EDITOR'S ANALYSIS: The court identified two bases for authentication of pictorial evidence. The first instance involves pictorial evidence which merely depicts events based upon sworn testimony. The second involves the use of the pictorial evidence as probative in and of itself. The latter type was presented in this case. Photographic evidence of any type, whether videotape or ordinary photographs, are treated as writings under the evidence rules of most jurisdictions.

[For more information on authentication by chain of custody, see Casenote Law Outline on Evidence, Chapter 13, § III, Authentication of Objects.]

EVANSVILLE SCHOOL CORP. v. PRICE
Ind. App. Ct., 138 Ind. App. 268, 208 N.E.2d 689 (1965).

NATURE OF CASE: Appeal from award of damages for wrongful death.

FACT SUMMARY: Evansville (D) contended that the trial court erred in allowing a photograph of the deceased child in his coffin to be introduced into evidence.

CONCISE RULE OF LAW: In order for a photograph to be admitted into evidence, it must be material and relevant.

FACTS: Alfred Price (P), the father of the deceased Alfred Lee Price, instituted a wrongful death action against Evansville (D) to recover damages for the death of his son, which occurred when he was struck on the head with a baseball while attending a baseball game. At the trial, Price (P) offered in evidence a color photograph of the deceased youth lying in his casket, after preparation by a mortician, and prior to internment. The photograph was not gruesome, nor did it depict any physical markings, wounds, defects, or other bodily abnormalities. Evansville (D) objected to the introduction of the photograph on the grounds that there was no triable issue as to the fact or cause of death, that the photograph was inflammatory, and that it was not material to any issue involved in the case. Price (P) alleged that the photograph was being offered into evidence to show the physical characteristics of the boy and to corroborate testimony that the boy was a "nice looking and healthy chap." After the photograph was admitted into evidence, the jury returned a verdict for Price (P), and Evansville (D) appealed, renewing its objection below to the introduction of the photograph.

ISSUE: In order for a photograph to be admitted into evidence, must it be material and relevant?

HOLDING AND DECISION: (Prime, J.) Yes. In order for a photograph to be admissible in evidence, it must first be accepted by the trial court as material and relevant, and must tend to prove or disprove some material fact in issue. The admission or rejection of photographs in evidence lies largely within the discretion of the trial court and will not be disturbed unless an abuse of discretion is shown to have occurred. Relevancy is determined by an inquiry into whether or not a witness would be permitted to describe the objects photographed. The fact that a photograph might arouse the passions of the jury and prejudice them against one of the parties is not a sufficient ground to justify its exclusion if the photograph is material and relevant. Here, it appears that the only legitimate purpose for admitting the photograph would have been to establish the fact of death, and this fact was admitted in the pleadings. Thus, the photograph should not have been admitted into evidence, and the trial court abused its discretion in permitting it to be admitted and exhibited to the jury. Reversed and remanded.

EDITOR'S ANALYSIS: As a general rule, a photograph that is entirely irrelevant and immaterial to any issue in the case and which might divert the minds of the jury to improper or irrelevant considerations should be excluded from evidence. Occasionally, a picture taken before death will be admissible as being relevant to the issue of damages in an action for wrongful death.

[For more information on discretionary exclusion of evidence, see Casenote Law Outline on Evidence, Chapter 2, § V, Discretionary Exclusion of Relevant Evidence.]

NOTES:

ENSOR v. WILSON
519 So.2d 1244 (1987).

NATURE OF CASE: Appeal from plaintiff's verdict in a medical malpractice action.

FACT SUMMARY: Ensor (D), a physician, objected to an in-court demonstration by Misty (P), a mentally retarded child who was suing him for malpractice, in which she exhibited her physical and mental limitations to the jury.

CONCISE RULE OF LAW: An in-court demonstration of an injured plaintiff conducted by a testifying witness or by counsel is permissible in the measurable discretion of the trial court.

FACTS: Ensor (D), a physician, was sued for medical malpractice by Misty Wilson (P), a child who was born prematurely and suffered from brain damage and retardation. At trial, the court allowed an in-court demonstration between Misty (P) and a special education therapist, showing Misty's (P) physical and mental abilities and limitations. The jury returned a verdict of $2.5 million for Misty (P). Ensor (D) appealed. On appeal, Ensor (D) claimed the demonstration put him at an unwarranted and unjust disadvantage. Ensor (D) complained that there was no opportunity to cross-examine Misty (P), she was not placed under oath, she was not competent to testify, and there were no adequate means for preserving, for appeals purposes, the effect the demonstration had on the jury.

ISSUE: Is an in-court demonstration of an injured plaintiff permissible in the measurable discretion of the trial court?

HOLDING AND DECISION: (Beatty, J.) Yes. An in-court demonstration of an injured plaintiff is permissible in the measurable discretion of the trial court. Here, the special education therapist who conducted the demonstration was sworn as a witness and was subjected to a searching cross-examination. It is also clear that Misty's (P) cognitive, as well as physical, ability was in issue on the matter of damages. Under the control of the trial judge, the demonstration here was not different in theory and practice from the relevant exhibition of wounds, movement, etc., whether by the witness himself or through the use of photographs. It would, after all, be difficult to exhibit cognition without a demonstration of vocal expression, physical response, and so on. Therefore, it was not erroneous to have such a demonstration guided by a witness skilled in ascertaining such relevant responses and explaining their meaning. In any event, the accuracy of such demonstrations should be tested by the requirement of relevancy, and such a demonstration should not be allowed when its probative worth is exceeded by its capacity for prejudice. In this case, there was no abuse in the trial court's permitting the demonstration. Affirmed.

EDITOR'S ANALYSIS: In Ensor, the Supreme Court of Alabama referred to an Ohio case in which the court had approved the demonstration in open court of an infant who allegedly had suffered brain damage. In that case, Heidbreder v. Northampton Township Trustees, 411 N.E.2d 825 (1979), the infant remained outside the courtroom during the entire trial except for the period of demonstration. He was brought before the jury only to show the extent of his motor paralysis and ability to communicate and do simple tasks. This evidence was relevant to the issue of damages and peripherally so to the liability issue. Prior to the demonstration, an in camera hearing was held and the proposed demonstration enacted for the trial court. The court found specifically that the evidentiary value of the appearance would not be outweighed by its prejudicial effect.

NOTES:

McDOWELL v. SCHUETTE
Mo. Ct. App., 610 S.W.2d 29 (1980).

NATURE OF CASE: Appeal from award of damages for breach of contract.

FACT SUMMARY: Schuette (D) contended the trial court erred in allowing the jury to view the house containing the disputed work, contending such viewing was improper lay evidence of the condition of the structure.

CONCISE RULE OF LAW: A jury viewing is not evidence; it is a vehicle to allow the digestion of competent evidence.

FACTS: Schuette (D) contracted with the McDowells (P) for the latter to construct a house. The McDowells (P) sued to recover payment for their work, and Schuette (D) countersued, contending the house was not constructed properly. The court allowed the jury to inspect the house, under strong cautionary directions concerning deliberating prematurely. A verdict for the McDowells (P) was returned, and Schuette (D) appealed. He contended that the jury view constituted the use of improper lay evidence.

ISSUE: Is a jury view of the situs of the pertinent act evidence?

HOLDING AND DECISION: (Stewart, J.) No. A jury view is not evidence. It is a vehicle of demonstration which allows the jury to better understand the actual evidence presented. It must be used as a supplement to otherwise competent evidence. The use of a viewing is within the discretion of the court. No abuse of discretion occurred here, thus the verdict must stand. Affirmed.

EDITOR'S ANALYSIS: This rule is not universally accepted. Many jurisdictions do consider a jury view to be the presentation of evidence. Many commentators are of the opinion that considering a jury view to be evidence is the preferable approach. Many problems arise in a jury view due to the difficulty in sheltering inadmissible evidence, however, it is a helpful tool in a complex case.

NOTES:

GEO. C. CHRISTOPHER & SON, INC. v. KANSAS PAINT & COLOR CO., INC.

Kan. Sup. Ct., 215 Kan. 185, 523 P.2d 709 (1974).

NATURE OF CASE: Appeal from award of damages for breach of implied warranty.

FACT SUMMARY: Kansas (D) contended that the jury erred in inspecting paint samples which had been introduced into evidence.

CONCISE RULE OF LAW: Jury misconduct which results in prejudice to a litigant and impairs his right to a fair and impartial trial requires a new trial.

FACTS: Christopher (P) sued Kansas (D) for breach of an implied warranty to furnish a suitable paint to prime steel. The jury found for Christopher (P), and, in support of its motion for a new trial, Kansas (D) filed the affidavit of one of its attorneys stating that he had conferred with several jury members following the verdict and that the foreman of the jury had performed certain tests on a paint sample panel submitted as evidence. The foreman scraped paint from Christopher's (P) exhibit with a pocket knife and discussed these results with the jury, but did not perform tests on any of Kansas' (D) exhibits. The affidavit contended that the jurors admitted that those tests were influential factors in their decision for Christopher (P). The trial court denied the motion for new trial saying the facts stated in the affidavit were insufficient grounds upon which to order a new trial, and Kansas (D) then brought this appeal on the same grounds.

ISSUE: Does misconduct of the jury which results in prejudice to a litigant and impairs his right to a fair and impartial trial require a new trial?

HOLDING AND DECISION: (Owsley, J.) Yes. Misconduct of jurors per se does not necessitate a new trial, but misconduct which results in prejudice to a litigant and impairs his right to a fair and impartial trial requires a new trial. It is for the trial court to determine whether misconduct on the part of the jury has resulted in prejudice to a litigant, and its judgment on that issue will not be overturned unless abuse of discretion is manifest. Litigants have a right to expect that with respect to evidence, juries will confine themselves to the evidence introduced, and that members of a jury will not engage in any extracurricular activities. Here, the jurors duplicated tests performed in the courtroom on exhibits sent with them to the jury room. The object of sending exhibits to the jury is to enable the jurors to make a more thorough examination of them than was possible when the exhibits were offered in evidence. The salient question is whether the experiment or investigation made by the jury out of the presence of the parties, and while they were deliberating, can be said to be within the scope or purview of the evidence introduced at trial, or whether it amounts to the taking of evidence outside the presence of the parties. Here, the exhibit was before the jury, and it was permissible to take it to the jury room and examine it for the purpose of testing the validity of statements made in open court with respect to it. Affirmed.

EDITOR'S ANALYSIS: The majority view in most American jurisdictions supports the sending of formally offered and admitted tangible exhibits along with the jury when it retires, subject in some jurisdictions to some discretionary control of the practice by the trial court. This case illustrates one of the uses to which exhibits may properly be put by a jury.

NOTES:

CHAPTER 11
WRITINGS AND RELATED MATTERS

QUICK REFERENCE RULES OF LAW

1. **Authentication of a Writing.** A writing must be authenticated in some manner before it will be admitted into evidence. (City of Randleman v. Hinshaw)

   [For more information on the authentication of a writing, see Casenote Law Outline on Evidence, Chapter 13, § II, Authentication of Documents.]

2. **Authentication of Handwriting.** A handwriting may be proved by a witness' show of familiarity with it. (Buckingham Corp. v. Ewing Liquors Co.)

   [For more information on the authentication of handwriting, see Casenote Law Outline on Evidence, Chapter 13, § II, Authentication of Documents.]

3. **Authentication of Documents.** Only a prima facie case of an alleged author's identity must be established in order for documents to be admitted. (United States v. American Radiator & Standard Sanitary Corp.)

   [For more information on the authentication of documents, see Casenote Law Outline on Evidence, Chapter 13, § II, Authentication of Documents.]

4. **Authentication of a Writing.** Authorship of writings may be shown by circumstantial evidence. (United States v. Sutton)

   [For more information on the authentication of a writing, see Casenote Law Outline on Evidence, Chapter 13, § II, Authentication of Documents.]

5. **Authentication of a Phone Conversation.** Authentication of a phone conversation may be achieved if the surrounding circumstances indicate to the court that it is improbable anyone other than the purported participants were involved. (People v. Lynes)

   [For more information on the authentication of a phone conversation, see Casenote Law Outline on Evidence, Chapter 13, § IV, Authentication of Voices.]

6. **Authentication of Ancient Documents.** Writings purporting to be 30 years or more old, if relevant to the inquiry, are admissible in evidence without proof of execution or handwriting. (Town of Ninety Six v. Southern Ry. Co.)

   [For more information on the authentication of ancient documents, see Casenote Law Outline on Evidence, Chapter 13, § II, Authentication of Documents.]

7. **Chain-of-Custody.** Proper authentication of a document requires testimony from personal knowledge concerning how the custodian came into possession of the document. (State v. Day)

   [For more information on the chain-of-custody, see Casenote Law Outline on Evidence, Chapter 13, § III, Authentication of Objects.]

8. **Best Evidence Rule.** The best evidence rule covers writings and provides that the original writing must be produced unless it is shown to be unavailable for some reason other than the serious fault of the proponent. (United States v. Duffy)

   [For more information on the best evidence rule, see Casenote Law Outline on Evidence, Chapter 14, § I, The Best Evidence Rule Stated.]

9. **The Best Evidence Rule.** The best evidence rule is limited to cases where the contents of a writing are to be proved. (Meyers v. United States)

   [For more information on the best evidence rule, see Casenote Law Outline on Evidence, Chapter 14, § I, The Best Evidence Rule Stated.]

10. **The Best Evidence Rule.** Testimony concerning whether a record does not contain certain entries is admissible and not violative of the best evidence rule. (State v. Nano)

    [For more information on the use of the best evidence rule, see Casenote Law Outline on Evidence, Chapter 14, § III, "To Prove the Content of a Writing".]

11. **Admissibility of Copies.** A photostatic copy of a document is admissible as the original, unless a genuine issue of authenticity is raised. (Wilson v. State)

    [For more information on the admissibility of copies, see Casenote Law Outline on Evidence, Chapter 14, § II, Definitions.]

12. **Voluminous Writings.** Summary charts based upon previously admitted evidence are admissible. (United States v. Stephens)

    [For more information on voluminous writings, see Casenote Law Outline on Evidence, Chapter 14, § IV, Absence of Originals Excused.]

13. **Scope of the Best Evidence Rule.** Pictures and nonverbal facsimiles are writings and are covered by the best evidence rule. (Seiler v. Lucasfilm)

    [For more information on the scope of the best evidence rule, see Casenote Law Outline on Evidence, Chapter 14, § I, The Best Evidence Rule Stated.]

14. **Secondary Evidence.** There are no degrees of secondary evidence. (Doe D. Gilbert v. Ross)

    [For more information on secondary evidence, see Casenote Law Outline on Evidence, Chapter 14, § V, The "Second Best" Evidence Rule.]

CITY OF RANDLEMAN v. HINSHAW
N.C. App. Ct., 2 N.C. App. 381, 163 S.E.2d 95 (1968).

NATURE OF CASE: Appeal from judgment condemning an easement.

FACT SUMMARY: Hinshaw (D) contended that the trial court erred in allowing an unauthenticated document to be introduced into evidence.

CONCISE RULE OF LAW: A writing must be authenticated in some manner before it will be admitted into evidence.

FACTS: The City (P) brought a special proceeding to condemn an easement for water and sewer lines through Hinshaw's (D) property. All issues were stipulated except the issue of damages, upon which conflicting evidence was introduced. The City (P) maintained that Hinshaw's (D) property would be enhanced in value as a result of the installation of water and sewer lines onto which Hinshaw (D) would have the right to tap, but some question existed as to whether Hinshaw (D) would have such a right in view of the location of her property outside the city limits. The City (P) then offered in evidence a writing purporting to be an offer by the City (P) to allow Hinshaw (D) to tap onto the lines on payment of ordinary fees charged for the privilege. The writing was purportedly signed by the Mayor of the City (P) and attested by the City Secretary. However, the writing was introduced without any identification and read to the jury before the City (P) had presented oral testimony. Hinshaw (D), on appeal, sought a new trial on the grounds that the trial court erred in allowing this unauthenticated document to be introduced.

ISSUE: Must a writing be authenticated in some manner before it will be admitted into evidence?

HOLDING AND DECISION: (Britt, J.) Yes. Before any writing will be admitted in evidence, it must be authenticated in some manner, i.e., its genuineness or execution must be proved. Even a competent public record or document must be properly identified, verified, or authenticated by some recognized method before it may be introduced in evidence. The writing which is the subject of this appeal raises many questions, including the genuineness of the signatures of the Mayor and City Secretary, and whether those officials were authorized to sign such a document. Accordingly, the trial judge erred in introducing this evidence. New trial ordered.

EDITOR'S ANALYSIS: It is interesting to note that the court in this case did not appear to attribute any significance to the fact that the writing was acknowledged before a notary public. The notary's attestation is often used to provide evidence as to the genuineness of the signature of the purported signer of the document. This holding would seem to reflect a minority view regarding the significance of an acknowledgement executed by a notary public, which usually gives rise to a presumption of a valid signature.

[For more information on the authentication of a writing, see Casenote Law Outline on Evidence, Chapter 13, § II, Authentication of Documents.]

NOTES:

BUCKINGHAM CORP. v. EWING LIQUORS CO.
Ill. App. Ct., 15 Ill. App. 3d 839, 305 N.E.2d 278 (1973).

NATURE OF CASE: Appeal from issuance of permanent injunction.

FACT SUMMARY: Ewing (D) contended that Buckingham (P) had failed to prove the existence of a fair trade agreement, which was an essential element of its cause of action because a signature had not been properly authenticated.

CONCISE RULE OF LAW: A handwriting may be proved by a witness' show of familiarity with it.

FACTS: Ewing (D) appealed from an order granting Buckingham (P) a permanent injunction enjoining Ewing (D) from advertising, offering for sale or selling Buckingham's (P) products in Illinois at prices less than those stipulated by Buckingham (P) pursuant to a fair trade agreement. At the hearing, Buckingham (P) introduced evidence of a fair trade agreement between it and Ewing (D). Ted Herbik, a marketing director for Buckingham Distributors, was called as a witness and testified that he recognized the signature of William Gallagan, Buckingham's (P) vice-president, on the agreement. Herbik testified that he was familiar with Gallagan's signature because he had received correspondence from him in the past, although he had never actually seen Gallagan sign his name. On appeal, Ewing (D) contended that because the alleged agreement had not been properly authenticated, Buckingham (P) had failed to prove an essential element of its cause of action, the existence of a fair trade agreement.

ISSUE: May a handwriting be proved by a witness' show of familiarity with it?

HOLDING AND DECISION: (Stamos, J.) Yes. A handwriting may be proved by a witness' show of familiarity with it. This familiarity may be gained from having seen the party actually write or from having been acquainted with the handwriting in the course of business dealings. Ewing (D) contended that Buckingham (P) failed to adequately prove an essential element of its cause of action, the existence of a fair trade agreement. Ewing's (D) answer demanded strict proof of all allegations of Buckingham's (P) complaint, and one of Ewing's (D) affirmative defenses stated that Ewing (D) had no knowledge of Buckingham's (P) alleged fair trade agreement. Buckingham (P) was therefore required to prove the execution, existence, and authenticity of the agreement before it was admitted into evidence. Herbik's testimony was competent evidence of his knowledge of Gallagan's signature in addition to the testimony regarding his having seen the signature on correspondence in the regular course of business. This testimony was that Gallagan had told him that he had signed the agreement. Thus, Buckingham (P) adequately proved the execution of the fair trade agreement. However, because Buckingham (P) failed to adequately prove notice of the fair trade agreement to Ewing (D), the decision granting a permanent injunction must be reversed.

EDITOR'S ANALYSIS: In general, the identification of a signature by a lay witness is held to be sufficient for purpose of authentication.

The requirement that a witness be familiar with the purported author's writing has tended to be liberally interpreted. Familiarity with a writing based upon a single observation has often been held sufficient for authentication purposes.

[For more information on the authentication of handwriting, see Casenote Law Outline on Evidence, Chapter 13, § II, Authentication of Documents.]

NOTES:

UNITED STATES v. AMERICAN RADIATOR & STANDARD SANITARY CORP.

433 F.2d 174 (3d Cir. 1970);
cert. denied, 401 U.S. 948 (1971).

NATURE OF CASE: Appeal from convictions under the Sherman Antitrust Act.

FACT SUMMARY: Standard (D) contended that the trial court erred in admitting documents on which the handwriting had been identified by a nonexpert witness.

CONCISE RULE OF LAW: Only a prima facie case of an alleged author's identity must be established in order for documents to be admitted.

FACTS: Standard (D) was indicted for allegedly violating provisions of the Sherman Antitrust Act. The indictment charged, among other acts, that Standard (D) and other coconspirators had met at various conventions of the Plumbing Fixtures Manufacturers Association (PFMA) and entered into various specified illegal agreements, including one to discontinue the manufacture of regular enameled cast iron plumbing fixtures which were lower-priced than acid-resistant enameled cast iron plumbing fixtures. As evidence of the illegal agreement, the Government (P) offered a document which consisted of six pages of undated and unsigned notes on hotel stationery, which contained figures and statements on the plumbing items in question, and which were allegedly written by Raymond Pape, an official of the Crane Company, which had also been indicted. The Government (P) called a former secretary in Pape's department to make a lay handwriting identification. She testified that she had done work for Pape and was familiar with his handwriting. She identified the handwriting on four of the six pages as resembling Pape's, but could not identify the writing on the other two pages. The entire document was then introduced into evidence, and Standard (D) was convicted. On appeal, Standard (D) argued that the document was not identified with sufficient certainty.

ISSUE: Must only a prima facie case of an alleged author's identity be established in order for documents to be admitted?

HOLDING AND DECISION: (Seitz, J.) Yes. The weight of authority requires only that a prima facie case of the alleged author's identity be established for documents to be admitted. The ultimate issue of their authorship and the probative weight to be afforded them is for the jury. Because the requisite prima facie case as to the four pages identified by the secretary was established, the trial court did not abuse its discretion in admitting them. The jury was instructed that it could compare the two unauthenticated pages of the document with the other four pages in order to determine authorship. When documents are admitted for purposes other than handwriting comparison, they may be used by the jury as a standard for handwriting comparison if the handwriting is admitted or proved to be that of the alleged author. The vast weight of authority requires that the trial judge determine whether the genuineness of the handwriting on the documents to be used as the standard has been sufficiently proved. The evidence supplied by the secretary, in conjunction with the fact that the notes were subpoenaed from

Crane's PFMA file, were stapled together, and were internally consistent in content supports the jury's finding that the four pages were in Pape's hand and could be used as a handwriting standard. Affirmed.

EDITOR'S ANALYSIS: While most writings may be authenticated by the testimony of a witness who is sufficiently familiar with the handwriting of the alleged signatory, different rules have evolved for writings whose execution is required to be attested by witnesses. Federal Rule of Evidence 903 provides that: "The testimony of a subscribing witness is not necessary to authenticate a writing unless required by the laws of the jurisdiction whose laws govern the validity of the writing."

_____

[For more information on the authentication of documents, see Casenote Law Outline on Evidence, Chapter 13, § II, Authentication of Documents.]

NOTES:

UNITED STATES v. SUTTON
426 F.2d 1202 (D.C.Cir. 1969).

NATURE OF CASE: Appeal from conviction of first-degree murder.

FACT SUMMARY: Sutton (D) contended that the trial court erred in admitting into evidence four writings which, it was contended, were not properly authenticated.

CONCISE RULE OF LAW: Authorship of writings may be shown by circumstantial evidence.

FACTS: Sutton (D) was indicted for the shooting death of Matilda Glass. Beside Mrs. Glass's body was found an envelope which stated that it was "From Alexander Sutton" to his wife and daughter. Inside the envelope were three notes which were introduced into evidence. One note indicated troubles between the author and "Matilda." A second note identified "Arthur" as the party who carried "her home Sunday night." The third note, not made by the same author, was an amorous note from "Arthur" to an unnamed party. Another note, which had been removed from Sutton's (D) pocket, which referred to his wife, mother, and daughter, was also introduced into evidence at trial. All four notes were introduced into evidence over the objections of counsel for Sutton (D) that they had not been properly authenticated. Sutton (D) was convicted by the jury of first-degree murder and the unlicensed carrying of a dangerous weapon, and then brought this appeal, renewing his objection to the introduction of the four notes into evidence.

ISSUE: May authorship of writings be shown by circumstantial evidence?

HOLDING AND DECISION: (Robinson, J.) Yes. Ordinarily, the genuineness of documentary evidence must be shown independently before it can be accepted as proof. The mere contents of a written communication, purporting to be a particular person's, are not of themselves sufficient evidence of genuineness. However, authorship of writings may be shown by circumstantial evidence, among the components of which the contents of the writing may play a significant role. In special circumstances, where the contents reveal a knowledge or other trait peculiarly referable to a single person, the contents alone may suffice for purposes of authentication. Here, the evidence points to Sutton (D) as the author of three of the notes. The envelope bore the name of Sutton (D) as the addressor and designated three persons, all described as close relatives, as the intended addressees. One of the notes discussed intimate business and personal affairs which, if true, would have been peculiarly within Sutton's (D) knowledge. One of the writings contained a summary statement of the status of the writer's financial affairs, and the dispositions he desired of his worldly estate, naming Sutton's (D) relatives as the beneficiaries of those bequests. Accordingly, the disputed exhibits were properly accepted into evidence, and were entitled to such consideration as the jury was inclined to give them. Affirmed.

EDITOR'S ANALYSIS: The court in this case analogized the issue presented to it to cases permitting the introduction into evidence of writings found in the possession of an accused as exemplars for purposes of expert comparison with the handwriting of a disputed document. In those cases, the court found, many jurisdictions have sanctioned receipt of the exemplar when there were additional circumstances supporting its authenticity.

[For more information on the authentication of a writing, see Casenote Law Outline on Evidence, Chapter 13, § II, Authentication of Documents.]

NOTES:

PEOPLE v. LYNES
N.Y. Ct. App., 49 N.Y.2d 286, 401 N.E.2d 405 (1980).

NATURE OF CASE: Appeal from conviction for rape.

FACT SUMMARY: Lynes (D) appealed his conviction on the basis that testimony concerning an incriminating phone call lacked sufficient foundation to establish that he made the call and thus was inadmissible.

CONCISE RULE OF LAW: Authentication of a phone conversation may be achieved if the surrounding circumstances indicate to the court that it is improbable anyone other than the purported participants were involved.

FACTS: Lynes (D) was arrested for rape, burglary, and other crimes. The evidence against him consisted of the victim's identification and testimony by a police officer that two hours after leaving a message with Lynes' (D) brother, he received an incriminating phone call from Lynes (D). The caller identified himself as Lynes (D) and asked for this specific officer. Although the officer was unfamiliar with Lynes' (D) voice, the court allowed the testimony and Lynes (D) was convicted. He appealed, contending the testimony lacked sufficient authentication and did not established that he was the caller.

ISSUE: May authentication of a phone conversation be achieved without the direct identification of the participant's voice?

HOLDING AND DECISION: (Fuchsberg, J.) Yes. Authentication of a phone conversation may be achieved if the surrounding circumstances indicate to the court it is improbable that anyone other than the purported participants were involved. In this case, the caller called within hours of the officer's leaving his number with Lynes' (D) brother, requesting Lynes (D) call him. Also the caller asked for the detective by name, even though they had no prior contact. These elements were sufficient for the trial court in its discretion to allow in the testimony. Affirmed.

EDITOR'S ANALYSIS: In the usual case, telephone conversations are admitted based on authentication through familiarity with the voice. The witness simply testifies that he recognized the voice as that of the person it purports to be. This recognition may be based on familiarity gained either before or after the phone call occurred.

[For more information on the authentication of a phone conversation, see Casenote Law Outline on Evidence, Chapter 13, § IV, Authentication of Voices.]

STATE v. DAY
La. Sup. Ct., 410 So.2d 741 (1982).

NATURE OF CASE: Appeal from conviction for firearm possession.

FACT SUMMARY: The State (P) contended that a parole release certificate was properly authenticated by its custodian and properly received in evidence.

CONCISE RULE OF LAW: Proper authentication of a document requires testimony from personal knowledge concerning how the custodian came into possession of the document.

FACTS: Day (D) was charged with being a felon in possession of a firearm. At trial, the State (P) attempted to introduce Day's (D) certificate of discharge from parole into evidence. Testimony was given by the custodian to authenticate the document. No testimony was given concerning how the custodian came into possession of the certificate. Day (D) was convicted and appealed, contending the document was not properly authenticated.

ISSUE: Must a custodian of documents testify as to how he came into possession of the document in order to properly authenticate it?

HOLDING AND DECISION: (Gulotta, J.) Yes. A custodian of documents must testify as to how he came into possession of the document in order to properly authenticate it. Such testimony must be from personal knowledge. In this case, no such testimony was offered, and the custodian had no personal knowledge of the chain of possession. Thus the document was not properly authenticated and was inadmissible. Reversed.

EDITOR'S ANALYSIS: Day (D) petitioned for a rehearing, however, such was denied. The court, per curiam, reinforced the proposition that the person in charge of custody must testify as to the creation and preservation of the document. This ensures the document is what its proponent says it is.

[For more information on the chain-of-custody, see Casenote Law Outline on Evidence, Chapter 13, § III, Authentication of Objects.]

NOTES:

TOWN OF NINETY SIX v. SOUTHERN RY. CO.
267 F.2d 579 (4th Cir. 1959).

NATURE OF CASE: Enjoining construction of building.

FACT SUMMARY: The Town (D) contended that the trial court erred in refusing to admit a document which pertained to the dispute.

CONCISE RULE OF LAW: Writings purporting to be 30 years or more old, if relevant to the inquiry, are admissible in evidence without proof of execution or handwriting.

FACTS: Southern (P) brought suit to enjoin the Town (D) from further construction of certain buildings upon Southern's (P) right of way. Southern (P) alleged that it was vested with a right of way 100 feet in width on each side of the center line of its main track in the Town (D). In its answer, the Town (D) alleged that Southern's (P) right of way was limited by written agreement to 30 feet from the center line of its track, and also alleged adverse possession and estoppel. At trial, the Town (D) sought to introduce a letter from James Gilliam, the owner of the land in question at the time the railroad was built, to T.C. Lipscomb, which stated that the railroad claimed a right of way some 60 feet in width on each side of the track. The letter was dated September 3, 1872, and had been recorded with the Court Clerk on May 29, 1905. The Town (D) offered the recorded copy of the letter as an ancient document, but that offer was rejected by the trial court. The court then granted Southern's (P) request for an injunction, and the Town (D) appealed, on the basis that the trial court should have admitted the copy of the document as an ancient document.

ISSUE: Are writings purporting to be 30 years or more old, if relevant to the inquiry, admissible in evidence without proof of execution or handwriting?

HOLDING AND DECISION: (Stanley, J.) Yes. Writings purporting to be 30 years or more old, if relevant to the inquiry, when produced from proper custody, and on their face free from suspicion, are admissible in evidence, without the ordinary requirements as to proof of execution or handwriting. The rule, except as it relates to documents purporting to transfer land or other property, deals only with the authentication of the document sought to be proved and not with its competency or admissibility. The doctrine of admitting ancient documents in evidence, without proof of their genuineness, is based on the ground that they prove themselves, the witness being presumed dead. The questions of its relevancy and admissibility as evidence are not affected by the fact that it is an ancient document. What has been offered in evidence is a purported copy of a letter which was written by a predecessor in title to the land in question and purports to claim a lesser right of way for Southern (P) than that specified in the charter granted by the state legislature. It is neither a deed nor a will and does not purport to deal with the transfer of land or other property. It is clearly inadmissible as evidence of the facts recited in it. Affirmed.

EDITOR'S ANALYSIS: The Federal Rules provide that "Extrinsic evidence of authenticity as a condition precedent to admissibility is not required with respect to . . . a copy of an official record or record or entry therein, or of a document authorized by law to be recorded or filed and actually recorded or filed in a public office." See, Federal Rule of Evidence 902(4).

[For more information on the authentication of ancient documents, see Casenote Law Outline on Evidence, Chapter 13, § II, Authentication of Documents.]

NOTES:

UNITED STATES v. DUFFY
454 F.2d 809 (5th Cir. 1972).

NATURE OF CASE: Appeal from a conviction for transporting a stolen vehicle in interstate commerce.

FACT SUMMARY: Two witnesses testified that a shirt found in a suitcase in the car Duffy (D) was accused of stealing had the laundry mark "D-U-F," but Duffy (D) objected to the testimony and claimed the best evidence rule required that the Government (P) produce the shirt.

CONCISE RULE OF LAW: The best evidence rule covers writings and provides that the original writing must be produced unless it is shown to be unavailable for some reason other than the serious fault of the proponent.

FACTS: A car that had been brought into the Florida body shop where Duffy (D) worked disappeared over the same weekend he did. Both were later found in California. Duffy (D) was convicted of transporting a motor vehicle in interstate commerce knowing it to have been stolen. On appeal, he complained of error in the admission of certain evidence. Specifically, two witnesses had testified that the trunk of the stolen car had contained two suitcases when found, and that in one of the suitcases was a white shirt with the laundry mark "D-U-F." Duffy (D) argued that the best evidence rule required the Government (P) to produce the shirt itself, because the laundry mark made it proper to treat the shirt as a "writing."

ISSUE: Does the Best Evidence Rule cover writings only?

HOLDING AND DECISION: (Wisdom, J.) Yes. Only writings are covered by the best evidence rule. According to McCormick, the rule, as it exists today, may be stated as follows: "In proving the terms of a writing, where such terms are material, the original writing must be produced, unless it is shown to be unavailable for some reason other than the serious fault of the proponent." When, as in this case, the disputed evidence is an object bearing a mark or inscription, and is, therefore, a chattel and a writing, the trial judge has discretion to treat the evidence as a chattel or as a writing. Here, the inscription on the shirt was simple and there was little danger it could not be accurately remembered. Furthermore, its terms were by no means central or critical to the case, the shirt being only collateral evidence of the crime and only one piece of evidence in a substantial case against Duffy (D). Thus, the policy considerations behind the rule are not present and the judge acted properly in treating the shirt as chattel instead of as a writing. Affirmed.

EDITOR'S ANALYSIS: A number of courts agree with Wigmore and McCormick that the trial judge should have the discretion to decide whether the best evidence rule should be applied in any individual case involving an inscribed chattel. However, the Uniform Rules of Evidence adopt the strident position that any object carrying an inscription should be treated as a "writing."

[For more information on the best evidence rule, see Casenote Law Outline on Evidence, Chapter 14, § I, The Best Evidence Rule Stated.]

NOTES:

MEYERS v. UNITED STATES

171 F.2d 800 (D.C. Cir. 1948);
cert. denied, 336 U.S. 912 (1949).

NATURE OF CASE: Appeal from conviction for perjury.

FACT SUMMARY: Meyers (D) contended that the Government (P) violated the best evidence rule by allowing testimony as to what was contained in a transcript.

CONCISE RULE OF LAW: The best evidence rule is limited to cases where the contents of a writing are to be proved.

FACTS: Lamarre testified before a committee of the United States Senate investigating fraud and corruption in the conduct of World War II that he, and not General Bennett Meyers (D), was the actual owner of Aviation Electric Corporation, which had held numerous lucrative contracts with the Army Air Force. Meyers (D) was a deputy chief procurement officer for the Army Air Force. Lamarre was indicted for perjury, and Meyers (D) was indicted for suborning the perjury of Lamarre. During the trial, William P. Rogers, the chief counsel to the senatorial committee, was permitted to testify as to what Lamarre had sworn to the subcommittee. Later in the trial, the Government (P) introduced in evidence a stenographic transcript of Lamarre's testimony at the Senate hearing. After being convicted of the charges, Meyers (D) appealed, arguing that the trial court violated the best evidence rule by allowing Rogers to testify, when the transcript of Lamarre's testimony was actually the best evidence of what had been stated before the subcommittee.

ISSUE: Is the best evidence rule limited to cases where the contents of a writing are to be proved?

HOLDING AND DECISION: (Miller, J.) Yes. The best evidence rule is limited to cases where the contents of a writing are to be proved. Here, there was no attempt to prove the contents of a writing; the issue was what Lamarre had said, not what the transcript contained. The transcript media from shorthand notes of his testimony was evidence of what he had said, but it was not the only admissible evidence concerning it. Rogers' testimony was equally competent and admissible whether given before or after the transcript was received in evidence. Statements alleged to be perjurious may be proved by any person who heard them, as well as by a reporter who recorded them in shorthand. Affirmed.

DISSENT: (Prettyman, J.) The testimony given by Lamarre before the Senate Committee was presented to the jury at trial in so unfair and prejudicial a fashion as to constitute reversible error. Rogers did not purport to be absolute in his reproduction but merely recited his unrefreshed recollection, and his recollection on each of the alleged incidents of perjury bears a striking resemblance to the succinct summation in the indictment. It is obvious that what Rogers gave as substance was an essence of his own distillation and not an attempt to reproduce the whole of Lamarre's testimony.

EDITOR'S ANALYSIS: The Federal Rules state that: "To prove the content of a writing, recording, or photograph, the original writing, recording, or photograph is required, except as otherwise provided in [the Federal] rules or by Act of Congress." See Federal Rule of Evidence 1002.

[For more information on the best evidence rule, see Casenote Law Outline on Evidence, Chapter 14, § I, The Best Evidence Rule Stated.]

NOTES:

STATE v. NANO
Or. Sup. Ct., en banc, 273 Or. 366, 543 P.2d 660 (1975).

NATURE OF CASE: Appeal from conviction for theft.

FACT SUMMARY: The court of appeals reversed Nano's (D) theft conviction, holding testimony concerning the absence of records of sale for the merchandise violated the best evidence rule.

CONCISE RULE OF LAW: Testimony concerning whether a record does not contain certain entries is admissible and not violative of the best evidence rule.

FACTS: Nano (D) was charged with the theft of a box of calculators. The State (P) called the manager of the department from which the calculators were missing. Testimony was elicited that, based upon a lack of entries in sales records, the calculators were not sold. Nano (D) objected that such testimony violated the best evidence rule. The court allowed it, and Nano (D) was convicted. He appealed.

ISSUE: Does testimony concerning an absence of entries in a writing violate the best evidence rule?

HOLDING AND DECISION: (Denecke, J.) No. Testimony concerning whether a record does not contain certain entries is admissible and not violative of the best evidence rule. In this case, the precise language of a writing was not a prima facie issue in the case. Thus production of the original records was not necessary. Testimony that the merchandise was not sold was sufficient to support the conviction. Thus, the court of appeals erred in reversing the conviction. Reversed.

EDITOR'S ANALYSIS: The best evidence rule seeks to require litigants to produce original writings so that their content can be determined. It is commonly said that a document "speaks for itself," and that testimony concerning its content is unnecessary and often inaccurate. However, where the precise language is not at issue and it is the absence of entries rather than the presence, the rule is less helpful.

[For more information on the use of the best evidence rule, see Casenote Law Outline on Evidence, Chapter 14, § III, "To Prove the Content of a Writing".]

WILSON v. STATE
Ind. Ct. App., 169 Ind. App. 297, 348 N.E.2d 90 (1976).

NATURE OF CASE: Appeal from conviction for theft.

FACT SUMMARY: Wilson (D) contended that the State (P) was bound to produce the original paycheck he was accused of stealing, and the use of a copy was insufficient.

CONCISE RULE OF LAW: A photostatic copy of a document is admissible as the original, unless a genuine issue of authenticity is raised.

FACTS: Wilson (D) knocked over a government employee and took her paycheck. He was charged with theft. At trial a Xerox copy of the check was introduced, and Wilson (D) was convicted. He appealed, contending the original check must be produced or shown to be unavailable.

ISSUE: Is a photostatic copy of a document admissible as an original in the absence of a genuine issue of authenticity?

HOLDING AND DECISION: (Garrard, J.) Yes. A photostatic copy of a document is admissible as an original in the absence of a genuine issue of authenticity. The rule requiring use of the original dates back to the use of hand copying where errors were common. The availability of electronic copying machines eliminates the rationale for the rule. Thus, in this case there was no issue of authenticity, and the copy was admissible. Affirmed.

CONCURRENCE: (Hoffman, J.) The copy was admissible only because proper foundation was presented concerning its authenticity.

EDITOR'S ANALYSIS: The electronic developments in computer-generated documentation has blurred the line between originals and copies of documents. Word processing allows for the creation of limitless "originals." Thus, the long-standing rationale behind the requirement of originals is no longer viable.

[For more information on the admissibility of copies, see Casenote Law Outline on Evidence, Chapter 14, § II, Definitions.]

NOTES:

UNITED STATES v. STEPHENS
779 F.2d 232 (5th Cir. 1985).

NATURE OF CASE: Appeal from conviction for mail fraud.

FACT SUMMARY: Stephens (D) contended that the trial court erred in admitting summary exhibits into evidence.

CONCISE RULE OF LAW: Summary charts based upon previously admitted evidence are admissible.

FACTS: Stephens (D) was charged with falsifying federal loan documents and mail fraud. Voluminous documentation was introduced into evidence at trial, along with summary charts of the evidence. Stephen's (D) objected to the summaries on the basis they were inadmissible as argumentative and pedagogical.

ISSUE: Are summary charts based upon previously admitted evidence admissible?

HOLDING AND DECISION: (Williams, J.) Yes. Summary charts based on previously admitted evidence are admissible. As long as proper instruction is given, such charts merely make the voluminous documentation understandable. The charts themselves are not evidence and must be viewed in light of the underlying documentation. As a result, the charts were admissible. Affirmed.

EDITOR'S ANALYSIS: Federal Rule of Evidence 1006 provides for the use of summary charts under certain circumstances. If they are used as argument or to teach the jury, they may not be used. Their proper use is as summaries of previously admitted evidence. The rule requires also that the documentation summarized be voluminous and production be inconvenient.

[For more information on voluminous writings, see Casenote Law Outline on Evidence, Chapter 14, § IV, Absence of Originals Excused.]

NOTES:

SEILER v. LUCASFILM, LTD.
797 F.2d 1504 (9th Cir. 1986).

NATURE OF CASE: Appeal from a denial of damages for copyright infringement.

FACT SUMMARY: Seiler (P) contended that pictures of his creations were not covered by the best evidence rule.

CONCISE RULE OF LAW: Pictures and nonverbal facsimiles are writings and are covered by the best evidence rule.

FACTS: Seiler (P) sued Lucasfilm (D), contending that characters he created in 1976 and copyrighted in 1981 were used by Lucasfilm (D) in the 1980 film, "The Empire Strikes Back." Seiler (P) was precluded from showing copies of his work to the jury on the basis of the best evidence rule. He could produce no original evidence that the characters existed prior to 1980. He appealed from entry of summary judgment, contending his work was artwork and not subject to the best evidence rule.

ISSUE: Are pictures and other nonverbal facsimile writings subject to the best evidence rule?

HOLDING AND DECISION: (Farris, J.) Yes. Pictures and other nonverbal facsimiles are writings covered by the best evidence rule. In this case, the key issue is the similarity between the two characters. Facsimiles created after the Lucasfilm (D) characters were created are of dubious probative value. Because they are subject to the best evidence rule, it must be shown that the originals were lost or destroyed by no fault of Seiler (P). Because this was not done, the facsimiles cannot be used. Affirmed.

EDITOR'S ANALYSIS: Writings are often defined extremely broadly under most jurisdictions' evidence codes. The term includes traditional verbal communications as well as motion pictures, audio recordings, and videotape. Any type of recording method may be classified as a writing and be made subject to the best evidence rule.

[For more information on the scope of the best evidence rule, see Casenote Law Outline on Evidence, Chapter 14, § I, The Best Evidence Rule Stated.]

DOE d. GILBERT v. ROSS

Eng. Exch. Pleas, 7 M. & W. 102, 151 Eng. Rep. 696 (1840).

NATURE OF CASE: Appeal from order of ejectment.

FACT SUMMARY: Ross (D) contended that the trial court had not received the best evidence of ownership of the property in question.

CONCISE RULE OF LAW: There are no degrees of secondary evidence.

FACTS: Gilbert (P), claiming to be the heir at law of Arthur Gramer Miller, instituted an action in ejectment against Ross (D). Miller had died in 1832 without issue, and it therefore became necessary for Gilbert (P) to prove that he had acquired the fee simple of the property in question before the time of Miller's death. For this purpose, Gilbert (P) sought to introduce the marriage settlement of Miller, in order to show that he had acquired the fee by exercising the power of appointment. However, this settlement was in the possession of Mr. Baxter, the attorney for Ross (D), who refused to produce it at trial. Gilbert (P) then introduced secondary evidence of the deed. After a copy of the deed had been refused, because it did not have an official stamp, Gilbert (P) was allowed to read into evidence the notes made by the court reporter at a previous hearing at which the deed had been introduced. After the court found for Gilbert (P), Ross (D) appealed, arguing that there were degrees of secondary evidence, and that since an attested copy of the deed could have been produced if Gilbert (P) had had the deed stamped, the trial court was in error, and its decision should be reversed.

ISSUE: Are there degrees of secondary evidence?

HOLDING AND DECISION: (Parke, B.) No. If an attested copy is to be one degree of secondary evidence, the next will be a copy not attested; and then an abstract; then would come an inquiry, whether one man has a better memory than another, and we should never know where to stop.

CONCURRENCE: (Lord Abinger, C.B.) There are no degrees of secondary evidence. The rule is, that if you cannot produce the original, you may give parol evidence of its contents. If indeed the party giving such parol evidence appears to have better secondary evidence in his power, which he does not produce, that is a fact to go to the jury, from which they might sometimes presume that the evidence kept back would be adverse to the party withholding it. But the law makes no distinction between one class of secondary evidence and another.

EDITOR'S ANALYSIS: The Federal Rules provide that "The contents of an official record, or of a document authorized to be recorded or filed and actually recorded or filed, including data compilations in any form, if otherwise admissible, may be proved by (certified) copy . . . or testified to be correct by a witness who has compared it with the original. If a copy which complies with the foregoing cannot be obtained by the exercise of reasonable diligence, then other evidence of the contents may be given." See, Federal Rule of Evidence 1005.

NOTES:

NOTES

CHAPTER 12
TESTIMONIAL EVIDENCE

QUICK REFERENCE RULES OF LAW

1. **Coconspirator Admissions.** The Sixth Amendment, as applied to the states through the Fourteenth Amendment, guarantees a defendant the right, under any circumstances, to put his witnesses on the stand, as well as the right to compel their attendance in court. (Washington v. Texas)

   [For more information on coconspirator admissions, see Casenote Law Outline on Evidence, Chapter 9, § VIII, Exemption: Statements by Parties.]

2. **Witness Testimony.** Promising to tell the truth is a sufficient method of ensuring truthful testimony and swearing or affirmation is not necessary. (Gordon v. Idaho)

   [For more information on witness testimony, see Casenote Law Outline on Evidence, Chapter 11, § III, Oath.]

3. **Competency of a Witness.** The decision whether to order a psychiatric examination of a witness is committed to the discretion of the trial court. (United States v. Heinlein)

   [For more information on the competency of a witness, see Casenote Law Outline on Evidence, Chapter 11, § II, Witness Competence.]

4. **Exclusion of Witnesses.** If either party requires it, the judge may exclude from the courtroom any witness of the adverse party not at that time under examination, so that he may not hear the testimony of other witnesses. (State v. Bishop)

   [For more information on the exclusion of witnesses, see Casenote Law Outline on Evidence, Chapter 11, § X, Exclusion and Sequestration of Witnesses.]

5. **The Form of Witness Examination.** While it is within the discretion of the court to allow a witness to give his testimony in narrative form, it is the right and duty of counsel objecting to such testimony to interpose and arrest the narrative by calling it to attention of the court, and making a motion to strike it from the case. (Northern Pacific R. v. Charless)

   [For more information on the form of witness examination, see Casenote Law Outline on Evidence, Chapter 11, § VI, The Form of Questions.]

6. **Leading Questions.** The principal test of a leading question is whether it suggests the answer desired. (State v. Scott)

   [For more information on leading questions, see Casenote Law Outline on Evidence, Chapter 11, § VI, The Form of Questions.]

7. **Leading Questions.** The use of leading questions is a decision left to the discretion of the trial judge. (United States v. Brown)

   [For more information on leading questions, see Casenote Law Outline on Evidence, Chapter 11, § VI, The Form of Questions.]

8. **Past Recollection Recorded.** Any writing may be used to refresh the recollection of a witness. (Ward v. Morr Transfer & Storage Co.)

[For more information on past recollection recorded, see Casenote Law Outline on Evidence, Chapter 10, § VI, Past Recollection Recorded.]

9. **Disclosure of Refreshing Documents.** A party, against whom a witness testifies, has a right to see a writing used by the witness to refresh his memory. (Winters v. Winters)

   [For more information on disclosure of refreshing documents, see Casenote Law Outline on Evidence, Chapter 11, § IX, The Restroom Rule.]

10. **Witness and Testimony.** A witness, other than the defendant himself, may not offer testimony to the extent that it has been enhanced through hypnosis. (People v. Zayas)

    [For more information on witnesses and testimony, see Casenote Law Outline on Evidence, Chapter 11, § I, "Witness" Defined.]

11. **Testimonial Capacity.** Testimony of a witness is admissible when it is possible for the witness to have obtained personal knowledge of the facts related. (Strickland Transportation Co. v. Ingram)

    [For more information on testimonial capacity, see Casenote Law Outline on Evidence, Chapter 5, § II, Preliminary Questions of Fact.]

12. **Testimony from Lay Witnesses.** Testimony from a lay witness concerning the speed of a vehicle is admissible if the witness has a sufficient opportunity to observe the vehicle in motion. (Jackson v. Leach)

    [For more information on testimony from lay witnesses, see Casenote Law Outline on Evidence, Chapter 12, § II, Lay Witness Opinions.]

13. **Opinion Testimony.** The conclusion, judgment, or opinion of a witness may be testified to where the facts underlying them are of such a character that they cannot be presented with proper force to anyone without the benefit of personal observation. (Parker v. Hoefer)

    [For more information on opinion testimony, see Casenote Law Outline on Evidence, Chapter 12, § II, Lay Witness Opinions.]

14. **Testimony of Lay Witnesses.** Lay opinion testimony is admissible, in the discretion if the court, where it will be helpful to a clear understanding of the testimony given concerning the facts of the case. (Krueger v. State Farm Mutual Automobile Insurance Co.)

    [For more information on testimony of lay witnesses, see Casenote Law Outline on Evidence, Chapter 12, § II, Lay Witness Opinions.]

15. **Opinion Testimony of Lay Witnesses.** A layperson who is sufficiently acquainted with the accused may give an opinion as to the sanity of the accused. (Rupert v. People)

    [For more information on opinion testimony of lay witnesses, see Casenote Law Outline on Evidence, Chapter 12, § II, Lay Witness Opinions.]

16. **Qualifications of an Expert Witness.** To qualify as an expert witness, a lay person must demonstrate specialized knowledge or particularized qualifications in that field of expertise. (Smith v. Hobart Manufacturing)

    [For more information on qualifications of an expert witness, see Casenote Law Outline on Evidence, Chapter 12, § III, Expert Opinions.]

17. **Admission of Expert Testimony.** Expert testimony concerning the reliability of photographic evidence is admissible. (United States v. Alexander)

[For more information on the admission of expert testimony, see Casenote Law Outline on Evidence, Chapter 12, § III, Expert Opinions.]

18. **Hypothetical Questions and Expert Testimony.** Hypothetical questions must be based on the facts rather than upon other expert opinion. (Harris v. Smith)

[For more information on hypothetical questions and expert testimony, see Casenote Law Outline on Evidence, Chapter 12, § III, Expert Opinions.]

19. **Expert Witness Testimony.** Expert witnesses may base opinions on inadmissible testimony. (Thomas v. Metz)

[For more information on expert witness testimony, see Casenote Law Outline on Evidence, Chapter 12, § III, Expert Opinions.]

20. **Opinion Testimony from Expert Witnesses.** A witness may testify concerning the mental condition and ability of a testator, but may not offer testimony which involves definitions, tests, or concepts of a purely legal nature. (Carr v. Radkey)

[For more information on opinion testimony from expert witnesses, see Casenote Law Outline on Evidence, Chapter 12, § III, Expert Opinions.]

21. **The Use of Court-appointed Experts.** The Constitution requires the state to provide an indigent defendant access to a psychiatrist to aid in proving an insanity defense. (Ake v. Oklahoma)

[For more information on the use of court-appointed experts, see Casenote Law Outline on Evidence, Chapter 12, § III, Expert Opinions.]

22. **"Surprise" Testimony.** A party may impeach his own witness in the event of genuine surprise and hostility. (State v. Green)

[For more information on "surprise" testimony, see Casenote Law Outline on Evidence, Chapter 11, § VII, Impeachment of Witnesses.]

23. **Attacking the Credibility of a Witness.** When a party calls the opposing party as a witness, he is not bound by the testimony of that opposing party. (Becker v. Eisenstodt)

[For more information on attacking the credibility of a witness, see Casenote Law Outline on Evidence, Chapter 11, § VII, Impeachment of Witnesses.]

24. **Prior Inconsistent Statements.** Impeachment by prior inconsistent statement is impermissible if used to get otherwise inadmissible evidence before the jury. (United States v. Webster)

[For more information on prior inconsistent statements, see Casenote Law Outline on Evidence, Chapter 9, § VII, Exemption: Prior Statements of Witnesses.]

25. **Evidence of Witness Bias.** The existence of bias is a proper subject for cross-examination. (Alford v. United States)

[For more information on evidence of witness bias, see Casenote Law Outline on Evidence, Chapter 11, § VII, Impeachment of Witnesses.]

26. **Evidence of Witness Bias.** A party has the right to cross-examine a witness about possible bias or interest, even though the disclosure will also reveal the presence of liability insurance in the case. (Barton Plumbing Co. v. Johnson)

   [For more information on evidence of witness bias, see Casenote Law Outline on Evidence, Chapter 11, § VII, Impeachment of Witnesses.]

27. **The Treatise Exception.** Treatises or books may be used to impeach an expert witness when that witness has used the treatise in giving his testimony. (Ross v. Foss)

   [For more information on the treatise exception, see Casenote Law Outline on Evidence, Chapter 10, § IX, Miscellaneous Hearsay Exceptions.]

28. **Impeachment through Prior Convictions.** A witness may be impeached through introduction of evidence of a prior conviction of any crime. (Marshall v. Martinson)

   [For more information on impeachment through prior convictions, see Casenote Law Outline on Evidence, Chapter 6, § V, Character to Impeach.]

29. **Character to Impeach.** A prior narcotics conviction may be used to impeach a defendant if probative on the issue of credibility. (United States v. Ortiz)

   [For more information on character to impeach, see Casenote Law Outline on Evidence, Chapter 6, § V, Character to Impeach.]

30. **Impeachment Using a Prior Conviction.** A witness may be impeached by proof that he was convicted of a crime if the manner in which the witness committed the offense involved deceit. (Altobello v. Borden Confectionary Products, Inc.)

   [For more information on impeachment using a prior conviction, see Casenote Law Outline on Evidence, Chapter 6, § V, Character to Impeach.]

31. **Evidence of Misconduct.** Past incidents of violent behavior are not probative of veracity and cannot be used to impeach the truthfulness of the witness. (State v. Morgan)

   [For more information on evidence of misconduct, see Casenote Law Outline on Evidence, Chapter 6, § IV, The "Other Crimes" Loophole.]

32. **Admission of Rape Victim's Character.** Evidence of sexual reputation and opinion evidence of sexual behavior may not be used to show an alleged rape victim's state of mind. (Doe v. United States)

   [For more information on admission of rape victim's character, see Casenote Law Outline on Evidence, Chapter 6, § III, Character to Prove Conduct.]

33. **Miscellaneous Quasi-privileges.** Evidence of specific instances of an alleged victim's past sexual behavior is admissible if offered to show the source of injury to the victim. (United States v. Azure)

   [For more information on miscellaneous quasi-privileges, see Casenote Law Outline on Evidence, Chapter 7, § VII, Miscellaneous Quasi-Privileges.]

34. **Federal Rules of Evidence and Rape Shield.** Evidence of past accusations of sexual assault are not admissible under the rape-shield rule. (United States v. Cardinal)

   [For more information on Federal Rules of Evidence and rape shield, see Casenote Law Outline on Evidence, Chapter 7, § VII, Miscellaneous Quasi-Privileges.]

35. Using Character to Impeach. The credibility of a witness may be impeached by evidence of his reputation for truth and veracity in the community. (State v. Baker)

[For more information on using character to impeach, see Casenote Law Outline on Evidence, Chapter 6, § V, Character to Impeach.]

36. Competency of a Witness. The decision whether to order a psychiatric examination of a witness is committed to the discretion of the trial court. (United States v. Heinlein)

[For more information on the competency of a witness, see Casenote Law Outline on Evidence, Chapter 11, § II, Witness Competence.]

37. Prior Inconsistent Statements. A witness may be impeached by the use of prior self-contradictory statements. (Central Mutual Insurance Co. v. Newman)

[For more information on prior inconsistent statements, see Casenote Law Outline on Evidence, Chapter 9, § VII, Exemption: Prior Statements of Witnesses.]

38. Prior Inconsistent Statements. A proper foundation must be established before a witness may be impeached by prior inconsistent statements. (Nichols v. Sefcik)

[For more information on prior inconsistent statements, see Casenote Law Outline on Evidence, Chapter 9, § VII, Exemption: Prior Statements of Witnesses.]

39. Evidence of Good Character. Where an attack is made on the veracity of a witness, it is proper to permit testimony that the witness has a good reputation for truth and veracity. (Rodriguez v. State)

[For more information on evidence of good character, see Casenote Law Outline on Evidence, Chapter 6, § III, Character to Prove Conduct.]

40. Evidence of Motive. A witness should be permitted to explain briefly the circumstances of a prior criminal conviction. (United States v. Boyer)

[For more information on evidence of motive, see Casenote Law Outline on Evidence, Chapter 6, § IV, The "Other Crimes" Loophole.]

41. Prior Inconsistent Statements. An impeached witness must always be afforded the opportunity to explain or deny a prior inconsistent statement. (Bradford v. State)

[For more information on prior inconsistent statements, see Casenote Law Outline on Evidence, Chapter 9, § VII, Exemption: Prior Statements of Witnesses.]

WASHINGTON v. TEXAS
388 U.S. 14 (1967).

NATURE OF CASE: Appeal of conviction for murder with malice.

FACT SUMMARY: Washington (D) challenged the constitutionality of Texas statutes which provided that persons charged or convicted as coparticipants in the same crime could not testify for one another.

CONCISE RULE OF LAW: The Sixth Amendment, as applied to the states through the Fourteenth Amendment, guarantees a defendant the right, under any circumstances, to put his witnesses on the stand, as well as the right to compel their attendance in court.

FACTS: Washington (D) was charged with a shotgun shooting. At his trial for murder, he sought to have a codefendant, Fuller, testify that he, Fuller, had taken the gun from Washington (D), and that Washington (D) had unsuccessfully tried to prevent the shooting. Because two Texas statutes prohibited persons charged or convicted as coparticipants in the same crime from testifying for one another, Fuller was not produced as a witness for Washington (D). Texas law would have permitted Fuller to testify for the state.

ISSUE: Does a defendant in a criminal case have the right to have compulsory process for obtaining witnesses in his behalf under the Sixth Amendment, and is that right violated by a state procedural statute preventing persons charged as principals, accomplices, or accessories in the same crime from being introduced as witnesses for each other?

HOLDING AND DECISION: (Warren, C.J.) Yes. The right to compulsory process for obtaining witnesses is so fundamental and essential to a fair trial that it is incorporated in the Due Process Clause of the Fourteenth Amendment. This right is, in plain terms, the right to present a defense. Although a defendant has the right to produce favorable witnesses in the courtroom, the right is frustrated if these witnesses cannot take the stand. The general theory against permitting this is that if two persons charged with the same crime were allowed to testify on behalf of each other, each would try to swear the other out of the charge, and thus the right to present witnesses is subordinate to the court's interest in preventing perjury. The absurdity of this reasoning is demonstrated by the exception allowing a coparticipant to testify on behalf of the state. Common sense would suggest that he often has a greater interest in lying for the prosecution, particularly if he is still awaiting trial or sentencing. Furthermore, should the coparticipant be acquitted, he may testify under Texas law. He would then be free to perjure himself, completely secure in the knowledge that he could not be reprosecuted for the same offense.

EDITOR'S ANALYSIS: At common law, where a witness had been convicted of treason, a crime of fraud or deceit, or a felony, he was absolutely disqualified from testifying. This has been changed by statute in most states, and the U.S. Supreme Court has ruled that disqualification will no longer be permitted in criminal trials at the federal level. The jury should be the safeguard against a lying witness. Arguably, those state statutes which still recognize disqualification for perjury and subornation are invalid because of the decision in the present case. Commentators have generally viewed Washington v. Texas as clearly establishing a defendant's right to compulsory process. Under this expansive view, state regulations which prevent a wife from testifying against her husband may be unconstitutional. However, the right to compulsory process does have some limits. One court has held that a defendant is not entitled to compel the presence of a witness who had already indicated that he would rely on the privilege against self-incrimination. Under Washington v. Texas, this decision would follow since a witness who will refuse to testify cannot deprive the defendant of relevant and material testimony.

[For more information on coconspirator admissions, see Casenote Law Outline on Evidence, Chapter 9, § VIII, Exemption: Statements by Parties.]

NOTES:

STATE v. BISHOP
Or. App. Ct., 17 Or. App. 568, 492 P.2d 509 (1972).

NATURE OF CASE: Appeal from conviction for sale and possession of dangerous drugs.

FACT SUMMARY: Before trial, counsel for Bishop (D) requested that all witnesses be excluded from the courtroom.

CONCISE RULE OF LAW: If either party requires it, the judge may exclude from the courtroom any witness of the adverse party not at that time under examination, so that he may not hear the testimony of other witnesses.

FACTS: Bishop (D) was convicted of the sale and possession of dangerous drugs. When the case was called for trial, counsel for Bishop (D) requested that all witnesses, including police officers scheduled to testify against Bishop (D), be excluded. Counsel for Bishop (D) argued that Bishop (D) would be prejudiced if the police officers were allowed to remain in the courtroom because they would be able to determine the theory of the defense and adjust their testimony accordingly. The trial judge denied the motion, explaining that it was desirable that the "officers have an opportunity to learn what it is about their police practices that is being questioned." Bishop (D) appealed, arguing that the motion to exclude should have been granted.

ISSUE: If either party requires it, may the judge exclude from the courtroom any witness of the adverse party not at that time under examination?

HOLDING AND DECISION: (Schwab, J.) Yes. When one party moves to exclude witnesses and the other party voices no objection, the motion should always be granted. When the motion is opposed, the trial court must weigh the good cause shown for not excluding witnesses against the policy favoring exclusion. The practice of excluding witnesses is designed to prevent one witness from being influenced, consciously or unconsciously, by hearing the testimony of prior witnesses. However, a party to a proceeding who will later be called as a witness cannot be excluded. Here, the reasons advanced by the trial court to explain its refusal to exclude are inadequate. These reasons, while undoubtedly salutary as an educational device, were not relevant to the purpose of the trial, namely the determination of whether Bishop (D) was guilty of the crime charged. Here, the trial court abused its discretion by not excluding witnesses as requested. Reversed and remanded for new trial.

EDITOR'S ANALYSIS: The Federal Rules provide that "At the request of a party the court shall order witnesses excluded so that they cannot hear the testimony of other witnesses, and it may make the order of its own motion." The Rules provide for several exceptions to the general rule, including the prohibition for excluding "a person whose presence is shown by a party to be essential to the presentation of his cause." See, Federal Rule of Evidence 615.

[For more information on the exclusion of witnesses, see Casenote Law Outline on Evidence, Chapter 11, § X, Exclusion and Sequestration of Witnesses.]

GORDON v. IDAHO
778 F.2d 1397 (9th Cir. 1985).

NATURE OF CASE: Appeal from dismissal of civil rights action.

FACT SUMMARY: The trial court dismissed Gordon's (P) civil rights action for his failure to swear to his testimony after being ordered to do so.

CONCISE RULE OF LAW: Promising to tell the truth is a sufficient method of ensuring truthful testimony and swearing or affirmation is not necessary.

FACTS: Gordon (P) was cited for civil contempt for failing to swear or affirm his testimony. He sued, contending this violated his First Amendment right of freedom of religion. Within his civil rights suit, the court ordered him to swear or affirm his deposition testimony. When he refused, the court dismissed his case as a discovery sanction. He appealed the dismissal on First Amendment religion grounds.

ISSUE: Is promising to tell the truth sufficient to ensure truthful testimony?

HOLDING AND DECISION: (Pregerson, J.) Yes. Promising to tell the truth is a sufficient method of ensuring truthful testimony and swearing or affirmation is not necessary. In this case, the religious beliefs of Gordon (P) precluded his use of the words "swear" or "affirm." However, he agreed to testify under penalty of perjury and knew that if he testified falsely, he could have been subject to criminal penalties. This was sufficient to ensure truthful testimony, and the dismissal was improper. Reversed.

DISSENT: (Weigel, J.) Affirming testimony is the alternative to swearing to it. It should be required in cases of this sort.

EDITOR'S ANALYSIS: A person's capacity to testify usually rests upon their ability to appreciate truth from falsity. It would appear from this case that any manifestation of this ability along with an agreement to tell the truth would be sufficient. It appears practical that the mere recitation of certain words need not be adhered to and the substance of the agreement to be truthful be upheld.

[For more information on witness testimony, see Casenote Law Outline on Evidence, Chapter 11, § III, Oath.]

NOTES:

UNITED STATES v. HEINLEIN
490 F.2d 725 (D.C. Cir. 1973).

NATURE OF CASE: Appeal from felony-murder conviction.

FACT SUMMARY: Heinlein (D) and two others were convicted of two criminal charges, after a motion to subject a witness to a psychiatric examination was denied.

CONCISE RULE OF LAW: The decision whether to order a psychiatric examination of a witness is committed to the discretion of the trial court.

FACTS: Heinlein (D) and the two Walker brothers were convicted of felony-murder and assault with intent to commit rape while armed. Because Heinlein (D) and the Walker brothers chose not to testify at trial, the only purported eyewitness to the events in question was James Harding, a chronic alcoholic. Harding underwent direct examination for one day and was cross-examined for one day by counsel for Heinlein (D). At the beginning of the third day, counsel for Heinlein (D) moved that Harding be subjected to a psychiatric examination with respect to his competency on the basis that Harding's testimony had been highly confusing and that medical testimony showed that Harding's memory had been affected by chronic brain syndrome associated with alcoholic intoxication. The motion was denied, and the propriety of the ruling was raised upon appeal.

ISSUE: Is the decision to order a psychiatric examination of a witness committed to the discretion of the trial court?

HOLDING AND DECISION: (McGowan, J.) Yes. The competency of a witness to testify before the jury is a threshold question of law committed to the trial court's discretion. The decision as to whether a court should order a psychiatric examination in order to aid it in resolving the issue of competency must be entrusted to the sound discretion of the trial judge in light of the particular facts of the case. Here, the trial judge ruled on the motion for psychiatric examination after seeing Harding testify on the stand for two full days, during which he gave his direct testimony in full, and was subjected to extensive and vigorous cross-examination. There were discrepancies and gaps in Harding's testimony. But the court, noting that Harding's various statements, despite some differences, related essentially to the same event and described all three defendants as active participants, concluded that these differences were not such as to shake significantly Harding's account of what happened to the victim. Thus, it appears that the trial court did not abuse its discretion in refusing to treat Harding as a witness of actual or potential incompetency. Affirmed.

EDITOR'S ANALYSIS: Determinations as to the competency of a particular witness are usually made by the trial judge on the basis of his own observations of the witness. The trial judge does have the discretion to admit extrinsic evidence which bears on the competency of the witness, including mental and psychiatric tests, and the expert testimony of psychiatrists and psychologists.

[For more information on the competency of a witness, see Casenote Law Outline on Evidence, Chapter 11, § II, Witness Competence.]

NOTES:

UNITED STATES v. BROWN
603 F.2d 1022 (1st Cir. 1979).

NATURE OF CASE: Appeal from conviction for theft.

FACT SUMMARY: Brown (D) was convicted of stealing 16 birds, after leading questions were asked of a hostile witness.

CONCISE RULE OF LAW: The use of leading questions is a decision left to the discretion of the trial judge.

FACTS: Brown (D) was convicted of stealing 16 birds worth more than $100 from the Delta Airlines air freight terminal at Logan Airport. At trial, one Jerome Proulx was permitted to be examined as a hostile witness, allowing the prosecution to use leading questions during his examination. Proulx testified to having been at a pet store when Brown (D) may have learned that a shipment of birds had arrived at the airport. Proulx also testified to his driving to the airport with Brown (D), where Brown (D) picked up a box. Proulx, while testifying, was hesitant, confused, and reluctant to volunteer information. On appeal, Brown (D) argued that the government (D) should not have been permitted to use leading questions in its direct examination of Proulx.

ISSUE: Is the decision whether to permit the use of leading questions left to the discretion of the trial judge?

HOLDING AND DECISION: (Bownes, J.) Yes. The use of leading questions must be left to the sound discretion of the trial judge who sees the witness and can, therefore, determine in the interest of truth and justice whether the circumstances justify leading questions to be propounded to a witness by the party producing him. In general, leading questions are undesirable on direct-examination, although permissible on cross-examination. Leading questions may be used in the direct examination of hostile witnesses. Here, the trial judge did not abuse his discretion in allowing the prosecutor to use leading questions in the direct examination of Proulx. Proulx and Brown (D) were good friends, and the evidence shows that Proulx was a participant in the crime. Proulx's testimony is replete with lapses of memory attributed to alcohol and drugs. While Proulx was not hostile in the sense of being contemptuous or surly, he was both evasive and adverse to the government. Affirmed.

EDITOR'S ANALYSIS: The Federal Rules state that "Leading questions should not be used on the direct examination of a witness except as may be necessary to develop his testimony. Ordinarily, leading questions should be permitted on cross-examination. When a party calls a hostile witness, an adverse party, or a witness identified with an adverse party, interrogation may be by leading questions." Federal Rule of Evidence 611.

[For more information on leading questions, see Casenote Law Outline on Evidence, Chapter 11, § VI, The Form of Questions.]

NORTHERN PAC. R. v. CHARLESS
51 F. 562 (9th Cir. 1892).

NATURE OF CASE: Appeal of damages for personal injuries.

FACT SUMMARY: Charless (P), an employee of Northern (D) suing for on-the-job injuries, related his testimony in narrative form to which Northern (D) objected.

CONCISE RULE OF LAW: While it is within the discretion of the court to allow a witness to give his testimony in narrative form, it is the right and duty of counsel objecting to such testimony to interpose and arrest the narrative by calling it to attention of the court, and making a motion to strike it from the case.

FACTS: Charless (P) sued Northern (D) for personal injuries sustained while employed as a section hand. At trial, Charless (P) appeared as a witness in his own behalf. His counsel asked him to give a narrative account of the circumstances upon which he brought suit. Northern (D) did not object. As the narrative continued, Northern (D) objected claiming that Charless (D) was making a statement of matters immaterial to the issues involved in the case, incompetent as being hearsay, and not the best evidence. Further, since the testimony was narrative, Northern (D) claimed it had no opportunity to interpose such objections before the testimony was out. Northern (D) appealed the award of $18,250 to Charless (P).

ISSUE: When testimony is being given in narrative form, is it the duty of counsel objecting to such testimony to arrest the narrative, call the objectionable matter to the court's attention, and move to strike it out?

HOLDING AND DECISION: (Morrow, J.) Yes. It is within the court's discretion to allow the witness to give his testimony in narrative form. But if a witness giving such testimony states irrelevant, immaterial, incompetent or hearsay matters, it is the duty of counsel objecting to such testimony to interpose and arrest the narrative by calling it to the court's attention, and, making a motion to strike it from the case. As it does not appear that Northern's (D) counsel was deprived of the opportunity to make such a motion, there was no error.

EDITOR'S ANALYSIS: Most courts prefer that witnesses testify from specific questions. Narrative testimony is usually more accurate and wastes less time, however. Should a narrative be given, the court should instruct the witness to stick to what he saw for himself and not discuss what he learned from hearsay sources. It has been suggested that narrative testimony be followed by specific questions so that accuracy and completeness will balance. In the instant case, it appears that counsel's objections were not specific as to the particular testimony desired to be struck.

[For more information on the form of witness examination, see Casenote Law Outline on Evidence, Chapter 11, § VI, The Form of Questions.]

STATE v. SCOTT
Wash. Sup. Ct., 20 Wash. 2d 696, 149 P.2d 152 (1944).

NATURE OF CASE: Appeal from conviction for statutory rape.

FACT SUMMARY: Scott (D) contended that the trial judge erroneously allowed the prosecutor to use leading questions during the direct examination of a witness.

CONCISE RULE OF LAW: The principal test of a leading question is whether it suggests the answer desired.

FACTS: Scott (D) was convicted by a jury on the charge that he carnally knew a female child of the age of 14 years who was not his wife. On appeal, Scott (D) argued that the trial court erred in allowing leading questions to be asked of the complaining witness. The questions claimed by Scott (D) to have been of a leading character, and to which timely objections were made, were what is known as the alternative forms of questions. In three separate interrogatories, the prosecutor asked "whether or not" Scott (D) had said why he had done what he had done, "whether or not" Scott (D) had said anything relative to his being the first to touch the complaining witness, and "whether or not" Scott (D) had suggested that the complaining witness be examined by a doctor. The trial court upheld the use of this type of question, and Scott (D) appealed.

ISSUE: Is the principal test of a leading question whether it suggests the answer desired?

HOLDING AND DECISION: (Grady, J.) Yes. The principal test of a leading question is whether it suggests the answer desired. In order to elicit the facts, a trial lawyer may find it necessary to direct the attention of a witness to the specific matter concerning which his testimony is desired, and, if the question does not suggest the answer, it is not leading. Even though the question may call for a yes or a no answer, it is not leading for that reason, unless it is so worded that, by permitting the witness to answer yes or no, he would be testifying in the language of the interrogator rather than on his own. The alternative form of question is not a leading question, because both affirmative and negative answers are presented for the witness' choice. Such a question may or may not be improper, according to the amount of palpably suggestive detail which it embodies. Here, the questions propounded were not leading. The witness gave fully explanatory answers in response to the questions posed. The trial court has a wide discretion in determining what is a proper form of question and as to permitting the asking of a question that is leading. The trial court in this case properly allowed the challenged questions to be asked. Affirmed.

EDITOR'S ANALYSIS: The Federal Rules of Evidence provide that "Leading questions should not be used on the direct examination of a witness except as may be necessary to develop his testimony. Ordinarily leading questions should be permitted on cross-examination. When a party calls a hostile witness, an adverse party, interrogation may be by leading questions." Federal Rule of Evidence 611(c).

[For more information on leading questions, see Casenote Law Outline on Evidence, Chapter 11, § VI, The Form of Questions.]

NOTES:

WINTERS v. WINTERS
Tx. Ct. Civ. App., 282 S.W.2d 749 (1955).

NATURE OF CASE: Appeal from judgment denying a divorce.

FACT SUMMARY: When Dorothye Winters (P) sued her husband, Elmer Winters (D), for divorce the trial court did not permit her counsel to examine the notes used by an opposing witness when he testified.

CONCISE RULE OF LAW: A party, against whom a witness testifies, has a right to see a writing used by the witness to refresh his memory.

FACTS: Dorothye Winters (P) sued her husband, Elmer Winters (D), for divorce on the grounds of harsh, cruel, and unkind treatment. Elmer (D) denied the allegations, and charged that Dorothye's (P) association with a man named Carl Maberry was the sole cause of the troubles between them. At trial, a witness, Ray Converse, Jr., testified that Elmer (D) had employed him to follow and observe Dorothye (P) and Carl Maberry. Converse testified that he had seen Dorothye (P) and Maberry together seven times, that each time he made notes on what he observed, and had these notes with him when he testified. Converse referred to these notes while testifying; and when Dorothye's (P) counsel sought to examine these notes for use in cross-examining Converse, the court refused this request. On appeal, Dorothye (P) argued that this ruling constituted reversible error.

ISSUE: Does a party, against whom a witness testifies, have a right to see a writing used by the witness to refresh his memory?

HOLDING AND DECISION: (Pitts, J.) Yes. Notes or memoranda personally made by the witness at or near the time of the trans-actions concerning the matters about which the witness is called to testify may be used to refresh his memory. However, where a witness uses any paper or memoranda to refresh his memory in giving his testimony, the opposing side, upon proper demand, has a right to see and examine that paper or memoranda, and to use the same in cross-examination of the witness. Here, Converse was employed as a detective by Elmer (D), and he apparently made the notes or memoranda for the purpose of testifying from them. Dorothye (P) should have been permitted to examine those notes or memoranda, and to use them, if desired, upon cross-examination of Converse. Reversed and remanded for new trial.

EDITOR'S ANALYSIS: The Federal Rules provide that "If a witness uses a writing to refresh his memory for the purpose of testifying, either while testifying, or before testifying, if the court in its discretion determines it is necessary in the interests of justice, an adverse party is entitled to have the writing produced at the hearing, to inspect it, to cross-examine the witness thereon, and to introduce in evidence those portions which relate to the testimony of the witness." Federal Rule of Evidence 612.

[For more information on disclosure of refreshing documents, see Casenote Law Outline on Evidence, Chapter 11, § IX, The Restroom Rule.]

WARD v. MORR TRANSFER & STORAGE CO.
Mo. App. Ct., 119 Mo. App. 83, 95 S.W. 964 (1906).

NATURE OF CASE: Appeal in action for conversion.

FACT SUMMARY: Ward (P), who charged that Morr (D) had wrongfully converted a lot of household goods which she had stored with them, used a list which she had made at various times after storing the goods to refresh her memory it trial.

CONCISE RULE OF LAW: Any writing may be used to refresh the recollection of a witness.

FACTS: Ward (P), who had stored a lot of household goods with Morr (D), a general storage and warehouse company, charged that Morr (D) had wrongfully converted the goods. In preparing for trial, Ward (P) had compiled a list of the articles which she claimed were stored with Morr (D). The list was not made at the time the articles were packed, nor at the time they were delivered to Morr (D). The list was made on separate pieces of paper at different times, when the article would come into Ward's (P) memory as being part of the goods stored. Before trial, Ward (P) arranged these various memoranda into one list, which she compiled on a typewriter. At trial, over objection, Ward (P) referred to the list in order to remember which items had been allegedly converted. On appeal, Morr (D) argued that Ward's (P) use of the list and other memoranda at trial was reversible error.

ISSUE: May any writing be used to refresh the recollection of a witness?

HOLDING AND DECISION: (Ellison, J.) Yes. Any writing may be used to refresh the recollection of a witness. Here, it was proper for Ward (P) to use either the typewritten list or the other slips of paper to refresh her memory. Either reminded her of things to and about which she testified, just as anything else may remind an individual of a fact now forgotten. The memoranda, in such case, are not evidence, but the memory of the witness is. There are two situations where a writing may be used to refresh recollection. First, a witness may refer to a memorandum which refreshes his recollection, so that he may testify to what he actually remembers about the facts in question. Second, if a witness cannot recall the events in question after examining the memorandum, he may still testify to the accuracy of the memorandum if he remembers it as an accurate depiction of the facts at the time the memorandum was made. Reversed and remanded, but on other grounds.

EDITOR'S ANALYSIS: Some courts have required that a writing which is utilized to refresh a witness' memory must have been prepared contemporaneously with the occurrence of the facts recollected. However, the majority rule is contra, perhaps reflecting confusion between the theory permitting introduction of writings representing past recollection recorded as an exception to the hearsay rule, and that justifying refreshing the recollection of witnesses.

PEOPLE v. ZAYAS
Ill. Sup. Ct., 131 Ill.2d 284, 546 N.E.2d 513 (1989).

NATURE OF CASE: Appeal from murder conviction.

FACT SUMMARY: Zayas (D) appealed his conviction on three counts of murder, contending that the testimony of a police detective, which was hypnotically induced and which was used against Zayas (D) to obtain his conviction, was inadmissible and that the trial court therefore committed reversible error.

CONCISE RULE OF LAW: A witness, other than the defendant himself, may not offer testimony to the extent that it has been enhanced through hypnosis.

FACTS: Zayas (D) was prosecuted by the People (P) for three counts of murder. The victims were shot to death on the front porch of a building in Chicago. At trial, the People (P) put a police detective on the stand to testify that, shortly after the murders, he responded to a call which stated that shots had been fired. As he proceeded on to a second call, he noticed a car containing four males pull in front of him, but nothing appeared unusual about the car except that one of the occupants continually looked over his shoulder. The detective then returned to the scene of the shootings, and some officers informed him that a car similar to that containing the four males, which he had seen earlier, might have been involved. The detective testified that, at this time, he was able to describe the car as a light blue Plymouth Sebring with a possible license number of XND 405. Shortly after the shootings, the detective was hypnotized by a psychiatrist to help him recall the license number of the vehicle he partially described earlier. Over Zayas' (D) objection, the detective testified that, under hypnosis, he recalled the license number of the vehicle as NXJ 402. The actual license number of the car was NXJ 240. Zayas (D) was convicted of the shootings and appealed the conviction, arguing that the detective's testimony, insofar as he related to the jury that which he recalled under hypnosis, was inadmissible. The appellate court agreed but held that any error in admission of the detective's testimony was harmless. Zayas (D) appealed.

ISSUE: May a witness, other than the defendant himself, offer testimony to the extent that it has been enhanced through hypnosis?

HOLDING AND DECISION: (Ryan, J.) No. A witness, other than the defendant himself, may not offer testimony to the extent that it has been enhanced through hypnosis. Because no one really understands it, hypnosis plays a rather dubious role in judicial proceedings. There are essentially three different rules this court could adopt regarding the admissibility of hypnotically refreshed recollections. The first is a per se rule of admissibility, which places the burden on the jury to determine the witness' credibility. This rule has been sparsely followed and has many flaws. The second approach calls for an elaborate set of procedural safeguards. However, these checks do not really detect whether the hypnotist intentionally or subconsciously implanted suggestions in the mind of the subject. Procedural safeguards also do nothing to eliminate the problems associated with bolstered witness confidence and erroneous juror perception. Finally, this approach puts considerable strain on a trial court as that court is forced to hear testimony from several competing experts and then make a rather sophisticated determination of whether the probative value of the testimony will outweigh its prejudicial effect. The third standard, per se inadmissibility, which relieves the trial judge of determining the quality of such evidence and relieves jurors of the responsibility of determining its credibility, has gained widespread acceptance. It properly applies the standard that a court should not allow into evidence a "scientific" test which the relevant scientific community has not recognized as reliable. The relevant scientific community does not generally accept that hypnotically induced recall is accurate. Therefore, because its reliability is suspect, and it is not amenable to verification due to the fact that even the experts cannot agree upon its effectiveness as a memory-restorative device, a witness' hypnotically induced testimony, other than that of the defendant, is not admissible in Illinois courts. Without the detective's hypnotically induced testimony, the jury could have reached a verdict of not guilty. Appellate court reversed; circuit court reversed; cause remanded.

EDITOR'S ANALYSIS: The case upon which the Illinois Supreme Court in Zayas based its standard of per se inadmissibility of hypnotically induced testimony was Frye v. United States, 293 F. 1013 (D.C. Cir., 1923). However, since this decision was handed down, the so-called "Frye Test" has been superseded by the Federal Rules of Evidence in all federal courts and in most state courts. To be admissible under Fed. R. Evid 104(a), proposed testimony must constitute scientific knowledge that will assist the trier of fact to understand or determine a fact or issue. See Daubert v. Merrell Dow Pharmaceutical, Inc., 113 S. Ct. 2786 (1993). The Daubert Court suggested that courts test reliability by ascertaining if the novel scientific technique has been tested, subjected to peer review, and generally accepted.

[For more information on witnesses and testimony, see Casenote Law Outline on Evidence, Chapter 11, § I, "Witness" Defined.]

NOTES:

STRICKLAND TRANSP. CO. v. INGRAM
Tx. Ct. Civ. App., 403 S.W.2d 192 (1966).

NATURE OF CASE: Appeal in venue action.

FACT SUMMARY: Ingram (P), who was injured when his car was struck by a truck allegedly owned by Strickland (D), testified that he learned after the accident that the truck was indeed Strickland's (D).

CONCISE RULE OF LAW: Testimony of a witness is admissible when it is possible for the witness to have obtained personal knowledge of the facts related.

FACTS: Ingram (P) was injured when his car was struck by a truck allegedly owned by Strickland (D). At the venue hearing, the trial court authorized trial in Panola County. The only issue on appeal was whether there was evidence that the driver of the truck figuring in the collision was at the time of the occurrence a servant, agent or representative of Strickland (D), and acting within the scope of his employment. At the venue hearing, Ingram (P) testified that he had learned after the accident that the truck was owned by Strickland (D). Strickland (D) contended that Ingram's (P) testimony was hearsay and had no probative value.

ISSUE: Is the testimony of a witness admissible when it is possible for the witness to have obtained personal knowledge of the facts related?

HOLDING AND DECISION: (Chadick, J.) Yes. First hand knowledge of the facts is a fundamental qualification of testimonial capacity. A witness may testify in accordance with his knowledge at the time his testimony is offered; he is not restricted to his knowledge at the time the event occurred. Testimony of a witness is admissible and, therefore, must be assumed to be endowed with probative value when it is possible under the record for the witness to have obtained personal knowledge of the facts related. Here, it appears that Ingram's (P) knowledge of the ownership of the truck was the result of facts perceptible to him, even though he learned of these facts subsequent to the collision. Thus, Ingram's (P) testimony was not hearsay and was properly admitted into evidence. Affirmed.

EDITOR'S ANALYSIS: The Federal Rules provide that "A witness may not testify to a matter unless evidence is introduced sufficient to support a finding that he has personal knowledge of the matter. Evidence to prove personal knowledge may, but need not, consist of the testimony of the witness himself." See, Federal Rule of Evidence 602.

[For more information on testimonial capacity, see Casenote Law Outline on Evidence, Chapter 5, § II, Preliminary Questions of Fact.]

JACKSON v. LEACH
Md. App. Ct., 160 Md. 139, 152 A. 813 (1931).

NATURE OF CASE: Appeal from award of damages for personal injuries.

FACT SUMMARY: At trial when Leach (P) sued to recover damages for personal injuries resulting from a collision between Leach's (P) car and Jackson's (D) car a lay witness testified as to the speed of Jackson's (D) car.

CONCISE RULE OF LAW: Testimony from a lay witness concerning the speed of a vehicle is admissible if the witness has a sufficient opportunity to observe the vehicle in motion.

FACTS: Leach (P) sued to recover damages for personal injuries which resulted from a collision between the automobile of Leach (P) and that of Howard Jackson (D) while Jackson's (D) car was being driven by Riall Jackson (D), the other defendant. The accident occurred at the intersection of Ellamont Street and Clifton Avenue in Baltimore. At trial, a witness, Hall, testified that he had seen Jackson's (D) car when it hit Leach's (P) car, and that Jackson's (D) car had been traveling at a "terrific speed." According to his own statement, Hall did not see Jackson's (D) car except at the moment of the collision, when he was half a block away from the point of impact. Judgment was rendered for Leach (P), and Jackson (D) appealed, contending that Hall's testimony should have been stricken, because it had no probative force.

ISSUE: Is testimony from a lay witness concerning the speed of a vehicle admissible if the witness had sufficient opportunity to observe the vehicle in motion?

HOLDING AND DECISION: (Adkins, J.) Yes. Testimony from a lay witness concerning the speed of a vehicle is admissible if the witness had a sufficient opportunity to observe the vehicle in motion. Here, the issue is whether the observation of the car which Hall had immediately before the collision was sufficient to give him any information as to the speed of the car. It should be noted that there was a clear space which afforded Hall at least a momentary view of the car before the collision. While under the circumstances it might be argued that the weight to be given to the testimony was slight, it is not possible to say that, as a matter of law, it was without any probative force, and that it should have been stricken.

EDITOR'S ANALYSIS: The majority of courts today will admit testimony concerning the speed of vehicles, provided that the lay witness is shown to have had a sufficient opportunity to observe the vehicle in motion. The witness need not be absolutely certain as to the exact speed of the vehicle, and this lack of certainty will not normally affect the admissibility of the evidence, unless the uncertainty appears to stem from a lack of opportunity to observe the matter related.

[For more information on testimony from lay witnesses, see Casenote Law Outline on Evidence, Chapter 12, § II, Lay Witness Opinions.]

PARKER v. HOEFER
Vt. Sup. Ct., 118 Vt. 1, 100 A.2d 434 (1953).

NATURE OF CASE: Appeal of award of damages for alienation of affections.

FACT SUMMARY: In an action for alienation of affections by enticement and criminal conversation, Parker (P) testified that her husband stayed out late at night, sometimes not returning the same day, and that he appeared exhausted, smelled of alcohol, and displayed intimacy toward Hoefer (D), who moved to strike this testimony as improper opinion evidence.

CONCISE RULE OF LAW: The conclusion, judgment, or opinion of a witness may be testified to where the facts underlying them are of such a character that they cannot be presented with proper force to anyone without the benefit of personal observation.

FACTS: Parker (P) brought an action against Hoefer (D) for alienation of affections by enticement and criminal conversation, alleging that Hoefer (D) was responsible for a breakdown of Parker's (P) marriage. Parker (P) testified that she became lonely and unhappy, lost sleep and weight, and became nervous when her husband began to come home very late and sometimes not until the following day after going out at night. She further testified that there was intimacy between Hoefer (D) and Parker's (P) husband, who appeared exhausted, looked haggard, and smelled of alcohol upon return, in addition to relating incidents of Hoefer's (D) "cozying off" with the husband at social functions. Another witness testified that Mr. Parker was not as kind and considerate toward Parker (P) as he had been before. Hoefer (D) appealed an award of damages to Parker (P), challenging the admission of the testimony as improper opinion evidence, admitted without foundation.

ISSUE: May the conclusion, judgment, or opinion of a witness be testified to where the facts underlying them are of such a character that they cannot be presented with proper force to anyone without the benefit of personal observation?

HOLDING AND DECISION: (Sherburne, J.) Yes. While there is a general rule that a witness must testify to facts and not opinions, there is an exception permitting such opinion testimony from a lay witness under certain circumstances. The conclusion, judgment or opinion of a witness may be testified to where the facts underlying them are of such a character that they cannot be presented with proper force to anyone without the benefit of personal observation. Therefore, since the kind of information Parker (P) sought to admit through her testimony could not be related by recitations of naked fact, her conclusions as to the facts based upon her observations were admissible. Affirmed.

EDITOR'S ANALYSIS: There is often a fine line between what is an "opinion" and what is a "fact." When someone is "tired," or "moving quickly," there may be no other effective way to explain what the witness saw. However, this notion (sometimes called the "collective facts" doctrine) cannot be extended to permit statements that a party "was negligent" or that otherwise invade the province of the trier of fact in drawing conclusions.

[For more information on opinion testimony, see Casenote Law Outline on Evidence, Chapter 12, § II, Lay Witness Opinions.]

NOTES:

KRUEGER v. STATE FARM MUTUAL AUTOMOBILE INS. CO.
707 F.2d 312 (8th Cir. 1983).

NATURE OF CASE: Appeal from denial of damages for wrongful death.

FACT SUMMARY: Krueger (P) contended that the trial court erred in refusing to admit lay opinion testimony.

CONCISE RULE OF LAW: Lay opinion testimony is admissible, in the discretion if the court, where it will be helpful to a clear understanding of the testimony given concerning the facts of the case.

FACTS: Mr. Krueger was killed when struck by Batchman's automobile. Castelli, a percipient witness, testified to the speed of the car and the distance between the car and Mr. Krueger when the driver first saw him. He was not allowed to testify whether, in his opinion, Batchman could have stopped and avoided the accident. The jury found against Mrs. Krueger (P) who appealed, contending the court erred in refusing to allow Castelli's lay opinion testimony.

ISSUE: Is lay opinion testimony admissible where it will be helpful to a clear understanding of the factual testimony?

HOLDING AND DECISION: (Per Curiam) Yes. Lay opinion testimony is admissible in the discretion of the court, where it will be helpful to a clear understanding of the testimony given concerning the facts of the case. Castelli provided testimony concerning the facts of the accident. His opinion could not have added to an understanding of these facts. It would have inappropriately suggested for the jury to use Castelli's lay opinion instead of their own evaluation of the evidence. As a result, the court correctly refused to admit it. Affirmed.

EDITOR'S ANALYSIS: The rule in this case derives from Federal Rule of Evidence 701. The determination of admissibility is in great part based on the discretion of the trial court. The danger exists that such opinion will be given too much weight, rather than used merely to explain the testimony.

[For more information on testimony of lay witnesses, see Casenote Law Outline on Evidence, Chapter 12, § II, Lay Witness Opinions.]

NOTES:

RUPERT v. PEOPLE
Colo. Sup. Ct., 163 Colo. 219, 429 P.2d 276 (1967).

NATURE OF CASE: Appeal from conviction for kidnapping.

FACT SUMMARY: Rupert (D) was initially found sane at the time of the crime, and then was found guilty of kidnapping, after a sanity trial where a lay person was permitted to testify that he thought Rupert was sane.

CONCISE RULE OF LAW: A layperson who is sufficiently acquainted with the accused may give an opinion as to the sanity of the accused.

FACTS: Rupert (D) was charged with kidnapping, to which he initially entered a plea of not guilty by reason of insanity. At the sanity trial, Durham, a lay witness, was permitted to testify as to his opinion of Rupert's (D) sanity. The jury then determined that Rupert (D) was sane at the time the alleged offense was committed. Rupert (D) then entered a general plea of not guilty. At the trial on the issues, Dr. Karcher, a psychiatrist, testified, that in his opinion, Rupert (D) was insane as of the date of the alleged commission of the crime. The trial court, sitting without a jury, found Rupert (D) guilty of the crime of kidnapping. On appeal, Rupert (D) argued that the trial court erred in permitting Durham to give opinion testimony, and in rejecting the "unrefuted" testimony of Dr. Karcher.

ISSUE: May a layperson who is sufficiently acquainted with the accused give an opinion as to the sanity of the accused?

HOLDING AND DECISION: (McWilliams, J.) Yes. One who, in the opinion of the trial court, shows adequate means of becoming acquainted with the person whose mental condition is in issue, after detailing the facts and circumstances concerning his acquaintance, and the acts, conduct, and conversation upon which his conclusion is based, may give his opinion on the question of sanity. The weight of that opinion is for the jury to decide. Here, the trial court committed no error in permitting Durham to express his opinion as to Rupert's (D) sanity. Durham related in considerable detail the facts and circumstances concerning his acquaintance with Rupert (D), as well as the acts, conduct, and conversation upon which his opinion was based. Further, the trial court committed no error in refusing to be bound by Dr. Karcher's testimony. While Karcher did opine that Rupert (D) was insane as of the date of the offense, Durham testified that, in his opinion, Rupert (D) was sane at the time of the kidnapping. Faced with conflicting testimony, the trier of fact could properly find that Rupert (D) was sane at the time of the offense. Affirmed.

EDITOR'S ANALYSIS: In most jurisdictions today, lay opinion testimony concerning mental condition is admitted, although usually subject to the requirement that an opinion supporting insanity must be prefaced by a recitation of the facts bolstering the opinion. Many American courts, as in the present case, continue to hold to the view that a verdict of sanity is sufficiently supported by lay testimony even where there is expert testimony to the contrary.

SMITH v. HOBART MFG. CO.
185 F. Supp. 751 (E.D. Pa. 1960).

NATURE OF CASE: Appeal from award of damages in products liability action.

FACT SUMMARY: Smith (P) sustained injuries to his hand and lower arm requiring amputation while operating a meat-grinding machine manufactured by Hobart (D), and, at trial, he called an expert who had not published on the subject to which he was to testify.

CONCISE RULE OF LAW: To qualify as an expert witness, a lay person must demonstrate specialized knowledge or particularized qualifications in that field of expertise.

FACTS: Smith (P) sustained injuries to his hand and lower arm requiring amputation while operating a meat-grinding machine manufactured by Hobart (D). Smith (P) alleged that his injuries were sustained because the machine was designed in an unsafe manner, and also that it was not manufactured in accordance with the requirements of the rules and regulations of the Pennsylvania Department of Labor and Industry. At trial, Smith (P) had called Davidlee Von Ludwig to testify as an expert witness, over strenuous objections by Hobart (D). Von Ludwig claimed to be a consulting materials and safety engineer. Although it was determined that he had not written about the subjects of meat grinders or safety in food machines, the court permitted Von Ludwig to testify. The jury found in favor of Smith (P), and Hobart (D) appealed.

ISSUE: To qualify as an expert witness, does a lay person have to demonstrate specialized knowledge or particularized qualifications in that field of expertise?

HOLDING AND DECISION: (Wood, J.) Yes. Traditionally, the qualifications of an expert are left to the discretion of the judge, while the weight and credibility of the testimony submitted after qualification is for the jury. However, the possession of the required qualifications must be expressly shown by the party offering the expert. In order to qualify as an expert, a lay person, in the absence of proven recorded achievements in his chosen field, should produce corroboration by another witness or submission of oral or documentary evidence confirming proof of his qualifications. Here, Von Ludwig had not qualified as an engineer because his educational background was in history, rather than the field of alleged expertise. Further, while Von Ludwig may have written over 150 articles on various technical subjects, there was no evidence to show that he ever wrote about meat grinders or safety in food machines. The lower court thus erred in ruling that Von Ludwig was qualified to testify as an expert reversed and remanded for new trial.

EDITOR'S ANALYSIS: Two separate issues are presented in this area. First, it is necessary to inquire whether the subject matter of the litigation is such that the trier of fact would be aided in its determination by the testimony of a person with specialized knowledge. Second, the trial judge must determine that the witness at hand is qualified in that area of specialized knowledge. Some examples of nontraditional expert testimony include a laborer held expert in the proper manner of shoring ditches, a wax salesman held expert in the proper application of wax to floors, and an iron worker held expert as to reasonable care in affixing retiling to the steps of a house.

[For more information on qualifications of an expert witness, see Casenote Law Outline on Evidence, Chapter 12, § III, Expert Opinions.]

NOTES:

UNITED STATES v. ALEXANDER
816 F.2d 164 (5th Cir. 1987).

NATURE OF CASE: Appeal from conviction for robbery.

FACT SUMMARY: The district court refused Alexander's (D) request to use expert testimony that photographic evidence against him was inconclusive.

CONCISE RULE OF LAW: Expert testimony concerning the reliability of photographic evidence is admissible.

FACTS: Alexander (D) was charged with bank robbery. The only evidence against him was the identification of a man in photographs as him. He was not allowed to present expert testimony that the individual in the photos could not be him. The court held that the jury could determine identification without such testimony. Alexander (D) was convicted and appealed.

ISSUE: Is expert testimony concerning the reliability of photographic evidence admissible?

HOLDING AND DECISION: (Williams, J.) Yes. Expert testimony concerning the reliability of photographic evidence is admissible. A jury of common experience is not as well qualified to evaluate the reliability of photographic evidence as the experts retained by Alexander (D). Subtle points of light and measurement can shade a lay person's ability to evaluate a photograph. Because such testimony was kept from the jury, the court committed reversible error. Reversed.

EDITOR'S ANALYSIS: Determinations of the propriety of expert testimony is usually left to the discretion of the trial court. In this case, the reviewing court determined the refusal to allow the expert testimony was an abuse of this discretion.

[For more information on the admission of expert testimony, see Casenote Law Outline on Evidence, Chapter 12, § III, Expert Opinions.]

NOTES:

THOMAS v. METZ
Wyo. Sup. Ct., 714 P.2d 1205 (1986).

NATURE OF CASE: Appeal from denial of damages for malpractice.

FACT SUMMARY: Thomas (P) contended that the trial court erred in allowing Metz (D) to present expert witnesses whose testimony was based on Metz's (D) deposition.

CONCISE RULE OF LAW: Expert witnesses may base opinions on inadmissible testimony.

FACTS: Thomas (P) sued Metz (D) for medical malpractice arising out of back surgery. Metz (D) presented expert testimony that the surgery was necessary and was competently performed. Thomas (P) objected to the admission of such testimony, arguing that the opinions were based on Metz's (D) deposition testimony, portions of which were inadmissible. The objections were overruled and a verdict for Metz (D) was returned. Thomas (P) appealed.

ISSUE: May expert witnesses base opinions on inadmissible testimony?

HOLDING AND DECISION: (Brown, J.) Yes. Expert witnesses may base opinions on inadmissible testimony. The opinions in this case were not rendered void merely because they were partially based on Metz's (D) deposition. The opinions were also based upon a review of the medical records and other admissible evidence. As a result, it was within the discretion of the trial court to admit the testimony. Affirmed.

EDITOR'S ANALYSIS: Many jurisdictions have liberal rules concerning what may serve as the basis for an expert opinion. They allow the expert to rely on anything, and leave impeachment to cross-examination. This often allows the existence of inadmissible evidence to come to the attention of the jury.

[For more information on expert witness testimony, see Casenote Law Outline on Evidence, Chapter 12, § III, Expert Opinions.]

HARRIS v. SMITH
372 F.2d 806 (8th Cir. 1967).

NATURE OF CASE: Appeal from denial of damages in malpractice action.

FACT SUMMARY: Harris (P) charged that Dr. Smith (D) was responsible for the amputation of his son Patrick's right arm.

CONCISE RULE OF LAW: Hypothetical questions must be based on the facts rather than upon other expert opinion.

FACTS: Harris (P), as father and guardian of Patrick Harris, sued Dr. Richard Smith (D), alleging that Dr. Smith's (D) negligence and malpractice had been responsible for the amputation of Patrick's right arm. Patrick, who had sustained a broken right arm in falling from a tree, had been treated by Dr. Smith (D). Three days after the accident, the arm had become infected by gangrene, necessitating amputation. At trial, counsel for Smith (D) had called and questioned two physicians who had not seen Patrick, but who were testifying as expert witnesses. Over objection, counsel for Smith (D) was permitted to ask each physician a hypothetical question which also included Dr. Smith's (D) own opinions. The jury found in favor of Smith (D), and Harris (P) appealed, claiming that improper hypothetical questions had been posed by counsel for Smith (D).

ISSUE: Must hypothetical questions be based upon the facts in evidence, rather than upon other expert opinion?

HOLDING AND DECISION: (Vogel, J.) Yes. It is improper, when asking a hypothetical question of an expert witness, to incorporate within the question being asked the opinion of other expert witnesses, for opinion upon opinion diverges much too far from the plain facts upon which all proper hypothetical questions must be grounded. Hypothetical questions must be based upon the facts rather than upon other expert opinion. A hypothetical question must assume all facts disclosed by the evidence material to the theory of the case as viewed from the side propounding the question. A question which assumes any material fact not supported by the evidence is inadmissible. A question which omits any material fact essential to the formation of a rational opinion is likewise incompetent. Here, the hypothetical questions under consideration were defective because they called for expert opinion based upon previously expressed expert opinion, rather than upon the plain facts; and the plain facts that were adduced did not portray a fair, complete picture for the jury's consideration. Accordingly, the case is remanded for a new trial.

EDITOR'S ANALYSIS: The Federal Rules, in addressing the topic of what constitutes a proper basis for expert testimony, states that "the facts or data in the particular case upon which an expert bases an opinion or inference may be those perceived by or made known to him at or before the hearing. If of a type reasonably relied upon by experts in the particular field in forming opinions or inferences upon the subject, the facts or data need not be admissible in evidence." Federal Rule of Evidence 703.

[For more information on hypothetical questions and expert testimony, see Casenote Law Outline on Evidence, Chapter 12, § III, Expert Opinions.]

NOTES:

CARR v. RADKEY
Tx. Sup. Ct., 393 S.W.2d 806 (1965).

NATURE OF CASE: Action to recover for personal injuries and damage to property.

FACT SUMMARY: Radkey (D) contested the probating of Hewlett's will, alleging that she had been incompetent at the time of its execution. The proponents (P) of the will sought to introduce expert testimony of a specialist in mental illnesses, but the court would not permit him to testify that the testatrix had been competent when she made her will.

CONCISE RULE OF LAW: A witness may testify concerning the mental condition and ability of a testator, but may not offer testimony which involves definitions, tests, or concepts of a purely legal nature.

FACTS: Radkey (D) and others (D) contested the probating of two holographic wills executed by Hattie Hewlett. Carr (P) and the State (P), as proponents of one of the wills, sought to introduce the testimony of Dr. Hoerster, an expert in mental illnesses. The court, however, refused to permit Hoerster to express any opinion as to whether or not the testatrix had comprehended the nature and effect of her act, and knew her beneficiaries and the extent of her property. Hoerster was permitted to testify that Hewlett was a manic depressive who often exhibited insane behavior, but that her affliction often vanished during periods of remission, and that on these occasions her behavior was normal. Hoerster was not, however, permitted to speculate as to whether Hewlett's will indicated that it had been executed during a lucid interval. For the record, but out of the hearing of the jury, Hoerster was permitted to respond to the questions which had been found objectionable, and his answers were favorable to the proponents (P) of the will. The jury found that Hewlett had lacked testamentary capacity. Therefore her will was denied probate, and Carr (P) and the State (P) appealed, alleging error in the exclusion of the testimony offered by Hoerster.

ISSUE: May a specialist in mental illnesses testify concerning either a testatrix' competency in general or her lucidity at the times that she executed her will?

HOLDING AND DECISION: (Greenhill, J.) Yes. Although the authorities sometimes fail to make a proper distinction between the two types of evidence, testimony relating to a witness's perceptions of a testator's mental condition is always admissible, but expressions of opinion concerning legal capacity will be excluded. Although several objections to the receiving of evidence of a testator's mental capacity have been suggested, they are largely spurious. For example, it is argued that testimony concerning the competency of the testator invades the province of the jury and also requires the witness to resolve the ultimate issue of the case. However, most authorities permit questions which call for opinions on ultimate issues, and the objection that the province of the jurors will be invaded is unrealistic since it ignores the fact that jurors can always choose to disbelieve any evidence offered, and will only accord it such weight as it deserves. Therefore, testimony concerning a testator's competency is inadmissible only to the extent that it involves the witness' expression of opinions concerning concepts which are purely legal in nature. In the present case, the testimony sought did not pertain to the testatrix' legal capacity to make a will, and therefore should have been admitted. Its exclusion constituted prejudicial error since it prevented Hoerster from properly developing his testimony. Therefore, the judgment denying probate of the will must be reversed and a new trial granted.

EDITOR'S ANALYSIS: It has been observed that the danger against which the rule of Carr v. Radkey guards will rarely present itself, since questions which arguably call for legal conclusions will rarely be asked except when the popular meaning of a concept is approximately the same as its legal definition. Otherwise, a question calling for an opinion based on the former will have no bearing on the latter. Carr v. Radkey seems to reject the recommendation that confusion be averted by requiring counsel to define all concepts referred to in his question. Traditionally, a witness was precluded from offering any testimony concerning an ultimate fact in issue, and this rule is still observed in some jurisdictions.

[For more information on opinion testimony from expert witnesses, see Casenote Law Outline on Evidence, Chapter 12, § III, Expert Opinions.]

NOTES:

AKE v. OKLAHOMA
470 U.S. 68 (1985).

NATURE OF CASE: Appeal from conviction for murder.

FACT SUMMARY: The trial court denied Ake's (D) request for access to a psychiatrist to prove his insanity defense.

CONCISE RULE OF LAW: The Constitution requires the state to provide an indigent defendant access to a psychiatrist to aid in proving an insanity defense.

FACTS: Ake (D) was charged with murder. He claimed he was insane at the time of the incident and requested the state be required to provide him with a psychiatrist to prove his defense. The request was denied. At trial, the court instructed the jury that Ake (D) had the burden of providing evidence of his insanity at the time of the offense. He was convicted and appealed, contending that the Constitution required the state to provide indigent defendants psychiatric access. The court of appeals affirmed, and the Supreme Court granted certiorari.

ISSUE: Does the Constitution require a state provide indigent criminal defendants access to a psychiatric evaluator where his sanity is in issue?

HOLDING AND DECISION: (Marshall, J.) Yes. The Constitution requires the state to provide an indigent criminal defendant access to psychiatric evaluation where his sanity at the time of the offense is a material aspect of his defense. The importance of accuracy in criminal proceedings is immeasurable. Placing the burden of showing a state of mind on a defendant without providing the basic tools to achieve it is unconstitutional. As a result, the denial of access to a psychiatrist rendered the conviction erroneous. Reversed.

CONCURRENCE: (Burger, C.J.) A capital case requires an indigent defendant be afforded such access.

DISSENT: (Rehnquist, J.) The rule enunciated by the Court is too broad and should be limited to capital cases.

EDITOR'S ANALYSIS: There is federal authority for providing indigent defendants access to expert testimony in general. Under 18 U.S.C. § 3006, expert assistance is available. This compliments Federal Rule of Evidence 706 which allows the court to appoint such experts.

[For more information on the use of court-appointed experts, see Casenote Law Outline on Evidence, Chapter 12, § III, Expert Opinions.]

STATE v. GREEN
Wash. Sup. Ct., 71 Wash. 2d. 372, 428 P.2d 540 (1967).

NATURE OF CASE: Appeal from burglary conviction.

FACT SUMMARY: Green (D) and two others were charged with burglarizing a pharmacy, and at trial, the State (P) impeached one of its own witnesses.

CONCISE RULE OF LAW: A party may impeach his own witness in the event of genuine surprise and hostility.

FACTS: Green (D) was charged with burglary after having been apprehended by police officers while fleeing from the scene of the crime, the Medical Center Pharmacy. Green (D) contended that the burglary had been undertaken by two of his companions, Gaither and Wilkerson, while Green (D), ignorant of the others' purpose, waited in a car. At trial, the State (P) called Gaither as a witness. After Gaither denied that Green (D) had participated in the burglary, the State (P) was permitted to impeach Gaither's testimony through the introduction of a confession by Gaither incriminating Green (D) as an accomplice. The State (P) was only allowed to impeach Gaither's testimony because it claimed surprise and unexpected hostility from him. Green (D) was convicted of burglary and argued that the trial court committed reversible error in allowing the State (P) to impeach its own witness, Gaither.

ISSUE: May a party impeach his own witness in the event of genuine surprise and hostility?

HOLDING AND DECISION: (Hale, J.) Yes. A party may impeach his own witness in the event of genuine surprise and hostility. A party may not impeach his own witness unless without warning the witness tells a story different from the one the party calling him had a reasonable right to expect of him. Here, at the time the State (P) called Gaither, the prosecuting attorney had in hand a detailed statement of the crime signed by Gaither and describing Green (D) as one of two accomplices. Made by Gaither without duress, coercion or fear, the statement recited Gaither's and his accomplice's step-by-step participation in the burglary, and corroborated in detail the mass of other evidence which the prosecuting attorney intended to offer in the State's (P) case in chief. Gaither had never, to the prosecuting attorney's knowledge, repudiated the statement nor had he ever intimated to the prosecuting attorney at any time before being put on the witness stand that he intended to do so.

EDITOR'S ANALYSIS: This case is illustrative of the traditional rule prohibiting a party from impeaching its own witness, except where there is present both surprise and damage to that party. The Federal Rules have adopted an opposite view, stating that "the credibility of a witness may be attacked by any party, including the party calling him." Federal Rule of Evidence 607.

[For more information on "surprise" testimony, see Casenote Law Outline on Evidence, Chapter 11, § VII, Impeachment of Witnesses.]

BECKER v. EISENSTODT
N.J. Super. 60 N.J. Super. 240, 158 A.2d 706 (1960).

NATURE OF CASE: Appeal from dismissal of negligence action.

FACT SUMMARY: Becker's (P) daughter, Arlene, allegedly suffered injuries during post-operative treatment, and Eisenstodt (D) was called by Becker (P) as a witness at trial.

CONCISE RULE OF LAW: When a party calls the opposing party as a witness, he is not bound by the testimony of that opposing party.

FACTS: Becker (P), individually and as guardian ad litem of his daughter Arlene, brought an action against Eisenstodt (D), a physician and surgeon, charging negligence in administering a caustic solution during post-operative treatment of Arlene, thereby severely burning and disfiguring her. Becker (P) contended that Eisenstodt (D) had negligently inserted a caustic solution into Arlene's right nostril. At trial, Becker (P) called Eisenstodt (D) to the stand. Eisenstodt (D) testified that he had inserted a normal medicinal solution of 10% cocaine into Arlene's nose and nothing else. Two medical expert witnesses called subsequently by Becker (P) contradicted this testimony. The trial judge granted Eisenstodt's (D) motion to dismiss with prejudice at the close of Becker's (P) case, and Becker (P) appealed. Eisenstodt (D) contended that because Becker (P) had called him as a witness, Becker (P) was therefore bound by Eisenstodt's (D) testimony.

ISSUE: When a party calls the opposing party as a witness, is he bound by the testimony of that opposing party?

HOLDING AND DECISION: (Goldmann, J.) No. The traditional rule held that a party, by calling a witness, represented him to be worthy of some credit and was therefore bound by his testimony. However, this rule must now yield to reason and common sense. If there is any situation in which any semblance of reason disappears for the application of the rule against impeaching one's own witness, it is when the opposing party is himself called by the first party and is sought to be compelled to disclose under oath that truth which he knows but is naturally unwilling to make known. The present situation, though, should be distinguished from one where a party is permitted to neutralize unexpectedly adverse testimony given by its own witness, damaging to his case. In the latter case, if the party is genuinely surprised, the trial court, in the sound exercise of its legal discretion, may be permitted to show that the witness had made prior statements inconsistent with, or contradictory to, the testimony presently given. Reversed and remanded for a new trial.

EDITOR'S ANALYSIS: The Advisory Committee's notes to Federal Rule of Evidence 607, which is in accord with the holding of this case, states that: "The traditional rule against impeaching one's own witness is abandoned as based on false premises. A party does not hold out his witnesses as worthy of belief, since he rarely has a free choice in selecting them. Denial of the right leaves the party at the mercy of the witness and the adversary."

[For more information on attacking the credibility of a witness, see Casenote Law Outline on Evidence, Chapter 11, § VII, Impeachment of Witnesses.]

NOTES:

CASENOTE LEGAL BRIEFS — EVIDENCE

UNITED STATES v. WEBSTER
734 F.2d 1191 (7th Cir. 1984).

NATURE OF CASE: Appeal from conviction of aiding and abetting a bank robbery and receiving stolen funds.

FACT SUMMARY: Webster (D) appealed from his conviction of aiding and abetting a bank robbery and receiving stolen funds, arguing it was impermissible to call a hostile witness for the purpose of introducing inadmissible evidence for impeachment purposes.

CONCISE RULE OF LAW: Impeachment by prior inconsistent statement is impermissible if used to get otherwise inadmissible evidence before the jury.

FACTS: Webster (D) was accused of aiding and abetting a bank robbery and receiving stolen funds. The Government (P) introduced the testimony of King, the bank robber, and then offered prior inconsistent statements by which King inculpated Webster (D). His testimony at trial would have exculpated Webster (D). The Government (P) attempted to introduce King's testimony outside the jury, but defense counsel objected. Webster (D) was convicted and appealed, contending it was impermissible to call a hostile witness for the purpose of introducing inadmissible evidence for impeachment purposes.

ISSUE: Is impeachment by prior inconsistent statement permissible if used to get otherwise inadmissible evidence before the jury?

HOLDING AND DECISION: (Posner, J.) No. Impeachment by prior inconsistent statement is impermissible if used to get otherwise inadmissible evidence before the jury. Using evidence in this way places hearsay evidence in as substantive evidence against Webster (D), a result neither contemplated nor authorized by Federal Rule of Evidence 607. Here, however, there was no bad faith on the part of the Government (P). The prosecutor did not know what King would say and offered to examine King outside the presence of the jury. The good faith standard strikes the proper balance among competing interests. Affirmed.

EDITOR'S ANALYSIS: Many articles have been written on the delicate subject of impeaching one's own witness. Some argue Webster's (D) position in the present case, that the courts should require surprise and harm before impeachment by prior inconsistent statement is allowed. See 3A Wigmore, Evidence §§ 896-918 (Chadbourn rev. 1970) for background on the issue of impeaching one's own witness.

[For more information on prior inconsistent statements, see Casenote Law Outline on Evidence, Chapter 9, § VII, Exemption: Prior Statements of Witnesses.]

BARTON PLUMBING CO. v. JOHNSON
Tx. Ct. Civ. App., 285 S.W.2d 780 (1955).

NATURE OF CASE: Appeal from award of damages for negligence.

FACT SUMMARY: Johnson (P), who sued Barton (D) for personal injuries arising out of an automobile collision, was allowed to show Barton's (D) doctor's interest in the case, which necessarily revealed that Barton (D) was insured.

CONCISE RULE OF LAW: A party has the right to cross-examine a witness about possible bias or interest, even though the disclosure will also reveal the presence of liability insurance in the case.

FACTS: Johnson (P) sued Barton (D) for personal injuries resulting from a collision between Johnson's (P) pick-up truck and another pick-up truck owned by Barton (D). The trial court, over Barton's (D) objections, allowed evidence to be introduced showing that Dr. Solomon David, one of Barton's (D) medical witnesses, had been a stockholder and director in the Traders and General Insurance Company, and that Barton (D) was indemnified against liability on the accident in question under a policy of automobile liability insurance which Barton (D) held with that insurance company. Dr. David was a stockholder and director at the time he examined Johnson (P) and made the written report concerning which he was called to testify. After the jury found for Johnson (P), Barton (D) appealed, arguing that the trial court erred in admitting this testimony into evidence.

ISSUE: Does a party have the right to cross-examine a witness about possible bias or interest, even though the disclosure will also reveal the presence of liability insurance in the case?

HOLDING AND DECISION: (Hamblen, J.) Yes. Ordinarily, it is error to inform a jury in a common law damage suit that the defendant is indemnified by liability insurance on the accident in question, unless such showing is made on a material issue. However, this principle was not intended to supersede the rule that a party has the right to cross-examine the witness produced by his adversary, touching every relation tending to show interest or bias. Here, Dr. David's status as an agent of the insurance company was a proper topic for cross-examination, inasmuch as it might provide the basis for an inference of bias. Because the testimony was highly relevant, its admission in evidence was not error. Affirmed.

EDITOR'S ANALYSIS: The present case reflects the great importance which the courts generally place upon the need for effective cross-examination. Thus, the majority of courts will allow an inquiry on cross-examination into any affiliations of a witness which might produce interest or bias, even when the testimony of the witness might reveal the existence of liability insurance in the case.

[For more information on evidence of witness bias, see Casenote Law Outline on Evidence, Chapter 11, § VII, Impeachment of Witnesses.]

ALFORD v. UNITED STATES
282 U.S. 687 (1931).

NATURE OF CASE: Appeal from conviction for mail fraud.

FACT SUMMARY: Alford (D) claimed that he had been denied the right to engage in effective cross-examination by not being allowed to show possible bias of a witness.

CONCISE RULE OF LAW: The existence of bias is a proper subject for cross-examination.

FACTS: Alford (D) was convicted of using the mails to defraud. At trial, the Government (P) called as a witness a former employee of Alford (D). On direct examination, he gave damaging testimony with respect to various transactions of Alford (D). On cross-examination, questions seeking to elicit the witness' place of residence were excluded on the Government's (P) objection that they were immaterial and not proper cross-examination. Counsel for Alford (D) argued that the jury was entitled to know who the witness was, what his business was, and argued that he had been informed that the witness was then in the custody of federal authorities, presenting the possibility of bias or prejudice. On appeal, the court of appeals upheld the trial court's ruling excluding that line of questioning on cross-examination.

ISSUE: Is the existence of bias a proper subject for cross-examination?

HOLDING AND DECISION: (Stone, J.) Yes. Cross-examination of a witness is a matter of right. Its permissible purposes, among others, are that the witness may be identified with his community so that independent testimony may be sought and offered of his reputation for veracity in his own neighborhood; that the jury may interpret his testimony in the light, reflected upon it by knowledge of his environment; and that facts may be brought out tending to discredit the witness by showing that his testimony in chief was untrue or biased. It is the essence of a fair trial that reasonable latitude be given the cross-examiner, even though he is unable to state to the court what facts a reasonable cross-examination might develop. The present case was a proper one for searching cross-examination. Counsel for Alford (D) should have been allowed to identify the witness with his environment. In addition, Alford (D) was entitled to show by cross-examination that his testimony was affected by fear or favor growing out of his detention. Although there is a duty to protect a witness from questions which go beyond the bounds of proper cross-examination merely to harass, annoy, or humiliate him, no such case is presented here. Because the actions taken by the trial court were an abuse of discretion and prejudicial error, its decision is reversed.

EDITOR'S ANALYSIS: There are several other ways in which the right to cross-examine may be lost. Sometimes, a witness will die or become physically incapacitated during the time between direct and cross-examination. Occasionally too, a witness will claim an evidentiary privilege which precludes inquiry into otherwise relevant matters.

[For more information on evidence of witness bias, see Casenote Law Outline on Evidence, Chapter 11, § VII, Impeachment of Witnesses.]

NOTES:

ROSS v. FOSS
S.D. Sup. Ct., 77 S.D. 358, 92 N.W.2d 147 (1958).

NATURE OF CASE: Appeal from award of damages for negligence.

FACT SUMMARY: Foss (P) sued Ross (D) for a whiplash injury received in an automobile accident.

CONCISE RULE OF LAW: Treatises or books may be used to impeach an expert witness when that witness has used the treatise in giving his testimony.

FACTS: Foss (P) sued Ross (D) to recover damages for a whiplash injury received in an automobile collision on July 27, 1956. A verdict was returned in favor of Foss (P). Ross (D) appealed, alleging that the trial court had erred in not permitting the use of medical treatises in the cross-examination of Dr. Walter Van Demark, an orthopedic physician who testified for Foss (P) as a medical expert. The treatises in question were an article by Dr. Gotten and Dr. Eggers in the Journal of the American Medical Association. Counsel for Ross (D) had proposed to read portions of the article to the witness and ask if he agreed.

ISSUE: May treatises or books be used to impeach an expert witness when that witness has used the treatise in giving his testimony?

HOLDING AND DECISION: (Rentto, J.) Yes. The general rule is that medical books or treatises are not admissible to prove the truth of the statements contained therein. However, books or treatises may be used on the cross-examination of a witness when he admittedly has used the treatise in giving his testimony. It is proper to show that the work he admits he relied on discredits his testimony. If the witness has not relied on or cited the treatise as supporting his opinion, it may not be used on his cross-examination unless its authoritative status is established either by his admission or otherwise. From the testimony given at trial, it does not appear that Dr. Van Demark relied on the Gotten article. Nor does it establish the article involved as authority. Accordingly, there was no foundation for the proposed cross-examination. Affirmed.

EDITOR'S ANALYSIS: The Federal Rules provide that "to the extent called to the attention of an expert witness upon cross-examination or relied upon him in direct examination, statements contained in published treatises, periodicals, or pamphlets on a subject of history, medicine, or other science or art, established as a reliable authority by the testimony or admission of the witness, or by other expert testimony or by judicial notice" constitute an exception to the hearsay rule. See, Federal Rule of Evidence 803.

[For more information on the treatise exception, see Casenote Law Outline on Evidence, Chapter 10, § IX, Miscellaneous Hearsay Exceptions.]

MARSHALL v. MARTINSON
Or. Sup. Ct., 98 Or. 1079, 518 P.2d 1312 (1974).

NATURE OF CASE: Appeal from denial of damages in personal injury action.

FACT SUMMARY: Marshall (P), who was injured in a collision with Martinson's (D) automobile, appealed the trial judge's refusal to admit evidence of Martinson's (D) prior drunk driving conviction.

CONCISE RULE OF LAW: A witness may be impeached through introduction of evidence of a prior conviction of any crime.

FACTS: Marshall (P) sued Martinson (D) for damages for personal injuries sustained in an automobile accident which occurred on an interstate highway as Martinson's (D) automobile was overtaking and passing Marshall's (P) pickup truck. At trial, the judge sustained Martinson's (D) objection to the introduction in evidence of a record of the conviction of Martinson (D) on a state charge for the crime of driving under the influence of intoxicating liquor. After the jury found for Martinson (D), Marshall (P) appealed, contending that the trial court erred in excluding the proffered impeachment evidence.

ISSUE: May a witness be impeached through introduction of evidence of a prior conviction of any crime?

HOLDING AND DECISION: (Tongue, J.) Yes. A witness may be impeached by the party against whom he was called by his examination or by the record of the judgment, that he has been convicted of a crime. This is because a jury may properly find that a person who has been convicted of any crime may be less reliable as a witness than a person who has never been convicted of any crime. It follows then that the trial court had no discretion to reject Marshall's (P) offer of proof of the prior conviction upon the ground that undue prejudice would result. Reversed and remanded for a new trial.

DISSENT: (O'Connell, J.) The conviction for the crime of driving under the influence of intoxicants is not probative of Martinson's (D) credibility, and the use of the evidence of the prior conviction could severely prejudice Martinson (D) in the eyes of the jury. Courts in other jurisdictions have construed similar rules to exclude evidence of prior convictions unless the offense was one involving moral turpitude.

EDITOR'S ANALYSIS: The Federal Rules provide that for purposes of impeaching a witness "evidence that he has been convicted of a crime shall be admitted . . . but only if the crime (1) was punishable by death or imprisonment in excess of one year under the law under which he was convicted, and the court determines that the probative value of admitting the evidence outweighs its prejudicial effect to the defendant, or (2) involved dishonesty or false statement, regardless of the punishment." See, Federal Rule of Evidence 609(a).

[For more information on impeachment through prior convictions, see Casenote Law Outline on Evidence, Chapter 6, § V, Character to Impeach.]

UNITED STATES v. ORTIZ
553 F.2d 782 (2d Cir. 1977), cert. denied, 434 U.S. 897 (1977).

NATURE OF CASE: Appeal from conviction for distributing cocaine, possessing cocaine with intent to distribute it, and conspiring to distribute.

FACT SUMMARY: Ortiz (D) argued that the lower court abused its discretion in ruling that the federal government (P) might use, for impeachment purposes, Ortiz' (D) four-year-old narcotics conviction, which caused Ortiz (D) to forgo taking the stand and testifying in his own behalf.

CONCISE RULE OF LAW: A prior narcotics conviction may be used to impeach a defendant if probative on the issue of credibility.

FACTS: Ortiz (D) was charged by the federal government (P) with distributing cocaine, possessing cocaine with intent to distribute it, and conspiracy to distribute. At trial, the judge ruled that the federal government (P) could use a four-year-old conviction for selling heroin to impeach Ortiz (D) should he decide to take the stand in his own defense. Based on this ruling, Ortiz (D) chose not to testify. He was convicted and appealed, claiming reversible error because the lower court had abused its discretion.

ISSUE: May a prior narcotics conviction be used to impeach a defendant if probative on the issue of credibility?

HOLDING AND DECISION: (Owen, J.) Yes. A prior narcotics conviction may be used to impeach a defendant if probative on the issue of credibility. Rule 609(a) of the Federal Rules of Evidence provides in pertinent part: "For the purpose of attacking the credibility of a witness, evidence that he has been convicted of a crime shall be admitted if elicited from him or established by public record during cross-examination but only if the crime was punishable by death or imprisonment in excess of one year under the law under which he was convicted, and the court determines that the probative value of admitting this evidence outweighs its prejudicial effect to the defendant." This Rule gives broad discretion to the trial judge. One factor to be considered is whether the crime, by its nature, is probative of lack of veracity. Here, the district judge in his discretion was entitled to recognize that a narcotics trafficker lives a life of secrecy and dissembling. From this, he could rationally conclude that such activity in a witness' past is probative on the issue of credibility. Moreover, to allow Ortiz (D), if he took the stand, to appear "pristine" would have been unfair and misleading to the jury, especially since the credibility of his accuser — a confidential informant — had also been called into question. Under the circumstances presented, the district court did not abuse its discretion. Affirmed.

DISSENT: (Mansfield, J.) In drafting Rule 609(a), Congress was torn between two conflicting interests. Letting the jury have information regarding a prior conviction to the extent that it might bear on a defendant's credibility as a witness competed with a drive to avoid deterring the defendant, because of the obvious prejudice that might be caused by the jury's learning of his prior conviction, from testifying in his own defense. Congress finally conceded that the credibility of a witness, whether a defendant or someone else, may be attacked by proof of prior conviction but only if the crime was (1) a felony or (2) involved dishonesty or false statement regardless of the punishment. Applying Rule 609(a) here, Ortiz' (D) prior conviction for a narcotics sale could not be used against him as a crime which involved dishonesty since there is no showing by the federal government (P) that fraud or dishonesty constituted elements of the prior crime itself.

EDITOR'S ANALYSIS: Most often, appellate courts have not required that trial judges make explicit findings regarding Fed. R. Evid. 609(a) rulings. The trial judge has wide discretion in this area, regardless of whether or not she makes explicit findings. Such discretion may be held to have been abused if the trial judge has not considered that the defendant might have been prejudiced. Under Rule 609(b), courts have required specific findings regarding rulings on the admissibility of convictions older that ten years.

[For more information on character to impeach, see Casenote Law Outline on Evidence, Chapter 6, § V, Character to Impeach.]

NOTES:

ALTOBELLO v. BORDEN CONFECTIONARY PRODUCTS, INC.

872 F.2d 215 (7th Cir. 1989).

NATURE OF CASE: Appeal from defense verdict action seeking damages for age discrimination.

FACT SUMMARY: When Altobello (P) sued Borden Confectionary Products, Inc. (D) for firing him because of his age, he argued that Borden (D) should not be permitted to impeach his credibility as a witness by questioning him about a prior misdemeanor conviction for meter tampering.

CONCISE RULE OF LAW: A witness may be impeached by proof that he was convicted of a crime if the manner in which the witness committed the offense involved deceit.

FACTS: Altobello (P) brought suit against Borden (D), charging that Borden (D) fired him because of his age, in violation of the Age Discrimination in Employment Act. At trial, Borden (D) presented evidence that it had fired Altobello (P) because he was a malingerer, and Altobello (P) responded with evidence that this alleged malingering was merely a pretext for an age-motivated discharge. The jury found in favor of Borden (D). On appeal, Altobello (P) argued that the district court erred in allowing Borden (D) to impeach his credibility on the stand by questioning him about a ten-year-old conviction for tampering with the electric meters of Commonwealth Edison.

ISSUE: May a witness be impeached by proof that he was convicted of a crime if the manner in which the witness committed the offense involved deceit?

HOLDING AND DECISION: (Posner, J.) Yes. Rule 609(a)(2) of the Fed. R. Evid. allows a witness to be impeached by proof that he was convicted of a crime that involved dishonesty or false statement, regardless of whether it was a felony or a misdemeanor. Altobello (P) contended that unless Borden (D) was required to show that the specific acts for which Altobello (P) was convicted involved dishonesty in the sense of deception, any misdemeanor conviction would be usable for impeachment regardless of how prejudice and probative value balanced out since all crimes are, in a sense dishonest acts. In the case of some crimes, such as perjury, deceit is an element of the crime. In the case of other crimes, the court must look to the way the offense was committed. A person who has used deceit to commit a crime is more likely than another type of criminal or a law-abiding person to perceive the witness stand as an attractive site for further deceit. Here, the deceitful nature of the crime is plain on the face of the indictment. Altobello (P) was convicted of a misdemeanor theft — meter tampering. Meter tampering is necessarily a crime of deception; the goal is always to deceive the meter reader. It is therefore securely within the scope of Rule 609(a)(2). Affirmed.

EDITOR'S ANALYSIS: The Altobello case was decided in 1989, and the Seventh Circuit Court of Appeals specifically stated in this case that Fed. R. Evid. 403 was applicable to Rule 609(a)(2). That is, the balancing test provided in Rule 403, which directs exclusion of evidence the prejudicial effects of which substantially outweigh its probative value, was not to be considered in a Rule 609(a)(2) analysis.

However, Rule 609(a)(2) was later amended to require such an analysis. It is doubtful, though, that the decision in Altobello would have been different under the Amended Rule 609(a)(2).

[For more information on impeachment using a prior conviction, see Casenote Law Outline on Evidence, Chapter 6, § V, Character to Impeach.]

NOTES:

DOE v. UNITED STATES
666 F.2d 43 (4th Cir. 1981).

NATURE OF CASE: Appeal from denial of injunctive relief.

FACT SUMMARY: A prosecution witness in a rape trial (Doe) sought to seal the record on evidence of her sexual activity.

CONCISE RULE OF LAW: Evidence of sexual reputation and opinion evidence of sexual behavior may not be used to show an alleged rape victim's state of mind.

FACTS: Doe accused Black (D) of rape. Black (D) compelled the use of evidence of Doe's past sexual reputation and behavior to prove she consented to intercourse. Doe sought to seal the record in the criminal trial and brought a civil action to obtain permanent sealing of the record. Both were denied, and she appealed.

ISSUE: Is evidence of sexual reputation and behavior of an alleged rape victim admissible to show her state of mind?

HOLDING AND DECISION: (Butzner, J.) No. Evidence of sexual reputation and opinion evidence of sexual behavior may not be used to show an alleged rape victim's state of mind. Such evidence is of doubtful probative value, and its inflammatory content clearly outweighs its probative value. Evidence of what Black (D) knew of Doe's reputation is admissible, however, because it goes to the issue of Black's (D) intent. Conversations between Black (D) and Doe are also admissible. However, beyond that, the balance of the evidence was inadmissible. Reversed in part; affirmed in part.

EDITOR'S ANALYSIS: The court indicated that in some extreme circumstances, the evidence rejected in this case might be admissible. In the absence of a rape shield statute, the evidence could be used for impeachment or substantively to prove a defense.

[For more information on admission of rape victim's character, see Casenote Law Outline on Evidence, Chapter 6, § III, Character to Prove Conduct.]

NOTES:

STATE v. MORGAN
N.C. Sup. Ct., 315 N.C. 626, 340 S.E.2d 84 (1986).

NATURE OF CASE: Appeal from conviction for murder.

FACT SUMMARY: Morgan (D) contended that the trial court erred in admitting evidence of his past assaultive behavior to impeach his truthfulness.

CONCISE RULE OF LAW: Past incidents of violent behavior are not probative of veracity and cannot be used to impeach the truthfulness of the witness.

FACTS: Morgan (D) was charged with murder. He contended that he acted in self-defense when his victim charged him. The State (P) presented evidence that on two prior occasions, Morgan (D) acted violently. He was convicted and appealed, contending evidence of specific prior acts of assaultive behavior was inadmissible to prove his veracity, as offered by the state.

ISSUE: Are past incidents of assaultive behavior probative of a person's veracity and thus admissible?

HOLDING AND DECISION: (Owens, J.) No. Past incidents of assaultive behavior are not probative of a person's veracity. Past specific behavior can be used to prove or disprove veracity only if the conduct is probative of credibility. Thus, if the acts do not involve instances of a lack of truthfulness, the evidence is inadmissible. Violence is not probative of truthfulness, thus the evidence in issue was improperly admitted. This was, however, harmless error. Affirmed.

EDITOR'S ANALYSIS: The problem with evidence of this type is that the jury could use it to determine that the person acted consistently with his past. Thus, it can be improperly used as character evidence. Thus, if it is offered to impeach, it must be specifically related to the person's veracity.

[For more information on evidence of misconduct, see Casenote Law Outline on Evidence, Chapter 6, § IV, The "Other Crimes" Loophole.]

UNITED STATES v. AZURE
845 F.2d 1503 (8th Cir. 1988).

NATURE OF CASE: Appeal from conviction for carnal knowledge of a female under sixteen.

FACT SUMMARY: Azure (D) argued that his conviction on charges of having sexual intercourse with a ten-year-old must be reversed because the district court erred in excluding evidence of the victim's past sexual behavior under Fed. R. Evid. 412.

CONCISE RULE OF LAW: Evidence of specific instances of an alleged victim's past sexual behavior is admissible if offered to show the source of injury to the victim.

FACTS: Azure (D) was charged by the United States (P) with having sexual intercourse with Empen, the ten-year-old daughter of his common law wife. Empen was examined by a physician and was found to have vaginal lacerations, a stretched hymenal ring, and gonorrhea. The physician concluded that she had been severely abused. Prior to Azure's (D) trial, he sought to introduce evidence of past sexual relations between Empen and one of her young male friends. The district court excluded such evidence, Azure (D) was convicted of having carnal knowledge of a female under sixteen, and he appealed. The Eighth Circuit Court of Appeals reversed. On retrial, Azure (D) was again found guilty and appealed, arguing that the court should have admitted evidence of Empen's past sexual behavior under the source-of-injury exception to Fed. R. Evid. 412.

ISSUE: Is evidence of a victim's past sexual behavior admissible if offered to show the source of injury to the victim?

HOLDING AND DECISION: (Larson, J.) Yes. Evidence of a victim's past sexual behavior is admissible if offered to show the source of injury to the victim. Fed. R. Evid. 412 provides that evidence of a victim's past sexual behavior is not admissible except in certain narrow circumstances. The effect of Rule 412 is to preclude the routine use of evidence of specific instances of a rape victim's prior sexual behavior. The relevant exception to Rule 412 states that, subject to procedural and relevancy requirements, evidence of specific instances of an alleged victim's past sexual behavior is admissible if offered upon the issue of whether the accused was or was not the source of semen or injury. However, exception does not apply to the evidence here. In this case, evidence that Empen had prior consensual sexual relations with her friend is irrelevant to the source of her vaginal injuries. She testified that all her contacts with Azure (D) were painful. Her friend testified that all contacts he had with the victim were consensual and that he had never hurt her. The physician who examined her testified that the vaginal injuries received by the victim would have been very painful and that they were an indication of force. Therefore, the district court did not abuse its discretion in excluding evidence of Empen's alleged prior sexual activities. Affirmed.

EDITOR'S ANALYSIS: Almost all states now have "rape shield" laws. Such laws place varying limitations on the defendant's ability to cross-examine the alleged victim but also set forth many different exceptions. Such exceptions include the two which were discussed in Azure: prior sexual activity with the accused and evidence regarding the source of the semen or injury. Others exceptions include attempts to show that the victim had fantasized about the event prior to its happening; a pattern of prior conduct; and offers of such evidence as a basis of expert opinion.

_____

[For more information on miscellaneous quasi-privileges, see Casenote Law Outline on Evidence, Chapter 7, § VII, Miscellaneous Quasi-Privileges.]

NOTES:

UNITED STATES v. CARDINAL
782 F.2d 34 (6th Cir. 1986).

NATURE OF CASE: Appeal from conviction for rape on an Indian reservation.

FACT SUMMARY: Cardinal (D) was convicted of rape of a thirteen-year-old girl, his niece, and appealed, contending that the trial court committed reversible error by refusing to admit evidence that the niece had reported and then recanted other alleged instances of sexual assault on her by family members.

CONCISE RULE OF LAW: Evidence of past accusations of sexual assault are not admissible under the rape-shield rule.

FACTS: Cardinal (D), an American Indian, was charged by the United States (P) with raping a thirteen-year-old girl, his niece, on an Indian reservation. The girl testified that Cardinal (D) forcibly raped her. A physician who thereafter examined the girl found evidence of seminal fluid but could not testify as to the time the sexual intercourse occurred. The girl had previously reported, and then recanted, other instances of sexual assault by family members. Cardinal (D) was convicted and sentenced to thirty years' imprisonment. On appeal, Cardinal (D) argued that the trial court committed reversible error by refusing to admit evidence of the girl's prior charges of sexual assault against other family members and the subsequent withdrawal of these charges. The United States (P) argued that the girl's charges, made against her stepfather and Cardinal (D), were true and were only withdrawn because the girl feared retaliation by her mother.

ISSUE: Is evidence of past accusations of sexual assault admissible under the rape-shield rule?

HOLDING AND DECISION: (Boyce, J.) No. Evidence of past accusations of sexual assault is not admissible under the rape-shield rule. Fed. R. Evid. 412 limits the admissibility of evidence of a rape victim's past sexual behavior to three situations: when constitutionally required; when relevant and more probative than prejudicial on the source of semen or injury; and when relevant and more probative than prejudicial on the issue of consent. Here, Cardinal (D) argues that the prior charges by his niece should not have been excluded under Rule 412, as the issue was one of credibility and not prior sexual conduct. He contends that the evidence is admissible to assess the credibility of the complainant and should have been admitted in cross-examination under Fed. R. Evid. 607 and 608(b). Even accepting Cardinal's (D) argument as excusing compliance with the procedural requirement of Rule 412(c)(1), his contention ignores the basic policy of Rule 412. Its principal purpose is to protect rape victims from degrading and embarrassing disclosure of intimate details about their private lives. This case offers no reason to curtail the trial court's wide discretion in evidentiary matters. Affirmed.

EDITOR'S ANALYSIS: Fed. R. Evid. 412 was amended in 1994. These amendments require that the Rule apply in all criminal cases, not just those that involve sexual offenses. The Commentary to the amended Rule 412 states that "evidence offered to prove allegedly false prior claims by the victim is not barred by Rule 412. However, this evidence is subject to the requirement of Rule 404." Rule 404, generally, dictates that evidence of a person's character is not admissible to prove the conduct of the person.

[For more information on Federal Rules of Evidence and rape shield, see Casenote Law Outline on Evidence, Chapter 7, § VII, Miscellaneous Quasi-Privileges.]

NOTES:

STATE v. BAKER
Wis. Sup. Ct., 16 Wis. 2d 364, 114 N.W.2d 426 (1962).

NATURE OF CASE: Appeal from conviction for child molestation.

FACT SUMMARY: Baker (D) contended that the trial court improperly excluded evidence of the accusing witness' bad reputation for truth and veracity.

CONCISE RULE OF LAW: The credibility of a witness may be impeached by evidence of his reputation for truth and veracity in the community.

FACTS: Baker (D) was convicted of child molestation. At trial, the only evidence of Baker's (D) guilt was the uncorroborated testimony of James A., a 15-year-old boy, that Baker (D) took James into a shed behind Baker's (D) filling station, and there they cooperated in the acts with which Baker (D) was charged. Baker (D) denied James' accusations, and called as a witness the Rev. Clarence J. Schouten. However, the trial judge sustained an objection to a question asking the witness whether he knew James' reputation in the community for truth and veracity. On appeal, Baker (D) argued that because a proper foundation had been laid showing that Rev. Schouten knew James, the judge acted improperly in sustaining the objection to the question regarding James' reputation.

ISSUE: May the credibility of a witness be impeached by evidence of his reputation for truth and veracity in the community?

HOLDING AND DECISION: (Brown, J.) Yes. The usual method of impeaching the credibility of a witness as one who will not tell the truth is to show the bad general reputation of the witness for truth and veracity in the community where he lives, by impeaching witnesses who know that reputation. However, a proper foundation must be laid by showing that the witness bases his conclusions upon his knowledge of the party's general reputation among those with whom he resides. The form of the inquiry must be restricted to the inquiry whether, in view of the party's general reputation for truth and veracity, the witness would believe him under oath. Here, when the court permitted the State (P) to shut out evidence bearing upon James' reputation for truthfulness, under the circumstances of the trial it was error going to the heart of Baker's (D) guilt or innocence.

EDITOR'S ANALYSIS: The Federal Rules provide that impeaching evidence as to the truthfulness may be given in terms of the witness' personal opinion. The Rules state that "the credibility of a witness may be attacked or supported by evidence in the form of opinion or reputation, but subject to these limitations: (1) the evidence may refer only to character for truthfulness or untruthfulness, and (2) evidence of truthful character is admissible only after the character of the witness for truthfulness has been attacked by opinion or reputation evidence or otherwise." Federal Rule of Evidence 608(a).

[For more information on using character to impeach, see Casenote Law Outline on Evidence, Chapter 6, § V, Character to Impeach.]

CENTRAL MUTUAL INS. CO. v. NEWMAN
Fla. Ct. App., 117 So. 2d 41 (1960).

NATURE OF CASE: Appeal from award of proceeds of an insurance policy.

FACT SUMMARY: When Newman (P) sued Central Mutual (D) to recover proceeds from it as insurer on a jewelry "floater" policy, Central Mutual (D) was not allowed to introduce evidence of Newman's (P) prior inconsistent statements.

CONCISE RULE OF LAW: A witness may be impeached by the use of prior self-contradictory statements.

FACTS: Newman (P) sued Central Mutual (D) to recover proceeds from it as the insurer on a jewelry "floater" policy. Newman (P) claimed that four pieces of jewelry which he and his wife owned had disappeared in an unknown manner. During the trial, Central Mutual (D) offered into evidence prior inconsistent statements of Newman (P), consisting of a sworn statement given by Newman (P) to Central Mutual's (D) counsel pursuant to provisions of the policy and a signed statement made by Newman (P). Both offers were refused by the trial court. Because the jewels were under Newman's (P) exclusive control, the only defense upon which Central Mutual (D) could rely was that Newman's (D) story was inherently improbable, illogical, and unworthy of credit. After the court held in favor of Newman (P), Central Mutual (D) appealed, arguing that the court had improperly refused the prior inconsistent statements.

ISSUE: May a witness be impeached by the use of prior self-contradictory statements?

HOLDING AND DECISION: (Barns, J.) Yes. A witness may be impeached by the use of prior self-contradictory statements. When a witness has testified to facts material in the case, it is provable by way of impeachment that he has previously made statements relating to these same facts which are inconsistent with his present testimony. The theory of attack by prior inconsistent statements is not based on the assumption that the present testimony is false and the former statement true, but rather because such inconsistency raises doubts as to the truthfulness of both statements. Here, the trial court erred in refusing to admit the prior statements of Newman (P). Reversed and remanded for new trial.

EDITOR'S ANALYSIS: A prior inconsistent statement may be brought out during cross-examination of the witness; or, if the witness denies making the previous statement, the making of the statement may be proved by another witness. The Federal Rules provide that the prior statement need not be shown to the witness during cross-examination, but must be shown to opposing counsel upon request. See, Federal Rule of Evidence 613(a).

[For more information on prior inconsistent statements, see Casenote Law Outline on Evidence, Chapter 9, § VII, Exemption: Prior Statements of Witnesses.]

NICHOLS v. SEFCIK
N.M. Sup. Ct., 66 N.M. 449, 349 P.2d 678 (1960).

NATURE OF CASE: Appeal from judgment denying real estate commission.

FACT SUMMARY: Nichols (P) contended that a witness at trial should have been allowed to relate the contents of a prior statement.

CONCISE RULE OF LAW: A proper foundation must be established before a witness may be impeached by prior inconsistent statements.

FACTS: Nichols (P) sued to recover a commission from Sefcik (D) for producing a customer to whom Sefcik (D) sold the Circle S Motel owned by them in Tucumcari, New Mexico. A crucial issue in the litigation was whether a written contract had been entered into between Nichols (P) and Sefcik (D) giving Nichols (P) a listing on the Circle S. At trial, a witness, Hutchens, testified that McReynolds, another plaintiff, and he had never discussed the Circle S transaction. McReynolds was then placed on the stand and asked whether he ever had conversations with Hutchens regarding the Circle S. The court ruled that he could say whether or not he had the conversations, but could not detail the substance of these conversations. After the jury found for Sefcik (D), Nichols (P) appealed, alleging that the court's ruling had been erroneous, and that McReynolds should have been allowed to relate the substance of the conversations.

ISSUE: Must a proper foundation be established before a witness may be impeached by prior inconsistent statements?

HOLDING AND DECISION: (Moise, J.) Yes. In order to impeach a witness for prior inconsistent statements, there must first be laid a foundation of the time, place, and details of the statement in the examination of the witness being impeached. Here, the witness being impeached had not been asked whether or not at the time and place in question he had said certain things, other than to deny a quotation price on the property. The court properly excluded the interrogatory by counsel for Nichols (P) which merely asked McReynolds to relate what was said without asking him directly if the specific statement inquired about had been made. To permit the impeaching witness to freely state anything that he claims to recall would in effect open the doors to statements never before made or claimed to have been made, and would throw down all bars of restraint. Affirmed.

EDITOR'S ANALYSIS: The Federal Rules provide that "extrinsic evidence of a prior inconsistent statement by a witness is not admissible unless the witness is afforded an opportunity to explain or deny the same and the opposite party is afforded an opportunity to interrogate him thereon, or the interests of justice otherwise require." Federal Rule of Evidence 613(b).

[For more information on prior inconsistent statements, see Casenote Law Outline on Evidence, Chapter 9, § VII, Exemption: Prior Statements of Witnesses.]

RODRIGUEZ v. STATE
Tx. Ct. Civ. App., 165 Tex. Cr. 179, 305 S.W.2d 250 (1957).

NATURE OF CASE: Appeal from conviction for aggravated assault.

FACT SUMMARY: Rodriguez (D), who was convicted of aggravated assault for attempting to molest a seven-year-old girl, argued that the State (P) should not have been permitted to show the reputation for truth and veracity of its witness against him.

CONCISE RULE OF LAW: Where an attack is made on the veracity of a witness, it is proper to permit testimony that the witness has a good reputation for truth and veracity.

FACTS: Rodriguez (D) was convicted of aggravated assault. Cathalina Gavia testified that she had come into a room and found Rodriguez (D) attempting to remove the pants off her seven-year-old foster daughter. Rodriguez (D) denied the charge of assault and testified that on the day before the incident he had seen Cathalina in a car on a country road with a man lying on her legs; that when he came to see Cathalina's father, Rodriguez (D) spoke to her about what he had seen, she denied it angrily, and shortly thereafter charged Rodriguez (D) with assaulting the child. Cathalina was then recalled and denied the incidents testified to by Rodriguez (D). After the testimony was given by Rodriguez (D) and Gavia, the State (P) was permitted over objection to prove that Cathalina's reputation for truth and veracity in the community was good. On appeal, Rodriguez (D) argued that the admission of this testimony was error.

ISSUE: Is it proper to permit testimony that a witness has a good reputation for truth and veracity when an attack is made on the veracity of that witness?

HOLDING AND DECISION: (Woodley, J.) Yes. The general rule is that where there is no evidence to impeach the testimony of a witness except contradictory evidence, it is not permissible to bolster the testimony of the witness by proof of his good reputation for truth and veracity. However, where an attack is made upon the veracity of the witness, such as by evidence that the witness has conspired with another to falsely accuse the defendant, or where it is attempted to be shown that the witness is testifying under corrupt motives, or is fabricating testimony, it is proper to permit testimony that the witness has a good reputation for truth and veracity. Here, the introduction of the reputation evidence was under proper circumstances. Affirmed.

EDITOR'S ANALYSIS: In general, a witness will be given an opportunity to explain or deny those facts which are alleged to give rise to bias or interest. In addition, evidence of a witness' good reputation for veracity and truthfulness is usually admissible to rehabilitate that witness when he has been impeached by the showing of a prior criminal conviction.

[For more information on evidence of good character, see Casenote Law Outline on Evidence, Chapter 6, § III, Character to Prove Conduct.]

UNITED STATES v. BOYER
150 F.2d 595, 166 A.L.R. 209 (D.C. 1945).

NATURE OF CASE: Appeal from reversal of conviction for obtaining money by false pretenses.

FACT SUMMARY: Boyer (D) contended that the trial court erred in refusing to allow him to explain the circumstances of a prior conviction for embezzlement.

CONCISE RULE OF LAW: A witness should be permitted to explain briefly the circumstances of a prior criminal conviction.

FACTS: Boyer (D) was convicted of obtaining money by false pretenses. There was ample evidence that he cashed a check which he knew to be worthless. He was cross-examined about previous convictions on other bad check charges and was allowed to say in explanation that those charges were due to a mistake of his secretary. However, the court did not allow him to explain the circumstances of a previous conviction for embezzlement. The court of appeals reversed the conviction on the grounds that this refusal constituted reversible error and ordered a new trial. The Government (P) then brought this appeal.

ISSUE: Should a witness be permitted to explain briefly the circumstances of a prior criminal conviction?

HOLDING AND DECISION: (Edgerton, J.) Yes. The fact that a witness has been convicted of a crime may be shown on the theory that it diminishes the value of his testimony. It is unfair to the witness to permit no explanation of the prior conviction, particularly when he is at the same time a defendant in a criminal case and the prior conviction, though permitted solely for the purpose of affecting the credibility of the defendant, may have some tendency in the minds of the jury to prove his guilt of the crime for which he is then on trial. Whether the witness is or is not a defendant, if the opposing party introduces his previous convictions, that witness should be allowed to make reasonably brief protestations on his own behalf. In order to save time and avoid confusion of issues, the inquiry into a previous crime must be stopped before its logical possibilities are exhausted. The witness cannot call other witnesses to corroborate his story and the opposing party cannot call other witnesses to refute it. The trial judge has a wide discretion in drawing the line on the amount of explanatory testimony which may be introduced. Here, the trial court's refusal to let Boyer (D) offer any explanation whatever of one conviction, while technically wrong, does not justify a reversal. It related to a different kind of offense from the one for which Boyer (D) was on trial. There was convincing proof of Boyer's (D) guilt of the bad check charge which was the only issue to be tried. Boyer (D) was permitted to explain all his convictions but one. Reversed.

EDITOR'S ANALYSIS: The trial court's exercise of discretion in excluding evidence of extenuating circumstances of the kind discussed in this case is rarely held to be reversible error. However, once a witness has been impeached by a showing of a prior conviction, evidence of good reputation for truthfulness is generally admissible to rehabilitate that witness.

[For more information on evidence of motive, see Casenote Law Outline on Evidence, Chapter 6, § IV, The "Other Crimes" Loophole.]

NOTES:

BRADFORD v. STATE
Ala. Ct. App., 90 So. 2d 96 (1956).

NATURE OF CASE: Appeal from conviction for manslaughter.

FACT SUMMARY: Bradford (D), who was convicted of manslaughter, argued that it was error that this witness was not permitted to explain his prior inconsistent statements.

CONCISE RULE OF LAW: An impeached witness must always be afforded the opportunity to explain or deny a prior inconsistent statement.

FACTS: Bradford (D) was convicted of manslaughter for the shooting death of Jack Tate. At trial, three witnesses who had been eyewitness to the incidents and circumstances surrounding the actual shooting testified against Bradford (D). David Trammel, the fourth eyewitness to the event, testified on behalf of Bradford (D). There was direct conflict between the testimony of Trammel on direct examination and the testimony of the other three witnesses. During cross-examination, Trammel admitted to twice telling Mr. Troy Tate, the uncle of the deceased, that he had not been at the scene of the homicide. On redirect examination, over objection Trammel was not permitted to explain why he had made these inconsistent statements to Troy Tate. On appeal, Bradford (D) argued that the court erred in not allowing Trammell to explain his motive or reason for making the prior statements.

ISSUE: Must an impeached witness always be afforded the opportunity to explain or deny a prior inconsistent statement?

HOLDING AND DECISION: (Bone, J.) Yes. Where a witness has been cross-examined respecting his former statements with a view of impairing his credit, the counsel who called him has the right to reexamine him, so as to afford him an opportunity to explain such statements. Common justice requires that a witness, after recollecting the facts, should have the opportunity to explain the nature, circumstances, meaning, and design of a prior inconsistent statement. Where only one side is heard, it is highly unlikely that the case will be decided justly. Here, the denial of the right to rehabilitate the witness Trammel could well have been the reason for the adverse decision against Bradford (D). The trial court erred in sustaining the objection of the State (P) to the questions posed by Bradford's (D) attorney. Reversed and remanded for new trial.

EDITOR'S ANALYSIS: This case represents the majority view regarding rehabilitation of a witness who has made prior inconsistent statements. The case quotes Wigmore, who states that "The impeached witness may always endeavor to explain away the effect of the supposed inconsistency by relating whatever circumstances would naturally remove it." 3 Wigmore on Evidence 1044, p. 737 (3rd ed. 1940)

[For more information on prior inconsistent statements, see Casenote Law Outline on Evidence, Chapter 9, § VII, Exemption: Prior Statements of Witnesses.]

NOTES:

NOTES

CHAPTER 13
FOUNDATIONS OF THE RULE AND CONFRONTATION

QUICK REFERENCE RULES OF LAW

1. **Purpose of the Hearsay Rule.** Unless it falls within a recognized exception to the hearsay rule, hearsay evidence is not admissible and cannot be relied on in determining a defendant's innocence or guilt. (Moore v. United States)

   [For more information on purpose of the hearsay rule, see Casenote Law Outline on Evidence, Chapter 9, § I, Policy and Elements.]

2. **State of Mind Exception.** The hearsay rule does not apply to testimony offered to prove state of mind. (Player v. Thompson)

   [For more information on the state of mind exception, see Casenote Law Outline on Evidence, Chapter 10, § IV, Present State-of-Mind Exception.]

3. **Out-of-court Statements.** Out-of-court statements not offered for their truth are not hearsay. (United States v. Gibson)

   [For more information on out-of-court statements, see Casenote Law Outline on Evidence, Chapter 9, § III, The Out-of-Court ("O.C.C.") Statement.]

4. **"Silent Hound" Exception.** Evidence of no complaints is too remote to show a lack of defect unless there is evidence of similar circumstances of the persons not complaining, and that they had an opportunity to complain. (Silver v. New York Cent. Ry. Co.)

   [For more information on the "silent hound" exception, see Casenote Law Outline on Evidence, Chapter 10, § VII, The Business Records Exception.]

5. **State of Mind Exception.** Declarations in a will are evidence of the testator's feelings and, thus, are admissible. (Loetsch v. New York City Omnibus Corp.)

   [For more information on the state of mind exception, see Casenote Law Outline on Evidence, Chapter 10, § IV, Present State-of-Mind Exception.]

6. **Out-of-Court Declarations.** Written or oral evidence of the opinion of an out-of-court declarant which is not made subject to an oath or cross-examination is inadmissible as hearsay. (Wright v. Doe Dem. Tatham)

   [For more information on out-of-court declarations, see Casenote Law Outline on Evidence, Chapter 9, § IV, Hearsay Defined.]

7. **Nonassertive Verbal Conduct.** Nonassertive verbal conduct is not covered by the hearsay rule and is therefore admissible. (United States v. Zenni)

   [For more information on nonassertive verbal conduct, see Casenote Law Outline on Evidence, Chapter 9, § II, "Statement" Defined.]

8. **Hearsay Exceptions.** Evidence which has independent reliability and furthers the ends of the Federal Rules of Evidence may be admissible even if in the form of hearsay. (United States v. Muscato)

   [For more information on hearsay exceptions, see Casenote Law Outline on Evidence, Chapter 9, § II, "Statement" Defined.]

9. **Prior Inconsistent Statement.** If accompanied by certain procedural safeguards, a prior inconsistent statement is admissible for its probative value if made under oath before a grand jury. (Commonwealth v. Daye)

    [For more information on prior inconsistent statement, see Casenote Law Outline on Evidence, Chapter 9, § VII, Exemption: Prior Statements of Witnesses.]

10. **Prior Statements of Witnesses.** Fed. R. Evid. 801(d)(1)(B) permits prior consistent statements to be used for substantive purposes after the statements are admitted to rebut the existence of an improper influence or motive. (Tome v. United States)

    [For more information on prior statements of witnesses, see Casenote Law Outline on Evidence, Chapter 9, § VII, Exemption: Prior Statements of Witnesses.]

11. **Identification Testimony.** A witness may testify that another witness had earlier picked out a defendant's photograph from a photo spread. (United States v. Lewis)

    [For more information on identification testimony, see Casenote Law Outline on Evidence, Chapter 9, § VII, Exemption: Prior Statements of Witnesses.]

12. **Statements by Parties.** Admissions made by a party opponent are not subject to the rule against hearsay. (Olson v. Hodges)

    [For more information on statements by parties, see Casenote Law Outline on Evidence, Chapter 9, § VIII, Exemption: Statements by Parties.]

13. **Statements by Attorneys.** An opening statement by a defendant's attorney in a prior trial may be used as an admission in a later trial. (United States v. McKeon)

14. **Vicarious Admissions.** Federal Rule of Evidence 801(d)(2)(D) makes statements made by agents within the scope of their employment admissible and there is no implied requirement that the declarant have personal knowledge of the facts underlying his statement. (Mahlandt v. Wild Canid Survival & Research Center, Inc.)

    [For more information on vicarious admissions, see Casenote Law Outline on Evidence, Chapter 9, § VIII, Exemption: Statements by Parties.]

15. **Declarations against Interest.** An alleged trespasser's failure to deny that he has no interest in the subject property may act as an admission of assertions of such a lack of interest. (Wilson v. City of Pine Bluff)

    [For more information on declarations against interest, see Casenote Law Outline on Evidence, Chapter 10, § XIV, Declarations Against Interest.]

16. **Coconspirator Admissions.** A court may, in determining whether a conspiracy existed, consider the out-of-court statements which themselves are the subject of the inquiry into admissibility. (Bourjaily v. United States)

    [For more information on coconspirator admissions, see Casenote Law Outline on Evidence, Chapter 9, § VIII, Exemption: Statements by Parties.]

17. **Confrontation of a Witness.** The Confrontation Clause does not preclude the introduction of an out-of-court statement, taken under oath and subject to cross-examination, to prove the truth of the matter asserted, when the declarant is available as a witness at trial. (California v. Green)

    [For more information on confrontation of a witness, see Casenote Law Outline on Evidence, Chapter 9, § X, Hearsay and the Right of Confrontation.]

18. **The Right of Confrontation.** The transcript of testimony from a prior proceeding of a witness unavailable after a good faith effort to locate him is admissible in a criminal trial against a defendant who availed himself of an opportunity to challenge such testimony. (Ohio v. Roberts)

> *[For more information on the right of confrontation, see Casenote Law Outline on Evidence, Chapter 9, § X, Hearsay and the Right of Confrontation.]*

19. **Excited Utterances.** The Sixth Amendment Confrontation Clause does not prohibit the admission of testimony under the "spontaneous declaration" and "medical examination" exceptions to the hearsay rule. (White v. Illinois)

> *[For more information on excited utterances, see Casenote Law Outline on Evidence, Chapter 10, § III, Excited Utterances.]*

MOORE v. UNITED STATES
429 U.S. 20 (1976).

NATURE OF CASE: Appeal from a conviction for possessing heroin with intent to distribute it.

FACT SUMMARY: In a trial where Moore (D) was convicted of possession of heroin with intent to distribute it, the court relied on hearsay evidence that he occupied the apartment where the heroin was found.

CONCISE RULE OF LAW: Unless it falls within a recognized exception to the hearsay rule, hearsay evidence is not admissible and cannot be relied on in determining a defendant's innocence or guilt.

FACTS: An informant came to the police and said he had knowledge, from personal observation, that Moore (D) resided at a certain apartment in El Paso and was in possession of a certain amount of heroin. After obtaining a search warrant, the police entered the apartment. They found Moore (D) lying face down near a coffee table in the living room. A woman was sitting on the couch. Bags of heroin were on top of and beneath the coffee table. Moore (D) was convicted of possession of heroin with intent to distribute it. He appealed the conviction, citing as error the court's express reliance on the informant's hearsay declaration that Moore (D) lived at the apartment to arrive at the conclusion that he had been in possession of the heroin. The court of appeals summarily affirmed the judgment of conviction.

ISSUE: Can hearsay evidence normally be admitted or relied on in determining a defendant's guilt?

HOLDING AND DECISION: (Per Curiam) No. Hearsay evidence is not admissible unless it falls within a recognized exception to the hearsay rule. Thus, it cannot be relied on in determining a defendant's innocence or guilt, as it was in this case. The trial judge expressly relied upon the inadmissible evidence in finding Moore (D) guilty, so the judgment must be vacated and the case remanded to the court of appeals for a determination as to whether the wrongful admission of the hearsay evidence was harmless error.

EDITOR'S ANALYSIS: One of the reasons hearsay is not generally admissible is that it deprives the defendant of the opportunity to cross-examine the declarant. The other is that the out-of-court declarant who made the hearsay statement did not make the statement under the influence of an oath of truthfulness.

[For more information on purpose of the hearsay rule, see Casenote Law Outline on Evidence, Chapter 9, § I, Policy and Elements.]

PLAYER v. THOMPSON
S.C. Sup. Ct., 259 S.C. 600, 193 S.E.2d 531 (1972).

NATURE OF CASE: Appeal from nonsuit in negligence action.

FACT SUMMARY: Player (P), who was a passenger in a car driven by Carder and was injured when the car skidded on wet pavement, sought to introduce a vehicle inspection report made before the accident stating that two tires were unsafe.

CONCISE RULE OF LAW: The hearsay rule does not apply to testimony offered to prove state of mind.

FACTS: Bobby Thompson (D) furnished an automobile to his then-estranged wife, Geraldine Thompson (D), who entrusted the car to Nancy Carder. Player (P), a passenger in the car driven by Carder, was injured when the car skidded on wet pavement. Player (P) sued Carder and the Thompsons (D) for negligence, alleging that the car's tires were slick and dangerous. At trial, Player (P) attempted to introduce a sworn statement previously made by Carder, stating that two or three weeks prior to the collision, she had gone with Geraldine Thompson (D) to a motor vehicle inspection station, where an inspector allegedly told Thompson (D) that the car needed two new tires in order to pass inspection. The statement, which Player (P) sought to introduce against Carder alone, was not allowed into evidence because Carder had no personal knowledge of the tires being slick, because the inspection station incident was too remote in point of time; and because it was hearsay against Thompson and prejudicial to Thompson. Player (P) was nonsuited and appealed.

ISSUE: Does the hearsay rule apply to testimony offered to prove state of mind?

HOLDING AND DECISION: (Per Curiam) No. The hearsay rule does not apply to testimony offered to prove state of mind. Here, because Carder's testimony was not offered to prove the truth of the matter stated, but solely to prove notice, which is a state of mind, the hearsay rule does not apply. Carder's testimony should have been admitted to show whether Thompson (D) or Carder had notice of the two slick tires. Further, the trial judge was in error in excluding the statement allegedly made by Carder. This is because when a statement is admissible against one defendant and not against others, the trial judge must admit the statement against the defendant, and instruct the jury to disregard it as to the other defendants. The admission as it affects Carder should not have been excluded because Carder did not have personal knowledge that the tires were slick. The rule is that personal knowledge of the person making an admission is immaterial. Remanded for new trial.

EDITOR'S ANALYSIS: The Hearsay Rule, in general, prohibits the introduction of statements, other than one made by the declarant while testifying at the trial or hearing, which are offered to prove the truth of the matter asserted. "A statement is (1) an oral or written assertion, or (2) nonverbal conduct of a person, if it is intended by him as an assertion." Federal Rule of Evidence 801.

[For more information on the state of mind exception, see Casenote Law Outline on Evidence, Chapter 10, § IV, Present State-of-Mind Exception.]

UNITED STATES v. GIBSON
690 F.2d 697 (9th Cir. 1982);
cert. denied, 460 U.S. 1046 (1983).

NATURE OF CASE: Appeal from conviction for fraud.

FACT SUMMARY: Gibson (D) contended that the trial court erred in allowing witnesses to testify about conversations with his salesmen, on the basis such conversations were hearsay.

CONCISE RULE OF LAW: Out-of-court statements not offered for their truth are not hearsay.

FACTS: Gibson (D) was charged with mail fraud arising out of his marketing of franchises for a fast food chain. Testimony was offered by the Government (P) through investors concerning conversations with Gibson's (D) salesmen. The testimony related representations by the salesmen concerning the enterprise. Gibson (D) was convicted and appealed, contending such testimony was inadmissible hearsay,

ISSUE: Are out-of-court statements which are not offered for their truth hearsay?

HOLDING AND DECISION: (Reinhardt, J.) No. Out-of-court statements which are not offered to prove the truth of the matter asserted are not hearsay. The Government (P) offered the testimony to prove the representations were made, not that the statements were not hearsay and were admissible. Affirmed.

EDITOR'S ANALYSIS: Hearsay is an out-of-court statement offered for its truth, or to prove the matter asserted. The same evidence can lose its hearsay character depending upon the purpose for which it is offered. Otherwise, hearsay statements, if offered for credibility or another nonsubstantive reason, are admissible.

[For more information on out-of-court statements, see Casenote Law Outline on Evidence, Chapter 9, § III, The Out-of-Court ("O.C.C.") Statement.]

NOTES:

SILVER v. NEW YORK CENTRAL RAILROAD CO.
Mass. Sup. Jud. Ct., 329 Mass. 14, 105 N.E.2d 923 (1952).

NATURE OF CASE: Action for damages for personal injuries resulting from low temperature.

FACT SUMMARY: In order to prove that the temperature on New York Central's (D) train was not too low, New York Central (D) sought to introduce evidence that no one else complained to the porter of the lack of heat.

CONCISE RULE OF LAW: Evidence of no complaints is too remote to show a lack of defect unless there is evidence of similar circumstances of the persons not complaining, and that they had an opportunity to complain.

FACTS: Silver (P) alleged that an ailment she had was worsened because the temperature on New York Central's (D) railroad car was too low. In order to prove that the temperature was not too low, New York Central (D) sought to have the porter testify that none of the other passengers complained of the cold. The court would not allow this evidence.

ISSUE: Does the hearsay rule prevent evidence of the lack of complaints to show the lack of a defect?

HOLDING AND DECISION: (Wilkins, J.) No. The hearsay rule does not prevent such testimony. However, such evidence should be considered to be too remote, and inadmissible, unless the noncomplaining parties were in a similar position as the plaintiff, and they had an adequate opportunity to complain. In this case, the passengers on the train were all in a similar position with Silver (P), and it is not likely that they would refrain from complaining if the temperature dropped below what was proper. The porter was also the proper person to testify to such matters because he would be the person that would probably hear the complaints. Therefore, as there was an opportunity for the passengers to complain, the evidence of the lack of complaints was wrongfully excluded from evidence.

EDITOR'S ANALYSIS: The situation in this case, and the food situation the court talked about, are the classic areas in which a silence is the basis of an affirmative inference. While some courts have treated such cases as hearsay, most courts ignore any hearsay problem and base exclusion solely on relevancy. This is the way this court handled the problem. This explains the large number of courts which allow the lack of complaints to be admitted to show the lack of a defective condition. The trend is in the direction of admitting such evidence as nonhearsay. This trend finds support in recent statutes and rules.

[For more information on the "silent hound" exception, see Casenote Law Outline on Evidence, Chapter 10, § VII, The Business Records Exception.]

LOETSCH v. NEW YORK CITY OMNIBUS CORP.
N.Y. Ct. App., 291 N.Y. 308, 52 N.E.2d 448 (1943).

NATURE OF CASE: Action for wrongful death.

FACT SUMMARY: In an action for wrongful death, as part of the issue of damages, Omnibus Corp. (D) attempted to introduce into evidence the will of decedent to show the relations between decedent and her husband (P) and, thereby, the amount of loss to the husband (P).

CONCISE RULE OF LAW: Declarations in a will are evidence of the testator's feelings and, thus, are admissible.

FACTS: Husband (P) brought suit to recover damages for the wrongful death of wife. On the issue of damages, Omnibus Corp. (D) sought to introduce the wife's will, wherein the wife limited her bequest to one dollar because of his "cruelty." The trial court excluded the will, and Omnibus Corp. (D) appealed.

ISSUE: Is a will admissible, as a nonhearsay declaration, in order to prove the testator's feelings and relations with his beneficiary?

HOLDING AND DECISION: (Thacher, J.) Yes. Where, as in an action for damages for wrongful death, there is an issue as to the amount of damages to a wife or husband, occasioned by the death of a spouse, a will may be used to show the relationship between decedent and plaintiff. Such proof has a direct bearing on the amount of pecuniary loss suffered by the plaintiff. Declarations in a will, whether true or false, establish the feelings decedent held toward plaintiff, and, as such, are proof of their relationship. Since the declarations are evidence of the declarant's feelings or state of mind, they are not hearsay, and are admissible as verbal acts, as such.

EDITOR'S ANALYSIS: The declarations contained in the will in Loetsch now come under a recognized exception to the hearsay rule (i.e., the state of mind exception). Under this exception, declarations of a person tending to show his state of mind or feelings, at the time the statements are made, are admissible, and can be the basis for circumstantially inferring certain feelings or actions at a later time.

[For more information on the state of mind exception, see Casenote Law Outline on Evidence, Chapter 10, § IV, Present State-of-Mind Exception.]

NOTES:

WRIGHT v. DOE dem. TATHAM
Exchequer Ch., 7 Adolph. & E. 313, 112 Eng. Rep. 488 (1837).

NATURE OF CASE: Action to contest a will on the ground of the testator's incompetency to make a will.

FACT SUMMARY: At trial letters written to the testator, one of which concerned business, were introduced to demonstrate the testator's competency to make a will.

CONCISE RULE OF LAW: Written or oral evidence of the opinion of an out-of-court declarant which is not made subject to an oath or cross-examination is inadmissible as hearsay.

FACTS: Tatham (P) contested Marsden's, the testator, will on the grounds of Marsden's medical incompetency. At the trial, certain letters written to Marsden between 1784 and 1799, one of which concerned business matters, were rejected as inadmissible. Wright (D) wanted to introduce the letters to show that the writers of the letters treated Marsden as a sane man. Marsden executed his will in 1822 and a codicil in 1822.

ISSUE: Are letters expressing the opinion of out-of-court declarants not subject to oath or cross-examination inadmissible as hearsay?

HOLDING AND DECISION: (Parke, B.) Yes. The general rule is that evidence must be given under oath, and this case does not fall within any of the established exceptions to that rule. The letters express the writers' opinions which were formed from facts which were not before the jury. The issue of competency is a question of fact to be decided by the jury on the basis of the evidence of the facts before it, not on the basis of opinions formed by facts which are not known to the jury. Further, there is no opportunity for Tatham (P), the opposing party, to test by cross-examination the foundation upon which the opinions in the letter rest. Without the writers of the letters being present to testify as to what factors shaped their opinions of Marsden's competency, the letters are inadmissible. Further, the issue in this case is not what Marsden's mental capacity was reputed to be, but what it actually was. The letters are inadmissible as to this issue. Finally, the letters are not made admissible by the reason that the writers do not merely express their opinions in the letters but prove their belief of it by acting upon it to the extent of sending the letters. The opinion of a person is inadmissible. The act which proves that the person believed the truth of the opinion, and which is irrelevant to the issue, except for that purpose, cannot render the act admissible.

EDITOR'S ANALYSIS: This landmark case held nonassertive conduct to be excludable as hearsay. In subsequent cases, the hearsay issue has often gone unrecognized, especially where the conduct in question was nonverbal. When the issue has been raised the rulings have been divided. The current trend seems to oppose exclusion.

[For more information on out-of-court declarations, see Casenote Law Outline on Evidence, Chapter 9, § IV, Hearsay Defined.]

UNITED STATES v. ZENNI
492 F. Supp. 464 (E.D. Ky. 1980).

NATURE OF CASE: Prosecution for illegal bookmaking.

FACT SUMMARY: Humphrey (D) contended that testimony of Government (P) agents concerning phone conversations they had with callers to Humphrey's (D) premises after his arrest, wherein the callers stated directions for placing bets, was inadmissible hearsay.

CONCISE RULE OF LAW: Nonassertive verbal conduct is not covered by the hearsay rule and is therefore admissible.

FACTS: While executing a search warrant on Humphrey's (D) premises, Government (P) agents answered the phone several times pursuant to the warrant's authority to search for illegal bookmaking activities. The unknown callers stated directions for placing bets on various sporting events. Humphrey (D) was arrested, and at trial the Government (P) proposed to introduce the conversations to show that the callers believed that the premises were being used in betting operations, and that the existence of such belief tends to prove they were so used. Humphrey (D) objected, contending the conversations were offered for their truth and were inadmissible hearsay.

ISSUE: Is nonassertive verbal conduct covered by the hearsay rule?

HOLDING AND DECISION: (Bertelsman, J.) No. Nonassertive verbal conduct is not considered to be an effort on the part of the actor to communicate any fact inferable from the conduct. Therefore the hearsay rule does not apply. Fed. R. Evid. 801 defines hearsay as an out of court statement offered to prove its truth. A statement is then defined as an assertion intended to be an assertion. In this case, the callers did not by their calls intend to assert that Humphrey's (D) premises were being used for bookmaking. That fact is inferred from the callers' unassertive conduct and therefore was not hearsay. Therefore, the conversations are not rendered inadmissible as hearsay.

EDITOR'S ANALYSIS: A statement for purposes of the hearsay rule may be written or oral, or it may be manifested by conduct. A policeman who raises his hand with his palm forward is intending to communicate or assert a message to another to stop. This is clearly a statement also. Hand motions indicating acquiescence are also statements and if offered to prove the actor agreed to a particular thing are hearsay, yet they fall within the exception. The difference between these statements and the nonassertive conduct illustrated in this case is the intent to communicate the inferred fact.

[For more information on nonassertive verbal conduct, see Casenote Law Outline on Evidence, Chapter 9, § II, "Statement" Defined.]

UNITED STATES v. MUSCATO
534 F. Supp. 969 (E.D.N.Y. 1982).

NATURE OF CASE: Appeal from conviction for illegal firearms manufacture conspiracy.

FACT SUMMARY: Muscato (D) contended that an out-of-court description of a gun used to prove his guilt was inadmissible hearsay.

CONCISE RULE OF LAW: Evidence which has independent reliability and furthers the ends of the Federal Rules of Evidence may be admissible even if in the form of hearsay.

FACTS: Muscato (D) was charged with illegally manufacturing firearms. Testimony was presented by the prosecution that Muscato (D) was approached by two individuals to participate in the manufacture of guns shaped like pens. A prototype was given to him by Gollender who did not want to part with it. Muscato (D) gave him another gun, which Gollender marked distinctively to remind him how it was used. The scheme was discovered, and Gollender, without prompting, admitted that Muscato (D) gave him the gun. Because the police had already seized the gun from another participant, a fact unknown to Gollender, this admission implicated Muscato (D) in the scheme. At trial, Muscato (D) contended that the Gollender testimony was inadmissible hearsay. He was convicted and appealed.

ISSUE: May evidence with independent reliability be admissible even if it is hearsay?

HOLDING AND DECISION: (Weinstein, J.) Yes. Evidence which has independent reliability and furthers the ends of the Federal Rules of Evidence may be admissible even if it is in the form of hearsay. Because the gun was identified based on the unique markings placed there by Gollender, it could be verified by viewing the physical object. Also, the testimony was given under circumstances wherein the witness had no basis to determine the importance of the testimony to Muscato's (D) guilt. Thus he had no inducement to lie. This testimony came directly from the witness' memory, and no attack on his recall was launched. It thus was internally reliable and admissible.

EDITOR'S ANALYSIS: This case represents a court adopting a very liberal application of the nonapplicability of the hearsay rule. It indicates that in a particular case the hearsay rule will be secondary to the pursuit of clear justice. Some commentators indicate that form should not rule over substance, but that the hearsay rule should not be so liberally eroded.

[For more information on hearsay exceptions, see Casenote Law Outline on Evidence, Chapter 9, § II, "Statement" Defined.]

COMMONWEALTH v. DAYE
Mass. Sup. Jud. Ct., 393 Mass. 55, 469 N.E.2d 483 (1984).

NATURE OF CASE: Appeal from conviction in criminal proceeding.

FACT SUMMARY: Daye (D) appealed from his conviction in a criminal proceeding, and the Commonwealth (P), on appeal, argued that the admission of prior inconsistent statements made by a witness at a grand jury proceeding for probative use was proper.

CONCISE RULE OF LAW: If accompanied by certain procedural safeguards, a prior inconsistent statement is admissible for its probative value if made under oath before a grand jury.

FACTS: Daye (D) was convicted in a criminal proceeding. The conviction was based in part on his identification as the gunman in this particular crime. The Commonwealth (P) was able to identify Daye (D) as the gunman through the use of the testimony of Prochilo at trial (who was later impeached as to this testimony), and through the use of statements made by witnesses prior to trial which were inconsistent with their testimony at trial to the effect that they could not identify Daye (D) as the gunman. There were indications that these witnesses had been intimidated into changing their testimony. Daye (D) appealed, contending in part that the trial court erred in admitting evidence of the prior inconsistent statements made by these witnesses at a grand jury proceeding for their use as probative value. The Commonwealth (P) argued that the admission of this evidence for its probative value was proper.

ISSUE: If accompanied by certain procedural safeguards, is a prior inconsistent statement admissible for its probative value if made under oath before a grand jury?

HOLDING AND DECISION: (Abrams, J.) Yes. If accompanied by certain procedural safeguards, a prior inconsistent statement is admissible for its probative value if made under oath before a grand jury. [The court first found reversible error in the admission of testimony by a police officer concerning pretrial identification of Daye (D) by two witnesses who denied making the identification at trial.] The orthodox view prohibits the use of prior inconsistent statements for their probative value, while the modern view permits the probative use of prior inconsistent statements. The position taken here is on middle ground. The major argument of the orthodox view is that the prior inconsistent statement was not made under oath, the declarant was not subject to cross-examination at the time of the statement, and the statement was not made in the presence of the trier of fact. Therefore, the orthodox view only allows the use of such statements for impeachment purposes. But these restrictions are unnecessary with respect to inconsistent grand jury statements. If the statement is made under oath, as grand jury testimony is, if the statement is not coerced, and if the declarant is subject to cross-examination at the time of trial, there is no reason to have jurors attempt the mental gymnastics of distinguishing between the use of these grand jury statements for impeachment purposes as opposed to their use for probative value. [The court also held that the prior inconsistent statement should be more than an affirmation or a denial of an allegation by the grand jury interrogator.] Reversed and remanded for new trial.

EDITOR'S ANALYSIS: Rule 801(d)(1)(A) of the Federal Rules of Evidence requires that the prior inconsistent statement be made at trial, hearing, or other proceeding. The courts are currently considering what other types of "proceedings" satisfy this requirement. It should be noted that the courts are not in accord as to whether an affirmation or denial of a leading question would constitute an inconsistent prior statement.

[For more information on prior inconsistent statement, see Casenote Law Outline on Evidence, Chapter 9, § VII, Exemption: Prior Statements of Witnesses.]

NOTES:

TOME v. UNITED STATES
513 U.S. __, 115 S. Ct. 696 (1995).

NATURE OF CASE: Appeal from conviction of felony sexual abuse of a child.

FACT SUMMARY: Tome (D), convicted of felony sexual abuse of a child, appealed, contending that the trial court abused its discretion by admitting out-of-court consistent statements made by his daughter to six prosecution witnesses who testified as to the nature of Tome's (D) sexual assaults on his daughter.

CONCISE RULE OF LAW: Fed. R. Evid. 801(d)(1)(B) permits prior consistent statements to be used for substantive purposes after the statements are admitted to rebut the existence of an improper influence or motive.

FACTS: Tome (D) was charged by the United States (P) with felony sexual abuse of his daughter, A.T., who was four years old at the time of the alleged crime. Tome (D) and the child's mother were divorced in 1988, and the mother was finally awarded custody in 1990. Thereafter, the mother contacted authorities with allegations that Tome (D) had committed sexual abuse against A.T. Tome (D) argued that A.T.'s allegations were concocted so that the child would not be returned to Tome (D) for visitation purposes. At trial, A.T. testified first for the United States (P). Thereafter, cross-examination took place over two trial days. On the first day, A.T. answered all questions placed to her. Under cross-examination, however, A.T. was questioned regarding her conversations with the prosecutor but was reluctant to discuss them. The United States (P) then produced six witnesses who testified about seven statements made by A.T. describing Tome's (D) sexual assaults upon her. A.T.'s out-of-court statements, recounted by these witnesses, were offered by the United States (P) under Fed. R. Evid. 801(d)(1)(B). The trial court admitted all of the statements over Tome's (D) objections, accepting the United State's (P) argument that they rebutted the implicit charges that A.T.'s testimony was motivated by a desire to live with her mother. Tome (D) was convicted and sentenced to twelve years' imprisonment. On appeal, the Tenth Circuit Court of Appeals affirmed, and Tome (D) again appealed, contending that the district court judge had abused his discretion in admitting A.T.'s out-of-court statements.

ISSUE: Does Fed. R. Evid. 801(d)(1)(B) permit prior consistent statements to be used for substantive purposes after the statements are admitted to rebut the existence of an improper motive?

HOLDING AND DECISION: (Kennedy, J.) Yes. Fed. R. Evid. 801(d)(1)(B) permits prior consistent statements to be used for substantive purposes after the statements are admitted to rebut the existence of an improper motive. The prevailing common law rule, before adoption of the Federal Rules of Evidence, was that a prior consistent statement introduced to rebut a charge of recent fabrication or improper influence or motive was admissible if the statement had been made before the alleged fabrication, influence, or motive came into being but inadmissible if made afterward. Rule 801 defines prior consistent statements as nonhearsay only if they are offered to rebut a charge of recent fabrication or improper influence or motive. Prior

consistent statements may not be admitted to counter all forms of impeachment or to bolster the witness merely because she has been discredited. Here, the question is whether A.T.'s out-of-court statements rebutted the alleged link between her desire to be with her mother and her testimony, not whether they suggested that A.T.'s testimony was true. The Rule speaks of a party's rebutting an alleged motive, not bolstering the veracity of the story told. However, the requirement is that consistent statements must have been made before the alleged influence or motive to fabricate arose. The language of the Rule suggests that it was intended to carry over the common law premotive rule. If the Rule were to permit introduction of prior statements as substantive evidence to rebut every implicit charge that a witness' in-court testimony results from recent fabrication, improper influence, or motive, the whole emphasis of the trial could shift to the out-of-court statements rather than the in-court ones. In response to a rather weak charge that A.T.'s testimony was a fabrication so that she could stay with her mother, the United States (P) was allowed to present a parade of witnesses who did no more than recount A.T.'s detailed out-of-court statements to them. Although those statements might have been probative on the question of whether the alleged conduct had occurred, they shed minimal light on whether A.T. had the charged motive to fabricate. Reversed and remanded.

DISSENT: (Breyer, J.) The basic issue here concerns not hearsay, but relevance. The majority believes that a hearsay-related rule, Fed. R. Evid. 801(d)(1)(B), codifies this absolute timing requirement. It does not. Rule 801(d)(1)(B) has nothing to do with relevance. Rather, that Rule carves out a subset of prior consistent statements that were formerly admissible only to rehabilitate a witness. It thus says that members of such a subset are "not hearsay." That is, if such a statement is admissible for a particular rehabilitative purpose, its proponent may use it substantively, for a hearsay purpose, as well. The Federal Rules do authorize a district court to allow (where probative in respect to rehabilitation) the use of postmotive prior consistent statements to rebut a charge of recent fabrication, improper influence, or motive.

EDITOR'S ANALYSIS: Justice Breyer, in his dissent, commented that prior consistent statements may rehabilitate a witness whose credibility has been questioned. Justice Breyer also cited Judge Friendly's opinion in United States v. Rubin, 609 F.2d 51 (2d Cir. 1979). In that case, Judge Friendly argued that Rule 801(d)(1)(B)'s timing requirement applied exclusively to those prior consistent statements offered for their truth after a challenge of recent fabrication or improper influence or motive. When used just to rehabilitate after other varieties of challenge and credibility, the statement is admissible under Rule 801(c) for a limited purpose of questioning credibility rather than for the truth of the statement. Friendly argued that Rule 801(d)(1)(B)'s timing restrictions were inapplicable. In these circumstances, no improper influence or motive is alleged, and the prior statement does not need to precede it.

[For more information on prior statements of witnesses, see Casenote Law Outline on Evidence, Chapter 9, § VII, Exemption: Prior Statements of Witnesses.]

OLSON v. HODGES
Iowa Sup. Ct., 236 Iowa 612, 19 N.W.2d 676 (1945).

NATURE OF CASE: Appeal from award of damages for negligence.

FACT SUMMARY: Olson (P), who had been a passenger in an automobile driven by Hodges (D), sued to recover for personal injuries.

CONCISE RULE OF LAW: Admissions made by a party opponent are not subject to the rule against hearsay.

FACTS: Olson (P), who had been a passenger in an automobile driven by Hodges (D), sued to recover for personal injuries sustained when the car skidded out of control and crashed into a bridge bannister. At trial, Hodges (D) introduced a written statement which had been signed by Olson (P) nine days after the accident. This evidence contained statements which indicated that Hodges (D) had been exercising due care in the operation of the automobile, including the following: "Hodges (D) was a good careful driver . . . he had not been driving fast or carelessly . . . we were all sober." Olson (P) explained that the statements contained in this writing, which were contrary to his sworn testimony, were obtained while Olson (P) was under the influence of painkillers. The trial court told the jury that the written statement could be considered only as bearing upon the credibility of Olson (P) as a witness and not as proving any substantive fact. After a verdict was returned in favor of Olson (P), Hodges (D) appealed, alleging that the judge's jury instruction was unduly restrictive.

ISSUE: Are admissions made by a party opponent subject to the rule against hearsay?

HOLDING AND DECISION: (Bliss, J.) No. Admissions made by a party opponent are not subject to the rule against hearsay. Therefore, the judge's instruction unduly and improperly limited the consideration of the statement by the jury. Because the evidence was a deliberate statement signed by Olson (P), it was admissible not only for purposes of determining Olson's (P) credibility as a witness, but also as substantive evidence against Olson (P). Olson (P) was not only a witness but a party-opponent of Hodges (D), and even though he had not taken the stand as a witness, the statement was admissible against Olson (P) and his case, as a discrediting inconsistency on his part. Reversed.

EDITOR'S ANALYSIS: "Admissions by a party opponent are excluded from the category of hearsay on the theory that their admissibility in evidence is the result of the adversary system rather than satisfaction of the conditions of the hearsay rule. No guarantee of trustworthiness is required in the case of an admission. A party's own statement is the classic example of an admission." Advisory Committee's Note to Federal Rule of Evidence 801.

[For more information on statements by parties, see Casenote Law Outline on Evidence, Chapter 9, § VIII, Exemption: Statements by Parties.]

UNITED STATES v. LEWIS
565 F.2d 1248 (2d Cir. 1977).

NATURE OF CASE: Appeal of conviction of armed bank robbery and conspiracy.

FACT SUMMARY: A trial court admitted testimony that a witness had picked out a photograph of Lewis (D) from a photo spread.

CONCISE RULE OF LAW: A witness may testify that another witness had earlier picked out a defendant's photograph from a photo spread.

FACTS: Lewis (D) was accused of armed bank robbery and conspiracy. After the crime, Sharpe had picked out Lewis' (D) photo from a photo spread. At trial, she was unable to identify Lewis in the courtroom. However, FBI Agent Farrell, who was present when she identified Lewis' (D) photo, testified that this was the photo she had selected. Lewis (D) was convicted and he appealed, arguing that Farrell's testimony was hearsay.

ISSUE: May a witness testify that another witness had earlier picked out a defendant's photograph from a photo spread?

HOLDING AND DECISION: (Feinberg, J.) Yes. A witness may testify that another witness had earlier picked out a defendant's photograph from a photo spread. In 1975, Congress amended the Federal Rules of Evidence to include Rule 801(d)(1)(C) which excludes from hearsay a statement by a witness present at trial, subject to cross-examination, relating to identification of a person after perceiving him. Lewis (D) argues that this exception should apply only to corporeal identification, but this court sees no reason not to apply it to photographic identification. The Rule reflects a generally accepted notion that identifications made soon after an event are more trustworthy than in-court identifications. Here, Sharpe had made an earlier identification and was present in court. The fact that she could not identify Lewis (D) in court is of no matter. Affirmed.

EDITOR'S ANALYSIS: Pretrial identification has had a mixed reception in the courts. Before the advent of the Federal Rules of Evidence, most courts held such identification to be hearsay. A number of states, notably California, carved out exceptions. Under Fed. R. Evid. 801(d)(1)(C), such identifications are no longer hearsay.

[For more information on identification testimony, see Casenote Law Outline on Evidence, Chapter 9, § VII, Exemption: Prior Statements of Witnesses.]

WILSON v. CITY OF PINE BLUFF
Ark. App. Ct., 6 Ark. App. 286, 641 S.W.2d 33 (1982).

NATURE OF CASE: Appeal of conviction for criminal trespass.

FACT SUMMARY: Wilson (D) accused by a woman of being on her property without her consent was arrested and tried for trespass and did not deny it was her property.

CONCISE RULE OF LAW: An alleged trespasser's failure to deny that he has no interest in the subject property may act as an admission of assertions of such a lack of interest.

FACTS: Police responded to an emergency call. Upon arriving, a woman told them she owned the premises and that she wanted Wilson (D) to leave. Wilson (D) did not deny the woman's assertions that he had no possessory interest in the property. When he refused to leave, he was arrested for trespass. At trial, over Wilson's (D) objections, the police officers were permitted to testify that the woman claimed Wilson (D) had no interest in the premises. No other evidence of possessory interest was admitted. Wilson (D) was convicted, and he appealed.

ISSUE: May an alleged trespasser's failure to deny that he has no interest in the subject property act as an admission of assertions of such a lack of interest?

HOLDING AND DECISION: (Cooper, J.) Yes. An alleged trespasser's failure to deny that he has no interest in the subject property may act as an admission of assertions of such a lack of interest. Silence may act as an adoptive admission of a statement. For this to occur, it must be shown that the statement must have been heard by the party against whom it is offered, it must have been understood, the subject matter must have been within his personal knowledge, he must have been physically able to deny the statement, and the circumstances must have been such that he reasonably could have been expected to deny it. Here, it appears that all these conditions were in fact met. For this reason, Wilson's (D) silence was properly submitted to the jury as an adoptive admission. Affirmed.

EDITOR'S ANALYSIS: There are constitutional limits to the extent to which a criminal defendant's silence may be construed against him. Of course, no inference can be drawn from an accused's refusal to testify. Also, silence during a police interrogation is likewise inadmissible to prove any sort criminal offense.

[For more information on declarations against interest, see Casenote Law Outline on Evidence, Chapter 10, § XIV, Declarations Against Interest.]

UNITED STATES v. McKEON
738 F.2d 26 (2d Cir. 1984).

NATURE OF CASE: Appeal of conviction for conspiracy to export firearms.

FACT SUMMARY: Following a mistrial, the Government (P) was allowed to introduce evidence of factual inconsistencies in McKeon's (D) two opening statements.

CONCISE RULE OF LAW: An opening statement by a defendant's attorney in a prior trial may be used as an admission in a later trial.

FACTS: McKeon (D) was accused of illegal exportation of firearms, as well as conspiracy. The first two trials ended in mistrials. In the third trial, McKeon's (D) lawyer made certain factual assertions substantively different from factual assertions made in the opening statement of the second trial. Over McKeon's (D) objection, evidence of these inconsistencies was admitted. McKeon (D) was convicted on the conspiracy count, and he appealed.

ISSUE: May an opening statement by a defendant's attorney in a prior trial be used as an admission in a later trial?

HOLDING AND DECISION: (Winter, J.) Yes. An opening statement by a defendant's attorney in a prior trial may be used as an admission in a later trial. It is established that, as a general rule, an attorney's statements have a binding effect within the four corners of a single trial, as do a party's pleadings. It is also established that superseded pleadings are also admissible in an action. From this, it is a small step to conclude that inconsistent assertions of fact by a party's attorney in subsequent opening statements should be admissible. To hold otherwise would be to invite sharp practice and lack of confidence in the judicial system. For this reason, as long as the inconsistencies go to facts, not argument, and the facts asserted are those which were likely to have had input from a defendant the evidence of inconsistent assertions should be admitted. Here, it appears that the inconsistencies did go to substantive facts, not argument. Affirmed.

EDITOR'S ANALYSIS: Different types of evidence and inconsistencies therein get different sorts of treatment in the courts. Interrogatories are handled much the same way as a party's testimony. Testimony by independent witnesses is not admissible in a subsequent proceeding for other than impeachment. Some courts treat a party's own statement as evidentiary, while others treat it as conclusive.

NOTES:

MAHLANDT v. WILD CANID SURVIVAL & RESEARCH CENTER, INC.
588 F.2d 626 (8th Cir. 1978).

NATURE OF CASE: Appeal from denial of damages for negligence.

FACT SUMMARY: The trial court hearing Daniel Mahlandt's (P) civil action against the Center (D) refused to let into evidence certain conclusionary statements against interest made by an employee of the Center (D).

CONCISE RULE OF LAW: Federal Rule of Evidence 801(d)(2)(D) makes statements made by agents within the scope of their employment admissible and there is no implied requirement that the declarant have personal knowledge of the facts underlying his statement.

FACTS: Nobody actually saw what happened, but young Daniel Mahlandt (P), who was just under four-years-old at the time, wound up in the enclosure where Mr. Poos (D), the Director of the Center (D), kept Sophie — a wolf belonging to the Center (D) but which he took around to schools and institutions where he showed films and gave programs regarding the nature of wolves. Sophie had been raised at the children's zoo and had there acted in a good natured and stable manner while in contact with thousands of children. Sophie apparently bit Mahlandt (P) causing him serious injuries. There was some evidence indicating that the child might have crawled under the fence and thereby received his injuries. An offer was made to disprove this theory by introducing evidence that Poos (D) had left a note on the door of the Center's (D) president saying the wolf had bitten a child and that he had made a similar statement later that day when he met the president and was asked what happened. There was also an offer to introduce minutes of a meeting of the Center's (D) board that reflected a great deal of discussion about the legal aspects of the incident of Sophie biting the child. None of this was let into evidence, the judge reasoning that in each case those making the statements had no personal knowledge of the facts and the statements were thus hearsay. A judgment for the Center (D) followed.

ISSUE: Is it necessary to show that the agent had personal knowledge of the facts underlining his statement for a statement made by an agent within the scope of his employment to be admissible under Federal Rule of Evidence 801(d)(2)(D)?

HOLDING AND DECISION: (Van Sickle, J.) No. Federal Rule of Evidence 801(d)(2)(D) makes admissible statements made by agents within the scope of their employment. Rule 403 provides for the exclusion of relevant evidence if its probative value is substantially outweighed by the danger of unfair prejudice, etc. Rule 805 recites, in effect, that a statement containing hearsay within hearsay is admissible if each part of the statement falls within an exception to the hearsay rule. While each provides additional bases for excluding otherwise acceptable evidence, neither rule mandates the introduction into Rule 801(d)(2)(D) of an implied requirement that the declarant have personal knowledge of the facts underlying his statement. Thus, the two statements made by Poos (D) (one in the

note he wrote and one he made verbally) were admissible against the Center (D). As to the minutes of the Center's (D) board meeting, there was no servant or agency relationship which justified admitting the evidence of these minutes as against Poos (D) (who was a nonattending, nonparticipating employee). The only remaining question is whether the trial court's rulings excluding these three items of evidence are at all justified under Rule 403. It is true that none of the statements involved were based on the personal knowledge of the declarant. However, it was recognized by the Advisory Committee on Proposed Rules that this does not necessarily mean they must be rejected as too unreliable to be admitted into evidence. In its discussion of 801(d)(2) exceptions to the hearsay rule, the Committee said: "the freedom which admissions have enjoyed from technical demands of searching for an assurance of trustworthiness in some against-interest circumstances, and form the restrictive influences of the opinion rule and the rule requiring first-hand knowledge, when taken with the apparently prevalent satisfaction with the results, calls for generous treatment of this avenue to admissibility." 28 U.S.C.A., Volume of Federal Rules of Evidence, Rule 801, p. 527, at p. 530. So here, remembering that relevant evidence is usually prejudicial to the cause of the side against which it is presented, and that the prejudice which concerns us is unreasonable prejudice — and applying the spirit of Rule 801(d)(2) — Rule 403 does not warrant the exclusion of the evidence of Poos' (D) statements as against himself or the Center (D). But the limited admissibility of the corporate minutes, coupled with the repetitive nature of the evidence and the low probative value of the minute record, all justify supporting the judgment of the trial court, under Rule 403, not to admit them into evidence. Reversed and remanded for a new trial.

EDITOR'S ANALYSIS: One of the questions courts have struggled with in this area is whether or not in order to qualify as an admission the statement must have been made by the agent to an outsider (i.e., one other than his principal or another agent). This often comes up when the opposing party in a suit against the principal wants to introduce into evidence a report written or given orally by an agent to the principal or another agent. Just as many courts have refused to let such evidence in as have let it in against principal as an admission. The Federal Rules of Evidence have been interpreted as recognizing what Wigmore observed: that "communication to an outsider has not generally been thought to be an essential characteristic of an admission." See, Wigmore on Evidence, § 1557.

[For more information on vicarious admissions, see Casenote Law Outline on Evidence, Chapter 9, § VIII, Exemption: Statements by Parties.]

BOURJAILY v. UNITED STATES
107 U.S. 2775 (1987).

NATURE OF CASE: Appeal from conviction for conspiracy to distribute drugs.

FACT SUMMARY: Bourjaily (D) contended that the trial court erred in considering statements by an accomplice in determining whether a conspiracy existed, as such a finding was a prerequisite to determining the admissibility of the statements.

CONCISE RULE OF LAW: A court may, in determining whether a conspiracy existed, consider the out-of-court statements which themselves are the subject of the inquiry into admissibility.

FACTS: Bourjaily (D) was charged with conspiracy to distribute cocaine. The Government (P) introduced out-of-court statements made by Lonardo, an accomplice, which arguably implicated Bourjaily (D) in the conspiracy. Under Federal Rule of Evidence 801, out-of-court statements by a coconspirator against a party, made during the course of the conspiracy, are not hearsay. The court made a preliminary evidentiary ruling based in part on Lonardo's out-of-court statements, that a conspiracy existed and that Bourjaily (D) was a conspirator. This ruling was solely as a preliminary step to finding the out-of-court statements fell under Rule 801, and were thus admissible. Bourjaily (D) was convicted and appealed, contending the court could not consider the statements themselves in determining whether a conspiracy existed where such determination was the threshold consideration in the statement's admissibility.

ISSUE: May a court, in making a preliminary determination of admissibility under Federal Rule 801, consider the subject statements?

HOLDING AND DECISION: (Rehnquist, C.J.) Yes. A court may, in making a preliminary determination of admissibility under Federal Rule of Evidence 801 consider the subject statements to determine if a conspiracy exists. Although case authority exists to the contrary, the amendments to the Federal Rules have made it clear that the statements may be used. Once it is shown by a preponderance of the evidence that a conspiracy existed and that the defendant was involved, the statements are not hearsay. The statements themselves may be highly probative of the existence of a conspiracy and may be used. Affirmed.

CONCURRENCE: (Stevens, J.) Rule 104 clearly requires that a trial court be able to use the statements in its evaluation under 801.

DISSENT: (Blackmun, J.) Rules 801 and 104 conflict. Thus, one cannot be used to supplement the plain meaning of the other.

EDITOR'S ANALYSIS: Rule 104 allows trial courts to consider hearsay evidence in making evidentiary determinations. Thus the Court read 104 in conjunction with 801 to arrive at its decision. It has been held, however, that if an agency relationship must be proved, the statements at issue cannot be considered. Commentators have argued that this case may change that rule.

[For more information on coconspirator admissions, see Casenote Law Outline on Evidence, Chapter 9, § VIII, Exemption: Statements by Parties.]

NOTES:

157

CALIFORNIA v. GREEN
399 U.S. 149 (1970).

NATURE OF CASE: Appeal from conviction for selling marijuana.

FACT SUMMARY: Green (D) was convicted of selling marijuana to Porter, who later recanted his testimony against Green (D).

CONCISE RULE OF LAW: The Confrontation Clause does not preclude the introduction of an out-of-court statement, taken under oath and subject to cross-examination, to prove the truth of the matter asserted, when the declarant is available as a witness at trial.

FACTS: In January 1967, Melvin Porter, a 16-year-old minor, was arrested for selling marijuana to an undercover police officer. Porter later told Officer Wade that Green (D) had been his supplier, and he later repeated this testimony at Green's (D) preliminary hearing. Porter's story at the preliminary hearing was subjected to extensive cross-examination by the same counsel who represented Green (D) at his subsequent trial. At that trial, Porter became "uncooperative," and excerpts from his preliminary hearing testimony were read and admitted as substantive evidence after Porter indicated that he could not remember whether Green was his supplier. Green (D) was convicted of the crime charged, but the court of appeals reversed, holding that the use of Porter's prior statements for the truth of the matter asserted therein denied Green (D) his right of confrontation. The California Supreme Court affirmed the appellate decision, and the State (P) appealed.

ISSUE: Does the Confrontation Clause preclude the introduction of an out-of-court statement, taken under oath and subject to cross-examination, to prove the truth of the matter asserted, when the declarant is available as a witness at trial?

HOLDING AND DECISION: (White, J.) No. The Confrontation Clause is not violated by admitting a declarant's out-of-court statements, as long as the declarant is testifying as a witness and subject to full and effective cross-examination. Because the witness is available to testify, the penalty of perjury helps to insure the giving of truthful testimony. Any inability to cross-examine the witness at the time he made his prior statement is not crucial so long as the defendant is assured of full and effective cross-examination at the time of trial. Further, the witness who now relates a different story about the events in question must necessarily assume a position as to the truth value of his prior statement, thus giving the jury a chance to observe and evaluate his demeanor as he either disavows or qualifies his earlier statement. Here, Porter was under oath at the preliminary hearing, Green (D) was represented there by the same counsel who represented him at trial, Green (D) had every opportunity to cross-examine Porter as to his statement, and the proceedings were conducted before a judicial tribunal. The judgment of the California Supreme Court is vacated, and the case remanded.

CONCURRENCE: (Burger, C.J.) The states should be encouraged to experiment and innovate in procedures at criminal trials.

CONCURRENCE: (Harlan, J.) The Confrontation Clause of the Sixth Amendment reaches no farther than to require the prosecution to produce any available witness whose declarations it seeks to use in a criminal trial.

DISSENT: (Brennan, J.) Confrontation at a preliminary hearing cannot compensate for the absence of confrontation at trial because the nature and objectives of the two proceedings differ significantly. A preliminary hearing is ordinarily a much less searching exploration into the merits of a case than a trial, simply because its function is the more limited one of determining whether probable cause exists to hold the accused for trial.

EDITOR'S ANALYSIS: The Federal Rules provide that a prior statement by the witness is not hearsay if "the declarant testifies at the trial or hearing and is subject to cross-examination concerning the statement, and the statement is inconsistent with his testimony and was given under oath subject to the penalty of perjury at a trial, hearing or other proceeding, or in a deposition." See, Federal Rule of Evidence 801(d)(1)(A).

[For more information on confrontation of a witness, see Casenote Law Outline on Evidence, Chapter 9, § X, Hearsay and the Right of Confrontation.]

NOTES:

OHIO v. ROBERTS
488 U.S. 56 (1980).

NATURE OF CASE: Review of rejection of transcript evidence in a criminal trial.

FACT SUMMARY: In Roberts' (D) trial for forgery and receiving stolen property, the Ohio Supreme Court refused to admit the preliminary hearing transcript of a witness' testimony, after a diligent but fruitless search for her, to rebut Roberts' (D) allegation that that witness had given him her parents' checkbook and credit cards with permission to use them.

CONCISE RULE OF LAW: The transcript of testimony from a prior proceeding of a witness unavailable after a good faith effort to locate him is admissible in a criminal trial against a defendant who availed himself of an opportunity to challenge such testimony.

FACTS: Roberts (D) was indicted for forgery, receiving stolen property, and possession of heroin. He had forged a check of one Isaacs and possessed several of Isaacs' credit cards. At the preliminary hearing, Roberts' (D) counsel called Isaacs' daughter, Anita, to the stand as a defense witness. She admitted knowing Roberts (D), and letting him use her apartment while she was away, but denied, even in response to leading questions, giving Roberts (D) the checks and credit cards for his use. Roberts' (D) counsel did not ask to have her declared hostile nor request permission to place her on cross-examination. The Government (P) did not question her. After indictment and before trial, Anita was subpoenaed five times but to no avail. Her mother testified to limited short contacts with Anita and said she knew of no way to contact her. The Government (P) proffered Anita's preliminary hearing testimony in transcript form and the court admitted it. Roberts (D) was convicted. Later, the Ohio Supreme Court held that the transcript was inadmissible because Roberts (D) was unconstitutionally deprived of his right to confront the witness against him. The United States Supreme Court granted certiorari.

ISSUE: Is the transcript of testimony from a prior proceeding of a witness unavailable after a good faith effort to locate him admissible in a criminal trial against a defendant who availed himself of an opportunity to challenge such testimony?

HOLDING AND DECISION: (Blackmun, J.) Yes. The Sixth Amendment's Confrontation Clause is not applied so as to abrogate every hearsay exception in criminal trials. When a witness in such a case is unavailable, the Clause countenances only hearsay marked with such trustworthiness that the reason for the hearsay rule is served. We have held that where a witness was unavailable for trial but has testified at an earlier proceeding and was there subjected to cross-examination, the transcript of the prior testimony was admissible against a criminal defendant at trial. In this case, Anita Isaacs was subjected to the equivalent of significant cross-examination. Roberts' (D) counsel asked her leading questions and challenged her veracity along with the accuracy of her recollections. The transcript of testimony from a prior proceeding of a witness unavailable after a good faith effort to locate him is admissible in a criminal trial against a defendant who availed himself of an opportunity to challenge such testimony. The efforts by the prosecution to locate Anita Isaacs were reasonable and made in good faith. While more might have been done, the issuance of five subpoenas and conversing with Anita's mother was constitutionally sufficient to establish Anita's unavailability. Reversed and remanded.

DISSENT: (Brennan, J.) In order to use testimony obtained at a preliminary hearing at trial, the unavailability of the witness must be shown. The prosecution here did not attempt in good faith to secure the witness' presence at trial. The delivery of subpoenas to the witness' parents' home, knowing she did not live there, did not constitute a good faith attempt to locate her.

EDITOR'S ANALYSIS: Under Rule 804(b)(1) of the Federal Rules of Evidence "former testimony" of a witness in a criminal matter may be admitted in transcript form if given under oath and the witness is unavailable. An opportunity to cross-examination the witness by the defendant must have been afforded, and the incentive to cross-examine must have been the same at the earlier proceeding. (Actual cross-examination is not required.) Under the view held by the majority of state courts, the former testimony must have come from a prior trial of the same matter and be offered at retrial only.

[For more information on the right of confrontation, see Casenote Law Outline on Evidence, Chapter 9, § X, Hearsay and the Right of Confrontation.]

NOTES:

WHITE v. ILLINOIS
112 S. Ct. 736 (1992).

NATURE OF CASE: Appeal from denial of motion for a mistrial.

FACT SUMMARY: In Illinois' (P) criminal action against White (D), the appellate court, affirming the trial court's ruling, denied White's (D) motion for a mistrial based on the admissibility of out-of-court testimony, even though his accuser was present during trial.

CONCISE RULE OF LAW: The Sixth Amendment Confrontation Clause does not prohibit the admission of testimony under the "spontaneous declaration" and "medical examination" exceptions to the hearsay rule.

FACTS: After White (D) was convicted by a jury for aggravated criminal sexual assault, residential burglary, and unlawful restraint, the appellate court, affirming the trial court's ruling, denied his motion for a mistrial in light of the trial court's determination that out-of-court accusatory statements by S.G., his four-year-old alleged victim, were admissible under the spontaneous declaration and medical examination exceptions to the hearsay rule, despite her presence and failure to testify at trial.

ISSUE: Does the Sixth Amendment Confrontation Clause prohibit the admission of testimony under the "spontaneous declaration" and "medical examination" exceptions to the hearsay rule?

HOLDING AND DECISION: (Rehnquist, C.J.) No. The Sixth Amendment Confrontation Clause does not prohibit the admission of testimony under the "spontaneous declaration" and "medical examination" exceptions to the hearsay rule. The Confrontation Clause and the hearsay rule generally conform to the same purpose, which is the promotion of fact-finding integrity. In this end, certain "firmly rooted" exceptions to the hearsay rule carry sufficient corroborative weight so as to satisfy the reliability requirement posed by the Confrontation Clause. In the instant case, since the trial court determined that the statements S.G. made triggered the application of the spontaneous declaration and medical examination exceptions to the hearsay rule, and since these exceptions are "firmly rooted" in this country's jurisprudence, White's (D) motion for a mistrial is denied. Affirmed.

CONCURRENCE: (Thomas, J.) The Confrontation Clause is implicated by extrajudicial statements only insofar as they are contained in formalized testimonial materials, such as affidavits, depositions, prior testimony, or confessions.

EDITOR'S ANALYSIS: Despite having no textual basis in the Sixth Amendment to reach its result, the majority above assumes that the Confrontation Clause limits admission of hearsay evidence insofar as it does not bear a particularized guarantee of trustworthiness. Notwithstanding this ostensibly evenhanded rule, however, courts accordingly will have wide discretionary latitude in determining a statement's trustworthiness.

[For more information on excited utterances, see Casenote Law Outline on Evidence, Chapter 10, § III, Excited Utterances.]

NOTES:

CHAPTER 14
EXCEPTIONS TO THE HEARSAY RULE

QUICK REFERENCE RULES OF LAW

1. **Present Sense Impressions.** A statement recounting events of at least an hour prior thereto may not be admitted to prove the truth of the facts therein. (United States v. Cain)

   [For more information on present sense impressions, see Casenote Law Outline on Evidence, Chapter 10, § II, Present Sense Impressions.]

2. **The Excited Utterance Exception.** The excited utterance exception may authorize the admission of a statement by an anonymous declarant. (Miller v. Keating)

   [For more information on the excited utterance exception, see Casenote Law Outline on Evidence, Chapter 10, § III, Excited Utterances.]

3. **State-of-Mind Exceptions.** Declarations which are otherwise hearsay may be admitted to prove a person's mental or emotional state. (Wilkinson v. Service)

   [For more information on state-of-mind exceptions, see Casenote Law Outline on Evidence, Chapter 10, § IV, Present State-of-Mind Exception.]

4. **State-of-Mind Exceptions.** A statement of the declarant's then-existing state of mind constitutes an exception to the hearsay rule. (United States v. Day)

   [For more information on state-of-mind exceptions, see Casenote Law Outline on Evidence, Chapter 10, § IV, Present State-of-Mind Exception.]

5. **State-of-Mind Exceptions.** A declarant's contemporaneous statement describing what he thought he was doing is admissible. (United States v. DiMaria)

   [For more information on state-of-mind exceptions, see Casenote Law Outline on Evidence, Chapter 10, § IV, Present State-of-Mind Exception.]

6. **Intention of the Declarant.** Whenever a party's intention is, of itself, a distinct and material fact in a chain of circumstances, it may be proved by contemporaneous oral or written declarations of the party. (Mutual Life Insurance Co. v. Hillmon)

   [For more information on the intention of the declarant, see Casenote Law Outline on Evidence, Chapter 10, § IV, Present State-of-Mind Exception.]

7. **Admission of Testimony of a Declarant's Present Intention.** A decedent's statement as to whom he would be meeting is admissible. (State v. Terrovona)

   [For more information on the admission of testimony of a declarant's present intention, see Casenote Law Outline on Evidence, Chapter 10, § IV, Present State-of-Mind Exception.]

8. **Admissibility of Statements Made for Medical Diagnosis.** Under Fed. R. Evid. 803(4) an exception to the hearsay rule is created that permits admission of statements made for purposes of medical diagnosis or treatment. (United States v. Iron Shell)

   [For more information on the admissibility of statements made for medical diagnosis, see Casenote Law Outline on Evidence, Chapter 10, § V, Statements for Medical Diagnosis.]

9. **Past Recollection Recorded.** Past recollection recorded is one of the exceptions to the hearsay rule. (United States v. Booz)

   [For more information on past recollection recorded, see Casenote Law Outline on Evidence, Chapter 10, § VI, Past Recollection Recorded.]

10. **Recorded Recollection Exception.** A translated statement may not be admitted into evidence unless the preparer can testify that he no longer has an independent recollection thereof.(United States v. Felix-Jerez)

[For more information on the recorded recollection exception, see Casenote Law Outline on Evidence, Chapter 10, § VI, Past Recollection Recorded.]

11. **Admission of Business Records.** Business records, once properly verified, may be admissible as evidence. (Robertson v. Carlson)

   [For more information on the admission of business records, see Casenote Law Outline on Evidence, Chapter 10, § VII, The Business Records Exception.]

12. **Business Record Exception.** Long distance telephone tickets may be admitted as business record evidence. (Olesen v. Henningsen)

   [For more information on the business record exception, see Casenote Law Outline on Evidence, Chapter 10, § VII, The Business Records Exception.]

13. **Business Record Exception.** The absence of an entry concerning a particular transaction in a regularly maintained business record of such transactions is admissible under the business records exception. (United States v. De Georgia)

   [For more information on the requirements for the business record exception, see Casenote Law Outline on Evidence, Chapter 10, § VII, The Business Records Exception.]

14. **Admissibility of Business Records.** Computer printouts are not necessarily inadmissible hearsay. (United States v. Sanders)

   [For more information on the admissibility of business records, see Casenote Law Outline on Evidence, Chapter 10, § VII, The Business Records Exception.]

15. **The Business Records Exception.** (1) The statements of bystanders recorded in a policeman's report of accident are inadmissible as business records to show the facts reported. (2) Doctors' reports, although prepared specifically for litigation, are admissible if at the time they were made there was no motive to misrepresent. (Yates v. Bair Transportation, Inc.)

   [For more information on the business records exception, see Casenote Law Outline on Evidence, Chapter 10, § VII, The Business Records Exception.]

16. **Admissibility of Public Records.** Public records, kept pursuant to statutory requirements, constitute an exception to the hearsay rule. (Chesapeake and Delaware Canal Co. v. United States)

   [For more information on the admissibility of public records, see Casenote Law Outline on Evidence, Chapter 10, § VIII, The Official Records Exception.]

17. **Official Record Exception to Hearsay.** Fed. R. Evid. 803(8)(c) excludes from operation of the hearsay bar, records and reports from public offices or agencies that set forth factual findings, opinions, or conclusions resulting from an investigation made pursuant to authority granted by law, unless the sources of information or other circumstances indicate lack of trustworthiness. (Sabel v. Mead & Johnson Co.)

   [For more information on official records exception to hearsay, see Casenote Law Outline on Evidence, Chapter 10, § VIII, The Official Records Exception.]

18. **The Admission of Records Kept by Government Employees.** A deportation warrant is admissible in a prosecution for illegal reentry. (United States v. Quezada)

   [For more information on the admission of records kept by government employees, see Casenote Law Outline on Evidence, Chapter 10, § VIII, The Official Records Exception.]

19. **The Unavailability of a Declarant.** A declarant's assertion of his Fifth Amendment privileges may constitute unavailability for hearsay rule purposes. (United States v. MacCloskey)

> *[For more information on the unavailability of a declarant, see Casenote Law Outline on Evidence, Chapter 10, § XI, "Unavailability" of Declarant Exception.]*

20. **The Admissibility of Declarations against Interest.** The declaration against interest exception to the hearsay rule is unavailable when deposition testimony of the declarant is available. (Campbell v. Coleman Co., Inc.)

> *[For more information on the admissibility of declarations against interest, see Casenote Law Outline on Evidence, Chapter 10, § XIV, Declarations Against Interest.]*

21. **The Admission of Former Testimony.** Generally speaking, deposition testimony taken in a civil action may not be used in a criminal action in which charges had not been filed at the time of the deposition. (United States v. Feldman)

> *[For more information on the admission of former testimony, see Casenote Law Outline on Evidence, Chapter 10, § XII, The Former Testimony Exception.]*

22. **The Admission of Deposition Testimony.** A deposition taken in a previous lawsuit may be read into evidence if the party against whom it is offered is in a similar situation to a party in the previous lawsuit. (Dykes v. Raymark Industries, Inc.)

> *[For more information on the admission of deposition testimony, see Casenote Law Outline on Evidence, Chapter 10, § XII, The Former Testimony Exception.]*

23. **The Admission of Dying Declarations.** In order for a statement to be considered a dying declaration, the declarant must have spoken without hope of recovery and in the shadow of impending death. (Shepard v. United States)

> *[For more information on the admission of dying declarations, see Casenote Law Outline on Evidence, Chapter 10, § XIII, Dying Declarations.]*

24. **The Admission of Declarations against Pecuniary Interest.** Declarations against pecuniary interest are an exception to the hearsay rule. (Haskell v. Siegmund)

> *[For more information on the admission of declarations against pecuniary interest, see Casenote Law Outline on Evidence, Chapter 10, § XIV, Declarations Against Interest.]*

25. **The Admissibility of Declarations against Interest.** Declarations against interest are admissible to prove incidental facts contained within the scope of the declaration. (Knapp v. St. Louis Trust Co.)

> *[For more information on the admissibility of declarations against interest, see Casenote Law Outline on Evidence, Chapter 10, § XIV, Declarations Against Interest.]*

26. **Declarations against Interest.** Fed. R. Evid. 804(b)(3) does not allow admission of non-self-exculpatory statements, even if they are made within a broader narrative that is generally self-inculpatory. (Williamson v. United States)

> *[For more information on declarations against interest, see Casenote Law Outline on Evidence, Chapter 10, § XIV, Declarations against Interest.]*

27. Policy Governing Hearsay Exceptions. In matters of local interest, when the fact in question is of such a public nature it would be generally known throughout the community, and when the questioned fact occurred so long ago that the testimony of an eye witness would probably be less trustworthy than a contemporary newspaper account, a federal court may relax the hearsay exclusionary rules to the extent of admitting the newspaper article in evidence. (Dallas County v. Commercial Union Assurance Co.)

> *[For more information on policy governing hearsay exceptions, see Casenote Law Outline on Evidence, Chapter 10, § I, Definitions and Policy.]*

28. The "Catchall" Exceptions. In rare and exceptional circumstances, a hearsay statement which is not covered by any of the stated exceptions may be admissible. (United States v. Medico)

> *[For more information on the "catchall" exceptions, see Casenote Law Outline on Evidence, Chapter 10, § X, The "Wildcard" Exceptions.]*

UNITED STATES v. CAIN
587 F.2d 678 (5th Cir. 1979).

NATURE OF CASE: Appeal of conviction for interstate transportation of a stolen vehicle.

FACT SUMMARY: A statement recounting events of at least an hour prior thereto was admitted to prove the truth of the facts therein.

CONCISE RULE OF LAW: A statement recounting events of at least an hour prior thereto may not be admitted to prove the truth of the facts therein.

FACTS: Cain (D) escaped from prison and obtained a truck. With the help of "CB'ers," officers were able to locate the truck's whereabouts. One CB'er reported seeing two persons, one later identified as Cain (D), walk away from the truck. Shortly thereafter, the two were arrested about six miles down road from the vehicle, which had been abandoned. At trial, the officer who received the call testified about what the CB'er had said regarding seeing two men walking away from the truck. Cain (D) was convicted, and he appealed.

ISSUE: May a statement recounting events of at least an hour prior thereto be admitted to prove the truth of the facts therein?

HOLDING AND DECISION: (Hill, J.) No. A statement recounting events of at least an hour prior thereto may not be admitted to prove the truth of the facts therein. In order for such a hearsay statement to be admitted under the present sense impression exception to the hearsay rule, the statement must recount events nearly contemporaneous to the making of the statement. In this case, the CB'er stated that he saw two men walking away from the truck, yet they were very quickly apprehended about six miles from the vehicle. Therefore, at least an hour must have passed between the statement and the event. While the outer limits of the present sense impression exception are not clearly defined, an hour is certainly outside those limits. Reversed.

EDITOR'S ANALYSIS: The present sense impression exception is often lumped together with the excited utterance exception, yet they are distinct. The former does not require excitation, as does the latter. Because of this, very little time is allowed to lapse between the event and the statement, as the declarant can coolly reflect and therefore the danger of fabrication increases.

[For more information on present sense impressions, see Casenote Law Outline on Evidence, Chapter 10, § II, Present Sense Impressions.]

MILLER v. KEATING
754 F.2d 507 (3d Cir. 1985).

NATURE OF CASE: Appeal from denial of damages in personal injury action.

FACT SUMMARY: A trial court admitted a statement by an anonymous declarant, under the excited utterance exception.

CONCISE RULE OF LAW: The excited utterance exception may authorize the admission of a statement by an anonymous declarant.

FACTS: An auto accident occurred wherein a truck rear-ended Miller's (P) vehicle, pushing it into another vehicle. Miller sued Keating (D), the driver of the truck. Keating (D) contended that Miller (D) swerved into his lane. At trial, Parris testified that an individual walked up and said, "The s.o.b. tried to cut in." This individual was never identified. The jury found against Miller (P), who appealed based on a hearsay objection to the statement.

ISSUE: May the excited utterance exception ever authorize the admission of a statement by an anonymous declarant?

HOLDING AND DECISION: (Stern, J.) Yes. The excited utterance exception may authorize the admission of a statement by an anonymous declarant. The hearsay rule's exceptions offer no absolute right of cross-examination. However, where a declarant is anonymous, the party proffering the evidence bears a heavier burden to establish admissibility. In the context of an excited utterance, it requires (1) a starting event; (2) a statement concerning that event; (3) a declarant who appears to have had personal knowledge of the event; and (4) lack of time to reflect and fabricate. Only if these criteria are met will the exception apply. Here, there was no evidence presented, other than what could be inferred from the statement itself, that the declarant had witnessed the event. Since the third criterion was not met, the statement was improperly admitted. Reversed.

EDITOR'S ANALYSIS: As with all hearsay exceptions, the basis of the excited utterance exception is trustworthiness. The view is that one who makes a statement in the heat of a stressful situation is less likely to fabricate. For this reason, a lack of reflection time is a necessary element for the exception, and the declarant's presence or absence makes no difference.

[For more information on the excited utterance exception, see Casenote Law Outline on Evidence, Chapter 10, § III, Excited Utterances.]

WILKINSON v. SERVICE
Ill. Sup. Ct., 249 Ill. 146, 94 N.E. 50 (1911).

NATURE OF CASE: Action to set aside a will.

FACT SUMMARY: Wilkinson (P) sought to set aside the will of her father on the ground that he was not of sound mind and memory when it was executed.

CONCISE RULE OF LAW: Declarations which are otherwise hearsay may be admitted to prove a person's mental or emotional state.

FACTS: Wilkinson (P) filed suit to set aside the will of her father on the ground that he was not of sound mind and memory when it was executed. The deceased, Charles Hews, had divided his property between Dr. James Kelly, a close friend, and Mary Service (D), his sister. Wilkinson (P) received nothing. At trial, the lawyer who drew Hews' will was permitted to testify that Wilkinson's (P) husband had written a letter in which he had directed Hews not to communicate with Wilkinson (P) in any way because he had never treated her right. The letter was also introduced into evidence. A trial before a jury resulted in a verdict that the writing was the last will and testament of Hews made while he was of sound mind and memory. Wilkinson (P) appealed.

ISSUE: Are declarations which are otherwise hearsay admissible to prove a person's mental or emotional state?

HOLDING AND DECISION: (Carter, J.) Yes. Declarations of a testator are competent, in a contest involving the validity of his will, to show the state of his mind, but not to prove the facts stated. Whatever is material to prove the state of a person's mind or what is passing in it, and what were his intentions, may be shown by his declarations and statements. The truth or falsity of such statements is of no consequence. Declarations, prior to the execution of the will, that certain of the testator's children were wanting in natural affection are properly considered as showing his state of mind. Here, the testimony as to Hews' feeling towards Wilkinson (P) and the causes for it were properly admitted to show the condition of his mind at the time the will was executed.

EDITOR'S ANALYSIS: It is firmly established that a person's mental or emotional condition may be proved by his contemporaneous declarations. In cases involving alienation of affections, declarations of the alienated spouse are inadmissible to prove the alleged wrongful alienating acts, but are admissible to prove the state of mind of the alienated spouse before separation, the effect produced on the alienated spouse, and the reasons why the alienated spouse left the home.

[For more information on state-of-mind exceptions, see Casenote Law Outline on Evidence, Chapter 10, § IV, Present State-of-Mind Exception.]

UNITED STATES v. DiMARIA
727 F.2d 265 (2d Cir. 1984).

NATURE OF CASE: Appeal from conviction for receiving stolen cigarettes.

FACT SUMMARY: DiMaria (D), accused of receiving stolen cigarettes, was not allowed to introduce a contemporaneous statement purportedly describing what he thought he was doing.

CONCISE RULE OF LAW: A declarant's contemporaneous statement describing what he thought he was doing is admissible.

FACTS: DiMaria (D) was arrested by FBI agents while attempting to purchase a substantial number of stolen cigarettes. At the scene, he stated, "I only came here to get some cigarettes real cheap." DiMaria (D) attempted to introduce this statement to prove that he did not believe (1) that the cigarettes were stolen or (2) that he intended to buy the jurisdictional number, 60,000. The district court excluded the statement. DiMaria (D) was convicted, and he appealed.

ISSUE: Is a defendant's contemporaneous statement describing what he thought he was doing admissible?

HOLDING AND DECISION: (Friendly, J.) Yes. A defendant's contemporaneous statement describing what he thought he was doing is admissible. Fed. R. Evid. 803(3) permits hearsay evidence tending to prove a declarant's then-existing state of mind. The only exception within this exception is that a statement of memory or belief introduced for the very purpose of proving the fact remembered or believed. Here, the statement was not introduced to prove itself, but rather to demonstrate what DiMaria's (D) motivations were. This fell properly within the hearsay exception of Fed. R. Evid. 803(3), and should have been admitted. Reversed.

DISSENT: (Mansfield, J.) The other evidence against DiMaria was so strong that any error was harmless.

EDITOR'S ANALYSIS: The exception to the exception described in the present case was first articulated by Justice Cardozo in 1933. Essentially, it prevents the state of mind exception from being used to imply the happening of the event which produced the state of mind. To hold otherwise would largely eviscerate the hearsay rule.

[For more information on state-of-mind exceptions, see Casenote Law Outline on Evidence, Chapter 10, § IV, Present State-of-Mind Exception.]

UNITED STATES v. DAY
591 F.2d 861 (D.C. Cir. 1979).

NATURE OF CASE: Interlocutory appeal from order excluding proposed evidence.

FACT SUMMARY: "Beanny" Day (D) was indicted for the murder of Williams and, before trial, the judge ruled that certain statements were to be excluded.

CONCISE RULE OF LAW: A statement of the declarant's then-existing state of mind constitutes an exception to the hearsay rule.

FACTS: Day (D) and Eric Sheffey were indicted for the murder of one Williams. In advance of trial, the judge made a ruling that excluded proposed testimony by the witness Mason for the Government (P) that Williams, a few minutes before he was killed, gave Mason a slip of paper on which he had written "Beanny, Eric 635-3135" and told Mason, "if he [Williams] wasn't back home by three the next day to call the police and tell them what he had told me and give them the number." The ruling also excluded testimony by Mason that at the same time Williams told him that Williams and "Beanny" Day (D) had a fight over stolen guns and coats and that "Beanny" and "his boy" were trying to "get out on him." The Government (P) appealed.

ISSUE: Does the statement of the declarant's then-existing state of mind constitute an exception to the hearsay rule?

HOLDING AND DECISION: (Mackinnon, J.) Yes. The state of mind exception to the hearsay rule allows the admission of extra-judicial statements to show the state of mind of the declarant at the time if that is the issue in the case. Here, the statement accompanying the delivery of the paper is inadmissible hearsay. While Williams' statements to Mason are some indication of his state of mind, the inference to be drawn from Williams' statement has too great a potential for unfair prejudice. However, no hearsay problem is presented by the introduction of the slip of paper and the writing on it. The words themselves do not assert anything except that Beanny and/or Eric might have a particular telephone number. Where statements by an out-of-court declarant which are neutral (not assertive of direct complicity in crime) are offered to show association and not to show the truth of the matters contained therein, and the evidence is not otherwise unfairly prejudicial, the statements should be admitted. Affirmed in part; reversed in part.

DISSENT: (Robinson, J.) The slip of paper bearing Day's (D) name and telephone number are inadmissible. If testimony showing the mere delivery and content of the slip is neutral, then by the same token it must also be quite irrelevant. In actuality, the Government (P) is attempting to infer that Williams feared Day (D) and Sheffey.

EDITOR'S ANALYSIS: The Federal Rules establish an exception to the hearsay rule for statements "of the declarant's then existing state of mind, emotion, sensation, or physical condition." Federal Rule of Evidence 803(3). In general, a declaration of state of mind may not be used to prove the occurrence of a prior act.

[For more information on state-of-mind exceptions, see Casenote Law Outline on Evidence, Chapter 10, § IV, Present State-of-Mind Exception.]

NOTES:

MUTUAL LIFE INS. CO. OF N.Y. v. HILLMON
145 U.S. 285 (1892).

NATURE OF CASE: Action to recover proceeds of insurance policy.

FACT SUMMARY: Mutual Life (D) refused to pay off on a life insurance policy on Hillmon's life because of a conflict over the identity of the decedent.

CONCISE RULE OF LAW: Whenever a party's intention is, of itself, a distinct and material fact in a chain of circumstances, it may be proved by contemporaneous oral or written declarations of the party.

FACTS: Hillmon was missing. A body which could have been his or another's was buried at Crooked Creek. Hillmon's wife (P), the beneficiary of his life insurance, filed suit against two insurance companies (D) to recover the policy proceeds. Mutual Life (D) defended on the basis that it could not adequately be established that Hillmon was dead, since the body could not be positively identified. Some evidence was admitted which tended to show that Hillmon had gone to Crooked Creek at the same time the body was discovered. Mutual Life (D) contended that Walters was the actual decedent at Crooked Creek. It tried to introduce a letter written to Walters' fiancee that he intended to go to Crooked Creek at the time the body was discovered. It was alleged that this was within the business record exception to the hearsay rule. The letter was not admitted, and the jury found for Hillmon (P).

ISSUE: Where an actor's intentions are a material factor in a controversy, is evidence admissible to establish his intent?

HOLDING AND DECISION: (Gray, J.) Yes. Where a party's intention is, of itself, a distinct and material fact in a chain of circumstances, it may be proved by contemporaneous oral or written declarations of the party. Here, there is a controversy over the identity of the decedent. Mutual Life (D) contends that the decedent was Walters. While the letters were not within the business records exception as Mutual (D) argued, they are admissible as falling within the state of mind exception. The evidence of Walters' intention is admissible to create the inference that since he intended to go there at the time the letter was written, that he did go there. It is not proof that he actually went, only that it is more likely than not that he did. Since the issue was in controversy, it might have tended to influence the jury. Where the bodily or mental feelings of an actor are material to be proved, the usual expression of them is competent and admissible as an exception to the hearsay rules. After death, there is no other way of establishing such facts. Since the letters were probative as to Walters' current state of mind, it was error to exclude them. Judgment is reversed and the cause is remanded.

EDITOR'S ANALYSIS: Regarding this case, McCormick has said, "Despite the failure until recently to recognize the potential value of declarations of state of mind to prove subsequent conduct, it is now clear that out-of-court statements which tend to prove a plan, design or intention of the declarant are admissible, subject to the usual limitations as to remoteness in time and apparent sincerity common to all declarations of mental state, to prove that the plan, design, or intention of the declarant was carried out by declarant."

[For more information on the intention of the declarant, see Casenote Law Outline on Evidence, Chapter 10, § IV, Present State-of-Mind Exception.]

NOTES:

UNITED STATES v. BOOZ
451 F.2d 719 (3d Cir. 1971).

NATURE OF CASE: Appeal from conviction for bank robbery.

FACT SUMMARY: Booz (D) was convicted of violating the Federal Bank Robbery Act by robbing a bank in Dublin, Pennsylvania.

CONCISE RULE OF LAW: Past recollection recorded is one of the exceptions to the hearsay rule.

FACTS: In January 1971, Booz (D) was convicted of the robbery of a bank in Dublin, Pennsylvania, which took place on April 21, 1967. He had observed a white pickup truck near the bank which was robbed and had seen a man get out of the truck, look around, and leave. FBI Agent Bass testified from his investigatory notes that Mr. Kulp gave him the license plate number S0633. The evidence showed that Booz (D) owned two pickup trucks with plate numbers S6003R and S6002R. At trial, Kulp was unable to recall the exact license number which he had given to Bass, and the judge refused to allow the FBI report containing that number into evidence. However, the judge did allow Agent Bass to testify to the prior identification by Kulp. Booz (D) was convicted of bank robbery, and the issue on appeal was whether Agent Bass impermissibly testified to the hearsay conversation with Kulp.

ISSUE: Is past recollection recorded one of the exceptions to the hearsay rule?

HOLDING AND DECISION: (Seitz, J.) Yes. Witnesses may use any aid to refresh their recollections. The rule in cases of refreshed recollection is that the writing may not be admitted into evidence or its contents ever seen by the jury. If Kulp's memory had not been refreshed on the stand, resort must be had to the hearsay exception for past recollection recorded. Where as here, a record is the joint product of two individuals, one who makes an oral statement and one who embodies it in a writing, if both parties are available to testify at trial as to the accuracy with which each performed his role, the recollection may be admitted. If Agent Bass can verify the accuracy of his transcription, and if Kulp can testify that he related an accurate recollection of the number to Agent Bass, sufficient indicia of the accuracy of the recollection exist to let the evidence go to the jury. Reversed and remanded for new trial.

EDITOR'S ANALYSIS: The Federal Rules exclude from the hearsay rule "a memorandum or record concerning a matter about which a witness once had knowledge but now has insufficient recollection to enable him to testify fully and accurately, shown to have been made or adopted by the witness when the matter was fresh in his memory, and to reflect that knowledge correctly." See, Federal Rule of Evidence 803(5).

[For more information on past recollection recorded, see Casenote Law Outline on Evidence, Chapter 10, § VI, Past Recollection Recorded.]

STATE v. TERROVONA
Wash. Sup. Ct., en banc, 105 Wash. 2d 632, 716 P.2d 295 (1986).

NATURE OF CASE: Appeal of conviction for first-degree murder.

FACT SUMMARY: A trial court allowed the admission of a decedent's statement as to whom he would be meeting.

CONCISE RULE OF LAW: A decedent's statement as to whom he would be meeting is admissible.

FACTS: Patton received a phone call. He then told his girlfriend that the caller was Terrovona (D), his stepson, who claimed to have run out of gas and requested aid. Patton indicated he was going to help. His body was found less than 30 minutes later. Terrovona (D) was charged with the murder. The statement of Patton was admitted into evidence. Terrovona (D) was convicted, and he appealed.

ISSUE: Is a decedent's statement as to whom he would be meeting admissible?

HOLDING AND DECISION: (Andersen, J.) Yes. A decedent's statement as to whom he would be meeting is admissible. The mental condition exception to the hearsay rule has been held to include statements regarding a declarant's present intention. There is authority for the proposition that such statements should only be admissible to prove the conduct of the declarant, not third parties. However, while such applications may be somewhat less trustworthy than first-party applications, this court believes that this should go to weight, not admissibility. Therefore, Patton's statement that he was meeting Terrovona (D) was properly admitted. Affirmed.

EDITOR'S ANALYSIS: The Washington rule of evidence applied here was identically phrased as Fed. R. Evid. 803(a)(3). While not textually so stating, advisory comments indicate that Fed. R. Evid. 803(a)(3) was not intended to prove third-party conduct. Despite the identity of phraseology, the court here preferred to hold to the contrary.

[For more information on the admission of testimony of a declarant's present intention, see Casenote Law Outline on Evidence, Chapter 10, § IV, Present State-of-Mind Exception.]

UNITED STATES v. IRON SHELL
633 F.2d 77 (8th Cir. 1980).

NATURE OF CASE: Appeal from conviction for assault with intent to commit rape.

FACT SUMMARY: Iron Shell (D) objected to the admission at his trial of statements made to an examining physician by the nine-year-old girl he allegedly tried to rape.

CONCISE RULE OF LAW: Under Fed. R. Evid. 803(4) an exception to the hearsay rule is created that permits admission of statements made for purposes of medical diagnosis or treatment.

FACTS: Lucy, the nine-year-old Indian girl the jury found Iron Shell (D) had assaulted with intent to commit rape, had made certain statements to the doctor who examined her on the night of the assault. He elicited various statements from her concerning the cause of her injuries. At trial, the doctor was permitted to testify that she had told him she was dragged into the bushes, then her clothes were removed, that the man had tried to force something into her vagina that hurt, and that she had tried to scream but was unable to because he put his hand over her mouth and neck. Lucy was unable to detail what happened to her after she was assaulted but did manage to respond to a series of leading questions on direct and thus tell some of her story. Defense counsel did not explore any of the substantive issues on cross-examination, nor did he examine Lucy concerning her statements to the doctor. On appeal, Iron Shell (D) argued that these statements were not ones falling within the hearsay exception for statements made for purposes of medical diagnosis or treatment.

ISSUE: Are statements made for purposes of medical diagnosis or treatment admissible?

HOLDING AND DECISION: (Stephenson, J.) Yes. Federal Rule 803(4) significantly liberalized prior practice concerning admissibility of statements made for purposes of medical diagnosis or treatments (i.e., those reasonably pertinent to diagnosis or treatment). To ascertain if this exception to the hearsay rule applied, it must be determined if the statement communicated a fact of the type reasonably relied upon by experts in a particular field in forming opinions. Actually, a two-part test is appropriate in these cases: first, is the declarant's motive consistent with the purpose of the rule; and second, is it reasonable for the physicians to rely on the information in diagnosis or treatment. Both parts of the test seem satisfied by the circumstances of this case. Thus, admission of the statements Lucy made to the examining doctor was proper.

EDITOR'S ANALYSIS: While a number of states have adopted the federal rule, others have maintained a more orthodox and restrictive stance. The federal rule dropped the distinction between the doctor who was consulted for the purpose of treatment and one consulted only in order to testify as a witness. Many states have not.

[For more information on the admissibility of statements made for medical diagnosis, see Casenote Law Outline on Evidence, Chapter 10, § V, Statements for Medical Diagnosis.]

NOTES:

ROBERTSON v. CARLSON
Ill App. Ct., 181 Ill. App. 251 (1913).

NATURE OF CASE: Appeal from award of damages for repair of automobile.

FACT SUMMARY: Robertson (P), the owner of a garage, sought to recover damages for work, labor, and material furnished in repairing Carlson's (D) automobile.

CONCISE RULE OF LAW: Business records, once properly verified, may be admissible as evidence.

FACTS: Robertson (P), the owner of a garage, was asked by Carlson (D) to repair Carlson's (D) automobile. In order to repair the automobile's engine, it was necessary to send the crank shaft to a welding company. Considerable delay resulted, and when the crank shaft was returned to Robertson (P) it did not fit properly, and a number of the engine parts had to be filed and readjusted, and the machine put together in running order. To prove the time spent in making the extra repairs, Robertson's (P) workmen's time books were offered in evidence. Carlson (D) objected to the introduction of the time books on the ground that no proper foundation had been laid, but the objection was overruled. Carlson (D) appealed from the judgment granted in favor of Robertson (P).

ISSUE: Are business records, once verified properly, admissible as evidence?

HOLDING AND DECISION: (Fitch, J.) Yes. Here, some of the time books were properly identified by the workmen themselves as containing original entries made by them in the ordinary course of business contemporaneously with the doing of the work for which the charges were made. These books were properly admitted. However, several entries in the books were made by workers no longer employed by Robertson (P). In order to make the books kept by the absent workmen admissible, there must be proof that the entries were made by a deceased person, by a disinterested person, or by a nonresident of the state at the time of the trial. It was error to admit these books because there is no competent evidence showing that the entries were made by persons who were either dead, or nonresidents of the state at the time of the trial. The judgment is reversed and remanded for new trial.

EDITOR'S ANALYSIS: The Federal Rules make an exception to the Hearsay Rule for "a memorandum, report, record, or data compilation, in any form, of acts, events . . . made at or near the time by . . . a person with knowledge, if kept in the course of a regularly conducted business activity, and if it was the regular practice of that business activity to make the memorandum (or) report . . . all as shown by the testimony of the custodian or other qualified witness." See, Federal Rule of Evidence 803(6). This decision, though based upon a statute, accurately reflects the requirements for the introduction of business records.

[For more information on the admission of business records, see Casenote Law Outline on Evidence, Chapter 10, § VII, The Business Records Exception.]

UNITED STATES v. FELIX-JEREZ
667 F.2d 1287 (9th Cir. 1982).

NATURE OF CASE: Appeal of conviction for prison escape.

FACT SUMMARY: A translated, transcribed confession was admitted into evidence despite the fact that the preparer did not testify that he no longer had a recollection of its contents.

CONCISE RULE OF LAW: A translated statement may not be admitted into evidence unless the preparer can testify that he no longer has an independent recollection thereof.

FACTS: Felix-Jerez (D) escaped from a federal prison. He was soon arrested. He later signed a waiver which was written in Spanish. Tolavera, a trilingual guard, served as an interpreter during the interrogation. Hardeman, the interrogator, later made a statement out of his questions and the translated answers. He typed the statement himself. At trial, Hardeman testified about the procedure whereby the statement was taken. He did not testify that he no longer had a recollection of the statement. The trial court admitted the statement, and Felix-Jerez (D) was convicted. He appealed.

ISSUE: May a translated statement be admitted into evidence if the preparer cannot testify that he no longer has an independent recollection thereof?

HOLDING AND DECISION: (Skelton, J.) No. A translated statement cannot be admitted into evidence unless the preparer can testify that he no longer has an independent recollection thereof. Such a statement is hearsay, and to be admissible, an exception thereto must be found. The only potentially applicable exception is found in Fed. R. Evid. 803(5), the recorded recollection exception. This concerns a record concerning a matter about which a witness once had knowledge but no longer does. An element of this exception is that the witness who wrote the record no longer recalls its substance. Here, Hardeman did not testify that he no longer recalled the matters recorded in the statement, so the exception was inapplicable. Reversed.

EDITOR'S ANALYSIS: Arguably, the statement could have been considered an adopted admission. The problem was lack of adoption. Felix-Jerez (D), because of the language barrier, never adopted the admission, according to the court.

[For more information on the recorded recollection exception, see Casenote Law Outline on Evidence, Chapter 10, § VI, Past Recollection Recorded.]

OLESEN v. HENNINGSEN
Iowa Sup. Ct., 247 Iowa 883, 77 N.W.2d 40 (1956).

NATURE OF CASE: Appeal from denial of damages for negligence.

FACT SUMMARY: Olesen (P), who sued to recover damages for personal injuries sustained when the car he was driving struck the rear of a wagon load of corn owned by Henningsen (D), argued that a long distance telephone ticket was inadmissible.

CONCISE RULE OF LAW: Long distance telephone tickets may be admitted as business record evidence.

FACTS: Olesen (P) sued to recover damages for personal injuries sustained when the car he was driving struck the rear of a wagon load of corn which had been temporarily parked on a public highway. The wagon was owned by Henningsen (D). At the time of the collision, no lighted red tail lamp was being exhibited on the rear of the wagon, and a principal issue of fact was whether the collision had occurred at a time of day at which exhibition of such a light was required by Iowa statute. At trial, a long distance telephone ticket was introduced showing that a call had been made from the Olesen (P) farm residence to the sheriff about the accident at 5:45 p.m. of the day of the accident. The introduction of the ticket tended to impeach Olesen's (P) testimony and bolstered Henningsen's (D) defense. An official of the telephone company testified that the ticket was part of their permanent records. The trial court admitted the ticket into evidence, the jury found for Henningsen (D), and Olesen (P) appealed.

ISSUE: Are long distance telephone tickets admissible as business record evidence?

HOLDING AND DECISION: (Peterson, J.) Yes. Long distance telephone tickets, as well as railway ticket records and hospital records, may be admitted as business record evidence. The elements necessary for admission of a telephone ticket in a case such as this, are identification by one or more telephone employees who either make or have supervision and charge of the records, and who know the ticket to be a genuine part of the records of the company, and who can testify it was made at or about the time shown thereon. The evidence submitted in this case meets this test because a telephone company employee identified the ticket, verified the time, and testified that the ticket was part of the company's permanent records. Thus, the trial court did not commit reversible error. Affirmed.

EDITOR'S ANALYSIS: The Uniform Business Record as Evidence Act, which preceded the adoption of the Federal Rules of Evidence, provided for the introduction of business records into evidence. It provided that a business record was competent evidence if a qualified witness testified to its identity and the mode of its preparation, if it was made in the regular course of business, at or near the time of the event, and if the court felt that these factors justified its admission.

[For more information on the business record exception, see Casenote Law Outline on Evidence, Chapter 10, § VII, The Business Records Exception.]

NOTES:

UNITED STATES v. DE GEORGIA
420 F.2d 889 (9th Cir. 1969).

NATURE OF CASE: Appeal from conviction of violation of Dyer Act.

FACT SUMMARY: De Georgia (D), who was convicted of stealing a 1968 Mustang from the Hertz Corporation in New York City, appealed, arguing that Hertz computer records regarding the car in question were hearsay and inadmissible at trial.

CONCISE RULE OF LAW: The absence of an entry concerning a particular transaction in a regularly maintained business record of such transactions is admissible under the business records exception.

FACTS: De Georgia (D) was convicted of violating the Dyer Act, for stealing a 1968 Mustang automobile from the Hertz Corporation in New York City, and driving it to Tucson, Arizona. At trial, Tony Gratta, the security manager for Hertz's New York operations, produced documentary evidence showing that the Mustang in question was owned by Hertz, and that the car had last been returned to a Hertz lot on June 30, 1968. Gratta further testified that Hertz's business records concerning rental and lease transactions were kept in a central computer system, and that information from the computer showed that the Mustang in question had been returned to the Hertz office at the New York airport on June 30, 1968, and that there was no subsequent rental or lease activity recorded. Gratta testified that this indicated that the vehicle had been stolen. On appeal, De Georgia (D) argued that this evidence should not have been admitted on the ground that it was hearsay.

ISSUE: Is the absence of an entry concerning a particular transaction in a regularly maintained business record of such transactions admissible under the business records exception?

HOLDING AND DECISION: (Hanley, J.) Yes. Regularly maintained business records are admissible in evidence as an exception to the hearsay rule because the circumstance that they are regularly maintained records upon which the company relies in conducting its business assures accuracy not likely to be enhanced by introducing into evidence the original documents upon which the records are based. This same circumstance offers a like assurance that if a business record designed to note every transaction between specified dates, no such transaction occurred between those dates. Thus, it follows that Gratta's testimony to the effect that the Mustang was a stolen vehicle when it was transported across state lines after July 2, 1968, was properly received in evidence. Affirmed.

CONCURRENCE: (Ely, J.) The Federal Business Records Act should never be construed as authorizing carte blanche admission into evidence of any and all information that can be obtained from the records of a business. It is essential that the trial court be convinced of the trustworthiness of the particular records before admitting them into evidence.

EDITOR'S ANALYSIS: The scope of what constitutes a record made in the regular course of business has been enlarged over the years. Among the items which have been admitted under the business records exception are personal check records, letters between officials of local governmental units, a report of an incident involving a prisoner by a prison counselor to a staff psychiatrist, a Postal Service report on security procedures at a substation where theft occurred, and a combination appointment calendar and business diary.

[For more information on the requirements for the business record exception, see Casenote Law Outline on Evidence, Chapter 10, § VII, The Business Records Exception.]

NOTES:

CHESAPEAKE & DELAWARE CANAL CO. v. UNITED STATES
250 U.S. 123 (1919).

NATURE OF CASE: Action to recover dividends.

FACT SUMMARY: The United States (P) sought to recover dividends due on shares of stock held by it in Canal Co. (D) and, at trial, introduced Treasury records pertaining to the matter.

CONCISE RULE OF LAW: Public records, kept pursuant to statutory requirements, constitute an exception to the hearsay rule.

FACTS: The United States (P) sued to recover dividends claimed to be due and unpaid on shares of stock held by it in Canal Co (D). At trial, the Government (P) produced a witness who testified that he and others had conspired to embezzle the amount of the dividends, and that, to conceal their crime, they placed in the files of the Canal Co. (D) forged drafts purporting to have been drawn by assistant treasurers of the United States. The Government (P) also introduced Treasury Department books into evidence and produced employees of the Treasury Department who testified as to the authenticity of the records and the manner of their preparation. The records showed the receipt of prior dividends from Canal Co. (D), but no record of the payment of any of the dividends sued upon. The Canal Co. (D) appealed the introduction of certain of the records which were not original entries, but compilations.

ISSUE: Do public records, which are kept pursuant to statutory requirements, constitute an exception to the hearsay rule?

HOLDING AND DECISION: (Clarke, J.) Yes. Public records, kept pursuant to constitutional and statutory requirements, are admissible under the exception to the hearsay rule for official records and reports. Here, their character as public records required by law to be kept, the official character of their contents, the obvious necessity for regular contemporaneous entries, and the reduction to a minimum of motive on the part of public officials and employees to either make false entries or to omit proper ones, all unite to make these books admissible as unusually trustworthy sources of evidence. The books are admissible into evidence to prove both the truth of the statements of entries contained in them, and as evidence tending to show that because the receipt of the dividends was not entered in them, they were not received and therefore were not paid. Affirmed.

EDITOR'S ANALYSIS: The Federal Rules create an exception to the Hearsay Rule for "records, reports, statements, or data compilations, in any form, of public offices or agencies, setting forth (a) the activities of the office or agency, or (b) matters observed pursuant to duty imposed by law as to which matters there was a duty to report." See, Federal Rule of Evidence 803(8).

[For more information on the admissibility of public records, see Casenote Law Outline on Evidence, Chapter 10, § VIII, The Official Records Exception.]

UNITED STATES v. SANDERS
749 F.2d 195 (5th Cir. 1984).

NATURE OF CASE: Appeal of conviction for fraud.

FACT SUMMARY: Sanders (D) was convicted of Medicaid fraud, largely on the basis of certain computer printouts.

CONCISE RULE OF LAW: Computer printouts are not necessarily inadmissible hearsay.

FACTS: Sanders (D), a, physician, was accused of fraudulently submitting phony Medicaid-covered prescription claims to the Government (P). The major portion of the evidence against him consisted of certain computer printouts. These printouts reflected claim information which was stored in the normal course of business by the Texas Department of Human Resources. Sanders (D) argued that these printouts were hearsay. They were admitted nonetheless, and Sanders (D) was convicted. He appealed.

ISSUE: Are computer printouts necessarily inadmissible hearsay?

HOLDING AND DECISION: (Higginbotham, J.) No. Computer printouts are not necessarily inadmissible hearsay. These types of records are admissible if (1) they are routinely kept pursuant to a procedure designed to assure their accuracy, (2) they are created for motives tending to assure their accuracy, and (3) they are not mere accumulations of hearsay. Here, the records reflected by the printouts were kept by official sources as part of routine procedure, and no reason to doubt their accuracy exists. They are not mere accumulations of hearsay because to the extent the underlying information is hearsay the business record exception would apply. Affirmed.

EDITOR'S ANALYSIS: Sanders (D) argued that the printouts had been made expressly for use as evidence and therefore were not made pursuant to usual business practices. The court disagreed. Said the court, it was not the printouts themselves, but rather the underlying information that was to be scrutinized for hearsay purposes.

[For more information on the admissibility of business records, see Casenote Law Outline on Evidence, Chapter 10, § VII, The Business Records Exception.]

YATES v. BAIR TRANSPORT, INC.
249 F. Supp. 681 (S.D.N.Y. 1965).

NATURE OF CASE: Action to recover damages for personal injuries.

FACT SUMMARY: Yates (P) sought to introduce a policeman's report containing statements of bystanders who witnessed an accident, and reports prepared by his own physicians, and those hired by Bair (D).

CONCISE RULE OF LAW: (1) The statements of bystanders recorded in a policeman's report of accident are inadmissible as business records to show the facts reported. (2) Doctors' reports, although prepared specifically for litigation, are admissible if at the time they were made there was no motive to misrepresent.

FACTS: Yates (P) suffered a job-related injury. In an action brought by him against his employer, Bair Transport (D), to recover damages for personal injury, Yates (P) sought to introduce two principal pieces of evidence. The first was a policeman's report. The policeman not witness the accident, but based his report on the statements of eyewitnesses present at the scene. The Federal Business Records Act, 28 U.S.C. § 1732, provided for the admissibility of any writing or record of any act or event, made in the regular course of business where it was the regular course of such business to make such an entry. Section 1732 further provided that "lack of personal knowledge by the entrant or maker may be shown to affect its weight, but . . . shall not affect its admissibility." The second piece of evidence were several doctors' reports which had been submitted in a prior worker's compensation case as required by law. Two reports were made by Bair's (D) insurer; two others were prepared by Yates' (P) own physicians.

ISSUES: (1) Are statements of ordinary bystanders included in a policeman's report inadmissible hearsay? (2) Are doctors' reports, made specifically for litigation, ever admissible?

HOLDING AND DECISION: (Tenney, J.) (1) No. Where the informant to the entrant of a business record is under no duty to anyone to make a truthful account of the facts thus recorded, the record will not be admissible as proof of such facts. Thus, § 1732 notwithstanding, statements of ordinary bystanders recorded in a policeman's report of accident are inadmissible. Section 1732 merely authorizes an entrant or maker to include statements from witnesses to any accidents who were themselves under a duty, as part of their regular course of business, to report to him what they knew. Where the hearsay information instead comes from unauthorized persons — ordinary bystanders — the memorandum or record is inadmissible not because it contains hearsay, but because it was not made in the regular course of business. (2) Yes. Although doctors' reports made specifically for litigation are self-serving, they are nonetheless admissible if they were prepared at a time, or under circumstances, when the motive to misrepresent was not present. Thus, in the present case, the fact that two of the reports were made by Bair's (D) insurer enhances their value since it is Yates' (P) and not Bair (D) who seeks their introduction. The

party who seeks the admission into evidence of these reports has an interest adverse to that of the party on whose behalf the reports were made. However, this element of added trustworthiness is not present in the situation of the two reports prepared by Yates' (P) own doctors, and hence they, but not the reports prepared by Bair's (D) insurer, are inadmissible.

EDITOR'S ANALYSIS: Other courts, and some commentators, have specifically rejected the Yates court's refusal to give § 1732 a literal reading, and have criticized the result reached as a twisted attempt to invoke the double hearsay rule. As for the holding on the doctors' reports, the Federal Rule of Evidence § 803(6) provides for the admissibility of all business records "unless the sources of information or other circumstances indicate lack of trustworthiness."

[For more information on the business records exception, see Casenote Law Outline on Evidence, Chapter 10, § VII, The Business Records Exception.]

NOTES:

SABEL. v. MEAD JOHNSON & CO.
737 F. Supp. 135 (Mass. 1990).

NATURE OF CASE: Action against a pharmaceutical manufacturer seeking recovery for negligence and breach of warranty.

FACT SUMMARY: In his negligence and breach of warranty suit against the drug manufacturer Mead Johnson & Co. (D), Sabel (P) sought to introduce, under the public record exception to the hearsay rule, an FDA warning letter.

CONCISE RULE OF LAW: Fed. R. Evid. 803(8)(c) excludes from operation of the hearsay bar, records and reports from public offices or agencies that set forth factual findings, opinions, or conclusions resulting from an investigation made pursuant to authority granted by law, unless the sources of information or other circumstances indicate lack of trustworthiness.

FACTS: Sabel (P) sued Mead (D), a drug manufacturer, for negligence and breach of warranty concerning warnings for its drug Desyrel, alleging that this antidepressant drug caused Sabel (P) to develop a priapism, a prolonged, painful erection, which ultimately required surgery and left him impotent. At trial, Sabel (P) sought to introduce a letter from Dr. Leber of the Federal Drug Administration recommending that a boxed warning be included in Desyrel's label to emphasize the risk of priapism and the potential need for surgery and threat of impotence. Mead (D) objected on hearsay grounds.

ISSUE: Does Fed. R. Evid. 803(8)(c) exclude from operation of the hearsay bar records, reports, and statements from public offices or agencies that set forth factual findings resulting from an investigation made pursuant to authority granted by law, unless the circumstances indicate lack of trustworthiness?

HOLDING AND DECISION: (Wolf, J.) Yes. Fed. R. Evid. 803(8)(c) excludes from operation of the hearsay bar records and statements from public offices or agencies that set forth factual findings, opinions, or conclusions resulting from an investigation made pursuant to authority granted by law, unless the sources of information or other circumstances indicate lack of trustworthiness. The Rule 803(8(c) exception rests on the assumption that a public official will perform her duty properly without bias or improper motivation. The burden is on the party opposing admission to demonstrate the statement's untrustworthiness. Even factually based conclusions or opinions are not excluded from the scope of Rule 803(8)(c). This includes opinions on the ultimate factual issue in a lawsuit as long as the public report contains factual findings and satisfies Rule 803(8)(c)'s trustworthiness requirement. There are four factors for determination of trustworthiness under the Rule: (1) timeliness of the investigation; (2) the investigator's skill or expertise; (3) whether a hearing was held; and (4) the possible bias when reports are prepared with a view to possible litigation. Here, Dr. Leber's letter is admissible based on both prongs of Rule 803(8)(c). Dr. Leber's opinion is based on a factual investigation of the association between Desyrel and priapism and was prepared pursuant to the FDA's statutory responsibility to regulate the safe marketing of prescription drugs. Regarding Rule 803(8)(c)'s

second prong, trustworthiness, the Leber letter was not prepared in the context of litigation, and Dr. Leber's expertise cannot reasonably be questioned. The evidence also suggests that Mead (D) and the FDA had discussed other label changes relating to Desyrel and the risk of priapism in the past. The Leber letter, therefore, is trustworthy and otherwise satisfies Rule 803(8)(c)'s requirement for exception to the hearsay bar.

EDITOR'S ANALYSIS: In Sabel, Mead (D) also objected to the use of the Leber letter as an expert without foundation and the opportunity for cross-examination. The court decided that, even assuming the truth of the argument, the argument was unpersuasive given the U.S. Supreme Court's discussion in Beech Aircraft v. Raney, 488 U.S. 153 (1988), of the relationship between opinion testimony and Rule 803(8)(c) and the clear purpose of the hearsay exceptions to permit the admission of trustworthy evidence even when cross-examination of the declarant is not possible.

[For more information on official records exception to hearsay, see Casenote Law Outline on Evidence, Chapter 10, § VIII, The Official Records Exception.]

NOTES:

UNITED STATES v. QUEZADA
754 F.2d 1190 (5th Cir. 1985).

NATURE OF CASE: Appeal of conviction for illegal reentry after deportation.

FACT SUMMARY: Much of the evidence used to convict Quezada (D) of illegal reentry came from a deportation warrant, an official police document prepared upon his original deportation.

CONCISE RULE OF LAW: A deportation warrant is admissible in a prosecution for illegal reentry.

FACTS: Quezada (D), an illegal alien, was deported. Part of the deportation process involved serving upon him a warrant of deportation, which basically told him of his illegal status, that he was being deported, and that reentry was illegal. He did reenter, and when caught, was indicted on charges of illegal reentry after deportation. The Government (P) objected, calling it hearsay. The court admitted the document, and Quezada (D) was convicted. He appealed.

ISSUE: Is a deportation warrant admissible in a prosecution for illegal reentry?

HOLDING AND DECISION: (Brown, J.) Yes. A deportation warrant is admissible in a prosecution for illegal entry. Fed. R. Evid. 803(8)(B) creates as an exception to the hearsay rule public records and reports generated in the normal course of duty. Due to possible Confrontation Clause problems, the rule excludes in criminal cases matters observed by law enforcement personnel. Quezada (D) argues that this exception to the exception applies. However, the best view of this situation is that this applies to matters observed at the scene of a crime or apprehension of a defendant where a confrontational situation exists. Matters of a ministerial nature are more reliable and should not be excluded. Here, the warrant was not based on matters observed during a confrontation, but rather information obtained through a ministerial, clerical process. This being so, the warrant falls within the public records exception to the hearsay rule and was properly excluded. Affirmed.

EDITOR'S ANALYSIS: The rule here is not uniform among the circuits. At least one, the Second Circuit, has read the police record exception to the public records exception very broadly, holding all police records inadmissible under the public records exception. The Fifth Circuit expressly rejected the Second Circuit's approach.

[For more information on the admission of records kept by government employees, see Casenote Law Outline on Evidence, Chapter 10, § VIII, The Official Records Exception.]

UNITED STATES v. MacCLOSKEY
682 F.2d 468 (6th Cir. 1982).

NATURE OF CASE: Appeal from conviction for conspiracy to murder.

FACT SUMMARY: MacCloskey (D) attempted to introduce former testimony of Edwards, who subsequently refused to testify under the Fifth Amendment.

CONCISE RULE OF LAW: A declarant's assertion of his Fifth Amendment privileges may constitute unavailability for hearsay rule purposes.

FACTS: MacCloskey (D) and Edwards were indicted on conspiracy to commit murder charges. Edwards testified in a voir dire hearing, giving evidence exculpatory to her and MacCloskey (D). The charges against Edwards were dismissed. Edwards was then subpoenaed to testify at MacCloskey's trial, but refused to answer questions based on her Fifth Amendment rights. MacCloskey (D) sought to introduce transcripts of her voir dire testimony. The trial court excluded the testimony, holding Edwards not to be unavailable. MacCloskey (D) was convicted, and he appealed.

ISSUE: May a declarant's assertion of his Fifth Amendment privileges constitute unavailability for hearsay rule purposes?

HOLDING AND DECISION: (Murnaghan, J.) Yes. A declarant's assertion of his Fifth Amendment privileges may constitute unavailability for hearsay rule purposes. Fed. R. Evid. 804(a) defines unavailability as including situations in which the declarant "is exempted by ruling of the court from testifying concerning the subject matter of the statement," or refuses to testify despite a court order. Here, Edwards did invoke her Fifth Amendment rights, a course with which the court must have agreed because it did not order her to answer. This being so, Edwards was unavailable for hearsay rule purposes, and her former testimony should have been admitted. Reversed.

EDITOR'S ANALYSIS: The concept of unavailability has broadened significantly over the years. At common law, only a declarant's death constituted unavailability. Now, privilege invocation and evasion of process may also constitute unavailability.

[For more information on the unavailability of a declarant, see Casenote Law Outline on Evidence, Chapter 10, § XI, "Unavailability" of Declarant Exception.]

UNITED STATES v. FELDMAN
761 F.2d 380 (7th Cir. 1985).

NATURE OF CASE: Appeal from convictions for mail fraud.

FACT SUMMARY: The transcript of a civil deposition was introduced into a criminal trial against Feldman (D) and Martenson (D).

CONCISE RULE OF LAW: Generally speaking, deposition testimony taken in a civil action may not be used in a criminal action in which charges had not been filed at the time of the deposition.

FACTS: Feldman (D), Martenson (D), and Sanburg were principals of a firm dealing in precious metals. At one point federal regulators filed a civil action against the firm. A deal was struck wherein Sanburg would testify against the others in exchange for no prosecution. His deposition was taken. Neither Feldman (D) nor Martenson (D) attended. Sanburg soon died. Criminal charges were later filed against Feldman (D) and Martenson (D) based on mail fraud and RICO violations. Sanburg's deposition was introduced. Feldman (D) and Martenson (D) were convicted, and they appealed.

ISSUE: May deposition testimony taken in a civil action be used in a criminal action in which charges had not been filed at the time of the deposition?

HOLDING AND DECISION: (Wisdom, J.) No. Generally speaking, deposition testimony taken in a civil action may not be used in a criminal action in which charges had not been filed at the time of the deposition. For former testimony to be introduced, the party against whom the testimony to be introduced must have had a similar opportunity and motive to cross-examine in the original proceeding. Criminal and civil actions differ greatly, and a party's motive in the civil actions might not be the same in the criminal action. Further, if the criminal action was not filed as of the time of the deposition, the issues to be addressed in the criminal action have not been framed. "Opportunity to cross-examine" contemplates meaningful opportunity, which cannot exist under these circumstances. For this reason, unless some unusual set of circumstances exists to negate the above concerns, a civil deposition transcript cannot be used in a subsequent criminal proceeding. Reversed.

EDITOR'S ANALYSIS: The Federal Rule involved here, 804(b)(1), speaks of "successors in interest" being liable to have former deposition transcripts used against them. Literally, this would require some form of privity. However, the majority of jurisdictions only require a substantive identity of interest.

[For more information on the admission of former testimony, see Casenote Law Outline on Evidence, Chapter 10, § XII, The Former Testimony Exception.]

CAMBELL v. COLEMAN CO., INC.
786 F.2d 892 (8th Cir. 1986).

NATURE OF CASE: Appeal of denial of damages for personal injury.

FACT SUMMARY: Certain hearsay statements were admitted as declarations against interest despite the fact that deposition testimony of the declarant was available.

CONCISE RULE OF LAW: The declaration against interest exception to the hearsay rule is unavailable when deposition testimony of the declarant is available.

FACTS: Campbell (P) sued Coleman Co., Inc. (D) on behalf of her two minor children who were burned by a Coleman (D) lantern. Coleman (D) contended the accident occurred when one Hayes had tossed the lamp at them. Hayes was deposed and denied this. By trial time he was unavailable. Coleman (D) introduced three witnesses who testified that Hayes had indicated he had in fact thrown the lantern. The trial court admitted the testimony as falling under the declaration against interest exception to the hearsay rule. A defense verdict ensued and Campbell (P) appealed.

ISSUE: Is the declaration against interest exception to the hearsay rule available when deposition testimony of the declarant is available?

HOLDING AND DECISION: (Murphy, J.) No. The declaration against interest exception to the hearsay rule is unavailable when deposition testimony of the declarant is available. The declaration against interest exception, codified at Fed. R. Evid. 804(b)(3), requires that a declarant be unavailable. However, this refers to a declarant's testimony, not his physical presence. Where deposition testimony exists and is admissible, the declarant may not be considered unavailable. Here, Hayes' deposition was taken, and his testimony therefore was available. Reversed.

EDITOR'S ANALYSIS: The absence of a witness must be real, not manufactured. If he was easily subpoenable but the proffering party failed to do so, it is very likely that the court would not consider the witness unavailable. The trial court has very wide discretion in ruling on this.

[For more information on the admissibility of declarations against interest, see Casenote Law Outline on Evidence, Chapter 10, § XIV, Declarations Against Interest.]

SHEPARD v. UNITED STATES
290 U.S. 96 (1933).

NATURE OF CASE: Appeal from conviction for murder.

FACT SUMMARY: Shepard (D) filed a writ of certiorari challenging the validity of his murder conviction, claiming that the court improperly admitted evidence of a dying declaration of his prejudice.

CONCISE RULE OF LAW: In order for a statement to be considered a dying declaration, the declarant must have spoken without hope of recovery and in the shadow of impending death.

FACTS: Shepard (D) was convicted of murdering his wife by poisoning. Two days after Mrs. Shepard had become ill, while she was lying in bed, she had a conversation with Brown, a nurse. Mrs. Shepard asked Brown to bring her a particular bottle of liquor, told Brown that was what she was drinking right before she collapsed, asked Brown to test it for poison, and then stated, "Dr. Shepard (D) has poisoned me." The conversation was admitted after Brown testified that Mrs. Shepard said she was not going to get well, that she was going to die. At the time the conversation took place, all prospects for Mrs. Shepard's recovery were good. A fortnight after the conversation, Mrs. Shepard gave an indication that she was still hopeful of recovery. Shepard (D) was convicted, and the conviction was affirmed by the court of appeals. Shepard (D) then filed a writ of certiorari.

ISSUE: In order for a statement to be considered a dying declaration, must the declarant have spoken without hope of recovery and in the shadow of impending death?

HOLDING AND DECISION: (Cardozo, J.) Yes. In order for a statement to be considered a dying declaration, the declarant must have spoken without hope of recovery and in the shadow of impending death. Fear or even belief that illness will result in death will not suffice. There must be a "settled" hopeless expectation that death is near at hand, and what is said must have been spoken in hush of its impending presence. Here, there was hope for recovery, and death was not imminent when the statement was made, and therefore it could not have been admitted as a dying declaration. It cannot be said that the admission of the declaration was mere unsubstantial error.

EDITOR'S ANALYSIS: There is no reason to believe that fear or even belief that one is going to die could not provide the guarantee of special reliability necessary to admit this type of hearsay evidence, since it is probably reasonable that persons so inclined would tell the truth. The strict application of the doctrine probably represents a basic lack of trust in "deathbed" statements generally.

[For more information on the admission of dying declarations, see Casenote Law Outline on Evidence, Chapter 10, § XIII, Dying Declarations.]

DYKES v. RAYMARK INDUSTRIES, INC.
801 F.2d 810 (6th Cir. 1986).

NATURE OF CASE: Appeal of award of damages for wrongful death.

FACT SUMMARY: A trial court permitted a party to enter into evidence a deposition taken in a previous similar lawsuit.

CONCISE RULE OF LAW: A deposition taken in a previous lawsuit may be read into evidence if the party against whom it is offered is in a similar situation to a party in the previous lawsuit.

FACTS: Dykes contracted asbestos-related cancer and died. His survivors (P) brought a wrongful death action. At trial, the survivors (P) sought to introduce the deposition testimony of an industry expert taken in a similar case. Raymark Industries (D) objected, based on hearsay. The trial court permitted introduction of the testimony. Raymark (D) appealed a subsequent damage award.

ISSUE: May a deposition taken in a previous lawsuit be read into evidence if the party against whom it is offered is in a similar situation to a party in the previous law suit?

HOLDING AND DECISION: (Engel, J.) Yes. A deposition taken in a previous lawsuit may be read into evidence if the party against whom it is offered is in a similar situation to a party in the previous lawsuit. Fed. R. Evid. 804(b)(1) creates an exception to the hearsay rule former testimony offered against a successor in interest to a party who had an adequate opportunity and motive to examine the witness. This court does not believe that "successor in interest" in this context refers to a party in privity with the previous party, but rather refers to a party placed in a similar position. Here, the two suits were similar, and it may be assumed that the defendant in the previous proceeding had a similar motive to cross-examine the deponent. The trial court properly applied Fed. R. Evid. 804(b)(1). [The court went on to remand on a different issue.]

EDITOR'S ANALYSIS: The rule followed here presents a potential danger. If a previous party had a similar motive for cross-examination but did so incompetently, a strong possibility of prejudice arises. However, as the court noted here, the possibility of a Fed. R. Evid. 403 objection mitigates this problem.

[For more information on the admission of deposition testimony, see Casenote Law Outline on Evidence, Chapter 10, § XII, The Former Testimony Exception.]

KNAPP v. ST. LOUIS TRUST CO.
Mo. Sup. Ct., 199 Mo. 640, 98 S.W. 70 (1906).

NATURE OF CASE: Action contesting the validity of a will.

FACT SUMMARY: The will of Margaret Gaffey was challenged on the grounds that she was not of sound mind, and that she was under undue influence.

CONCISE RULE OF LAW: Declarations against interest are admissible to prove incidental facts contained within the scope of the declaration.

FACTS: The validity of the will of Margaret Gaffey was challenged on the grounds that, at the time she executed the alleged will, she was not of sound and disposing mind and memory and was under undue influence. At trial, entries in the account book of a Dr. McWilliams were introduced into evidence. McWilliams, who had made the entries, was deceased at the time of trial. The entries showed Gaffey's name and address, medical charges, and indicated that she had been treated for hyperaemia of the brain. The trial court held that the entries in the account book were only admissible to show that at certain dates Dr. McWilliams had made certain charges for visits to Mrs. Gaffey. On appeal, it was argued that the entries should be admissible as evidence of the disease for which Mrs. Gaffey was treated.

ISSUE: Are declarations against interest admissible to prove incidental facts contained within the scope of the declaration?

HOLDING AND DECISION: (Gantt, J.) Yes. Declarations against interest are admissible not only as evidence of the fact directly asserted, but also of incidental facts contained within the scope of the declaration. Here, the entries were made by a person who had no interest in making them, and such entries against interest of the party making them are clearly evidence of the fact stated. Thus, the entries were admissible not only for the purpose of showing that at certain dates Dr. McWilliams rendered medical services to Mrs. Gaffey, but also for the purpose of showing that he treated her for hyperaemia of the brain, and for softening of the brain and paralysis. Reversed and remanded for new trial.

EDITOR'S ANALYSIS: The Federal Rules create an exception to the hearsay rule for "a statement which was at the time of its making so far contrary to the declarant's pecuniary or proprietary interest . . . that a reasonable man in his position would not have made the statement unless he believed it to be true." See, Federal Rule of Evidence 804(b)(3).

[For more information on the admissibility of declarations against interest, see Casenote Law Outline on Evidence, Chapter 10, § XIV, Declarations Against Interest.]

HASKELL v. SIEGMUND
Ill. App. Ct., 28 Ill. App. 2d 1, 170 N.E.2d 393 (1960).

NATURE OF CASE: Appeal from award of damages for negligence.

FACT SUMMARY: Haskell (P) was injured by an automobile driven by Siegmund (D).

CONCISE RULE OF LAW: Declarations against pecuniary interest are an exception to the hearsay rule.

FACTS: Haskell (P) recovered a judgment against Siegmund (D) for injuries sustained by Siegmund's (D) driving of an automobile owned by Peterson. Haskell (P) then sought to collect the judgment from Peterson's liability insurance company. Liability under the policy depended on whether Siegmund (D) was driving with Peterson's permission. Following the accident, Klophel, an investigator for the insurance company, obtained statements from Peterson to the effect that he had given Siegmund (D) permission to use the automobile. Peterson died before trial of the action to collect the insurance proceeds. The insurance company appealed from a judgment entered against it.

ISSUE: Are declarations against pecuniary interest an exception to the hearsay rule?

HOLDING AND DECISION: (Reynolds, J.) Yes. Peterson's written statements to Klophel that he loaned the automobile to Siegmund (D) were admissible as declarations against his pecuniary interest, a well established exception to the hearsay rule. In order for a statement to be admissible as a statement against pecuniary interest: (1) the declarant must be dead; (2) the declaration must have been against the pecuniary interest of the declarant at the time it was made; (3) the declaration must be of a fact in relation to a matter concerning which the declarant was immediately and personally cognizable; and (4) the court should be satisfied that the declarant had no probable motive to falsify the fact declared. Here, Peterson's statements to Klophel meet these tests: (1) Peterson was dead at the time of trial; (2) when Peterson stated that he owned the car being driven by Siegmund (D) on the night of the accident, he was exposing himself to liability for Siegmund's (D) negligence; (3) Peterson had personal knowledge of the circumstances under which he gave the car to Siegmund (D); and (4) Peterson had no motive to falsify statements concerning Siegmund (D), who was only a part-time employee. Affirmed.

EDITOR'S ANALYSIS: There are at least three views as to what type of statements satisfy the test for being against interest. The possibilities are that the facts stated be against interest, that the statement itself create an obligation, and that the declarant be creating evidence which may be used to his detriment.

[For more information on the admission of declarations against pecuniary interest, see Casenote Law Outline on Evidence, Chapter 10, § XIV, Declarations Against Interest.]

WILLIAMSON v. UNITED STATES
512 U.S. ___, 114 S. Ct. 2431 (1994).

NATURE OF CASE: Appeal from conviction of possession of cocaine with intent to distribute, conspiracy to possess cocaine with intent to distribute, and traveling interstate to promote the distribution of cocaine.

FACT SUMMARY: Williamson (D) contended that the district court erred in allowing the testimony of a DEA agent in court who related arguably self-inculpatory statements made out of court to him by Harris, one of Williamson's (D) employees, regarding the possession and transport of the cocaine.

CONCISE RULE OF LAW: Fed. R. Evid. 804(b)(3) does not allow admission of non-self-exculpatory statements, even if they are made within a broader narrative that is generally self-inculpatory.

FACTS: Harris, an employee of Williamson (D), was stopped by the police while he was driving. The police, after searching the car, found 19 kilograms of cocaine in the car and arrested Harris. After his arrest, Harris was interviewed by telephone by a DEA agent, Walton. Harris told Walton that he had gotten the cocaine from a Cuban, that the cocaine belonged to Williamson (D), and that Harris was delivering it to a particular dumpster for pickup. Shortly thereafter, Walton interviewed Harris personally; Harris then told Walton that he was transporting the cocaine to Atlanta for Williamson (D), that Williamson (D) was traveling ahead of him in another car at the time of the arrest, and that Williamson (D) had apparently seen the police searching Harris' car and had fled. Harris told Walton that he had initially lied about the source of the cocaine because he was afraid of Williamson (D). Harris implicated himself in his statements to Walton but did not want his story to be recorded and refused to sign a written transcript of the statement. Walton later testified that Harris was not promised any reward for cooperating. Williamson (D) was eventually charged and convicted of various drug-related offenses. When Harris was called to testify at Williamson's (D) trial, he refused to do so. The district court then ruled that, under Fed. R. Evid. 804(b)(3), Agent Walton could relate what Harris told him because Harris' statements were against his own interests. Williamson (D) was convicted, and the court of appeals affirmed. On appeal, Williamson (D) argued that both lower courts erred by allowing Walton to testify regarding Harris' out-of-court statements.

ISSUE: Does Fed. R. Evid. 804(b)(3) allow admission of non-self-inculpatory statements, even if they are made within a broader narrative that is generally self-inculpatory?

HOLDING AND DECISION: (O'Connor, J.) No. Fed. R. Evid. 804(b)(3) does not allow admission on non-self-inculpatory statements, even if they are made within a broader narrative that is generally self-inculpatory. The district court may not just assume, for purposes of Rule 804(b)(3), that a statement is self-inculpatory because it is part of a fuller confession, and this is especially true when the statement implicates someone else. The question under the Rule is always whether the statement was sufficiently against the declarant's penal interest that a reasonable person would not have made the statement unless believing it to be true. This question can only be answered in

light of all the surrounding circumstances. In this case, some of Harris' confession would clearly have been admissible under the Rule. For instance, when he said he knew there was cocaine in the car, he forfeited his only defense to the charge of cocaine possession — lack of knowledge. But other parts of his confession, especially those in which he implicated Williamson (D), did little to subject Harris to criminal liability. A reasonable person in Harris' position might think that implicating someone else would decrease his own exposure to criminal liability at sentencing. Nothing in the record shows that the district court or court of appeals inquired whether each of the statements in Harris' confession was truly self-inculpatory. Remanded to the court of appeals to conduct this inquiry.

CONCURRENCE: (Scalia, J.) A declarant's statement is not magically transformed from a statement against penal interest into one that is inadmissible merely because the declarant names another person or implicates a possible codefendant. The relevant inquiry, however — and one that is not furthered by clouding the waters with manufactured categories such as "collateral neutral" and "collateral self-serving" — must always be whether the particular remark at issue (and not the extended narrative) meets the standard set forth in the Rule.

CONCURRENCE: (Ginsburg, J.) Fed. R. Evid. 804(b)(3) excepts from the general hearsay rule only those declarations or remarks within a narrative that are individually self-inculpatory. However, Harris' statements, as recounted by Walton, do not fit, even in part, within the exception described in the Rule for Harris' arguably inculpatory statements are too closely intertwined with his self-serving declarations to be ranked as trustworthy. To the extent that some of these statements tended to incriminate Harris, they provided only marginal or cumulative evidence of his guilt. They project the image of a person's acting not against his penal interest but striving mightily to shift principal responsibility to someone else. Therefore, Harris' hearsay statements should not be admissible under Rule 804(b)(3).

CONCURRENCE: (Kennedy, J.) Rule 804(b)(3) establishes a hearsay exception for statements against penal, proprietary, pecuniary, and legal interest. The text of the Rule does not tell us whether collateral statements are admissible. The Court resolves this issue by adopting the extreme position that no collateral statements are admissible under the Rule. The Court reaches that conclusion by relying on the "principle behind the Rule" that reasonable people do not make statements against their interest unless they are telling the truth, and reasons that this policy "expressed in the statutory text" simply does not extend to collateral statements. To the contrary, three sources indicate that the Rule allows the admission of some collateral statements: first, the Advisory Committee Note to the Rule establishes that some collateral statements are admissible; second, at common law, collateral statements were admissible, and we can presume that Congress intended the principle and terms used in the Federal Rules of Evidence to be applied as they were at common law; third, absent a textual direction to the contrary, we should assume that Congress intended the penal interest exception for inculpatory statements to

Continued on next page

have some meaningful effect. The exclusion of collateral statements would cause the exclusion of almost all inculpatory statements.

EDITOR'S ANALYSIS: As indicated by the Court in Williamson, Rule 804(b)(3) requires that self-inculpatory statements should be examined in terms of the reasonable person and that the declarant believe the statement to be against interest. In order to analyze whether the declarant truly believes his statement was against interest, the identity of the person to whom the statement was made should be considered. Although the situation wherein a declarant makes his statement to the authorities is the prime example of a statement against interest, if such a statement was made to a trusted friend (who was expected to keep the information secret), it has not necessarily been held that this eliminates the disserving nature of the statement.

[For more information on declarations against interest, see Casenote Law Outline on Evidence, Chapter 10, § XIV, Declarations against Interest.]

NOTES:

DALLAS CNTY. v. COMMERCIAL UNION ASSUR. CO., LTD.
286 F.2d 388 (5th Cir. 1961).

NATURE OF CASE: Action to collect under insurance policy.

FACT SUMMARY: Insurer (D) offered into evidence a 1901 newspaper article.

CONCISE RULE OF LAW: In matters of local interest, when the fact in question is of such a public nature it would be generally known throughout the community, and when the questioned fact occurred so long ago that the testimony of an eye witness would probably be less trustworthy than a contemporary newspaper account, a federal court may relax the hearsay exclusionary rules to the extent of admitting the newspaper article in evidence.

FACTS: In 1957, the Dallas County (P) court house collapsed. In order to collect under an insurance policy which covered loss caused by lightning, the County (P) reported the presence of charcoal and charred timbers found in the building's ruins. To refute this at trial, the insurer (D), claiming that the charred remains were present in the building prior to its collapse, offered into evidence a local 1901 newspaper article, unsigned, which reported a fire in the court house. The County (P) objected to the introduction of the article on the ground of hearsay.

ISSUE: May a federal court ever admit into evidence a newspaper article?

HOLDING AND DECISION: (Wisdom, J.) Yes. Fed. R. Civ. P. 43(a) permits a federal court to follow any rule which favors the reception of evidence. Although nearly all newspaper articles constitute hearsay, a federal court may recognize its own exceptions. First, it is due to necessity that the article should be admitted. Witnesses to the 1901 fire would now either be dead or possess a faulty memory. Secondly, the article itself carries sufficient indicia of trustworthiness. A small town newspaper reporter in 1901 would not report a local fire unless there had, in fact, been one. The reporter would simply lack any motive to falsify. The article is admissible in evidence.

EDITOR'S ANALYSIS: Newspaper articles, printed books, or publications are usually not admissible in evidence. This is because, absent some special indication of reliability, as in the instant case, there is no opportunity to cross-examine their authors, and the statements within were not made under oath.

[For more information on policy governing hearsay exceptions, see Casenote Law Outline on Evidence, Chapter 10, § I, Definitions and Policy.]

UNITED STATES v. MEDICO
557 F.2d 309 (2d Cir. 1977);
cert. denied, 434 U.S. 986 (1977).

NATURE OF CASE: Appeal from bank robbery conviction.

FACT SUMMARY: Medico (D) was convicted in the armed robbery of the Chemical Bank in Queens, New York, after hearsay testimony describing the getaway car was admitted.

CONCISE RULE OF LAW: In rare and exceptional circumstances, a hearsay statement which is not covered by any of the stated exceptions may be admissible.

FACTS: Medico (D) was indicted and convicted of the May 27, 1976, armed robbery of the Chemical Bank in Queens, New York. At trial, William Carmody, a bank employee, testified that about five minutes after the robbers had fled a bank customer knocked on the bank door and gave Carmody a description of the getaway car as a "tan Dodge Valiant" with license plate number "700 CQA." The testimony was admitted after the Government (P) indicated that it could not find the customer nor the person who had given the description of the getaway car to the bank customer. In addition, William Cariola testified that he used to work with Medico (D) for a taxicab company and would see Medico (D) driving an off-white Dodge with license plate number 700 CQA. Medico (D) was convicted and claimed that the introduction of the hearsay testimony constituted reversible error.

ISSUE: In rare and exceptional circumstances, is a hearsay statement which is not covered by any of the stated exceptions admissible?

HOLDING AND DECISION: (Carter, J.) Yes. A statement not specifically covered by other hearsay exceptions, but having equivalent circumstantial guarantees of trustworthiness, may be admissible in rare and exceptional circumstances. Here, the testimony of the bank customer meets all the specific standards for admission as a present sense impression under Rule 803(1), but fails to meet all the criteria set forth in the supportive judicial rationale. Carmody's testimony was highly relevant, clearly material, and the need for that evidence was great. Carmody's testimony had several indicia of reliability, including two witnesses who were at the scene of the crime when the information was relayed to Carmody, and the very brief time frame in which the information was passed from the eyewitness to the bank customer to Carmody. Because of its trustworthiness and the necessity for its admission, the evidence was properly admitted. Affirmed.

DISSENT: (Mansfield, J.) The double hearsay identification of the getaway car admitted by the trial court lacked any guarantee of trustworthiness entitling it to admission under the residual hearsay exception. In the absence of any such guarantee, or of an opportunity to test the reliability of the proof through cross-examination, the admission of this evidence constituted an abuse of discretion and reversible error.

EDITOR'S ANALYSIS: The residual hearsay exception exempts "a statement not specifically covered by any of the foregoing exceptions but having equivalent circumstantial guarantees of trustworthiness, if the court determines that (a) the statement is offered as evidence of a material fact; (b) the statement is more probative . . . than any other evidence; and (c) the general purposes of these rules and the interests of justice will best be served by admission of the statement into evidence." Federal Rule of Evidence 804(b)(5).

[For more information on the "catchall" exceptions, see Casenote Law Outline on Evidence, Chapter 10, § X, The "Wildcard" Exceptions.]

NOTES:

NOTES

15

CHAPTER 15
PROTECTING RELATIONSHIPS BY MEANS OF PRIVILEGE

QUICK REFERENCE RULES OF LAW

1. **The Spousal Privilege.** A criminal defendant cannot prevent his spouse from voluntarily giving testimony against him because the privilege against adverse spousal testimony belongs to the testifying spouse. (Trammel v. United States)

   [For more information on the spousal privilege, see Casenote Law Outline on Evidence, Chapter 8, § V, Spousal Privileges.]

2. **The Spousal Privilege.** Confidential communications and information gained by reason of the marital relationship are privileged. (Shepherd v. State)

   [For more information on the spousal privilege, see Casenote Law Outline on Evidence, Chapter 8, § V, Spousal Privileges.]

3. **The Attorney-client Privilege.** Professional employment is established, so that ensuing communications are privileged, where a person consults an attorney with the view to obtaining professional advice or aid and where the attorney acquiesces in such consultation. (Denver Tramway v. Owens)

   [For more information on the attorney-client privilege, see Casenote Law Outline on Evidence, Chapter 8, § II, The Attorney-Client Privilege.]

4. **The Scope of Attorney-client Privilege.** Statements are privileged if an attorney-client relationship existed, based on the belief of the client at the time the statements were made. (In re Grand Jury)

   [For more information on the scope of the attorney-client privilege, see Casenote Law Outline on Evidence, Chapter 8, § II, The Attorney-Client Privilege.]

5. **The Application of Attorney-client Privilege to Corporations.** In the case of a corporation claiming the attorney-client privilege, whether the privilege protects any particular communication must be determined on a case-by-case basis; the "control group" test does not govern. (Upjohn Co. v. United States)

   [For more information on the application of the attorney-client privilege to corporations, see Casenote Law Outline on Evidence, Chapter 8, § II, The Attorney-Client Privilege.]

6. **The Scope of the Attorney-client Privilege.** The attorney-client privilege prevents the prosecution by a defendant to help prepare an insanity defense. (State v. Pratt)

   [For more information on the scope of the attorney-client privilege, see Casenote Law Outline on Evidence, Chapter 8, § II, The Attorney-Client Privilege.]

7. **Joint Clients and the Attorney-client Privilege.** Communications between joint clients and their attorney are not privileged in a later action between those clients or their representatives. (Henke v. Iowa Home Mutual Casualty Co.)

   [For more information on joint clients and the attorney-client privilege, see Casenote Law Outline on Evidence, Chapter 8, § II, The Attorney-Client Privilege.]

8. **The Attorney-client Privilege.** Matters concerning a person's competency are not ordinarily confidential; consequently, they are not made inadmissible by the attorney-client privilege, which protects communications made in confidence by a client to an attorney. (United States v. Kendrick)

9. **Application of the Attorney-client Privilege.** Generally speaking, the attorney-client privilege does not prevent compelled identification of a client. (In re Grand Jury Investigation No. 83-2-35)

[For more information on application of the attorney-client privilege, see Casenote Law Outline on Evidence, Chapter 8, § II, The Attorney-Client Privilege.]

10. **Limitations on the Attorney-client Privilege.** Communications made to a lawyer by one contemplating fraud or the commission of a crime, and seeking the lawyer's legal advice as to how to commit the fraud or crime, or how to escape its consequences, are not privileged. (Standard Fire Insurance Co. v. Smithhart)

[For more information on limitations on the attorney-client privilege, see Casenote Law Outline on Evi-dence, Chapter 8, § II, The Attorney-Client Privilege.]

11. **The Journalist's Privilege.** Newspeople are not constitutionally privileged to withhold duly subpoenaed documents. (In the Matter of Myron Farber)

[For more information on the journalist's privilege, see Casenote Law Outline on Evidence, Chapter 8, § IX, Novel Privileges.]

12. **The Psychotherapist-patient Privilege.** Under a properly limited interpretation, the litigant-patient exception to the psychotherapist-patient privilege does not unconstitutionally infringe the constitutional rights of privacy of either psychotherapists or their patients. (In re Lifschutz)

[For more information on the psychotherapist-patient privilege, see Casenote Law Outline on Evidence, Chapter 8, § IV, The Psychotherapist-Patient Privilege.]

TRAMMEL v. UNITED STATES
445 U.S. 40 (1980).

NATURE OF CASE: Appeal from convictions for conspiracy to import and importing heroin.

FACT SUMMARY: Trammel's (D) wife agreed to testify against her husband in return for lenient treatment for herself, but Trammel (D) argued he had the right to prevent her from testifying against him.

CONCISE RULE OF LAW: A criminal defendant cannot prevent his spouse from voluntarily giving testimony against him because the privilege against adverse spousal testimony belongs to the testifying spouse.

FACTS: In return for lenient treatment for herself, Mrs. Trammel, an unindicted coconspirator, agreed to testify against her husband at his trial for conspiracy to import and importing heroin. The district court ruled she could testify to any act she observed during the marriage and to any communication made in the presence of a third person but not as to confidential communications between herself and her husband because they fell within the privilege attaching to confidential marital communications. On appeal, Trammel (D) contended that he was entitled to invoke the privilege against adverse spousal testimony so as to exclude the voluntary testimony of his wife. The court of appeals rejected this contention and affirmed the convictions.

ISSUE: Can a criminal defendant invoke the privilege against adverse spousal testimony so as to prevent his spouse from voluntarily offering adverse testimony against him?

HOLDING AND DECISION: (Burger, C.J.) No. Inasmuch as the privilege against adverse spousal testimony belongs solely to the testifying spouse, a criminal defendant cannot invoke the privilege to prevent his spouse from offering adverse testimony against him. The Hawkins case left the federal privilege for adverse spousal testimony where it found it at the time, thus continuing a rule which barred the testimony of one spouse against the other unless both consented. However, since that 1958 decision, support for that conception of the privilege has eroded further and the trend in state law is toward divesting the accused of the privilege to bar adverse spousal testimony. The ancient foundations for so sweeping a privilege involved a conception of the wife as her husband's chattel to do with as he wished, and they have long since disappeared. Nor is the desire to protect the marriage a valid justification for affording an accused such a privilege. If his spouse desires to testify against him, simply preventing her from doing so is not likely to save the marriage. Affirmed.

CONCURRENCE: (Stewart, J.) The court is correct when it says that the ancient foundations for so sweeping a privilege have long since disappeared. But those foundations had disappeared well before 1958; their disappearance certainly did not occur in the few years that have elapsed between the Hawkins decision and this one.

EDITOR'S ANALYSIS: The Model Code of Evidence and the Uniform Rules of Evidence completely abolished the notion of a privilege against adverse spousal testimony and limited themselves to recognizing a privilege covering confidential marital communications. Several state legislatures have followed suit.

[For more information on the spousal privilege, see Casenote Law Outline on Evidence, Chapter 8, § V, Spousal Privileges.]

NOTES:

SHEPHERD v. STATE
Ind. Sup. Ct., 257 Ind. 229, 277 N.E.2d 165 (1971).

NATURE OF CASE: Appeal from conviction for burglary.

FACT SUMMARY: Shepherd (D) contended that knowledge obtained by her former husband during their marriage relating to the crime in question was privileged and therefore inadmissible.

CONCISE RULE OF LAW: Confidential communications and information gained by reason of the marital relationship are privileged.

FACTS: Shepherd (D) was convicted, in a trial before the court, of second-degree burglary. On appeal, she argued that knowledge obtained by the State's (P) witness during his marriage to her was privileged and therefore inadmissible. The State's (P) witness testified that he committed the burglary, and that Shepherd (D) aided and abetted by driving the automobile for him. This testimony was admitted, over timely objection, and was the only evidence implicating Shepherd (D).

ISSUE: Are confidential communications and information gained by reason of the marital relationship privileged?

HOLDING AND DECISION: (Prentice, J.) Yes. Although the Indiana statute refers to husbands and wives as being incompetent witnesses, the matter is actually one of privileged communication. It has been restricted in its application to confidential communication and information gained by reason of the marital relationship. Privileged communications between husbands and wives, however, are not limited to mere audible communications to each other but include knowledge communicated by acts that would not have been done by one in the presence of the other but for the confidence between them by reason of the marital relationship. Public policy favors the promotion and preservation of marital confidences, even at the expense, in certain instances, of depriving honest causes of upright testimony. There are exceptions to the rule of privilege as to communications between spouses, as, for example when the offense charged was committed by one against the other, and when the communication sought to be suppressed was not confidential. However, there is no exception for statements made between spouses who are accomplices in crime. Here, the trial judge admitted the testimony of the husband upon the premise that the driving of an automobile could not constitute the communication of information. However, the operation of the vehicle was Shepherd's (D) role, and in this context, it was information imparted in confidence. A divorce does not remove the privilege as to confidences which were communicated between the parties during their marriage. Reversed.

DISSENT: (Arterburn, C.J.) There can be no valid ground for granting a privilege to a husband and wife to conspire to commit a crime or act as an accomplice with the other in the commission of a crime as in this case. The evidence shows that they were engaged as cocriminals before their marriage. The marriage ought not give them an added shield or advantage.

EDITOR'S ANALYSIS: The Uniform Rules of Evidence state that: "A communication is confidential if it is made privately by any person to his or her spouse and is not intended for disclosure to any other person. An accused in a criminal proceeding has a privilege to prevent his spouse from testifying as to any confidential communication between the accused and the spouse." See, Uniform Rules of Evidence (Revised 1974), Rule 504.

[For more information on the spousal privilege, see Casenote Law Outline on Evidence, Chapter 8, § V, Spousal Privileges.]

NOTES:

DENVER TRAMWAY CO. v. OWENS
Colo. Sup. Ct., 20 Colo. 107, 36 P. 848 (1894).

NATURE OF CASE: Appeal from granting of privilege in personal injury action.

FACT SUMMARY: Owens' (P) objection to the testimony of an attorney, as to Owens' (P) statements regarding the manner in which she was injured, was sustained in her personal injury action against Denver Tramway Co. (D).

CONCISE RULE OF LAW: Professional employment is established, so that ensuing communications are privileged, where a person consults an attorney with the view to obtaining professional advice or aid and where the attorney acquiesces in such consultation.

FACTS: Owens (P) was allegedly injured when alighting from a cable car operated by Denver Tramway Co. (D). Soon after, she conversed with Mead, an attorney. Although Owens (P) had no prior relationship with Mead and had not talked about fees or compensation of any kind, she talked with him about her injuries, consulting him "as an attorney in relation to her case." When defense counsel asked Mead what Owens (P) had related regarding the manner in which she had received her injuries, Owens (P) objected. The objection was sustained, and Denver Tramway Co. (D) appealed this ruling.

ISSUE: If one consults an attorney with a view to obtaining professional assistance, and if the attorney allows such consultation, are the communications between them privileged?

HOLDING AND DECISION: (Elliot, J.) Yes. At common law, a privilege was granted to attorney-client communications relating to the clients business affairs. Moreover, Colorado statutory law extends such a privilege to any communications made at a time when the attorney was employed in his or her professional capacity, with respect to the subject matter of the communication. To establish professional employment, one need not have had a previous relationship with the attorney, nor have paid any amount nor have filed suit; one need not even engage the attorney after the consultation. Professional employment is established, so that the ensuing communications are privileged, when an individual consults an attorney with a view towards obtaining professional aid or advice, if the attorney acquiesces in the consultation. Here, though the attorney was not subsequently engaged to represent Owens (P), Owens (P) consulted him "as an attorney in relation to her case." Thus, professional employment was established, and the communications which ensued were privileged and inadmissible. Affirmed.

EDITOR'S ANALYSIS: Denver Tramway Co. v. Owens is in accord with the weight of authority in holding that the attorney-client privilege turns on the client's consulting a lawyer in his or her legal capacity, with the intention of seeking legal advice. Preliminary communications are privileged although the employment is subsequently not accepted; otherwise, no one could safely consult an attorney for the first time. The burden of proving that the consultation was in the attorney's professional capacity rests on the party seeking to assert the privilege.

[For more information on the attorney-client privilege, see Casenote Law Outline on Evidence, Chapter 8, § II, The Attorney-Client Privilege.]

NOTES:

STATE v. PRATT
Md. Ct. App., 284 Md. 516, 398 A.2d 421 (1979).

NATURE OF CASE: Appeal of reversal of conviction for murder.

FACT SUMMARY: Pratt (D) was convicted of murder after the State (P) introduced, to rebut her insanity defense, testimony of a psychiatrist who had once been retained on her behalf.

CONCISE RULE OF LAW: The attorney-client privilege prevents the prosecution by a defendant to help prepare an insanity defense.

FACTS: Pratt (D) shot and killed her husband. Charged with murder, she raised the insanity defense. Three psychiatrists were retained, only one of whom concluded she was legally insane when the killing occurred. At trial, the State (P) introduced the testimony of one of the psychiatrists who thought her legally sane. She was convicted, but the state appellate court reversed, finding the use of the psychiatrist violative of the attorney-client privilege. The State (P) appealed.

ISSUE: Does the attorney-client privilege prevent the prosecution from employing the testimony of a mental health expert originally retained by a defendant to help prepare an insanity defense?

HOLDING AND DECISION: (Digges, J.) Yes. The attorney-client privilege prevents the prosecution from employing the testimony of a mental health expert originally retained by a defendant to help prepare an insanity defense. The attorney-client privilege has long been recognized as vital to promoting the policy that an individual in a free society be able to consult with his attorney without fear of compelled disclosure. Due to the complexity of modern litigation, this rule has been broadened to include a host of nonlegal advisors and support staff necessary for a lawyer to function. A mental health professional certainly must be included here, as few attorneys can venture into this sophisticated field without expert advice. Further, this court sees no reason to hold that a defendant putting his psychiatric condition into issue constitutes a waiver of the privilege. Finally, a prosecution's use of a professional originally retained by a defendant would be highly prejudicial. For these reasons, it must be held that the attorney-client privilege extends to mental health professionals employed by a defendant. Affirmed.

EDITOR'S ANALYSIS: A patient-psychotherapist privilege is recognized in most jurisdictions. In civil matters, this privilege is waived if the patient puts his mental state into issue by, for instance, claiming emotional distress damages. The privilege asserted here, that of attorney and client, is quite distinct conceptually.

[For more information on the scope of the attorney-client privilege, see Casenote Law Outline on Evidence, Chapter 8, § II, The Attorney-Client Privilege.]

IN RE GRAND JURY
106 F.R.D. 255 (N.H.D. 1985).

NATURE OF CASE: Motion to quash subpoena of attorney-client communications.

FACT SUMMARY: Boeckeler contended a Grand Jury subpoena should be quashed as compliance would violate the work-product privilege.

CONCISE RULE OF LAW: Statements are privileged if an attorney-client relationship existed, based on the belief of the client at the time the statements were made.

FACTS: Wallace retained attorney Boeckeler to represent him regarding Grand Jury proceedings. In the course of such representation, Boeckeler interviewed witness Doe and made a memorandum concerning the substance of such. Subsequently Wallace waived his attorney-client privilege. The Grand Jury subpoenaed the statement, and Boeckeler argued such should be quashed. Doe contended he believed Boeckeler was representing his interests in the interview, thus an attorney-client relationship existed making the statements privileged.

ISSUE: Are statements privileged if in the belief of the client, an attorney-client relationship existed at the time they were made?

HOLDING AND DECISION: (Loughlin, J.) Yes. Statements are privileged if in the belief of the client, an attorney-client relationship existed at the time the statements were made. Thus, because Doe believed Boeckeler was representing him, the statements were made in confidence and are privileged. Thus, the subpoena must be quashed.

EDITOR'S ANALYSIS: The basis for the motion to quash was identified by Boeckeler as work product privileges. The court indicated that even though Wallace had waived his attorney-client privilege, he had not lost all protection. However, the subpoena was quashed on the basis of Doe's attorney-client privilege.

[For more information on the scope of the attorney-client privilege, see Casenote Law Outline on Evidence, Chapter 8, § II, The Attorney-Client Privilege.]

UPJOHN CO. v. UNITED STATES
449 U.S. 383 (1981).

NATURE OF CASE: Appeal from denial of privilege in tax investigation.

FACT SUMMARY: Upjohn (D) claimed the IRS was not entitled to production of its questionnaires to and interviews of Upjohn (D) employees concerning possibly illegal payments made by Upjohn (D), as they were privileged communications and an attorney's work product.

CONCISE RULE OF LAW: In the case of a corporation claiming the attorney-client privilege, whether the privilege protects any particular communication must be determined on a case-by-case basis; the "control group" test does not govern.

FACTS: In January 1976, independent accountants discovered that a foreign subsidiary of Upjohn (D) had made payments to or for the benefit of foreign government officials. Upjohn's (D) general counsel conducted an investigation of these "possibly illegal" payments, which included interviews of all foreign general and area managers, and various other Upjohn (D) employees, and questionnaires to the foreign managers. The IRS conducted its own investigation to determine the tax consequences of the payments. It demanded production of all Upjohn's (D) relevant files, including the questionnaires and memoranda of the interviews. Upjohn (D) claimed these were privileged and also protected as the work product of an attorney in anticipation of litigation. Upjohn (D) appealed the enforcement of the summons. The Sixth Circuit affirmed to the extent that officers and employees not responsible for directing Upjohn's (D) actions in response to legal advice were not "clients" whose communications could come within the attorney-client privilege. The case was remanded to district court for a determination as to who was not within the "control group." The district court was not to consider the work-product doctrine, which the Sixth Circuit found inapplicable to administrative summonses. Upjohn (D) appealed.

ISSUE: In the case of a corporation claiming the attorney-client privilege, does the privilege for any communication turn on whether the employee making the communication was responsible for directing the corporations actions?

HOLDING AND DECISION: (Rehnquist, J.) No. The "control group" test adopted by the Sixth Circuit, which grants the attorney-client privilege to only those communications made by employees responsible for directing the corporation's actions in response to legal advice, frustrates the very purpose of the privilege; this is so because it discourages communication of relevant information by employees of the client corporation to attorneys seeking to render their best legal advice to the corporate control group. Further, it invites unpredictability of application, as those whose communications receive the privilege must play a "substantial role" in directing corporate actions in response to the advice. Thus, in the case of a corporation claiming the privilege, the control group test does not govern; whether any particular communication is privileged must be determined on a case-by-case basis. Here, the communications in question were made by Upjohn (D) employees to its counsel at the direction of its officers, so that they might get advice from the counsel. Thus, these communications, the questionnaires and notes reflecting responses to interviews, are privileged. Regarding the notes which go beyond recording responses to interviews, Federal Rule 26 offers special protection to work product revealing an attorney's mental processes. While a sufficient showing of necessity can overcome protection as to tangible items and documents, a far stronger showing is required as to material revealing a lawyer's mental impressions. Here, the lesser standard was erroneously applied by the district court to the attorney's memoranda of interviews which went beyond the recording of responses. Reversed and remanded.

CONCURRENCE: (Burger, C.J.) The majority is right to reject the "control group" test, but it should articulate a standard: A communication should be privileged whenever an employee speaks at the direction of management regarding conduct within the scope of employment.

EDITOR'S ANALYSIS: Before the Upjohn case, the weight of authority favored the control group test. A broader test that some courts employed extended the privilege to embrace any communication by an employee involving his corporate duties and made at the direction of his corporate employer. This latter test was favored by Burger in Upjohn, although the majority declined to formulate a standard. While avoiding some of the problems of the control group test, the broader test seems to unduly extend the shield of privilege.

[For more information on the application of the attorney-client privilege to corporations, see Casenote Law Outline on Evidence, Chapter 8, § II, The Attorney-Client Privilege.]

NOTES:

IN RE GRAND JURY INVESTIGATION NO. 83-2-35
723 F.2d 477 (6th Cir. 1983).

NATURE OF CASE: Appeal of contempt citation.

FACT SUMMARY: Durant, an attorney, refused to identify his client to a grand jury, invoking attorney-client privilege.

CONCISE RULE OF LAW: Generally speaking, the attorney-client privilege does not prevent compelled identification of a client.

FACTS: Certain checks fraudulently drawn on a certain account were traced to the law offices of Durant, who had endorsed them on a second-party basis. Federal prosecutors, investigating the fraud, subpoenaed Durant to ascertain from where the checks had been obtained. Durant refused to disclose the identity of this individual, stating that he was his client and that this information was protected under the attorney-client privilege. When Durant refused a court order to disclose the client's identity, the court held Durant in contempt. Durant appealed.

ISSUE: Generally speaking, does the attorney-client privilege prevent compelled identification of a client?

HOLDING AND DECISION: (Krupansky, J.) No. Generally speaking, the attorney-client privilege does not prevent compelled identification of a client. The circuits are in complete accord that, as a general rule, the attorney-client privilege goes only to content and does not concern identification of a client. Several exceptions have been carved out in the circuits. The one relevant to this case is the rule first stated in the Ninth Circuit and adopted in several others that if a strong possibility exists that disclosure of the identity would implicate the client in the matter for which legal advice was sought in the first place, confidentiality may be maintained. Durant asserts that this is so in this case. However, the burden is on the attorney asserting the privilege to show this to be the case, and something more than his own representations must be put forward, such as a request for an in camera review of the evidence. This was not done here, and therefore Durant did not meet his burden in demonstrating the applicability of the exception to the general rule. Affirmed.

EDITOR'S ANALYSIS: There are several additional exceptions to this rule. One is where disclosure of identity is tantamount to disclosure of the otherwise protected contents of a communication. Another exception exists when identification would constitute the last necessary link in a chain of evidence sufficient to support an indictment. The Sixth Circuit expressly rejected the latter exception.

[For more information on application of the attorney-client privilege, see Casenote Law Outline on Evidence, Chapter 8, § II, The Attorney-Client Privilege.]

HENKE v. IOWA HOME MUTUAL CAS. CO.
Iowa Sup. Ct., 249 Iowa 614, 87 N.W.2d 920 (1958).

NATURE OF CASE: Appeal from denial of privilege.

FACT SUMMARY: Iowa Home Mutual Cas. Co. (D), in an action for bad faith and negligence in failing to settle two cases against Henke (P), the insured, refused to produce various communications concerning the two cases.

CONCISE RULE OF LAW: Communications between joint clients and their attorney are not privileged in a later action between those clients or their representatives.

FACTS: Two suits were brought against Henke (P), the insured. The insurer, Iowa Home Mutual Cas. Co. (D), failed to settle the cases, and judgment was rendered against Henke (P) in an amount that greatly exceeded the limits of his policy. Henke (P) sued Iowa Home (D) for bad faith and negligence in failing to settle and requested that Iowa Home (D) produce all communications concerning the two previously tried cases. Iowa Home (D) refused to comply, claiming the communications were privileged. The trial court ruled that, because the communications in question had been made to a law firm which had represented both Henke (P) and Iowa Home (D) in the earlier actions, no privilege existed. Iowa Home (D) appealed.

ISSUE: Are communications between joint clients and their attorney privileged in a later action between those clients or their representatives?

HOLDING AND DECISION: (Larson, J.) No. It is well established in Iowa that communications between an attorney and those persons jointly consulting an attorney are not privileged in a later action between those persons or their representatives. An attorney who has a duty to act for the benefit of joint parties cannot be allowed or compelled to withhold important information affecting the rights of one of the parties simply because it involves the other. Duty, loyalty and fairness, as well as public policy considerations, require that these communications not be privileged. Here, Henke (P) and Iowa Home (D) were originally represented by the same law firm; therefore, the documents requested were not, as between the parties, privileged. Affirmed.

EDITOR'S ANALYSIS: Henke v. Iowa Home Mutual Cas. Co. illustrates the majority rule. The rationale is that the joint consultation of the parties precludes any argument suggesting that they intended to keep the communications secret from each other.

[For more information on joint clients and the attorney-client privilege, see Casenote Law Outline on Evidence, Chapter 8, § II, The Attorney-Client Privilege.]

UNITED STATES v. KENDRICK
331 F.2d 110 (4th Cir. 1964).

NATURE OF CASE: Appeal from denial of motion to vacate sentence.

FACT SUMMARY: At a post-conviction competency hearing, Kendrick (D) claimed his trial counsel's testimony, as to Kendrick's (D) competency to stand trial, should have been excluded on the basis of the attorney-client privilege.

CONCISE RULE OF LAW: Matters concerning a person's competency are not ordinarily confidential; consequently, they are not made inadmissible by the attorney-client privilege, which protects communications made in confidence by a client to an attorney.

FACTS: Kendrick (D) was convicted and sentenced in 1960. At a post-conviction hearing to determine his competency to stand trial, his counsel from the 1960 trial testified regarding Kendrick's (D) responsiveness, his logical abilities, and his understanding of everything that occurred before and during trial. Kendrick (D) objected to this testimony, claiming that it should have been excluded on the basis of the attorney-client privilege. The district court denied Kendrick's (D) motion to vacate his sentence. This appeal followed.

ISSUE: Are matters unrelated to the substance of the attorney-client communications, such as a client's responsiveness, reasoning ability, and powers of understanding, confidential matters that are protected by the attorney-client privilege?

HOLDING AND DECISION: (Per Curiam) No. The attorney-client privilege protects communications made in confidence by a client to his attorney. It does not protect matters concerning a person's competency, which are ordinarily observable by anyone who might come into contact with the client. These matters include a client's responsiveness, logical abilities, and capacity for comprehension, unless there is any reason to believe that the attorney's observations of such characteristics are confidential. Here, the attorney made no mention of the substance of any communication between him and Kendrick (D). He only testified as to Kendrick's (D) demeanor and awareness. Since the matters testified to were not confidential in nature, they were not protected by the privilege. While the attorney's testimony was properly received, further inquiry into Kendrick's (D) medical history, diagnosis, treatment, and response is warranted. Vacated and remanded.

CONCURRENCE: (Sobeloff, J.) An opinion as to the client's competency necessarily requires more than facts observable by just anyone. Here, the opinion was formed from observations inextricably intertwined with the client's confidential and privileged communications.

EDITOR'S ANALYSIS: The general rule appears to be that a client's appearance and demeanor are not privileged. Further, several cases besides United States v. Kendrick have held that questions of competence are no more than observations of appearance and demeanor and so are not privileged. E.g., State v.

Jensen, 286 Minn. 65, 174 N.W. 2d 226 (1970); Smith v. Smith, 222 Ga. 694, 152 S.E. 2d 560 (1966).

_____

[For more information on application of the attorney-client privilege, see Casenote Law Outline on Evidence, Chapter 8, § II, The Attorney-Client Privilege.]

NOTES:

STANDARD FIRE INS. CO. v. SMITHHART
Ky. App. Ct., 183 Ky. 679, 211 S.W. 441 (1919).

NATURE OF CASE: Appeal from denial of motion for new trial.

FACT SUMMARY: In a case brought for refusal of Standard Fire Ins. Co. (D) to pay damages due to fire, Smithhart's (P) attorney was not allowed to testify as to conversations suggesting Smithhart (P) had procured the destruction of the insured property.

CONCISE RULE OF LAW: Communications made to a lawyer by one contemplating fraud or the commission of a crime, and seeking the lawyer's legal advice as to how to commit the fraud or crime, or how to escape its consequences, are not privileged.

FACTS: Smithhart's (P) house and its contents, insured by Standard Fire Ins. Co. (D), were destroyed by fire. When Standard Fire Ins. Co. (D) refused to pay damages, Smithhart (P) brought suit. At trial, an attorney whom Smithhart (P) had first employed was called to testify as to communications he had with Smithhart (P). These tended to show that (1) Smithhart (P) had arranged to have her house burned while she was out of town, and that (2) she had attempted to defraud Standard Fire Ins. Co. (D) by pretending that the burning was accidental. The court refused to allow this testimony and Smithhart (P) was awarded damages. Standard Fire Ins. Co.'s (D) motion for a new trial was denied. This appeal followed.

ISSUE: Are communications privileged if made to a lawyer by one contemplating fraud or the commission of a crime, and seeking the lawyer's legal advice as to how to commit the crime or fraud, or how to escape its consequences?

HOLDING AND DECISION: (Hurt, J.) No. It is not within the professional character of a lawyer to advise a client as to how to commit a fraud or crime, or how to avoid its consequences; hence, a lawyer cannot be professionally employed to give such advice. This being so, communications made to a lawyer by one contemplating fraud or the commission of a crime, and seeking legal advice as to how to commit the fraud or crime or how to avoid its consequences, are not privileged. The situation is, of course, different, where the fraud or crime has already been committed, but that is not the case here with respect to the alleged attempt to defraud Standard Fire Ins. Co. (D). Here, communications made to the attorney to seek his assistance in defrauding the insurance company were not made to the lawyer in his professional capacity; thus, they were not privileged. This much of the testimony was, therefore, wrongfully excluded. Reversed and remanded.

EDITOR'S ANALYSIS: It is well established that a lawyer's communications with those seeking aid in carrying out illegal or fraudulent acts stand on different footing from communications with those seeking aid in presenting legitimate defenses to charges of past crimes. In the former case, the advice the attorney gives would not be a professional service but participation in conspiracy. Thus, the attorney-client privilege does not extend to such communications.

[For more information on limitations on the attorney-client privilege, see Casenote Law Outline on Evidence, Chapter 8, § II, The Attorney-Client Privilege.]

NOTES:

IN THE MATTER OF MYRON FARBER

N.J. Sup. Ct., 78 N.J. 259, 394 A.2d 330;
cert. denied, 439 U.S. 997 (1978).

NATURE OF CASE: Appeal from contempt citation.

FACT SUMMARY: Farber (D), a reporter for the New York Times, was cited for contempt after refusing to disclose certain investigative documents.

CONCISE RULE OF LAW: Newspeople are not constitutionally privileged to withhold duly subpoenaed documents.

FACTS: The New York Times Company and Myron Farber, a reporter employed by the newspaper, challenged judgments of civil and criminal contempt entered against them. The proceedings were instituted in an ongoing murder trial of Dr. Mario E. Jascalevich, as a result of their failure to comply with two subpoenas duces tecum, directing them to produce certain documents and materials compiled by one or both of them in the course of Farber's (D) investigative reporting of certain allegedly criminal activities. Farber (D) claimed a First Amendment privilege to refrain from revealing information sought by the subpoenas duces tecum for the reason that, if the material were divulged, confidential sources of such information would be made public.

ISSUE: Are newspeople constitutionally privileged to withhold duly subpoenaed documents?

HOLDING AND DECISION: (Mountain, J.) No. The Supreme Court, in Branzburg v. Hayes, 408 U.S. 665 (1972), held that the First Amendment affords no privilege to a newsman to refuse to appear before a grand jury and testify as to relevant information he possesses, even though in so doing he may divulge confidential sources. Thus, there is no authority for the proposition that newsmen are constitutionally privileged to withhold duly subpoenaed documents material to the prosecution or defense of a criminal case. Further, the Sixth Amendment and the New Jersey constitution afford a defendant in a criminal prosecution the right to compel the attendance of witnesses and the production of documents and other material for which he may have, or may believe he has, a legitimate need in preparing or undertaking his defense. It also means that witnesses properly summoned will be required to testify, and that material demanded by a properly phrased subpoena duces tecum will be forthcoming and available for appropriate examination and use. These constitutional provisions override any state laws designed to protect the confidentiality of a reporter's sources of information. Affirmed.

EDITOR'S ANALYSIS: In this case, Farber (D) and the New York Times argued that the New Jersey "shield" law protected against the disclosure of confidential sources of information. That statute read in part "a person engaged in the gathering or procuring . . . of news for the general public . . . has a privilege to refuse to disclose, in any legal or quasi-legal proceeding . . . the source, author, means, agency, or person from or through whom any information was procured." N.J.S.A. 2A: 84A-21 and 21a.

[For more information on the journalist's privilege, see Casenote Law Outline on Evidence, Chapter 8, § IX, Novel Privileges.]

NOTES:

IN RE LIFSCHUTZ
Cal. Sup. Ct., 2 Cal. 3d 415, 467 P.2d 557 (1970).

NATURE OF CASE: Petition for a writ of habeas corpus after refusal to answer questions and produce records in an action for personal injuries caused by an assault.

FACT SUMMARY: Housek (P) alleged that Arabian's (D) assault caused him mental and emotional stress. Dr. Lifschutz (petitioner) refused to produce any medical records or to answer any questions relating to his treatment of patients.

CONCISE RULE OF LAW: Under a properly limited interpretation, the litigant-patient exception to the psychotherapist-patient privilege does not unconstitutionally infringe the constitutional rights of privacy of either psychotherapists or their patients.

FACTS: Housek (P) alleged that Arabian's (D) assault caused him severe mental and emotional stress. Arabian (D) deposed Housek (P), who stated that he had received psychiatric treatment from Dr. Lifschutz over a six-month period about ten years before. He did not reveal the nature or contents of any conversation with Lifschutz. Arabian (D) subpoenaed Lifschutz for deposition and all his medical records relating to Housek (P). Lifschutz refused to answer any questions relating to his treatment of patients or to produce any of his medical records. Neither Housek (P) nor his lawyer were present at the deposition or the subsequent hearings and Housek (P) neither expressly claimed a psychotherapist-patient privilege nor expressly waived it. Relying on the patient-litigant exception of the Evidence Code, the Superior Court determined that because Housek (P) had tendered as an issue his mental and emotional condition, the statutory psychotherapist-patient privilege did not apply. Lifschutz claimed that the patient-litigant exception violated his constitutional rights of privacy and equal protection.

ISSUE: Does the patient-litigant exception to the psychotherapist-patient privilege violate the psychotherapist's or the patient's right to privacy, the psychotherapist's right to practice his profession, or the psychotherapist's right to equal protection?

HOLDING AND DECISION: (Trobiner, J.) No. Lifschutz claims that the Constitution grants him an absolute right to refuse to disclose communications with his patients, regardless of the wishes of a patient in a particular case. His claim is based on Griswold, wherein a doctor was allowed to challenge the constitutionality of a statute prohibiting the distribution of contraceptives. However, the constitutional rights underlying the Griswold decision belonged to the patients rather than the doctor. The doctor or psychotherapist does not have a significant privacy interest apart from his patients. Nor does the Evidence Code's requirement that a psychotherapist reveal confidential matters under some circumstances unconstitutionally impair the practice of his profession. The impairment that does occur is not so severe as to constitute an unconstitutional taking of a valuable property right, the doctor's right to practice. Nor is it sufficient to render the practice of psychotherapy impossible, thereby unconstitutionally restricting the realm of available medical treatment. Obviously, psychotherapy has grown and flourished in the past when the exception was in effect and also before the privilege was recognized. Nor does the existence of a legislatively created absolute clergy person-penitent privilege render the absence of such an absolute psychotherapist-patient privilege a denial of equal protection. Although in some circumstances clergy persons and psychotherapists perform similar functions and serve similar needs, fundamental and significant differences remain. It is true that a psychotherapist may assert the statutory privilege on behalf of a patient as long as that privilege has not been waived and does not fall into a statutory exception. Here, Housek (P) disclosed that he had consulted Lifschutz. Hence, he waived whatever privilege he may have had to keep such information confidential. Arabian (D) contended that any communication between Housek (P) and Lifschutz had lost its privileged status because of the patient-litigant exception, since Housek (P) has put his mental condition in issue by seeking to recover damages for mental and emotional distress. However, the patient-litigant exception allows only limited inquiry into the confidences of the psychotherapist-patient relationship. It compels disclosure of only those matters directly relevant to the specific emotional or mental condition which the patient has voluntarily disclosed. Griswold recognized that various guarantees of the Bill of Rights create zones of privacy. The confidentiality of the psychotherapeutic session falls within such a zone. However, since only the patient-litigant knows both the nature of the ailments for which recovery is sought and the content of the psychotherapeutic communications, the patient must show that a given communication is not directly related to issues the patient has tendered to the court.

EDITOR'S ANALYSIS: At common law, communications between physician and patient were not privileged. In many of the states, statutes have created such a privilege. The purpose of the privilege is to encourage freedom of disclosure by the patient so as to aid in the effective treatment of disease and injury. To attain this objective, the privilege protects the patient from the embarrassment and invasion of privacy which disclosure would entail. The patient-litigant exception to the privilege is based on two grounds. First, the patient, in raising the issue of a specific ailment or condition in litigation, has, in effect, dispensed with the confidentiality of that ailment and may no longer seek protection from the humiliation of its exposure. Second, in all fairness, a patient should not be permitted to establish a claim while simultaneously foreclosing inquiry into relevant matters.

[For more information on the psychotherapist-patient privilege, see Casenote Law Outline on Evidence, Chapter 8, § IV, The Psychotherapist-Patient Privilege.]

CHAPTER 16
PRIVILEGES DESIGNED TO SAFEGUARD GOVERNMENTAL OPERATIONS

QUICK REFERENCE RULES OF LAW

1. **The Informer Privilege.** When the issue is not guilt or innocence, but the question of probable cause for an arrest or search, police officers need not invariably be required to disclose an informant's identity if the officers did rely in good faith upon credible information supplied by a reliable informant. (McCray v. Illinois)

   [For more information on the informer privilege, see Casenote Law Outline on Evidence, Chapter 8, § VII, Government Privileges.]

2. **"Secrets of State" Privilege.** It is well settled that a privilege to protect military and state secrets belongs to the government, and where the court may find, from all the circumstances, that there is a reasonable danger that compulsion of evidence formally claimed to be so privileged would be contrary to the interests of national security, no disclosure may be required. (United States v. Reynolds)

   [For more information on the "secrets of state" privilege, see Casenote Law Outline on Evidence, Chapter 8, § VII, Government Privileges.]

3. **The Executive Privilege.** While all private presidential communications are presumptively privileged, the fundamental demands of due process of law in the fair administration of criminal justice take precedence where the privilege is invoked on only a generalized interest in confidentiality. (United States v. Nixon)

   [For more information on the executive privilege, see Casenote Law Outline on Evidence, Chapter 8, § VII, Government Privileges.]

4. **The Official Information Privilege.** Confidential statements obtained during military investigation of an accident are not subject to FOIA disclosure. (United States v. Weber Aircraft)

   [For more information on the official information privilege, see Casenote Law Outline on Evidence, Chapter 8, § VII, Government Privileges.]

5. **Juror Competency.** Following a verdict in a criminal action a court is not required to consider evidence of juror intoxication in a motion for new trial. (Tanner v. United States)

   [For more information on juror competency, see Casenote Law Outline on Evidence, Chapter 11, § II, Witness Competence.]

6. **Privilege Procedure.** A court may not order the disclosure of grand jury records under Fed. R. Crim. Pro. 6(e) unless it has access to all relevant information regarding the necessity of the requested material of another judicial proceeding as opposed to the necessity of continued secrecy of the grand jury proceedings. (Douglas Oil Co. of California v. Petrol Stops N.W.)

   [For more information on privilege procedure, see Casenote Law Outline on Evidence, Chapter 8, § X, Privilege Procedure.]

NOTES

McCRAY v. ILLINOIS
386 U.S. 300;
reh'g denied, 386 U.S. 1042 (1967).

NATURE OF CASE: Appeal from conviction of possession of narcotics.

FACT SUMMARY: At McCray's (D) trial, arresting officer refused to disclose name of informant who had tipped police that McCray (D) was carrying narcotics on his person.

CONCISE RULE OF LAW: When the issue is not guilt or innocence, but the question of probable cause for an arrest or search, police officers need not invariably be required to disclose an informant's identity if the officers did rely in good faith upon credible information supplied by a reliable informant.

FACTS: Officer Jackson, acting upon a tip from an informant that McCray (D) "was selling narcotics and had narcotics on his person" and could be found in a certain area at a particular time, arrested McCray (D), searched him, and found narcotics. No warrant had been obtained. At McCray's trial for possession, Jackson testified, with specificity, that he had known the informant for a year, and that on at least fifteen occasions, the informant had supplied him with accurate information resulting in numerous arrests and convictions. When Jackson was asked for the informant's name and address, the prosecutor objected, and this objection was sustained by the court.

ISSUE: Must police testifying at a trial on the question of probable cause for an arrest and search disclose an informant's identity?

HOLDING AND DECISION: (Stewart, J.) No. If police officers rely in good faith upon credible information supplied by a reliable informant who provides the probable cause for an arrest or search, they need not be required to disclose an informant's identity. Unlike during a trial where the informer's presence and testimony might disclose an entrapment, throw doubt on the accused's or the seized evidence's identity, reveal that the defendant lacked the requisite knowledge, or cast further doubt on the accused's guilt, a distinction should be made when the accused seeks to avoid the truth. Furthermore, a genuine privilege, on fundamental principle, must be recognized for the identity of persons supplying the government with information concerning the commission of crimes. Informants would, out of fear for their own or their family's safety or reputation, be discouraged if their identity were disclosed. Finally, nothing in the Constitution requires a judge in every suppression hearing, or trial, to assume the arresting officers are committing perjury. Jackson did not have to disclose his informant's identity.

DISSENT: (Douglas, J.) An arrest without a warrant should not be given as much weight as an arrest with a warrant. An arrest without a warrant bypasses the safeguards provided by an objective predetermination of probable cause. There is no way to determine the reliability of Old Reliable, the informer, unless he is produced at the trial, and cross-examined.

EDITOR'S ANALYSIS: In United States v. Jackson, 384 F.2d 825 (1967), the trial court had adopted a middle ground approach by requiring that the informant's identity be disclosed in camera. The

trial judge had questioned the informant "as to the possible physical danger he would encounter if disclosure were allowed and as to any evidence he could offer that might aid the defendant's cause." At 827.

_____

[For more information on the informer privilege, see Casenote Law Outline on Evidence, Chapter 8, § VII, Government Privileges.]

NOTES:

UNITED STATES v. REYNOLDS
345 U.S. 1 (1953).

NATURE OF CASE: Appeal of an order to disclose military information.

FACT SUMMARY: Reynolds (P) sought discovery of an Air Force accident report, containing classified military information.

CONCISE RULE OF LAW: It is well settled that a privilege to protect military and state secrets belongs to the government, and where the court may find, from all the circumstances, that there is a reasonable danger that compulsion of evidence formally claimed to be so privileged would be contrary to the interests of national security, no disclosure may be required.

FACTS: Reynolds (P) brought a wrongful death action under the Federal Tort Claims Act to recover damages for the death of her husband, who was killed in a plane crash while acting as a civilian observer on an Air Force test flight. At pretrial, she moved to discover (per Fed. R. Civ. P. 34) the official Air Force Accident Report. Over government objections, the judge found "good cause" for the discovery. Following this, the Secretary of the Air Force filed a formal "Claim of Privilege," asserting that the flight was involved in a "secret mission," the disclosure of which would not be in the national interest. The court rejected this claim and ordered the government to produce the report. When the government refused, the court ordered (per Fed. R. Civ. P. 37b) that the facts on the issue of negligence would be taken as established in Reynolds' (P) favor. From judgment for Reynolds (P), the government appealed.

ISSUE: May the United States be required to produce, in court, information classified as secret, by a mere showing of need for discovery by the adverse party?

HOLDING AND DECISION: (Vinson, C.J.) No. It is well settled that a privilege to protect military and state secrets belongs to the government, and where the court may find, from all the circumstances, that there is a reasonable danger that compulsion of evidence formally claimed to be so privileged would be contrary to the interests of national security, no disclosure may be required. It is true that judicial control over evidence in a case may not be abdicated to the mere caprice of judicial officers. This does not mean, however, that the court becomes automatically entitled to receive and review any and all evidence, regardless of the nature and extent of any privilege which it may be subject to. Here, the trial court was justified in finding "good cause" for discovery upon the showing of necessity by Reynolds (P). Once the Secretary filed his formal claim of privilege, however, the court should have taken judicial notice of contemporary national defense needs and granted the claim. The decision must be reversed.

EDITOR'S ANALYSIS: This case points up the general and common law rule that the government has a right to protect military and state secrets for the public interest. Note that this rule survives U.S. v. Nixon.

[For more information on the "secrets of state" privilege, see Casenote Law Outline on Evidence, Chapter 8, § VII, Government Privileges.]

NOTES:

UNITED STATES v. NIXON
418 U.S. 683 (1974).

NATURE OF CASE: Motion to quash subpoena duces tecum.

FACT SUMMARY: Incident to a federal trial of seven individuals for various violations of federal law, a subpoena duces tecum was issued for certain presidential documents and tapes. The president resisted the subpoena on a claim of privilege.

CONCISE RULE OF LAW: While all private presidential communications are presumptively privileged, the fundamental demands of due process of law in the fair administration of criminal justice take precedence where the privilege is invoked on only a generalized interest in confidentiality.

FACTS: In connection with the federal criminal trials of seven individuals for conspiracy to defraud the United States (P) and to obstruct justice, a subpoena duces tecum was issued for certain presidential documents and tapes. The President (D) had been named as an unindicted coconspirator in the original indictments. The President (D) resisted the subpoena by claiming the materials requested were constitutionally protected confidential communications.

ISSUE: Must the President of the United States (D) honor a subpoena for documents relating to private presidential communications issued in connection with a criminal trial where the communications involved do not pertain to military or diplomatic secrets or otherwise involve national security?

HOLDING AND DECISION: (Burger, C.J.) Yes. Notwithstanding the deference each branch of our government must show to the independent acts of the other branches, it is emphatically the province and the duty of this court to say what the law is with respect to the claim of privilege asserted in this case. While there is no explicit constitutional reference to presidential privilege in the area of confidential communications, it is clear that the privilege devolves from the necessary implementation of his enumerated powers. However, the privilege is not absolute as regards nonmilitary and nondiplomatic discussions. It cannot be asserted in a manner that would unduly disrupt the workings of another branch. Because the President (D) and his advisors must feel free in their private discussions to speak candidly and bluntly, any private presidential communications are presumptively privileged. This presumptive privilege must be weighed in this case against the constitutional mandate that an accused shall have the right "to be confronted with the witnesses against him" and "to have compulsory process for obtaining witnesses in his favor." Further, no man is to be deprived of liberty without due process of law. In the face of these constitutional requirements, a claim of privilege based on a generalized claim of confidentiality cannot prevail. The fundamental demands of due process of law in the fair administration of criminal justice require that the privilege must give way. The President (D) and his advisors cannot be affected in the candor of their remarks merely because there may be infrequent disclosures in the context of a criminal trial. It has been said, by Chief Justice Marshall, that "in no case of this kind would a court be required to proceed against

the president as against an ordinary individual." This is not to be read as placing the President (D) above the law, but as a recognition of the unique position of the office and its related duties. The trial judge correctly recognized that the requested material must be handled with the greatest care so that only the most relevant portions are produced at trial. All deliberations prior to selection of usable evidence must be made in camera, and any unused portions returned und·sclosed with the balance returned when their purpose is served.

EDITOR'S ANALYSIS: The Court, in a footnote, made clear that this decision had no application to civil litigation or the requests for information made by the Congress to the President (D). The case was limited to the conflict of a generalized assertion of confidentiality against the constitutional need for relevant evidence in criminal trials. The decision would appear to be in accord with Rule 508 of the 1974 Approved Draft of the Uniform Rules of Evidence relating to state secrets and governmental privilege. Rule 509 of the same Uniform Rules would have required dismissal of the charges against the defendants if the privilege were upheld.

[For more information on the executive privilege, see Casenote Law Outline on Evidence, Chapter 8, § VII, Government Privileges.]

NOTES:

UNITED STATES v. WEBER AIRCRAFT CORP.
465 U.S. 792 (1984).

NATURE OF CASE: Review of appellate court order mandating document disclosure under the Freedom of Information Act (FOIA).

FACT SUMMARY: Weber Aircraft (P) sought disclosure under the FOIA of confidential statements made during a military investigation of an accident.

CONCISE RULE OF LAW: Confidential statements obtained during military investigation of an accident are not subject to FOIA disclosure.

FACTS: A military investigation took place following a crash of an Air Force jet. As part of an investigation made solely for safety purposes, certain statements were taken from witnesses who were told the statements would be confidential. During a subsequent lawsuit, Weber Aircraft Corp. (P) requested the statements from the Air Force, which refused production. The trial court held the documents privileged from pretrial discovery. Weber Aircraft (P) then commenced an action under the Freedom of Information Act (FOIA) to obtain the statements. The district court refused to order production, but the court of appeals reversed. The Supreme Court granted review.

ISSUE: Are confidential statements obtained during military investigation of an accident subject to FOIA disclosure?

HOLDING AND DECISION: (Stewart, J.) No. Confidential statements obtained during military investigation of an accident are not subject to FOIA disclosure. It is already settled that such documents are not discoverable pursuant to Fed. R. Civ. P. discovery rules. Exception 5 to the FOIA protects from disclosure intra-agency memoranda not obtainable by non-FOIA procedures. Congress clearly did not intend the FOIA to be a vehicle for circumventing discovery privilege rules. To allow the production of the statements, which are not unquestionably intra-agency memoranda, would do precisely that. This cannot be permitted. Reversed.

EDITOR'S ANALYSIS: The Supreme Court has never expressly held documents of the type involved here privileged from disclosure by discovery under the Fed. R. Civ. P. However, the Court quoted approvingly Machin v. Zukert, 316 F.2d 336 (D.C. Cir. 1963), which came to that conclusion. It would seem, based on the Court's endorsement of this rule, that it should be applied in all circuits.

[For more information on the official information privilege, see Casenote Law Outline on Evidence, Chapter 8, § VII, Government Privileges.]

TANNER v. UNITED STATES
107 S. Ct. 2739 (1987).

NATURE OF CASE: Review of order denying post-conviction hearing and new trial.

FACT SUMMARY: Following his conviction, Tanner (D) attempted to demonstrate juror misconduct involving drug and alcohol consumption.

CONCISE RULE OF LAW: Following a verdict in a criminal action a court is not required to consider evidence of juror intoxication in a motion for new trial.

FACTS: Tanner (D) was convicted of mail fraud. After the conviction, a pair of jurors made it known to his attorney that, for much of the trial, some of the jurors ingested significant amounts of alcohol, cocaine, and marijuana. Tanner (D) submitted a declaration concerning this from a juror in support of a motion for a new trial. The district court held the declaration inadmissible under Federal Rule of Evidence 606, and denied the motion. The Eleventh Circuit affirmed. Tanner (D) obtained certiorari in the Supreme Court.

ISSUE: Is a court required, following a verdict in a criminal action, to consider evidence of juror intoxication in a motion for new trial?

HOLDING AND DECISION: (O'Connor, J.) No. Following a verdict in a criminal action, a court is not required to consider evidence of juror intoxication in a motion for new trial. It has long been the rule that, in order to guard the admittedly imperfect jury systems from a barrage of assaults from which it possibly could not survive, juror testimony may not be admitted to impeach a jury verdict, unless the testimony concerns some sort of extraneous influence, such as a bribe. This common law rule was codified in Fed. R. Evid. 606. Allegations of mental or physical incompetence have always been treated as internal rather than external matters, and the conduct called into question here fits into that category. It is clear that Congress intended that juror testimony not be admissible to impeach a jury verdict, as it specifically rejected a bill that would have so permitted. This being so, the district court was correct in refusing to consider the juror's declaration and denying the motion. Affirmed.

DISSENT IN PART: (Marshall, J.) A criminal defendant has a right, under the Sixth Amendment, to trial by a competent jury. Where evidence sufficient to raise a question whether a jury was competent exists, the court should be compelled to consider the evidence.

EDITOR'S ANALYSIS: Fed. R. Evid. 606 originally differed in its versions in the House of Representatives and the Senate. The House bill would have permitted juror testimony to be considered; the Senate bill did not. The Conference Committee eventually took the Senate side of the issue. Thus, in this instance the legislative history made the intent of Congress quite clear.

[For more information on juror competency, see Casenote Law Outline on Evidence, Chapter 11, § II, Witness Competence.]

DOUGLAS OIL CO. OF CALIFORNIA v.
PETROL STOPS NORTHWEST
441 U.S. 211 (1979).

NATURE OF CASE: Appeal from order granting disclosure of grand jury transcripts.

FACT SUMMARY: Petrol Stops Northwest (P) sought the production of grand jury transcripts containing testimony of Douglas Oil Co.'s (D) employees.

CONCISE RULE OF LAW: A court may not order the disclosure of grand jury records under Fed. R. Crim. Pro. 6(e) unless it has access to all relevant information regarding the necessity of the requested material of another judicial proceeding as opposed to the necessity of continued secrecy of the grand jury proceedings.

FACTS: Petrol Stops Northwest (Petrol) (P) sued Douglas Oil Co. (D) for antitrust violations, including charges of price-fixing, in an Arizona state court. In a separate criminal proceeding in California, Douglas (D) had pled nolo contendere to similar charges of price-fixing following a grand jury indictment. In its civil action, Petrol (P) requested that Douglas (D) produce grand jury transcripts detailing testimony of Douglas' (D) employees which Douglas (D) had previously obtained. Douglas (D) refused on the ground of irrelevance. Petrol (P) then petitioned the California district court as guardian of the grand jury transcripts, to order their production. The transcripts were released subject to several protective conditions. On appeal, the Ninth Circuit affirmed the disclosure order, finding that the lower court had followed the appropriate standard in making its determination, i.e., requiring the party seeking disclosure to show a particularized need for the documents which outweighs the need for continued secrecy of grand jury proceedings. Douglas (D) appealed, contending that the lower courts erred in allowing Petrol (P) to show only a slight need for disclosure and that, at any rate, the district court in California was not the proper court to order disclosure.

ISSUE: Must a court have access to all relevant information regarding both the need for the requested material in another judicial proceeding and the need for continued secrecy in the grand jury proceeding before ordering the disclosure of grand jury transcripts?

HOLDING AND DECISION: (Powell, J.) Yes. The courts below applied the correct standard in determining whether the grand jury transcripts should be released. The decision must be based on a balancing of the need for the material in other litigation against the acknowledged need for secrecy in a grand jury proceeding. The burden of showing that the need for disclosure outweighs the need for continued secrecy rests upon the party seeking disclosure. Where, as here, production of the grand jury records will result in little or no violation of grand jury secrecy since the records had already been disclosed to another party, the party seeking disclosure need only meet a lessened showing of necessity to another judicial proceeding in order to compel production. However, in order to properly determine whether production is proper, a court must have access to all relevant information regarding both the need for the

material in another proceeding and the need for continued secrecy in the grand jury proceedings. This was not evident in the present case. The district court in California was familiar with the grand jury proceedings and thus was best able to make an informed decision on the need for continued secrecy. However, the court was ignorant regarding the necessity of the material to the Arizona litigation. In this case, only the Arizona court could make that determination. Accordingly, the California court should have released the transcripts to the Arizona court, apprising it of the degree of need for continued secrecy, and then let the Arizona court judge the necessity of the information in the proceedings before that court. This procedure will not be necessary in all cases, only in those where one court is notable, by itself, to make an informed decision regarding all relevant factors. Reversed and remanded.

CONCURRENCE: (Rehnquist, J.) The majority correctly decided the case on its merits. However, the Court's jurisdiction in this case was uncertain and the question of whether the lower court's decision was a "final judgment," appealable to this Court, should have been discussed.

DISSENT: (Stevens, J.) The majority overstepped its bounds by reversing the lower court's order in the absence of any finding of abuse of discretion.

EDITOR'S ANALYSIS: As the Court points out, secrecy of grand jury proceedings has been an established part of our criminal justice system since its inception. There are several reasons advanced for this secrecy. By its nature, the grand jury process is a truth-seeking institution without the restraints imposed on the adversarial criminal justice system. It is often necessarily accomplished before the prospective defendant is in custody. Accordingly, many witnesses would be afraid to voluntarily testify if they knew that the prospective defendant might become aware of their testimony. Such witnesses, if they did testify, might be less likely to do so in a completely honest and forthright manner. The secrecy would also prevent those who are about to be indicted from fleeing. Finally, it would protect individuals who are not indicted from suffering from publicized but nonproven accusations.

[For more information on privilege procedure, see Casenote Law Outline on Evidence, Chapter 8, § X, Privilege Procedure.]

NOTES:

NOTES

NOTES

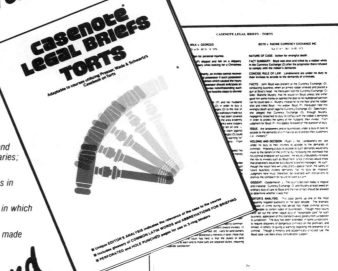
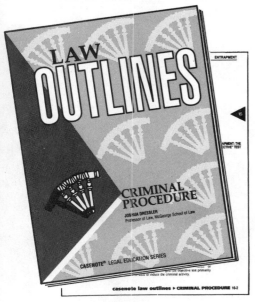